Mammals

Coyotes

BIOLOGY, BEHAVIOR, AND MANAGEMENT

Contributors

RONALD D. ANDREWS
DAVID L. ATKINS
MARC BEKOFF
WILLIAM E. BERG
EDWARD K. BOGGESS
C. A. BRADY
FRANZ J. CAMENZIND
ROBERT A. CHESNESS
GUY E. CONNOLLY
H. T. GIER
P. S. GIPSON
HENRY HILTON
JAMES J. KENNELLY
D. G. KLEIMAN
S. M. KRUCKENBERG
PHILIP N. LEHNER
R. J. MARLER
RONALD M. NOWAK
STEPHEN A. SHUMAKE
RAY T. STERNER
DALE A. WADE

Coyotes

BIOLOGY, BEHAVIOR, AND MANAGEMENT

EDITED BY

Marc Bekoff

Department of Environmental, Population, and Organismic Biology
University of Colorado
Boulder, Colorado

ACADEMIC PRESS New York San Francisco London 1978

A Subsidiary of Harcourt Brace Jovanovich, Publishers

ACADEMIC PRESS, INC.
111 Fifth Avenue, New York, New York 10003

United Kingdom Edition published by
ACADEMIC PRESS, INC. (LONDON) LTD.
24/28 Oval Road, London NW1

Library of Congress Cataloging in Publication Data

Main entry under title:

Coyotes : biology, behavior, and management.

Includes bibliographies and index.
1. Coyotes. 2. Coyotes–Behavior.
3. Coyotes–Control. I. Bekoff, Marc.
QL737.C22C68 599′.74442 77-13363
ISBN 0–12–086050–3

PRINTED IN THE UNITED STATES OF AMERICA

To my parents
for their unrelenting support

Contents

SECTION III ECOLOGY AND SYSTEMATICS

List of Contributors

Numbers in parentheses indicate the pages on which the authors' contributions begin.

RONALD D. ANDREWS (249), Iowa Conservation Commission, Clear Lake, Iowa

DAVID L. ATKINS (17), Department of Biological Sciences, The George Washington University, Washington, D.C.

MARC BEKOFF (97), Department of Environmental, Population, and Organismic Biology, University of Colorado, Boulder, Colorado

WILLIAM E. BERG (229), Section of Wildlife, Department of Natural Resources, Grand Rapids, Minnesota

EDWARD K. BOGGESS* (249), Department of Animal Ecology, Iowa State University, Ames, Iowa

C. A. BRADY (163), National Zoological Park, Smithsonian Institution Department of Zoology, Washington, D.C., and Ohio University, Athens, Ohio

FRANZ J. CAMENZIND† (267), Department of Zoology and Physiology, University of Wyoming, Laramie, Wyoming

ROBERT E. CHESNESS (229), Section of Wildlife, Department of Natural Resources, Grand Rapids, Minnesota

GUY E. CONNOLLY (327), U.S. Fish and Wildlife Service, Denver Wildlife Research Center, Denver, Colorado

H. T. GIER (37), Department of Anatomy and Physiology, College of Veterinary Medicine, Kansas State University, Manhattan, Kansas

P. S. GIPSON‡ (191), Poultry and Wildlife Sciences Department, University of Nebraska, Lincoln, Nebraska

HENRY HILTON (209), School of Forest Resources, University of Maine, Orono, Maine

* *Present address: Southwest Area Extension Office, Kansas State University, Garden City, Kansas.*

† *Present address: P. O. Box 1330, Jackson, Wyoming.*

‡ *Present address: Alaska Cooperative Wildlife Research Unit, U.S. Fish and Wildlife Service, University of Alaska, Fairbanks, Alaska.*

JAMES J. KENNELLY (73), U.S. Fish and Wildlife Service, Massachusetts Cooperative Wildlife Research Unit, University of Massachusetts, Amherst, Massachusetts

D. G. KLEIMAN (163), National Zoological Park, Smithsonian Institution, Washington, D.C.

S. M. KRUCKENBERG (37), Department of Pathology, College of Veterinary Medicine, Kansas State University, Manhattan, Kansas

PHILIP N. LEHNER (127), Department of Zoology and Entomology, Laboratory of Animal Behavior, Colorado State University, Fort Collins, Colorado

R. J. MARLER (37), Department of Pathology, College of Veterinary Medicine, Kansas State University, Manhattan, Kansas

RONALD M. NOWAK (3), Office of Endangered Species, Fish and Wildlife Service, U.S. Department of the Interior, Washington, D.C.

STEPHEN A. SHUMAKE (297), U.S. Fish and Wildlife Service, Wildlife Research Center, Denver, Colorado

RAY T. STERNER (297), U.S. Fish and Wildlife Service, Wildlife Research Center, Denver, Colorado

DALE A. WADE (347), Extension Wildlife Specialist, University of California, Davis, California

Foreword

Somewhere far out on a sprawling prairie, a tawny, medium-sized canid stretches, blinks, points its muzzle toward the twilight sky and howls—a quick series of high-pitched staccatos followed by a prolonged siren sound. It is the cry of the coyote (ký-oat, ky-ò-tee, ký-ute, or ky-úte). The howl might be regarded as a sort of reminder of the extreme success of the species.

Whereas the coyote's cousin, the wolf, long ago lost its battle with man throughout all but a tiny portion of the contiguous 48 United States, the coyote has actually extended its range and filled in where the wolf was exterminated. In the New England states for example, the coyote has even shown signs of having undergone a quick spurt of evolution. Some think this rapid change in size has helped the creature partly fill that food niche once preempted by the wolf.

To certain segments of society the coyote has been far too successful. "Eat lamb—10,000 coyotes can't be wrong" is a popular bumper sticker in much of the western United States. Although the actual value of sheep lost to coyotes has always been in dispute, there is no question that damage by coyotes has been significant to individual ranchers.

Thus, the U.S. Fish and Wildlife Service and its predecessor the Biological Survey have long been assigned the task of trying to control the coyote. Traps, poisons, chemosterilants, den-digging, aerial shooting, and numerous other techniques have been tried in an extensive campaign to minimize the damage caused by this very wary predator. Millions of dollars have been spent in the process and perhaps millions of dollars have been lost by the livestock industry.

Despite the extreme success of the coyote, its effect on the sheep ranching industry, and the prolonged official government attention to this species, it is only recently that much information has been gathered about this creature. Past books on the coyote, while interesting and provocative, offered little in the way of hard data and documented conclusions. Rather, they primarily provide what might be known as "coyote lore."

With the advent of the "Environmental Era" and much increased public consciousness about ecological matters, the general use of biocides has come under intense public scrutiny. Official coyote control programs have been questioned in a heated controversy over the need, ethics, and propriety of coyote control, itself a debate that may not die for decades.

No doubt the most important and valuable spin-off of this swirling controversy is the recognition that society knows relatively little about the coyote. Far more funds and manpower have been dedicated to destroying the animal than to studying it. Gradually, a logical resolution became apparent to the public: if more were known about the species, perhaps less money would be needed to control it.

To scientists this logic has been obvious for decades. However, it took public awareness to stimulate the financial support that researchers had been waiting for. During the past decade, therefore, coyote research began to flourish. Coyotes were weighed and measured as never before. They were live-trapped and ear-tagged, and some had radio transmitters attached to them. Their evolution, taxonomy, behavior patterns, communication, diseases, and parasites were investigated. Their ovaries and testes were sectioned for reproductive data, and their brains were dissected and described. Blood studies began. Some scientists even started taking a much closer look at coyote depredations, damages and control, and possible means of minimizing them.

The job of scientifically examining a creature as widespread and adaptable as the coyote has really just begun. No doubt another decade of research will be necessary before the creature is really understood. However, "Phase 1" is over, and this start has been encouraging.

In this book a cross section of recent coyote research is presented. Some of it is academic; some is of immediate practical value. All of it is new, well documented, and valuable to the ultimate understanding of the coyote.

I congratulate and thank the editor Marc Bekoff and his contributors for undertaking this first effort to draw together the rapidly accumulating knowledge about this species.

L. David Mech
Wildlife Research Biologist
Patuxent Wildlife Research Center
U.S. Fish and Wildlife Service

Preface

The purpose of this book is to bring together information on the coyote from a variety of disciplines with diverse research orientations, all of which are dedicated to learning more about this elusive canid. Existing literature on coyote biology is so scattered that it is beyond the power of one person to do it justice. As a reflection of this diversity of interest this book is divided into four main sections—I: Basic Biology: Evolution, Pathology, and Reproduction; II: Behavior; III: Ecology and Systematics; IV: Management. Each of these areas is given comprehensive scientific treatment by authorities in their respective fields.

In order to understand more completely the nature of any animal, we must study its basic biology. Evolution, pathobiology, and reproductive biology are all dealt with in detail in the first four chapters of this volume (Section I). The behavior of the coyote and related canids is then discussed in Section II (Chapters 5–7). Topics such as the development of behavior, hybridization, social communication, and comparative canid ethology are considered. The chapters in Section II deal mainly with "pure behavior"; those in Section III are more concerned with behavioral ecology, the geographic distribution of coyotes and related members of the genus *Canis*, and systematics. Topics such as hybridization, territoriality, population structure, size and dynamics, and food habits are given careful consideration. The last section deals with problems of management from different perspectives. It stresses primarily that systematic research in all areas of coyote biology is necessary for successful management practices to be instituted.

This volume should be useful to those interested in learning about coyotes (and predator biology) from different points of view, and should enable the reader to appreciate the kind of synthesis needed to come to terms with "the biology" of a selected species. The information contained will undoubtedly be applicable to other management problems in the United States and abroad (e.g., the "jackal problem" in South Africa).

The idea for this volume originated during the National Coyote Workshop (sponsored by the United States Fish and Wildlife Service) held in Denver in November 1974. After considerable consultation, various scientists were contacted (some of whom chose not to participate) and asked to contribute a "meaty" chapter within their area of specialization.

I would like to take this opportunity to thank Ms. Dorothea Slater, Ms. Nutan Pall, and Ms. Elizabeth Owen for much needed secretarial support and Professor David Wilson Crumpacker, Chairman of the Department of Environmental, Population, and Organismic Biology, University of Colorado, for financial support. Hope Ryden provided the cover photo. The assistance of the staff of Academic Press was extremely facilitative. Finally, I would like to thank all of the contributors for taking part in this venture. In particular, Phil Lehner was always a patient, responsive, and helpful sounding board.

Marc Bekoff

Introduction

> The ecological role of predators, that of the coyote, for example, seldom gets rational consideration, and unproven concepts are often perpetuated rather than challenged scientifically (Howard, 1973, p. 3).

> We have hope, but little optimism, that mankind will discard irrational and emotional hostility toward predators and substitute a scientific position on their management. But to people other than biologists or ecologists, the word *predator* has long meant something malicious—the wicked preying upon the good (McCabe and Kozicky, 1972, p. 383).

> Expediency for a solution to the coyote–livestock problem will undoubtedly force short cuts to careful investigations; however, we must be prepared to shoulder the consequences of grasping false panaceas (Lehner, 1976, p. 125).

In the past few years, an almost indigestable amount of information dealing with many aspects of the life of the ever-adaptable coyote has appeared in both the scientific and popular press (Ryden, 1975; Bekoff, 1977; Pringle, 1977; see Dolnick *et al.* for a bibliography containing over 4100 listings). Heightened interest in this animal has been paralleled by its rapidly expanding range (see Fig. 1), including large cities (Gill, 1965, 1970; *Time,* 1975). Yet we still know very little about the nature of this controversial carnivore. For example, most of what we know about the behavioral ecology of this elusive canid has been derived from telemeter "bleeps." We also know extremely little about the predatory behavior of the coyote with the exception of long lists documenting their catholic food habits.

Our lack of knowledge about the biology of the coyote and, in particular, its way of life is unfortunate. This book should help to bridge this gap. Much interest in the coyote, both now and historically (Young and Jackson, 1951), has been stimulated by the role of the coyote as a predator on domestic livestock, yet it is only recently that scientific studies of sheep killing by coyotes have appeared. For instance, the results of one study (Connolly *et al.,* 1976) indicate that sheep-killing ability and efficiency of individual captive coyotes vary over a broad range. Field work by myself and

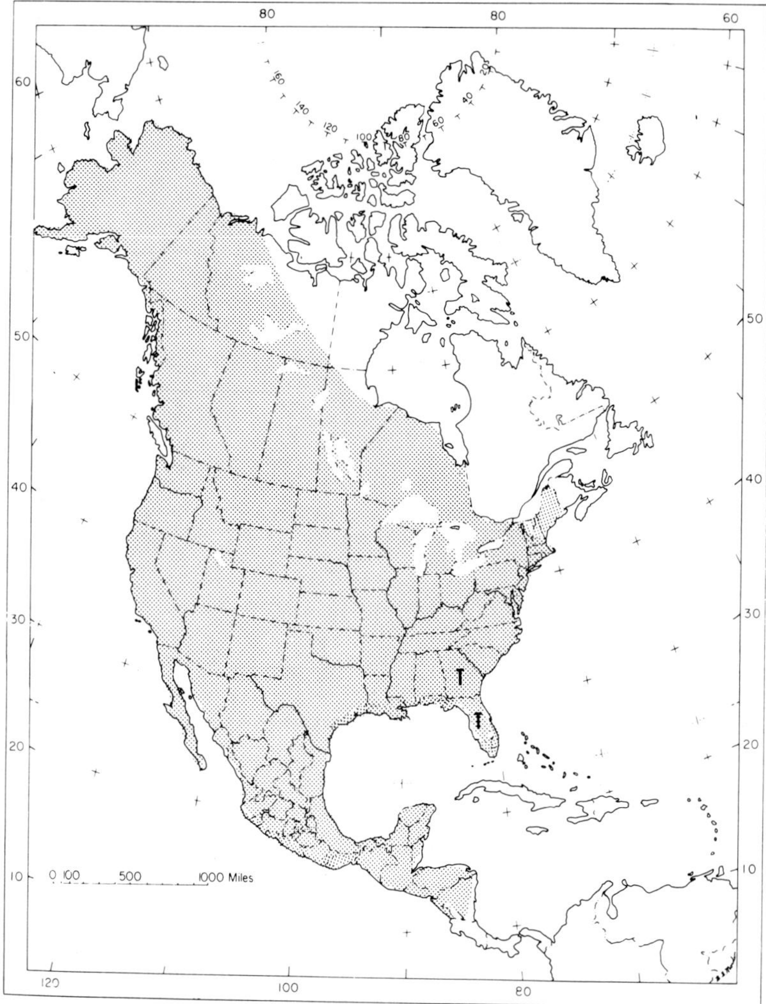

Fig. 1. Current estimated distribution of the coyote. T, probable transplants by man. (From Bekoff, 1977.)

several of my students also indicates that there is a good deal of variability in the predatory behavior of wild coyotes. In fact a common stumbling block to understanding and controlling the coyote is that of intraspecific variability. One cannot simply discuss "the coyote." Thus, future research will require hard work, with carefully controlled scientific methods, to come to terms with this elusive, intelligent, and protean predator. In particular, studies in a variety of habitats will be necessary, and, hopefully, funding will be made available (and increased) to allow these important studies to be performed in a rigorous fashion.

In addition to the nontrivial, subjective, emotion-laden question of whether or not we have the "right" to blame the coyote or any other predator for taking an "easy meal" (in Connolly's study, defensive behavior by sheep deterred coyotes less than one-third of the time), we must also deal with practical questions such as the following: (1) What proportion of a population of coyotes actually constitutes a threat to domestic livestock? (2) What is the magnitude of loss due to predation by coyotes? (3) To what extent do various control methods reduce the level of predation on domestic livestock? (4) Are there other, more important (and perhaps more easily managed) factors than predators? (5) Are the control methods selective for coyotes, are they safe, and what impact do they have on nontarget species and the environment? (6) Are the various management practices economically worthwhile? When there are answers to these and perhaps other questions (given the complexity of the problems, it is unlikely that the answers will be either "cut and dry" or of universal applicability) based on rigorous scientific approaches, then, and only then, can we attempt to cope efficiently with the existing problems.

We, *Homo sapiens,* have created the situation and consequently "the monster," and we continue to exercise our "evolutionary privilege" by punishing those species that take advantage of our poorly devised domestication practices that selected for increased productivity by livestock while sacrificing their defensive, life-sustaining, antipredatory behavioral responses. Indeed, the coyote has already been declared a dispensable species (Shelton, 1973) in man-made ecosystems. Of course economic considerations are justifiable considering the world's dependence on domestic livestock for food (Byerly, 1977), but indiscriminate attempts to deal with the complex problem of coyote predation simply have not worked. As Craighead and Craighead (1956, p. 328) have written:

> Perhaps the greatest misconceptions concerning predation have arisen through a misunderstanding of the biology of predation and a confusion of the biological with the economic aspects. No sound economic evaluation can be made without considering the general biological effects.

REFERENCES

Bekoff, M. (1977). *Mamm. Species* No. 79, 1–9.

Byerly, T. C. (1977). *Science* **195,** 450–456.

Connolly, G. E., Timm, R. M., Howard, W. E., and Longhurst, W. M. (1976). *J. Wildl. Manag.* **40,** 400–407.

Craighead, J. J., and Craighead, F. C. (1956). "Hawks, Owls and Wildlife." Stackpole, Harrisburg, Pennsylvania, [Reprinted: Dover, New York 1969].

Dolnick, E. H., Medford, R. L., and Schied, R. J. (1976). "Bibliography on the Control and Management of the Coyote and Related Canids with Selected References on Animal Physiology, Behavior, Control Methods, and Reproduction." Agric. Res. Serv., Beltsville, Maryland.

Gill, D. A. (1965). Coyote and Urban Man: A Geographic Analysis of the Relationship between the Coyote and Man in Los Angeles. Unpubl. M.A. Thesis, University of California, Los Angeles, 114 pp.

Gill, D. A. (1970). *Amer. Anthropol.* **72,** 821–826.

Howard, W. E. (1973). The biology of predator control. *Addison-Wesley Module Biol.* **11,**

Lehner, P. N. (1976). *Wildl. Soc. Bull.* **4,** 120–126.

McCabe, R. A., and Kozicky, E. L. (1972). *J. Wildl. Manag.* **36,** 382–394.

Pringle, L. (1977). "The Controversial Coyote." Harcourt, New York.

Ryden, H. (1975). "God's Dog." Coward, McCann, Geoghegan, New York.

Shelton, M. (1973). *BioScience* **12,** 719–720.

Time Magazine (1975), August 11, p. 44.

Young, S. P., and Jackson, H. H. T. (1951). "The Clever Coyote." Stackpole, Harrisburg, Pennsylvania.

Section I

BASIC BIOLOGY: EVOLUTION, PATHOLOGY, AND REPRODUCTION

With the decline and eventual extinction of the Borophaginae, the stage was set for the development of a new group of large canid predators. Although there are several views on the possible origin of *Canis,* it now seems most likely that the genus arose from foxlike ancestors in the early to middle Pliocene. In the late Pliocene and early Pleistocene (about 2–4 million years ago), as the Borophagine dogs disappeared, there was a corresponding radiation of *Canis*.

Only three named species of *Canis* are now known from the Pliocene of North America. Two of these, the mid-Pliocene *Canis davisii* from Nevada and Oregon, and *Canis condoni* from Oregon, are very small and may represent a link between the remainder of the genus and the foxes. Shotwell (1970) suggested that *C. davisii* and *C. condoni* might actually be referable to a single species. This species could have been the ancestor of all the wolves, coyotes, and jackals that subsequently appeared (the other Pliocene species, *Canis lepophagus,* is discussed below).

The living coyote (*Canis latrans*) is the most primitive member of its genus in North America. This is not to say that the species is in any way less intelligent or adaptable than the larger wolves (*Canis lupus* and *C. rufus*); indeed the opposite may be true. By the term primitive is meant that in those characters allowing comparison, the species resembles the ancestral, less specialized condition. In this respect the coyote is closer to the foxlike progenitors of the genus, and to the living foxes, than are the wolves. The jackals of the Old World (*Canis aureus, C. adustus,* and *C. mesomelas*) also are primitive species compared to the wolves. Both the coyote and jackals are relatively small animals, averaging closer in size to the foxes than to the gray wolf. The skull of the coyote, like that of the foxes, is comparatively narrow; the jaws have not spread to develop the great grasping power needed by a predator to attack an animal larger than itself. The sagittal crest is usually low or even flattened, indicating that the muscles controlling the jaws are relatively, if not absolutely, weak. The molar teeth of the coyote are deeply sculptured, retaining the primitive cusps and cones, and having large chewing surfaces. Such features suggest that the species still depends to some extent on vegetation for food, and has not become so specialized for flesh eating as the wolves. These various characters should not be considered handicaps, in the evolutionary sense. Its smaller size, and capability to utilize small prey and vegetation more efficiently, may help the coyote survive periods of adverse conditions under which the wolf would perish. Indeed, this process may be occurring today as the wolf progressively declines through competition with man, while the coyote continues to thrive and even expand its range.

The coyote might be considered part of the same central stock of unspecialized canids that has formed the basis of the evolution of the family since the Oligocene. These small animals seem to have maintained themselves with relatively little change, while the canids that became large, and specialized in habits, have disappeared. The bear-dogs of the Miocene, the hyena-dogs of the Pliocene, and the great dire wolf of the Pleistocene have all fallen by the wayside. Now even the gray and red wolves may be moving in this same direction, but the coyote shows no sign of becoming a has-been.

III. BLANCAN COYOTES

The term Blancan is based on a fossil faunal assemblage found in the Blanco deposits of Texas, and has been applied to various sites of the late Pliocene and early Pleistocene. The mammalian faunas of such sites usually seem to represent a transition between archaic Tertiary elements and modern species. Some Blancan sites contain the remains of huge Borophagine and Simocyonine dogs, but there also is abundant evidence that a coyote, not greatly different from that of today, had become widespread during this period.

The first detailed description of a Blancan coyote was provided by Johnston (1938) who named the species *Canis lepophagus* from the Cita Canyon site in Randall County, Texas. The specimens from this site still comprise the largest and most complete collection of material referred to *C. lepophagus*. The skulls from Cita Canyon are about the size of those of small *Canis latrans*, but have relatively smaller and less inflated braincases, more prominent sagittal crests, broader frontal and supraoccipital shields, and deeper mandibles. In these characters, the specimens demonstrated some approach to the condition in wolves, and Johnston (1938) thought that *C. lepophagus* might be the common ancestor of both coyotes and wolves.

The Cita Canyon site now is considered to date from relatively late in the Blancan. Following the description of *C. lepophagus* from that site, the species was reported from a number of other localities, including some of early Blancan age, in California, Idaho, Nebraska, Kansas, Texas, and Florida. Certain specimens, especially those from the earlier sites, are smaller and more delicate than those from Cita Canyon, and do not demonstrate the same approach to the wolflike condition. The mandibles from some of these sites actually are shallower, rather than deeper, than those of most modern *C. latrans*. The species *C. lepophagus* thus shows considerable variation, but this is not surprising considering the extensive geographical and geological distribution of the species, and it seems reasonable to assign all known coyotelike material from the Blancan to this species.

Specimens collected at the late Blancan Lisco Quarry in Garden County, Nebraska provide evidence of the unity of *C. lepophagus*. While the mandibles from this site are relatively shallow, like those from the earlier sites, the skull has a prominent sagittal crest, like that of the Cita Canyon specimens. The development of the sagittal crest in *C. lepophagus*, along with the relatively small braincase, suggests that at this stage in the evolution of the coyote, muscle power was ahead of brainpower. Subsequently, the braincase became more inflated, at the expense of the satittal crest. Taking into account what is known about the limb bones of *C. lepophagus*, the overall picture of the species is of a small, compact coyote, not so well adapted for long-distance running as *C. latrans*. The teeth, even in the more massive specimens, and especially in the earlier material, are small and suggest affinity to the Old World jackals and to the foxes. *Canis lepophagus*, thus, may have stood near the original foxlike line of the genus *Canis*, that gave rise to both the coyotes and jackals.

Kurten (1974) treated the entire species *C. lepophagus*, based mainly on data from the Cita Canyon specimens, as an evolutionary phase that eventually passed into a more advanced coyote. Another approach might be to consider the Cita Canyon animals as an evolutionary dead end that already had become too specialized to be regarded as ancestral to *C. latrans*. Modern coyotes may instead have been derived from the animals represented by the less massive specimens of the early Blancan. Possibly, both *C. lepophagus*, in the form of the Cita Canyon animals, and early *C. latrans*, coexisted for a certain period.

Although the Cita Canyon animals may not have been ancestral to *C. latrans*, they also do not appear to have been the ancestors of modern wolves, as suggested by Johnston (1938). It is true that in the characters mentioned above there is a slight approach to a wolflike condition, but the dentition of the specimens seems even less wolflike than that of modern *C. latrans*. Moreover, it now appears likely that the wolf line had separated from that of the coyote prior to the time in which the Cita Canyon animals lived, and that moderately large wolves already were established over a large region by the late Blancan. One of these wolves, the earliest described from North America, is *Canis edwardii*, based on a skull from Curtis Ranch, Cochise County, Arizona. Kurten (1974) assigned this specimen to *C. lepophagus*, but I disagree with that procedure. The skull is far larger and more massive than the contemporary material referred to *C. lepophagus*, and Hoffmeister and Goodpaster (1954, p. 34) actually synonymized *C. edwardii* with *C. lupus baileyi*, the modern Mexican gray wolf. Like the original describer of *C. edwardii* (Gazin, 1942), I think the species has closest affinity to the modern red wolf (*C. rufus*).

IV. IRVINGTONIAN COYOTES

The Irvingtonian period, named for a faunal assemblage found near the town of Irvington, Alameda County, California, extends through part of the early and middle Pleistocene. Many mammals of this period closely resembled modern species, though some of the larger kinds of the late Pleistocene had not yet appeared. The gray wolf (*Canis lupus*) may already have entered North America during the mid-Pleistocene, though fossil evidence is very scanty. The red wolf (*C. rufus*) was present, as was a closely related larger species (*C. armbrusteri*), which is well represented by fossil material from Maryland and Florida. There is no firm evidence of the presence of the dire wolf (*C. dirus*) in North America during the Irvingtonian.

Kurten (1974) examined canid specimens from a number of North American sites of Irvingtonian age. He recognized the presence of a remarkably large coyote during this period, which he thought represented a second evolutionary phase, subsequent to *C. lepophagus* and preceeding modern *C. latrans*. One of these specimens, from the Port Kennedy Cave deposit in Montgomery County, Pennsylvania, had been described by Cope (1899) under the name *Canis priscolatrans*. Since this name was the earliest available, Kurten applied it to the Irvingtonian coyotes of North America.

There is an alternative way of viewing *C. priscolatrans*, the type specimen of which consists only of four teeth. With respect to these teeth, the original description (Cope, 1899) stated: "The forms of the cusps and cingula in this species are like those of the corresponding teeth of the coyote, except as to the conules. The size is that of the large, but not largest wolves." This description agrees well with that of the modern red wolf by Goldman (1944), and Paradiso and Nowak (1972) who considered the red wolf to have coyotelike teeth, but to approach *C. lupus* in size. In fact, the teeth of *C. priscolatrans* are almost identical in size to those of *C. edwardii* and to the average in series of over 100 modern *C. rufus*. In structure the teeth seem closer to those of the red wolf, and it seems reasonable to consider *C. priscolatrans* as, at most, a subspecies of *C. rufus*. Under this interpretation, the animals represented by *C. priscolatrans* would have represented a stage in the development of the red wolf between the time of the Blancan *C. edwardii* and modern *C. rufus*. These animals would not have been in the line of modern *C. latrans*. Kurten (1974) assigned a number of other Irvingtonian specimens to *C. priscolatrans*, considering that they represented large coyotes. I have not examined all of this material, but it is possible that the specimens, like the type of *C. priscolatrans*, should be viewed as representing small wolves rather than large coyotes.

Savage (1951) described the species *Canis irvingtonensis*, based mainly on two mandibular fragments from Irvington, Alameda County, California.

He stated that the species had relatively deeper mandibles, and relatively wider and more closely spaced premolars than *C. latrans*. Kurten (1974) considered *C. irvingtonensis* as one of the large Irvingtonian coyotes that he grouped under the name *C. priscolatrans*. Although I agree that the mandibles of *C. irvingtonensis* have a more massive appearance than those of most coyotes, I have found that all their measurements fall well within the range of variation of both modern and late Pleistocene *C. latrans* from western North America. The length of the mandibles is about equal to that of modern *C. latrans*, and is exceeded by the average of coyotes from the late Pleistocene deposits at Rancho La Brea in California. The relative depth of the mandibles, and the width of the teeth, also are within the range of variation of the corresponding dimensions of *C. latrans*. The premolars are unusually close together, but this condition does occur occasionally in modern coyotes. In all other features that can be evaluated *C. irvingtonensis* matches series of *C. latrans*, and consequently I do not consider *C. irvingtonensis* a separate species.

In addition to the above material, specimens of coyotelike canids have been found at comparatively few sites of Irvingtonian age. These include localities in Alberta, California, Nebraska, Kansas, and Texas. None of these specimens suggest the presence of a species distinct from *C. latrans*. Considering all the evidence, it seems most likely that *C. latrans* already had developed by the end of the Blancan, and thereafter did not undergo any great changes.

V. RANCHOLABREAN COYOTES

The Rancholabrean period, named for the famed fossil deposits in Los Angeles, corresponds with late Pleistocene and early Recent times (about 8000–500,000 years ago). Many, perhaps nearly all, modern species of mammals had evolved by this period, but there also were a number of other species that were to become extinct as the Pleistocene ended. Horses, camels, mammoths, mastodons, saber-tooth tigers, lions, and giant ground sloths all roamed North America during the Rancholabrean, but none survived on the continent into modern times. *Canis armbrusteri* apparently disappeared early in this period, but the red and gray wolves remained. The most remarkable canid of the Rancholabrean was the dire wolf (*Canis dirus*), the largest species of the genus ever to exist. This great predator appeared suddenly all across North America during the late Pleistocene, and then, just as suddenly, vanished in the early Recent. Its origin and cause of disappearance are mysteries; it may have evolved from *C. armbrusteri* or been an invader from South America. Its extinction may be associated with that of other large animals which served as its prey.

Abundant fossil material shows that the coyote occurred nearly throughout North America during the Rancholabrean period, and that the species probably was even more variable than it is today. By far, the largest collection of coyote fossils is from Rancho La Brea itself. This remarkable site, in contrast to most, contains the remains of considerably more predators than prey. Dire wolves and saber-tooth tigers are the most common carnivores in the deposits, but the remains of over 200 individual coyotes also have been identified. Merriam (1912) described these specimens as representing a subspecies (*orcutti*) of modern *C. latrans*. This procedure seems reasonable because, while in size and all other characters there is considerable overlap between *orcutti* and modern coyotes, the former is more massive and larger, on the average, in all measurable dimensions. Several skulls from Rancho La Brea are larger than the largest Recent specimens that I examined. Major collections of equally large coyotes have been recovered from the McKittrick Tar Seeps and the Maricopa Brea in Kern County, California.

Two other coyotelike species have been described from Rancho La Brea, both based on single specimens. Merriam (1912) considered one small skull to represent a "coyote-like wolf," which he named *Canis andersoni*. In my own opinion, the specimen is that of a deformed, juvenile coyote that probably can be referred to *C. latrans orcutti*. Stock (1938) applied the name *Canis petrolei* to what he called a "coyote-like wolf jaw." This specimen is from one of the more recent deposits at Rancho La Brea, and probably represents a domestic dog (*Canis familiaris*). It is not surprising that the remains of this species have been found at Rancho La Brea, since domestic dogs are known from other late Pleistocene sites dating back about 11,000 years in North America and 14,000 years in the Middle East. It seems likely that *C. familiaris* was derived from the small wolves (*C. lupus*) of southwestern Asia, and subsequently spread throughout the world in association with the movements of man.

Several other named kinds of coyotes have been described from late Pleistocene sites in North America. *Canis caneloensis* was named by Skinner (1942) on the basis of a skull from the Papago Springs Cave, Santa Cruz County, Arizona. Among the characters said to distinguish this species are the relatively broad face, large tympanic bullae, and wide rear teeth. In all respects, however, the specimen can be matched by large series of modern coyotes, and there now seems little doubt that *caneloensis* is at most a subspecies of *C. latrans*.

Hay (1917) described the species *Canis riviveronis* from Vero, Indian River County, Florida, using a single skull fragment. Subsequently, specimens from a number of other late Pleistocene and early Recent sites in

Florida were referred to this species. Ray (1958), however, considered that there was no basis upon which *C. riviveronis* could be distinguished from *C. latrans*. I agree with Ray, but the material from Florida does average smaller than specimens of modern western coyotes, and fossil *C. latrans orcutti* from Rancho La Brea. One reason for the small size of late Pleistocene coyotes in Florida may have been the sympatric presence of the small red wolf (*C. rufus*), which could have restricted the ecological niche and hence the size of the coyotes. Whether competition from *C. rufus* could have contributed to the disappearance of the coyote from Florida is not known, but with the extermination of the modern red wolf by man, the coyote is returning to the southeast (see below).

Slaughter (1961) described the subspecies *Canis latrans harriscrooki* from the Lewisville site, Denton County, Texas. This site is thought to date from the Sangamon, the last major interglacial phase of the Pleistocene. Slaughter speculated that *harriscrooki* might have been a southern kind of coyote that could have inhabited Texas only during a warm climatic period. This possibility was supported by the presence of a posterior cusp on the second lower premolar of the type specimen, such as is absent from nearly all modern *C. latrans* except those of the extreme southern part of the range of the species. Slaughter implied possible affinity of *harriscrooki* to modern *C. latrans hondurensis* of Honduras, and I was able to examine six specimens of the latter subspecies. Five of these specimens had a prominent posterior cusp on the second lower premolar, and one had the cusp slightly developed. In contrast, only six of 250 Recent specimens from the western United States, and only one of 40 Pleistocene specimens from Rancho La Brea, which could be checked for this character, had any trace of the cusp. Slaughter (1966) reported that a Pleistocene skull from Laubach Cave, Williamson County, Texas, which he said might be referable to *harriscrooki,* had a relatively broader palate than modern *C. latrans,* a condition which is shared by most available skulls of *hondurensis*. Therefore, it seems a reasonable hypothesis that a warmth-adapted coyote was found in Texas during a part of the late Pleistocene, and might still be represented by the living coyote of Honduras. Subsequent to Slaughter's description, material from a number of other Texas fossil deposits has been referred to *harriscrooki*. That coyotes of this kind may also have occupied areas well to the east of the historical range of *C. latrans,* is suggested by two mandibles from the Frankstown Cave, Blair County, Pennsylvania, each of which has a prominent posterior cusp on the second lower premolar.

In addition to the above, coyotes have been reported from other Rancholabrean sites in Alaska, Alberta, Oregon, Idaho, California, Nevada, Arizona, New Mexico, Colorado, Wyoming, Nebraska, Kansas, Oklahoma, Texas, Missouri, Arkansas, Iowa or Wisconsin, Illinois,

Indiana, Maryland, Mississippi, Florida, Nuevo Leon, Estado de Mexico, Puebla, and Oaxaca. All of this material that I have examined apparently represents animals that were much the same as *C. latrans* of today. Only recently, however, Mooser and Dalquest (1975) described *Canis cedazoensis* on the basis of a maxillary fragment from what is thought to be an early Rancholabrean site in Aguascalientes, Mexico. The specimen reportedly is small and is not considered a coyote, but apparently is nearer to *C. latrans* than to any other species of North American *Canis*.

VI. MODERN COYOTES

When the white man first arrived in North America, *C. latrans* was distributed mainly in the western half of the continent. The exact southern, northern, and eastern limits of its historical range are not known. Young (1951) thought that the species originally was found only as far as central Mexico, and that movement farther to the south occurred after the introduction of livestock into the region. Jackson (1951), however, recognized the presence of three separate subspecies in Central America, and it is questionable whether all could have evolved in only 400 years (see above discussion of *C. latrans hondurensis*). Also, according to Young (1951), the coyote did not become established in Alaska and northwestern Canada until the nineteenth and twentieth centuries. Jackson (1951) suspected, however, that the subspecies *C. latrans incolatus* had been a very long time resident of Alaska. It seems that coyote populations always have been relatively small, but highly cyclic in the northern portions of their range, and their history in these regions is not well understood.

The historical range of the coyote extended at least as far east as southern Wisconsin, northwestern Indiana, western Arkansas, and central Texas. Skeletal remains, identified as *C. latrans*, have been reported from archeological excavations in Illinois, Missouri, and Arkansas. Indian sites from farther east apparently have not yielded specimens of *C. latrans*, though as noted above the species occurred as far east as Pennsylvania and Florida during the late Pleistocene. Man's extermination of the larger wolves (*C. lupus* and *C. rufus*), and his disruption of the environment, has contributed to an expansion of the range of the coyote in the last 100 years.

The first major eastern movement of the coyote in historical time came in the late nineteenth century following a period of intensive commercial logging in the Great Lakes region. In 1900 the range of the species included northern Minnesota, southwestern Ontario, and southern Michigan. By 1920 coyotes had occupied all of Michigan and had spread into southeastern Ontario. From there the advance proceeded across southeastern Canada and into the northeastern United States. From the 1930's to the 1960's coyotes became well established in northern New England and New York, and also had begun to spread down the Appalachian chain into Pennsylvania. At present, coyotes seem to have taken hold over much of this region, and also have entered West Virginia.

While one major invasion route took the coyote in an arc through the Great Lakes region, across southeastern Canada, and back down into the northeastern U.S., another thrust was occurring in the southern United States. By the 1920's a small number of coyotes had entered the forests of southern Missouri, northern Arkansas, and eastern Oklahoma, but they were still outnumbered by red wolves. Twenty years later this situation had reversed itself, with the coyote abundant in the Ozark region and the red wolf nearly exterminated. Around 1950 coyotes began to appear in large numbers in eastern Texas and Louisiana, and by the early 1960's they had crossed into Mississippi. Recently, the species seems to have become established in parts of Alabama and southern Tennessee. The red wolf, in pure form, has disappeared from throughout the south, except possibly for a narrow strip of coastal prairie in extreme southeastern Texas and adjacent Louisiana. Its future survival seems doubtful, but in all likelihood the coyote will again occupy the entire eastern United States just as it did 10,000 years ago.

The latest taxonomic revision of Recent coyotes is that of Jackson (1951) who recognized 19 subspecies in North America. Hall and Kelson (1959) mapped the distribution of these subspecies. Although it is likely that a taxonomist of today would not consider all of these subspecies to be valid, we have no choice other than to accept them until a new revision is published and approved by the systematic community.

All species of *Canis* have a diploid chromosome number of 78, and viable offspring have been produced in captivity from hybridization between *C. familiaris* and *C. lupus*, *C. familiaris* and *C. latrans*, *C. familiaris* and *C. aureus*, *C. familiaris* and *C. dingo*, *C. latrans* and *C. aureus*, *C. latrans* and *C. lupus*, and *C. lupus* and *C. dingo* (Gray, 1972, pp. 45–51). There also is good evidence of hybridization in the wild between *C. familiaris* and *C. lupus*, *C. familiaris* and *C. latrans*, *C. lupus* and *C. latrans*, and *C. rufus* and *C. latrans*. Species of other genera within the Caninae, that have been analyzed, have been found to have diploid numbers different from that of *Canis*, and there is no evidence that viable offspring ever has resulted from hybridization between *Canis* and another genus.

Hybridization is thought to have modified at least parts of the coyote populations that have been spreading into eastern North America since the late nineteenth century. It is questionable, however, whether genetic influence from the domestic dog has been responsible for any of this modification. Wild hybrids between *C. latrans* and *C. familiaris* (coy-dogs) have been reported from many parts of the continent, including the northeastern United States. Mengel (1971), however, considered that a phase shift in the breeding cycle of coy-dogs prevented them from interbreeding with *C. latrans,* and thus that the introgression of dog genes into the wild coyote population was unlikely. Mengel's view has been challenged, and the question is still unresolved, but there is no substantial evidence of any large-scale leakage of dog genes into wild coyote populations.

Standfield (1970) reported the collection of specimens in southeastern Ontario which were intermediate in all measurable characters between *C. latrans* and *C. lupus,* and which probably represented hybridization between these two species. I also have examined a number of skulls from this region which suggest that wolf–coyote hybridization has occurred (Nowak, 1973). It is reasonable to suppose that such interbreeding has allowed the flow of genes from the wolf into the coyote population. Specimens of wild *Canis* recently taken in New England, New York, Pennsylvania, and West Virginia appear predominantly coyotelike, but show a definite shift in characters toward *C. lupus.* Evidently, these specimens demonstrate a phenotypic expression of the wolf genes that were incorporated into the coyote population through hybridization in southeastern Canada. Although a few specimens from the same region appear to represent interbreeding between *C. familiaris* and *C. latrans,* there is no proof that such individuals are other than first generation offspring.

Hybridization between *C. latrans* and *C. rufus* was suggested long ago by Goldman (1944) and Jackson (1951), but both thought the phenomenon to be very limited in occurrence. McCarley (1962), however, showed that interbreeding between the two species was so widespread that the process had practically eliminated the red wolf as a pure species in eastern Texas.

My own studies (Nowak, 1973) suggest that a breakdown in reproductive and ecological isolation between *C. rufus* and *C. latrans* occurred in the south-central United States, because of human environmental disruption and persecution of the red wolf. By the early twentieth century hybridization was occurring all along the line where the two species overlapped, but was especially pronounced in central Texas. The population of wild *Canis* in central Texas eventually was largely eliminated by predator control programs, but by the 1930's hybridization also was rampant in the Ozark region. This process led to the incorporation of red wolf genes into the expanding coyote population, and as the red wolf was eliminated by man, the modified coyote population pushed south and east to fill the vacuum. The current population of wild *Canis* in most of eastern Oklahoma, eastern Texas, Arkansas, Louisiana, Mississippi, and Alabama is predominantly coyotelike, but demonstrates a slight shift in characters toward *C. rufus.*

Along much of the Gulf Coast there are canid populations which show the entire range of characters from *C. latrans* to *C. rufus*. The red wolf in pure form may survive only in a narrow strip of coastal prairie in extreme southeastern Texas and southwestern Louisiana.

VII. SUMMARY

The genus *Canis* apparently arose from small foxlike ancestors in the early to middle Pliocene. By the late Pliocene the ancestral coyote *Canis lepophagus* was widespread in North America. This species was highly variable, and it appears likely that an element thereof gave rise to *Canis latrans*. In the middle Pleistocene coyotes much like those of today were present on the continent, as were several kinds of wolves. In the late Pleistocene the coyote occurred nearly throughout North America and was even more variable than the modern species. Several named kinds of fossil coyotes have been described from the middle and late Pleistocene, but all appear to be, at most, subspecies of *C. latrans*.

In historical time, coyotes were restricted mainly to western North America, but since the late nineteenth century have spread over much of the east. Large-scale hybridization with *C. lupus* in the northeast and *C. rufus* in the southeast has led to a modification of the expanding coyote populations.

REFERENCES

Cope, E. D. (1899). *J. Acad. Nat. Sci., Philadelphia* **11,** 193–267.

Gazin, C. L. (1942). *Proc. U.S. Natl. Mus.* **92,** 475–518.

Goldman, E. A. (1944). "The Wolves of North America" (S. P. Young and E. A. Goldman), Part II, pp. 389–636. Am. Wildl. Inst., Washington, D.C.

Gray, A. P. (1972). "Mammalian Hybrids." Common. Agric. Bur., Slough, England.

Hall, E. R., and Kelson, K. R. (1959). "The Mammals of North America." Ronald Press, New York.

Hay, O. P. (1917). *Annu. Rep. Fla. Geol. Surv.* **9,** 43–68.

Hoffmeister, D. F., and Goodpaster, W. W. (1954). *Ill. Biol. Monogr.* **24,** i–v, 1–152.

Jackson, H. H. T. (1951). "The Clever Coyote" (S. P. Young and H. H. T. Jackson), Part II, pp. 227–441. Wildl. Manage. Inst., Washington, D.C.

Johnston, C. S. (1938). *Am. J. Sci.* **35,** 383–390.

Kurten, B. (1974). *Acta Zool. Fenn.* **140,** 1–38.

McCarley, H. (1962). *Southwest. Nat.* **7,** 227–235.

Mengel, R. M. (1971). *J. Mammal.* **52,** 316–336.

Merriam, J. C. (1912). *Mem. Univ. Calif.* **1,** 217–272.

Mooser, O., and Dalquest, W. W. (1975). *J. Mammal.* **56,** 781–820.

Nowak, R. M. (1973). North American Quaternary Canis. Ph.D. Thesis, Univ. of Kansas, Lawrence.

Paradiso, J. L., and Nowak, R. M. (1972). *U.S. Bur. Sport Fish. Wildl. Spec. Sci. Rep.—Wildl.* **145,** i–ii, 1–36.

Ray, C. E. (1958). *Bull. Mus. Comp. Zool., Harvard Univ.* **119,** 421–451.

Savage, D. E. (1951). *Univ. Calif., Berkeley, Publ. Bull. Dep. Geol.* **28,** 215–314.

Shotwell, J. A. (1970). *Bull. Mus. Nat. Hist. Univ. Oregon* **17,** 1–103.

Skinner, M. F. (1942). *Bull. Am. Mus. Nat. Hist.* **80,** 143–220.

Slaughter, B. H. (1961). *J. Mammal.* **42,** 503–509.

Slaughter, B. H. (1966). *Am. Midl. Nat.* **75,** 475–494.

Standfield, R. (1970). *In* "Proceedings of a Symposium on Wolf Management in Selected Areas of North America" (S. E. Jorgensen, C. E. Faulkner, and L. D. Mech, eds.), pp. 32–38. U.S. Bur. Sport Fish. Wildl., Twin Cities, Minnesota.

Stock, C. (1938). *Bull. South Calif. Acad. Sci.* **37,** 49–51.

Young, S. P. (1951). "The Clever Coyote" (S. P. Young and H. H. T. Jackson), Part I, pp. 1–226. Wildl. Manage. Inst., Washington, D.C.

2

Evolution and Morphology of the Coyote Brain

David L. Atkins

I. THE NERVOUS SYSTEM AS AN EVOLUTIONARY INDICATOR

Nervous system anatomy is often a detailed guide to mammalian evolution. The microscopic and gross morphology of this system must be under fairly rigid genetic direction, since sensory appreciation and motor control are minutely complex, and viability depends upon precise intercellular relations. To quote duBrul (1960), it is truly a ". . . system, not an ensemble." However, since it is in direct or indirect contact with all aspects of the internal and external environments and governs the animal's response, the nervous system is subject to continuous selective pressure. These opposing forces produce a system that resists trivial change but is not unmutable.

The increased complexity of advanced mammals is reflected in greater size and more elaborate structure of the brain—particularly of the cerebrum and cerebellum. These latter organs have usurped many lower brain functions and added new ones, but their ensuing physical growth required a new method of expansion. There are practical limits to brain size—a head can only be so large, relatively, and still function. To a major extent, skull size and form are controlled by brain growth, and this process is dramatically illustrated by cranial deformations in such developmental anomalies as hydrocephalus and microcephalus. However, in normal growth and adult function, the size and shape of the maternal birth canal, the position of special sensory capsules in the skull, and the size and mechanical operation of the jaw also contribute to and determine the functional success (= evolution) of skull form.

Cerebrum and cerebellum can expand into a limited volume and skull shape by folding their cortices into gyri (cerebrum) or thinner folia (cerebellum). Many cortical functional interrelationships, both neural and vascular (Atkins and Goldberg, 1972), are two-dimensional, i.e., they occur in the plane perpendicular to, and one plane parallel to, the surface. In these gyrencephalic (folded) brains, such orientation is in the long axis of the fold. Thus, surface area and amount of convolution offer a measure of neural complexity.

Brain size is under genetic control, as shown by indices of brain weight/body weight [for dog, see Latimer (1942) and Fox (1966, 1971)] and of brain volume/foramen magnum area (Radinsky, 1967). These relationships are consistent in a species and may measure relative "intelligence" in interspecific comparisons as well.

Increase in mammalian brain size has placed it in close contact with the entire calvaria, changing its relationship to other elements of the skull and associated soft organs. This aspect has been examined by Weidenreich (1941), Seiferle (1966), and Hofer (1969), among others. duBrul (1960) points out that extraneural anatomical changes also affect evolution of neuroanatomy, citing especially the neural corollaries to reduction of jaw skeleton and musculature.

The intimate physical relationship of brain with skull is impressive. Not only do the skull foramena record the positions of cranial nerves, but also the boundaries between brain divisions as well as the surface folds of cerebrum and cerebellum are often displayed in negative relief on the inner face of the cranial cavity. This permits the formation of an endocranial cast of brain form—either by natural concretions or various casting media—

which accurately reflects much of the superficial gross anatomy of the brain in fossils or in rare species where only skeletal specimens are available. Such fossil brains in canids have been described by Jakway and Clement (1967) and especially by Radinsky (1969, 1973), among others. Unfortunately, there are limitations to this method, which will be noted below in discussion of the coyote cerebrum (Section III,A).

II. EARLY CANID BRAIN EVOLUTION

A. Canid Cerebral Evolution

The primitive mammalian cerebrum (improperly = "brain" in many publications) is lissencephalic (i.e., lacking sulci), and subsequent sulcus formation has proceeded in a variety of patterns among more advanced taxa—different but constant within each. Order Carnivora exhibits such a unitary pattern, although variations exist at all subordinal levels.

†*Hesperocyon,* from the mid-Oligocene, has the oldest canid endocast described (Tilney, 1931; Scott and Jepson, 1936; Radinsky, 1973). Its cerebrum is relatively small, and neocortical sulcation is primitive. Only the coronolateral and suprasylvian are present.

Radinsky (1973) has reviewed the subsequent appearance of sulci in later forms, and these data are summarized in Fig. 1. The series indicated in the

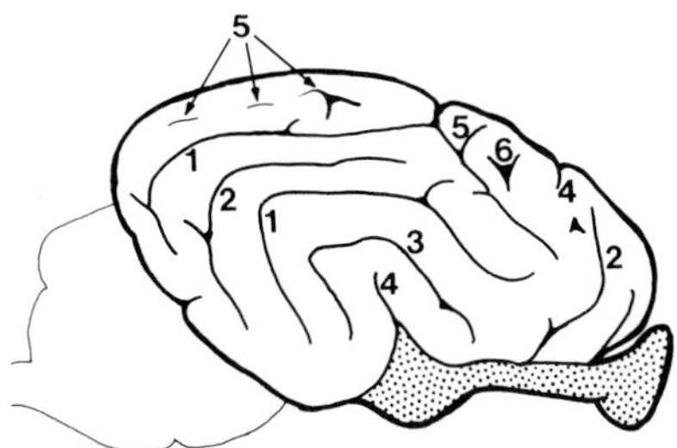

Fig. 1. Sequence of sulcal evolution in the Canidae. A lateral view of the cerebrum in *Canis latrans* illustrates the approximate temporal order of appearance of sulci in (1) †*Hesperocyon,* Middle Oligocene; (2) †*Leptocyon* and †*Nothocyon,* Early Miocene; (3) †*Cynodesmus,* Middle Miocene; †*Enhydrocyon,* Early Miocene and †*Mesocyon,* L. Olig–E. Mioc.; (4) †*Phlaocyon,* M.-L. Mioc.; (5) †*Tomarctus,* L. Mioc.–E. Plioc.; (6) †*Aelurodon,* M. Plioc. and *Canis,* E. Plioc.-Recent; (7) *Canis,* (on Fig. 2). Cerebellum and brainstem are shown in profile only. Sulci and gyri are identified on Fig. 2. Stippled area represents olfactory bulb and tract and the piriform lobe, which are not part of the cerebral neocortex.

figure caption is not intended as a linear phylogenetic progression to genus *Canis*, and some further interpretive caution is needed in that fossil preservation of brain structure is not always good. Also, there is some individual variation, especially in early evolutionary stages. Finally, the forces of sulcus formation are not fully understood, and Radinsky (1971) notes at least one instance of independent evolution of sulci. Nevertheless, a progressive appearance of homologous structures seems well documented in the case of the canid cerebrum which provides a reasonable picture of the early elaboration of this organ. Further evaluation of this series appears below in discussion of evolution of sulci.

B. Canid Cerebellar Evolution

Cortical subdivision of the cerebellum is vastly more complex than that of the cerebrum in all mammals. Further, much of this intricacy probably extends back to the reptilian ancestry of the mammals. No direct evidence exists to corroborate this, since the reptilian skull is not in close approximation to the brain surface, and modern reptiles have a simple cerebellum with two (Crocodilia) or no sulci (all others).

In mammals, however, the cerebellum is divided (1) into a midline vermis flanked by paired hemispheres—longitudinally, and (2) into three lobes transversely, the anterior-most two of these being further subdivided into several lobules. These, in turn, may be extensively sulcated into thin folial corrugations in more advanced taxa. This situation (to the lobule level) appears in all species, and the structural patterns seem homologous in therian mammals (Larsell, 1953, 1970; Dillon and Brauer, 1970); features of monotreme cerebellar evolution confirm the antiquity of this pattern (Dillion, 1962). In any event, the earliest canids already had a complicated cerebellar anatomy comparable to modern forms.

Due to overlap of this organ by the posterior cerebral pole, only a portion of cerebellar form is visible on endocasts, and the most instructive deep pattern, visible in midsagittal section (see Figs. 5 and 6), cannot be reconstructed. Thus, fossil cerebellar data are limited in scope, but several trends are evident in canid endocast specimens. The posterior vermian lobe is rather small in Oligocene and early Miocene endocasts, but by late Miocene, the dorsal part of this lobe has begun considerable expansion, as demonstrated by appearance of a sigmoid curve in the posterior vermis (Radinsky, 1973). This expansion has continued in modern canids, so that the dorsal posterior vermis is quite asymmetrical (see Fig. 5), a trait that appears independently in the Felidae and, irregularly, in other feloids and in the Mustelidae. The parafloccular process also appears late in the evolution of this organ, although it is generally present in modern canids.

III. THE GROSS NERVOUS SYSTEM OF THE COYOTE, *CANIS LATRANS*

The dog is a frequent subject of zoological experimentation, and the literature pertinent to anatomy and other aspects of its nervous system is enormous [see Miller (1964) for review of the older literature, and Fox (1971) for the more recent]. In contrast, relatively few comparative studies involving other canid or *Canis* species exist. The cerebrum of coyote was briefly described by England (1973) and compared with *C. dingo, C. lupus,* and *C. familiaris,* as well as with *Vulpes vulpes* and *Urocyon cinereoargenteus.* Radinsky (1973) illustrates several *Canis* species endocasts, including a fossil coyote, but he does not describe them individually.

Gross anatomy of the dog cerebellum has been examined comparatively by several authors, including Bolk (1906) and Larsell (1970); cerebella of *V. vulpes* and *C. latrans* were briefly examined and surrealistically illustrated by Riley (1928). Atkins (1970) described cerebella of *C. dingo,* †*C. dirus* (endocast), *Alopex lagopus, Chrysocyon brachyurus, Fennicus zerda, U. cinereoargenteus, V. chama, V. velox,* and *V. vulpes,* as well as (Atkins and Dillon, 1971) detailed cerebellar structure in *C. aureus, C. familiaris, C. latrans, C. lupus, C. mesomelas,* and *C. rufus.*

There are apparently no published studies of other central or peripheral nervous organs in coyote or other wild canids.

A. Anatomy of the Coyote Cerebrum

Many features of cerebrum and cerebellum indicate a common ancestry for the Recent Canidae, which is recent enough to preclude extensive anatomical divergence. The cerebrum seems particularly conservative in its evolution, creating the superficial impression that if you've seen one canid "brain," you've seen 'em all.

The sulcal pattern on the exposed cerebral surface does show several interspecific differences, however. Coyote seems a particularly appropriate subject for canid brain study in that its neural anatomy (both cerebral and cerebellar) appears primitive to other *Canis* species. Detailed comparisons herein will be made with brains (*sensu stricto*) of dog, *C. familiaris*, and red wolf, *C. rufus*. This latter species is included particularly because (1) its systematic status has been disputed (e.g., Paradiso, 1965, 1968; Lawrence and Bossert, 1967); (2) its precarious status due to reduced population size and apparent recent hybridization with other canids urges prompt scientific study and management; and (3) no descriptions of its nervous anatomy have been published, except on the cerebellum (Atkins and Dillon, 1971).

Seen from the lateral aspect (Fig. 2), most of the surface convolutions in the coyote cerebrum are visible, and all structures labeled on *C. latrans* (Fig. 2A) are found on the other species as well. This view and Fig. 3 (dorsal aspect) are the most instructive in comparisons with endocasts. Relationships with other brain divisions obscure surface features of most other cerebral regions; the posterior cerebellum offers little, and the ventral brainstem virtually no, information of phylogenetic value in endocasts.

The entolateral sulcus develops late in canid evolution (Fig. 1), just prior to the first fossil appearance of *Canis*, and this sulcus appears as a shallow and discontinuous series of grooves on the dorsal surface in coyotes. By

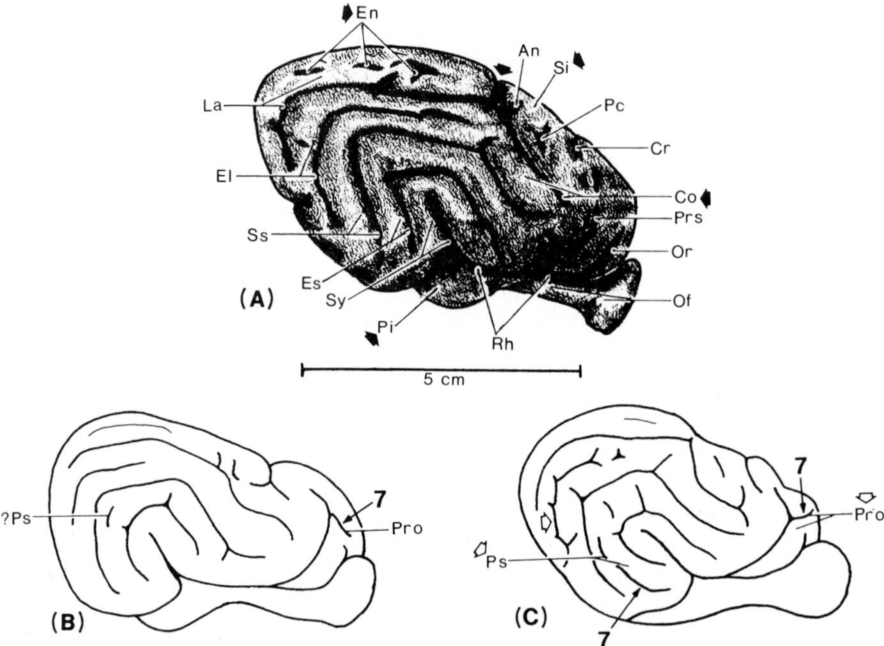

Fig. 2. Lateral view of the right cerebrum. (A) *Canis latrans*—An, ansate sulcus; Co, coronal s. & gyrus; Cr, cruciate s.; El, ectolateral s. & g.; En, entolateral s. & g.; Es, ectosylvian s. & g.; La, lateral s. & g.; Of, olfactory bulb and tract; Or, orbital s.; Pc, postcruciate s.; Pi, piriform lobe; Prs, presylvian s.; Rh, rhinal fissure; Si, sigmoid g.; Ss, suprasylvian s. & g.; Sy, sylvian s. & g. (B) *C. familiaris.* (C) *C. rufus*—Pro, prorean s.; Ps, postsylvian s. & g. (for "7," see Fig. 1). Scale refers to A only; A & C are the same length, with B being variable. Arrows indicate structures or relationships stressed in text.

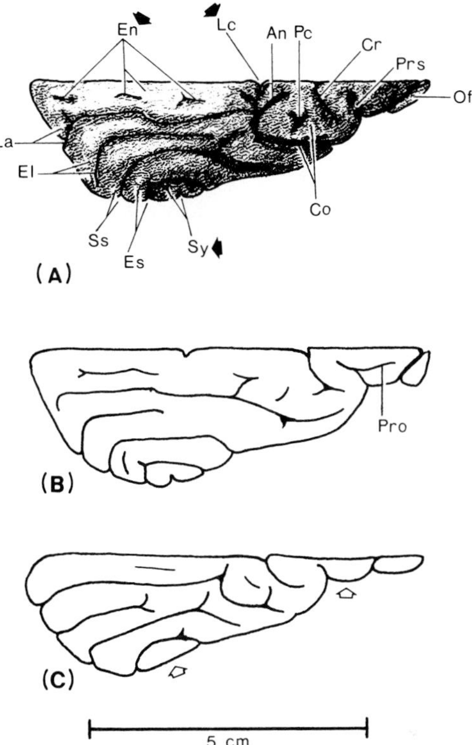

Fig. 3. Dorsal view of the cerebrum. (A) *Canis latrans*—Lc, lesser cruciate sulcus; all other abbreviations as in Fig. 2. (B) *C. familiaris*. (C) *C. rufus*. Scale refers to A and C.

contrast, it is a fully infolded sulcus—short in *C. rufus*, moderately long in the dog, and extending almost the entire *dorsal* length of the lateral gyrus in *C. lupus*. The piriform lobe (paleocortex) is still well exposed laterally in coyote and dog, but this has been more fully covered by ventrad expansion of the neocortex in red wolf. In coyote, the coronal suture may continue onto the medial face with the lesser cruciate sulcus (Fig. 2A, arrow; Figs. 3 and 4, labeled), completely separating the sigmoid and lateral gyri, although this is not a constant feature.

Three aspects of the red wolf lateral cerebrum should be noted. The prorean sulcus is well developed (as in dog and grey wolf); this appears inconsistently on coyote cerebra. A deep and long sulcus appears posterior to the ectosylvian, and this is here labeled the postsylvian. A series of shallow furrows occurs in the homologous site in *C. lupus*, and a short sulcus appearing in some dog specimens may be homologous (Fig. 2B). Finally, the gyral form is much more complex in *C. rufus* due to the

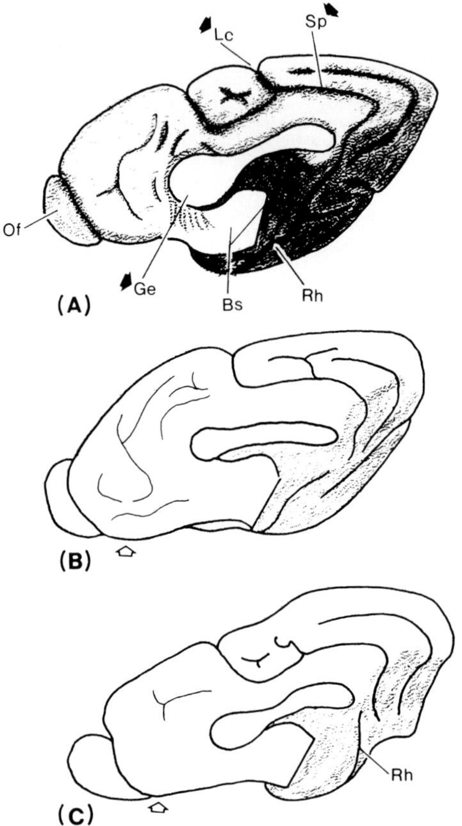

Fig. 4. Medial view of the cerebrum. (A) *Canis latrans*—Bs, cut faces (midsagittal and transverse) of brainstem; Ge, genu of corpus callosum (sectioned); Sp, splenial s.; all other abbreviations as in previous figures. (B) *C. familiaris*. (C) *C. rufus*.

presence of many sulcal spurs and dimples. Most of these have been omitted in Fig. 2C for the sake of simplicity, but the entolateral sulcus and gyrus exemplify this condition.

With the exception of the poorly formed entolateral sulcus, the coronal-lesser cruciate connection, and the variable prorean sulcus, the dorsal views of coyote and dog cerebra (Figs. 3A,B) are alike. In contrast, the elongate narrowness of the frontal region in *C. rufus* (Fig. 3C) can now be appreciated. England (1973) noted a similar elongation of the frontal gyrus in *C. lupus*, but comparison of the two species shows the grey wolf cerebral thickness is considerably greater in this region than that of the red. Only part of this added width is due to the greater size of the grey wolf brain. The ventrad expansion and rotation of the neocortex in *C. rufus* is emphasized by concealment of the sylvian sulcus in this view; this relationship applies to *C. lupus* also.

The medial faces are different in all three species (Fig. 4). The genu of the corpus callosum in coyote is considerably larger than in other canid species. The splenial sulcus continues onto the ventrolateral cortex (above the cerebellum) to join the rhinal fissure (in *C. rufus,* this latter is displaced posteriad by the neocortical expansion). The medial face of the frontal lobe in coyote is marked by several shallow sulci, and these appear at least partly homologous to fissures on the dog cerebrum. Red wolf presents a marked contrast, showing one small, faint indentation. This lack of sulcation in *C. rufus* accords with reduced frontal bulk noted above. This area is flat and rather bland in all three species.

Although the cerebral sulcal pattern develops rather late in ontogeny, the morphological pattern described above for coyote is fully formed in several *C. latrans* pups whose body sizes were about one-third that of adults.

B. Anatomy of the Coyote Cerebellum

Details of gross cerebellar anatomy for these species is described elsewhere (Atkins and Dillon, 1971). Even a brief glance at Fig. 5 indicates the extreme complexity of cortical folding in this organ among *Canis* species, but such intricacy offers numerous opportunities for interspecific variation. Further, there have been few comparative cerebellar studies between closely related species (Brauer, 1966; Dillon and Atkins, 1970). These factors naturally raise concern about *intra*specific variability as well; this question is discussed in a later section.

Figure 5 illustrates the right half only of a coyote cerebellum which has been detached from the remainder of the brain and "exploded" into its lobular divisions. This organ is bilaterally symmetrical except that the posterior vermis is distorted into an S-shaped twist (Fig. 5B). The midline vermis has been related neurologically to the lateral hemispheres as indicated. There is still some dispute over nomenclature and boundaries of divisions, but these problems do not affect the evolutionary matters under discussion.

Comparable cerebellar views of coyote, dog, and red wolf appear in Fig. 6. The following interspecific differences are notable, the numbers below being referrable to figure labels. Items 1–7 refer specifically to *C. latrans:*

1. The anterior lobe in coyote is more than one-half the total width.

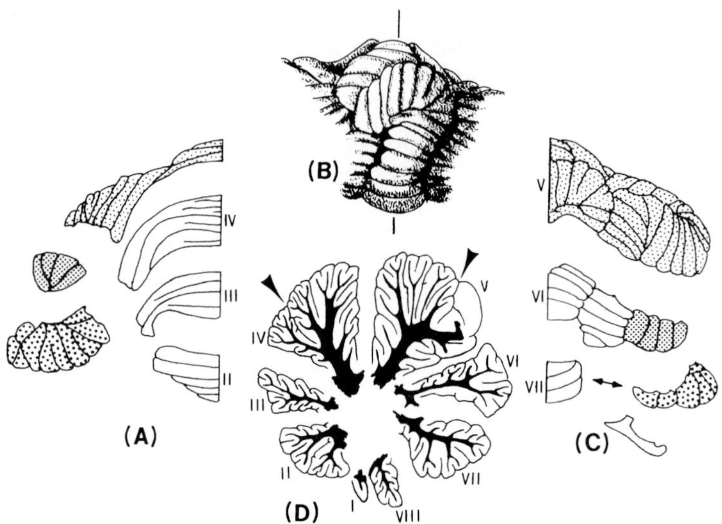

Fig. 5. Right half of cerebellum of *Canis latrans* dissected to show lobulation. (A) Anterior view. (B) Detail of posterior vermis, showing asymmetry; lines above and below indicate midsagittal plane. (C) Posterior view. (D) Midsagittal cut face. I- VIII, vermian lobules. Arrowheads on (D) indicate division of these segments according to nomenclature of Larsell (1953); enumeration would then change to I-X.

2. The parafloccular process is relatively prominent.
3. The paraflocculus is large; both 1 and 3 cause reduced anterior exposure of the ansiform lobule (Af).
4. Vermian lobule VII (uvula) reaches its greatest *Canis* size.
5. Posterior hemispheric folia are fewer in number and larger in coyote; those folia labeled "5" in Fig. 6 are merely exemplary.
6. Posterior ventral parafloccular limb is reduced in size.
7. The vermian twist is broadest in coyote.

The preceding traits distinguish *C. latrans* from all other species of *Canis* which have been examined. In the following traits, coyote and dog are alike, but *C. rufus* differs:

8. Lateral-most ansiform folia are vertical (*C. rufus*, lateral).
9. Anterior paraflocculus extends about one-half the width of each hemisection before recurving (*C. rufus*, greater than half).
10. Lobule I composed of a single folium (*C. rufus*, three; in a small proportion of coyote specimens examined, this lobule is also trifoliate).

11. Lobule II receives two principal tracts (black) from the central medullary body (*C. rufus*, one).

12. Lobule III is small and receives a single tract (*C. rufus*, large, with two tracts).

13. Tracts of lobule VI and VII branch from a short common stem (*C. rufus*, these tracts branch individually from that of lobule V).

14. Lobule VIII is fairly complex with about eight folia [*C. rufus*, lobule VIII is simpler (not smaller) with about three folia].

15. Vermis is more or less circular in midsagittal section (*C. rufus*, ovoid).

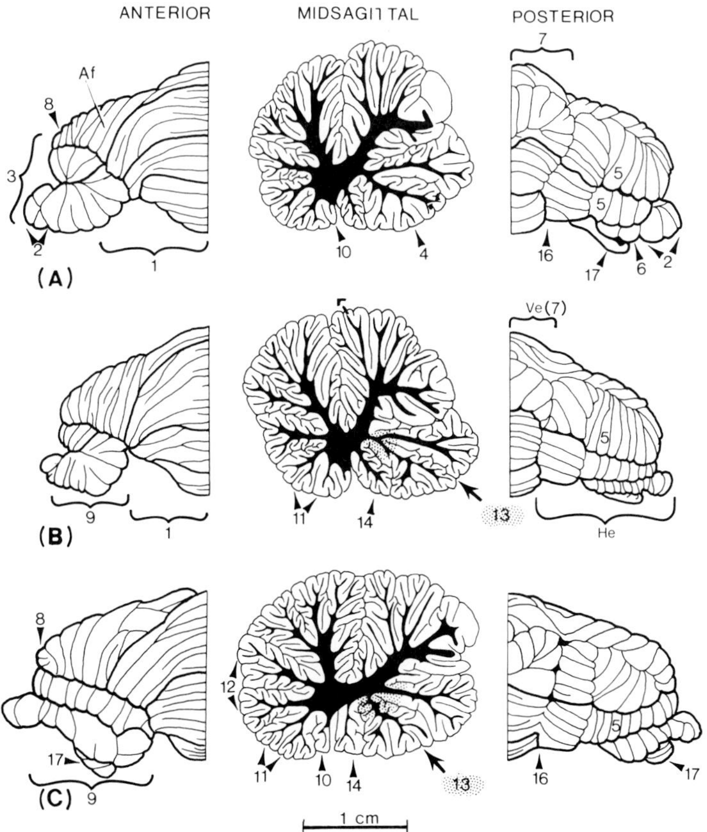

Fig. 6. Three views of the right half of the cerebellum. (A) *Canis latrans*. (B) *C. familiaris*. (C) *C. rufus*. Af, ansiform lobule; He, hemisphere; Ve, vermis; numbers refer to list of traits in text.

16. Paramedian sulcus is deep (*C. rufus*, the sulcus is merely a shallow furrow lateral to lobule VI).

17. Nodulus is narrow and poorly foliate; not visible anteriorly (*C. rufus*, well foliated and prominent anteriorly and posteriorly).

In all of these latter traits except 9 and 12, *C. rufus* and *C. lupus* agree. *Canis lupus* differs from other *Canis* species in having a small lobule VI.

C. Anatomy of the Coyote Brainstem and Cord

The remainder of the central nervous system is phylogenetically quite old, and tends to be stable in gross appearance. No outstanding variation occurs in the coyote brainstem when compared to that of dog. The spinal cord extends to the junction of vertebrae L-6 and L-7, as in the dog. Anatomy of peripheral nerves and of tracts and nuclei are beyond the scope of this chapter.

IV. COYOTE BRAIN EVOLUTION

A. Phylogenetic Considerations

Although differences occur, the cerebra of these three animals are very much alike. Fox (1971) examined the anatomy of the cerebrum in a large series (65) of dogs in several breeds; he found there was one basic sulcal pattern in all, which was present from birth. Principal variations noted related to brain size and shape, and these were a function of body size and skull form of the various breeds. All other *Canis* species conform to this same basic pattern but are more consistent because of greater internal homogeneity of body form and size. To the extent that variations occur between coyote, dog, and red wolf, *C. latrans* appears most closely similar to late Tertiary endocasts, and it can be proposed that coyote is closest to the primitive stem of the genus in cerebral structure.

Such a hypothesis also agrees with the cerebellar comparisons. Fifty-seven coyote cerebella were examined, plus 28 dogs, breed unknown, and five red wolves. Again, there was remarkable intraspecific consistency in the traits listed in Section III,B above, as well as in many nonlisted traits which did not vary among these three species or else within the genus or the family. In contrast to the cerebrum, there was considerable interspecific variation among cerebella of these animals. Dog and coyote were much alike, although not identical. Atkins and Dillon (1971) concluded from cerebellar comparisons that the dog was more closely related to the jackals, *C. aureus* and *C. mesomelas* and that coyote was primitive to all of these.

Brain comparisons with canids identified as red wolves indicate in both cerebral and, especially, cerebellar anatomy that these are quite distinct animals. The cerebral and, especially, cerebellar forms of *C. rufus* are in good agreement (but surely not identical) with *C. lupus*, and both of these are quite advanced in comparison to *C. latrans*.

B. Evolution of Cerebral Structure: Coyote, A Case in Point

These inter- and intraspecific comparisons are useful to describe evolution of the brain itself. The comparisons above have dealt in large part with the folding of cortex—either cerebral or cerebellar. The sagittal section of cerebellum demonstrates that folial, lobular, and lobar forms reflect distribution of nerve tracts deep to them; section of cerebral neocortex would show the same relationship, but the large size and consistently superficial location of gyri make this unnecessary.

The development of a genetically controlled, species-unique folding must have functional significance, and in the brain, this might relate to behavioral attributes. Since cerebral cortex often has precise point-to-point localization for sensory and motor innervation, it is possible to map the cortex surface by electrode measurements of peripheral stimulation or by observation of peripheral response to cortical excitation. In gyrencephalic cerebra, sulci frequently seem to bound distinct functional and, occasionally, cytoarchitectural areas.

Dog cortex has been mapped for neural function, but coyote has not. Although the conservative nature of the gross gyral pattern has been stressed, it can only be an error to infer coyote brain-periphery or brain-behavior relations from dog data, except in the most general and least informative way. This caution is emphasized by the electrophysiological comparisons of different procyonid species by Welker and associates (e.g., Welker and Campos, 1963; Welker *et al.*, 1964); the cerebra of raccoon (*Procyon lotor*), coati (*Nasua narica*), ringtail or cacomistle (*Bassariscus astutus*), kinkajou (*Potos flavus*), and red panda (*Ailurus fulgens*) have, again, a basic sulcal pattern that delimits areas generally similar in function, but *detailed* representations were quite individual and stable among these species. It would seem to follow, as Welker and Campos (1963) note, that functional extrapolation backward to endocranial casts is particularly hazardous.

Thus, neural activity should not be construed from anatomical form; however, the data of Welker and Campos (1963) do suggest a method of examining the evolution of behavior. Their results clearly indicate that sulcal formation is related to evolution of cortical specialization—that surface folding delimits physiological relationship. Relevant to this, they note that cacomistle "... has the least complicated fissural pattern ..." followed by kinkajou, then the other procyonid species.*

This exact kind of situation was noted above in comparisons of *C. latrans* and *C. rufus* cerebra. Coyote sulci tend to be simple and continuous; their gyri generally are smooth. by contrast, red wolf sulci include many short spurs and branches, and the gyri are frequently dented and dimpled. Dog is intermediate (in complexity, not phylogeny!). If these markings are electrophysiologically significant and genetically determined, mapping of their cerebral cortices correlated with behavior studies might indicate much about evolutionary divergence of these species.

C. Evolution of Cerebellar Structure: Coyote, A Case in Point

Interspecific variation in cerebellar lobar, lobular, and folial patterns are more difficult to examine or explain. Cerebellar cortex has a broad point-to-point reference with the periphery, but the differences in scale and complexity of the folding, plus the entirely different functional mode of this organ—cerebellum is generally inhibitory while cerebrum is generally excitatory—suggest that its responses to selection pressures are different.

In addition, there are certain contradictory findings from morphological and physiological studies. As Fig. 5 indicates, anatomical division and subdivision of the cerebellum tends to be transverse to the long axis of the brain. While the hierarchical ranking of some divisions is argued, the existence of these divisions is not disputed. The posterior vermian asymmetry of various carnivorans and ungulates are secondarily developed and do not affect the basic anatomical relationships.

The physiological projections, both afferent and efferent, are linear in the long axis of the cerebellum and of the entire CNS (Brodal, 1954; Jansen, 1954; Oscarsson, 1969; Voogd, 1969). Korneliussen (1967, 1968, 1969) confirms a longitudinal zonation of cerebellar corticogenesis and observes that function often does not correlate with lobular division.

The large series of coyote cerebella available provided an opportunity to test intraspecific constancy. The only variation noted from the "standard" coyote (described, in part, above; in part, see Atkins, 1970; Atkins and Dillon, 1971) appeared in the first vermian lobule. Usually, this includes a single folium, but in approximately 25% of the specimens, there are three

* Comparisons of cerebellar anatomy in the Procyonidae strongly suggest exactly this phylogenetic progression from extremely primitive (cacomistle) to more derived species, the red panda being most advanced.

folia, as in the two wolf species. This distribution could not be related to the several subspecies represented in the collection.

An attempt was made to quantify cerebellar descriptions by counting the number of vermian folia (per lobule, per lobe, and total) in the hope (and expectation) that there is a range characteristic of each species. For example, the coyote vermis illustrated in Figs. 5 and 6, contains 107 folia, including those not in the midsagittal section because of the vermian twist; the *C. rufus* shown has 122. After counting nine coyote specimens, the total folial count showed a range variation of approximately 30%. The tabulation was discontinued.

In spite of such variation, the basic anatomical form and relationships of each lobule is consistent within a species—not only in the canids, but also in every other mammal for which a large number of specimens is available. It is evident, then, that factors, which are independent of regional cortical function or patterns of cortical ontogeny are controlling cerebellar form, and that these patterns are not only stable, in a broad sense, but are subject to selection pressure.

The canids would be good subjects in which to characterize this genetic control. The 3:1 population ratio for folial variation in the first lobule of coyote cerebellum is suggestive, and analysis of a larger series of specimens might certify a variety of traits subject to genetic crosses. Further, several specimens were obtained in this survey which, from other physical criteria, were predicted to be hybrids; coyote–dog, coyote–red wolf, or dog–red wolf. Analysis of their cerebellar structure indicated wide variation from patterns normal for any canid species. Some of the variant traits did occur in one species or another (although the total "mix" was wrong), but in other instances, a blend seemed to occur. Since each canid species apparently has a distinctive cerebellum (and, to less extent, cerebrum) and since all *Canis* species apparently hybridize viably, these may be excellent experimental subjects to address such basic evolutionary questions as the role and mechanism of sulcation or the topographic development of nerve cell interrelationships during corticogenesis.

D. Formation of Sulcal Patterns

Welker and Campos (1963) support observations that surface folding of cerebral cortex often separates distinct physiological areas and that degree of utilization of a cortical area in behavior correlates positively with the proportion of CNS devoted to that activity. They hypothesize with Connolly (1950) that sulcal indentations represent relatively inactive areas (neurologically) which are overgrown by more active adjacent areas.

Such a theory is consistent with their observations but may not go far enough. All fissures do not demark unique physiological areas, and vice versa (especially in the lissencephalic cerebrum). Further, such observations have no relevance to cerebellar sulcation in which functional areas correlate poorly, if at all, with anatomical segregation.

Figure 1 may illustrate more than merely a historical progression. The temporal distribution of sulci over the face of the cerebrum, particularly when viewed on the size scale of the endocasts themselves, suggest a balance of growth in which distant if not antipodal areas underwent more or less simultaneous development. Adjacent areas did not seem to initiate such proliferation and sulcation at the same time although it seems likely that neighboring regions could simultaneously expand established growth patterns.

That particular sequence of evolution in the canid cerebrum or the distances separating incipient gyri may not be intrinsically important themselves, although they doubtless established many physiological and behavioral trends that ultimately produced modern canids. However, they do suggest a model for sulcation that includes the procyonid observations above but is more harmonious with evolutionary principles—namely, that regional overgrowth of a brain area resulting ultimately in gyrus–sulcus relationships is accomplished through significant change in the genome relative to regional cortical structure. This process will accomplish the same result as now reported by Welker and Campos (1963), but it places the anatomical–physiological horse before the ethological cart—it states that neurological potential precedes the nonneural components of an activity, although the developing activity–ability may then become a positive selective force for continued neural proliferation.

The human cerebral speech center may represent just such incipient evolution. The study of human–nonhuman interspecies communication is currently receiving much attention, and it has become evident that at least some nonhumans cannot talk mainly because they lack this proper neurological apparatus. This missing cortical center has little or nothing to do with basic intelligence or with basic communication; most animal species communicate with each other far better than sophisticated humans communicate with them. It seems, then, that advanced evolution of a small cortical area has made possible the use and further evolution of ordinary vocal–respiratory organs in an extraordinary way. This exact sequence can be applied with equal ease to observations on the sensory abilities of procyonid forepaw and procyonid cerebrum made by Welker and his associates, the principal difference being longer time for evolution with a more stable and efficient result in terms of operational error.

Thus, it is proposed that the evolution and proliferation of cortex or other neural complexes then permits development of abilities or processes, rather than abilities or behavior initiating cortical growth. This is less Lamarckian.

This hypothesis might also explain another extraordinary human and, to lesser degree, coyote attribute—intelligence.* Reed (1965) suggests that probably no evolutionary situation exists in which intelligence would have negative selective value. He is probably right, but it has been difficult to explain why, if intelligence is so good, it is so rare and so limited. In a half billion years of vertebrate CNS evolution, only human brains have made it big—literally and figuratively. From the preceding discussion the answer is suggested that evolution of the apparatus of intelligence (probably by the chance operation of genetic systems) must precede its realization.

The mechanics of sulcus formation, by extension, may relate not to discontinuities of neural function but to discontinuities of evolution in the form of local cortical metabolic activity. The proliferation of new regions by evolution as well as by ontogeny must represent an energy drain. The patterns of sulcal–gyral form may simply reflect the distribution systems of vascular supply. It is a common observation that major vessels ramify over the cerebral surface following the sulcal pattern. Deep to these, there is an extensive and intricate network of minor vessels which penetrate all cerebral and cerebellar sulci, ultimately branching perpendicularly into the cortex.

It has been assumed that these are merely the feeder vessels one would expect to encounter. To the contrary, they may determine sulcal patterns ontogenetically and phylogenetically through local supply of nutrients. Such a mechanism would clarify the phenomenon noted in the coyote cerebellum—viz., orderly and stable lobation and lobulation with inconstant foliation at sublobular levels. Sulcation, which does not follow neural function in the cerebellum and which does usually follow it in the cerebrum, may result from vascular rather than neural evolution.

V. SYNOPSIS

Nervous system evolution is both conservative and responsive. Precise anatomical relationships, both gross and microscopic, as well as complex, structure promote resistance to trivial change; however, the immediate contact of the nervous system to internal and external environments promotes flexibility. Impressions of genetically controlled folding of cerebral and cerebellar cortices onto the inner skull face permits production of endocasts of fossil species, and the sequential appearance of cerebral sulci in

* Intelligence is here used loosely to include all purposeful or innovative behavior not under genetic or physiological control.

canid fossils gives a good picture of canid cerebral evolution. Comparisons of these with modern canid cerebral and cerebellar anatomy indicates *C. latrans* (1) has a relatively primitive structure and (2) is systematically quite distinct from *C. rufus*, whose specific status has been disputed. Using details of coyote cortical anatomy, the evolutionary mechanisms governing morphological–physiological relationships is discussed, and a theory on the mode of sulcus formation is advanced which is consistent with both cerebral (functional) and cerebellar (nonfunctional) anatomical subdivision.

ACKNOWLEDGMENTS

Many specimens for this study were provided by John Steele, Alton Bridgewater, Professor Dr. Kurt Brauer, Glenn Chambers, David Zirub, Paul Speigler, the Division of Mammals of the U.S. National Museum of Natural History (Smithsonian), and the St. Louis Zoological Gardens. I am most grateful for their cooperation. Bill Bosley and Dan Goldberg provided much histological and dissection assistance. L. S. Dillon provided ready access to his brain collection and his wits. Part of this investigation was supported by U.S. Public Health Service Research Grant No. NB06525 from the Institute of Neurological Disease and Stroke.

REFERENCES

Atkins, D. L. (1970). Comparative Morphology and Evolution of the Cerebellum in the Mammalian Order Carnivora. Ph.D. Thesis, Texas A & M Univ., College Station.

Atkins, D. L., and Dillon, L. S. (1971). *J. Mammal.* **52,** 96–107.

Atkins, D. L., and Goldberg, D. J. (1972). *Am. Zool.* **12,** 728.

Bolk, L. (1906). "Das Cerebellum der Säugetiere." Bohn, Haarlem.

Brauer, K. (1966). *J. Hirnforsch.* **8,** 359–415.

Brodal, A. (1954). *In* "Aspects of Cerebellar Anatomy" (J. Jansen and A. Brodal, eds.), pp. 82–188. Johan Grundt Tanum Forlag, Oslo.

Connolly, C. J. (1950). "External Morphology of the Primate Brain." Thomas, Springfield, Illinois. [Cited in Welker and Campos (1963), p. 32.]

Dillon, L. S. (1962). *J. Comp. Neurol.* **118,** 343–353.

Dillon, L. S., and Atkins, D. L. (1970). *Anat. Rec.* **168,** 415–432.

Dillon, L. S., and Brauer, K. (1970). *J. Hirnforsch.* **12,** 217–232.

duBrul, E. L. (1960). *Perspect. Biol. Med.* **4,** 40–57.

England, D. R. (1973). The Phylogeny of the Order Carnivora Based on Cerebral Structure. Ph.D. Thesis, Texas A & M Univ., College Station.

Fox, M. W. (1966). *Experientia* **22,** 111–112.

Fox, M. W. (1971). "Integrative Development of Brain and Behavior in the Dog." Univ. of Chicago Press, Chicago, Illinois.

Hofer, H. O. (1969). *Ann. N.Y. Acad. Sci.* **167,** 341–356.

Jakway, G. E., and Clement, J. T. (1967). *Bull. South. Calif. Acad. Sci.* **66,** 39–45.

Jansen, J. (1954). *In* "Aspects of Cerebellar Anatomy" (J. Jansen and A. Brodal, eds.), pp. 189–248. Johan Grundt Tanum Forlag, Oslo.

Korneliussen, H. K. (1967). *J. Hirnforsch.* **9,** 151–185.

Korneliussen, H. K. (1968). *Brain Res.* **8,** 229–236.
Korneliussen, H. K. (1969). *In* "Neurobiology of Cerebellar Evolution and Development" (R. Llinás, ed.), pp. 515–523. Am. Med. Assoc., Chicago, Illinois.
Larsell, O. (1953). *J. Comp. Neurol.* **99,** 135–200.
Larsell, O. (1970). "The Comparative Anatomy and Histology of the Cerebellum from Monotremes through Apes." Univ. of Minnesota Press, Minneapolis.
Latimer, H. B. (1942). *Growth* **6,** 39–47.
Lawrence, B., and Bossert, W. H. (1967). *Am. Zool.* **7,** 223–232.
Miller, M. E. (1964). "Anatomy of the Dog." Saunders, Philadelphia, Pennsylvania.
Oscarsson, O. (1969). *In* "Neurobiology of Cerebellar Evolution and Development" (R. Llinás, ed.), pp. 525–537. Am. Med. Assoc., Chicago, Illinois.
Paradiso, J. L. (1965). *Southwest Nat.* **10,** 318–319.
Paradiso, J. L. (1968). *Am. Midl. Nat.* **80,** 529–534.
Radinsky, L. (1967). *Science* **155,** 836–837.
Radinsky, L. B. (1969). *Ann. N.Y. Acad. Sci.* **167,** 277–288.
Radinsky, L. (1971). *Evolution* **25,** 518–522.
Radinsky, L. (1973). *Brain. Behav. Evol.* **7,** 169–202.
Reed, S. C. (1965). *Am. Sci.* **53,** 317–326.
Riley, H. A. (1928). *Arch. Neurol. Psychiat.* **20,** 895–1034.
Scott, W. B., and Jepson, G. L. (1936). *Trans. Am. Phil. Soc.* **28,** 1–153.
Seiferle, E. (1966). *Acta Anat.* **63,** 346–362.
Tilney, F. (1931). *Bull. Neurol. Inst. N.Y.* **1,** 430–505.
Voogd, J. (1969). *In* "Neurobiology of Cerebellar Evolution and Development" (R. Llinás, ed.), pp. 493–514. Am. Med. Assoc., Chicago, Illinois.
Weidenreich, F. (1941). *Trans. Am. Phil. Soc.* **31,** 321–442.
Welker, W. I., and Campos, G. B. (1963). *J. Comp. Neurol.* **120,** 19–36.
Welker, W. I., Johnson, J. I., and Pubols, B. H. (1964). *Am. Zool.* **4,** 75–94.

3

Parasites and Diseases of Coyotes

H. T. Gier, S. M. Kruckenberg, and R. J. Marler

I. INTRODUCTION

A. General

Parasites are now known to have a much greater influence on coyote well-being than has been considered. The total influence is not yet fully understood, nor is the occurrence, rate of infestation, or immediate consequence of infestation known. A study of occurrence of parasites or incidence of disease in Texas cannot be interpolated to Nebraska or California. Neither can effects of infestations during the winter be transferred to summer, or those determined during times of nutritional stress be transferred to times of plenty.

Parasites are of extreme importance under conditions of poor nutrition (unusually low rabbit–rodent availability) and extremes in weather. Numerous authors have noted how low incidence of lice (*Trichodectes canis*) and of mange are continued over long time intervals; conditions then change and the louse–mange complex becomes a killer. In the Great Plains (1950–1970), lice and mange were evident on no more than 0.5% of the coyotes. By 1970, coyote populations across the prairies were at an all time high, bounties were removed as worthless, so take was reduced. In 1972, use of all toxicants for control was eliminated, and as pelts were essentially worthless, kill was farther reduced. With adequate rabbit–rodent populations, reproduction of coyotes continued unabated through the spring of 1973, essentially doubling the numbers of coyotes from May 1970 to May 1973. But, by late 1972, rabbits and rodents were noticeably reduced, and became scarce during the winter, but not scarce enough to inhibit reproduction. The big pup crop of April–May 1973 was too much for the food supply; many coyotes were distinctly underfed; there was a heavier than usual pup loss; and nearly one-third of the surviving pups were stunted (adult weight < 10 kg).

The shortage of natural food in 1972–1973, plus too frequent contact within the population provided the right conditions for rapid spread and heavy infestations of both lice (*Trichodectes*) and mange (sarcoptic). Continued poor nutrition in Fall 1973 enhanced the spread of the parasites such that reports of severe pelt damage ranged from 50% in Iowa, NW Missouri, and NE Kansas to 10% in SE Kansas and northern Oklahoma. Most dealers in the area refused to buy any pelts after Jan 1, 1974, because of the severity of pelt damage.

Severe blizzard conditions with nightly temperatures well below −15°C for 15 consecutive days, Jan 10–25, 1974, all the way down to Texas, resulted in death by freezing of many of the denuded and hair-matted "mangy" coyotes. Even with this heavy winter loss and three consecutive years of exceedingly low reproductive rate, inadequate nutrition, lice, and mange continued to be a coyote reduction syndrome across the Plains, and preconditioned coyotes to additional infections of parasites—viral, bacterial, protozoan, helminthic, or arthropod.

B. Approach

Materials for this report were gathered from all available sources: (1) our own combined experience of 40+ years of direct coyote research; (2) original research reports in scientific publications; (3) specific and personal communications from many of our friends about work not yet published; and (4) summaries in journals and books. Several recent books provided basic information that proved to be invaluable in our analysis of coyote problems, i.e., "Infectious Disease of Wild Animals," Davis, Karstad, and Trainer (1970); "Parasitic Diseases of Wild Mammals," Davis and Anderson (1971); "Veterinary Parasitology," Krull (1969); "Nematode Parasites of Domestic Animals and Man," Levine (1968); and "Parasites of Laboratory Animals," Flynn (1973). These books provide current information on epidemiology, pathology, life histories, and treatment, and are highly recommended for those readers who desire to gain more information about any phase of this work beyond the scope of the present treatise.

Terminology, although still confused, was simplified as much as possible, and to the limit of feasibility the nomenclature used by the authors of the above-listed references were used. Taxonomic relationships of tapeworms were taken from reports of Esch and Self (1965) and Verster (1969) and, on their authority, reports of invalid or synonomyzed species were changed to comply with the currently accepted nomenclature. Tick nomenclature follows Cooley and Kohls (1945) or Flynn (1973), and flea nomenclature, for the most part, follows Hubbard (1947) "Fleas of Western North America." Common names of mammals were used unless generic or family names better characterize the group under discussion.

II. ECTOPARASITES

A. Mange

Coyotes are afflicted with at least two kinds of mange (Table I). Demodectic mange results from infection of hair follicles by the mange mite, *Demodex canis*, resulting in loss of hair, scaly skin, and perhaps secondary bacterial infection. Sarcoptic mange (itch) occurs with *Sarcoptes scabei canis* burrowing into the epidermal layer of the skin, resulting in lymph oozing through the skin and intensive itch which causes much rubbing or biting of the infected area. Bacterial growth in the wet underfur produces a strong mousy to fetid odor; the wet, matted fur has little insulating value.

Demodectic mange has apparently not been specifically reported for the coyote, but "hairless coyotes" have been indicated throughout coyote country (Knowles, 1914; Young and Jackson, 1951) without determination as to which mange was involved. Sarcoptic mange appears to be the more common, and at present (since 1972) there is a rather severe scourge of Sarcoptic mange in coyotes (and red foxes) from Minnesota to Texas. Some of the effects of this epizootic are given in Section I,A.

TABLE I
Mites and Ticks Parasitic on Coyotes

Parasite	Normal host	Frequency on coyote[a]			Associate intermediate host for[b]	Geographic range and references
		1	2	3		
Demodicidae *Demodex canis*	Dogs, wolves, foxes	x	to	x	Bacterial and fungal infections	Cosmopolitan[c,d,e]
Sarcoptidae *Sarcoptes scabei canis*	Dogs, wolves, foxes	x	to	x	Staphylococcus infections	Cosmopolitan[c,d,e]; Kansas[f]; Montana[g]; Wisconsin[h]
Argasidae *Otobius megnini*	Birds, rodents, domestic animals	x	to	x	Unknown	Southwest U.S; Mexico[e,i]; Texas[j]
Ixodidae						
Ixodes angustus	Rodents	x			RMSF	British Columbia to Nova Scotia[k,l]; Rocky Mountain States[e,i,m]
Ixodes banksi	Prairie dogs, badgers	x			Unknown	Oklahoma[m]; Arkansas[e]
Ixodes cookei	Marmots, skunks, raccoons	x			Unknown	Nova Scotia to Oklahoma[i,l,m]; Texas[n]
Ixodes kingi	Raccoons, foxes, skunks	x			Unknown	Western U.S. to Canda[e,i,m]; Kansas[f]; Oklahoma[i]
Ixodes pacificus	Dogs, cows, deer		x		Tick fever	West Coast[i,m]; Mexico to British Columbia[e]

Ixodes rugosa	Dogs, skunks, foxes	x			Unknown	British Columbia to Mexico[e,k,l,m]
Ixodes scapularis	Dogs, raccoons, cows, lynxes	x			Anapl.	Texas and Oklahoma to East Coast[e,m]
Amblyomma americana	Deer, domestic mammals	x	to	x	RMSF, QF, tul. Theileria	Southern U.S. and Mexico[i,m]; west to central Texas[e]
Amblyomma cajennense	Domestic and wild mammals		?		RMSF, Q-F, tul., Theileria	Southern Texas and Mexico[e,m]
Rhipicephalus sanguines	Dogs	x			Q-F, babesiosis	Mexico, north to Oklahoma and Arkansas[e,i,m]; Texas[n]
Dermacentor albipictus	Caribou, elk		?		Tick fever	Nova Scotia[l,o]; British Columbia[k] to New Mexico[e,i]
Dermacentor andersoni	Mammals	x	to	x	RMSF, Q-F, tul.	Mountains, Canada to Mexico[e,i]
Dermaceto occidentalis	Deer, cows, horses, dogs		x			Southern Oregon and California[e,i]
Dermacentor variabilis	Rabbits, deer, nymphs on rodents		x		Tul., anapl.	Nova Scotia to British Columbia[k,o]; south to Mexico except Rocky Mountain States[e,i,p]

[a] 1 = Rare; 2 = occasional; 3 = common, in season.

[b] Abbreviations: RMSF = Rocky Mountain spotted fever; Q-F = Q-fever; tul. = tularemia; anapl. = anaplasmosis.

References: [c] Davis *et al.* (1970); [d] Flynn (1973); [e] Krull (1969); [f] Gier and Ameel (1959); [g] Knowles (1914); [h] Trainer and Hale (1969); [i] Bishopp and Trembly (1945); [j] Smith (1976 personal communication); [k] Gregson (1956); [l] Martell *et al.* (1969); [m] Cooley and Kohls (1945); [n] Eads (1948); [o] Dodds *et al.* (1969); [p] Stout *et al.* (1971).

We have found no authentic reports of psoroptic mange, chorioptic mange, nor otodectic mange in coyotes. No other mites are known to have more than incidental or accidental association with coyotes.

B. Ticks

Coyotes are infested with various species of ticks throughout the season of tick activity: May–August in the Northwest; March–November in Arkansas. Occasionally a tick may attach on the legs or in the soft skin of the axilla or groin, but most ticks are found in the short hair of the face and ears.

In general, the dominant tick of the area is the one found most frequently on the coyotes of that area (Table I). The eastern wood tick, *Dermacentor variabilis,* adult form only, comprised over 95% of all the ticks found on coyotes in Kansas, and apparently is the dominant coyote tick from the Rockies east to the Atlantic, and south into Texas. From Arkansas and Oklahoma south, *Amblyomma* sp., principally *A. americana* the "Lone Star tick," becomes the most frequent, with *A. cajennense* partially replacing the Lone Star from south central Texas through Mexico. Several other species of *Amblyomma,* mainly *A. inornatum* were listed by Cooley and Kohls (1945) as occuring on coyotes from Oklahoma south. In the Rocky Mountains *Dermacentor andersoni* (*venustus*) is the main coyote tick except that *D. variabilis* has become established in eastern Montana, and in western Idaho, Oregon, and California, (Stout *et al.*, 1971) and seems to be extending its range. *Dermacentor pacificus* and *D. occidentalis* are the principle coyote ticks from British Columbia southward into Mexico.

The brown dog tick, *Rhipicephalus sanguineus* has not been reported as occuring on coyotes, although it is a rather common tick on dogs from east Texas and Oklahoma north. As coyotes increase in number in the eastern United States and more studies are conducted, *R. sanguineus* will probably be found as regular guests on coyotes.

The spinous ear tick nymphs, *Otobius megnini* (*Ornithodorus megnini*), inhabit the external ear canal of various mammals. Bishopp and Trembley (1945) reported this tick in 3 or 17 coyotes examined from Arizona.

In the southern tier of Canadian provinces (British Columbia to Nova Scotia), *Dermacentor andersoni* is found in the Rockies, *D. albipictis* throughout, and *D. variabilis* from Saskatchewan east (Gregson, 1956).

In Mexico, at the present time, we can only interpolate the coyote tick situation. *Dermacentor variabilis* almost certainly extends well south into Mexico as does *Amblyomma americana. Amblyomma cajennense* is primarily a Mexican form. *Dermacentor pacificus*, *D. occidentalis*, and *Ixodes rugosa* are known to range from California and Arizona well south into Mexico. *Otobius megnini* should be much more common in Mexican coyotes than in those north of the border because of their predeliction for a warm, dry climate. Our records give no indication of *D. andersoni* in Mexico.

Various species of the genus *Ixodes* have been reported from coyotes but it appears that only *I. rugosa* and *I. cookei* occur with great enough frequency to merit comment. *Ixodes rugosa*, a west coast form, and *I. cookei*, an eastern form, have been reported several times (Table I) but seem to be primarily parasites of deer and rodents. *Ixodes kingi* nymphs were found on Kansas coyotes in midwinter. *Ixodes*, as a group, are not known to serve as intermediate hosts for parasites or diseases of coyotes, so are probably no more than a nusiance. *Ixodes pacificus* may carry tick paralysis, unknown in coyotes, and *I. angustus* has been blamed as a carrier of Rocky Mountain spotted fever.

Ticks of the genus *Dermacentor*, on the other hand, serve as intermediate hosts for tularemia; the rickettsial diseases: Rocky Mountain spotted fever, Erhlichiosis, and Q-fever; protozoan disease: babesiosis, viral tick fever, and possibly anaplasmosis, all of which affect the coyote to some extent (see Section III).

If enough coyotes are examined to get the total picture, probably every tick that occurs in coyote country will be found on coyotes, but only a few species (Table I) appear to thrive on coyote blood.

C. Lice

Reports of lice on coyotes are extremely scarce, possibly reflecting the resistance of coyotes to these parasites. One of us (H.T.G.) examined over 2000 coyotes for parasites over a 15 year span (1948–1963) and found only two coyotes severely infested. However, in the winter of 1973–1974, lousy coyotes became common, and approximately 30% of the coyotes examined from 1973 through 1976 had some lice, and 5–10% were severely infested with 5000 to 50,000 lice each. Some appeared to have 2 to 10 lice on each and every guard hair, frequently superimposed over a severe sarcoptic mange infection which resulted in wet, matted underfur. These lice were all the common dog louse, *Trichodectes canis*, also reported from Texas by Eads (1948). *Trichodectes canis* is generally distributed over all North America and undoubtedly will be found much more frequently on coyotes when observations are made specifically for it.

The only other louse that has been reported from coyotes is the tropical

TABLE II

Lice and Fleas Parasitic on Coyotes

Parasite	Normal host	Frequency on coyotes 1	2	3	Intermediate host for	Geographic range and references
Trichodectes canis	Dogs, wolves, foxes, coyotes	x	to	x	Tularemia, *Dipylidium caninum*	Entire North America[a]; Texas[b]; Kansas[c]
Heterodoxus spiniger (= *setosus*)	Dogs	x			Unknown	Southwest U.S.[a]; Mexico ? southern U.S.[a]; Texas[b,d]
Heteropsyllidae						
Echidnophaga gallinacea	Birds, rodents, deer	x			Unknown	Southern U.S.[e,f]; Texas[b]; New Mexico[g]
Pulicidae						
Cediopsylla simplex	Rabbits	x			Unknown	Oklahoma and Arkansas[e]; Kansas[c]; eastern U.S.[e]
C. i. inequalis	Rabbits	x			Plague	Western U.S.[f]; Montana[h]
Ctenocephalides canis	Dogs	x			Plague, *Dipylidium*	Alberta[i]; Kansas[c]
Hoplopsyllus affinis	Rabbits	x			Plague	Western U.S.[f] Alberta[f]; Kansas[c]; New Mexico[j]
H. anomalis	*Citellus*	x			Plague	Southwest U.S.[f]; New Mexico[j]
Pulex irritans	Rats, humans		?		Plague	Alberta[i]; Texas[b]; Colorado[k]; Montana[h]

Pulex simulans	N.A. Carnivores			x	?	North America[d]; Kansas[c]
Dolichopsyllidae						
Arctopsylla setosa	Cougars, bears	?			Plague	Alberta[h]; British Columbia[f]; Montana[h]
Chaetopsyllus lotorus	Raccoons	x			Unknown	Eastern U.S.[e]; Kansas[c]
Monopsyllus wagneri	*Peromyscus*		?		?	Montana[h]; western U.S.[f]
Oropsylla idahoensis	Ground squirrels	x			Plague ?	Montana[h]; western U.S.[f]
Oropsylla arctomys	Marmots	x			?	Montana[h]; Alaska to Montana[f]
Opisocrostis hirsutis	Prairie dogs, marmots	x			Plague ?	Montana[h]; Rocky Mountains[f]
Orchopeas leucopus	*Peromyscus*	x			?	U.S.[e,f]; Kansas[c]
Orchopeas s. sexdentatus	*Neotoma*	x			Plague, brucellosis	Alberta[i]; Texas[b]; New Mexico[g]; California[f]
Orchopeas howardii	Squirrels, *Peromyscus*	x			?	All U.S.[e,f]; Kansas[c]
Thrassis acamontis	Marmots	x			?	California to Alaska[f]
Hystrichopsyllidae						
Stenoponia americana	*Peromyscus, Microtus*	x			?	Eastern U.S.[e]; Kansas[c]; New Mexico[g]

References: [a] Krull (1969); [b] Eads (1948); [c] Gier and Ameel (1959); [d] Smith (1976 personal communication); [e] Fox (1940); [f] Hubbard (1947); [g] Williams and Hoff (1951); [h] Jellison and Kohls (1943); [i] Brown (1944); [j] Haas *et al.* (1973); [k] Ecke and Johnson (1952).

dog louse, *Heterodoxus spiniger* (= *H. setosus*), known from various areas in southern U. S. (Table II). *Heterodoxus spiniger* has been reported from one of 21 coyotes examined from Texas (Eads, 1948) and by Smith (1976 personal communication) from a limited area in Hopkins and Denton counties north of Dallas–Ft. Worth, Texas. Other areas of *H. spiniger* infestation will almost certainly be found when adequate observations are made.

D. Fleas

Fleas are almost always present in some numbers on every coyote from a few days old to old age. The coyote flea, apparently throughout North America, is *Pulex simulans* (not *Pulex irritans* as is so commonly designated),* with most if not all other species reported from coyotes being incidental, as primary parasites of coyote prey species (Table II). The stick-tight flea, *Echidnophaga gallinacea,* was reported by Smith (1976 personal communication) as common on coyotes, mostly on eyelids, in El Paso County, Texas. The dog flea, *Ctenocephalides canis* is occasionally found in some numbers where coyotes and dogs inhabit the same grounds, but probably is never resident on coyotes. The raccoon flea (*Chaetopsylla lotoris*), various rabbit fleas (*Hoplopsyllus, Cediopsylla,* etc.), mouse fleas (*Orchopeas, Stenoponia*), and others have been reported sporadically as having been collected from coyotes. As with *C. canis,* it is doubtful that any of these facultative parasites ever successfully reproduce in continuous association with coyotes.

Fleas apparently are more an irritating nusiance to coyotes than a real health hazard, although there is some indication that certain fleas may be vectors of tularemia, bubonic plaque, equine encephalitis, and possibly other diseases. Infestations of 100 to 400 fleas per coyote are not uncommon, but the continuity of infestations, reproductive success of the fleas, or health effects on the coyote can only be surmised.

* Speciation of fleas of the genus *Pulex* in North America was carefully reviewed (Smit, 1958) with the conclusion that most of the North American *Pulex* belonged to the species *simulans,* and that *irritans* probably did not occur on native mammals. Jellison (1976) on the other hand, considers that *P. irritans* has become thoroughly integrated into the flea populations of native mammals. Examination of several hundred *Pulex* from coyotes in Kansas has convinced me that I was observing a pure population of *P. simulans,* as determined by smaller size, longer maxillary palps, and broader dorsal sclerite of the aedeagus than are found in *P. irritans.* Furthermore, the coyote *Pulex* rarely bothered me (H. T. G.) or my helpers while we examined the coyotes, even though the fleas were abundantly present around us.

III. INTERNAL PARASITES

A. Flatworms

1. Flukes

Trematodes (flukes) are devastating when they gain entrance into coyotes but they are not common nor widespread. Only a few flukes are worthy of consideration here (Table III).

Salmon sickness occurs in coyotes from Minnesota (Erickson, 1944) to the Pacific from infections of the fluke *Nanophyethus salmincola* (from ingested fish, mostly salmon) which in turn carry the lethal agent *Neorickettsia.* Five to 10 days after infection, the temperature of the host rises to 105°F or above, and distemperlike symptoms appear—bloody diarrhea and weight loss—with 90% fatalities. Survivors are immune (Schlegel *et al.*, 1968).

The lung fluke *Paragonimus kellicotti* may occur locally in parts of eastern U. S. in coyotes as it has been reported in foxes and dogs in that area and in coyotes in Ontario (Ramsden and Presidente, 1975). The life cycle includes stages in snail, crayfish, and carnivore. Metacercaria penetrate the wall of the stomach, through the diaphragm into the lungs, where they grow to mature flukes about 10 × 5 mm, in the lumen of bronchioles. The liver fluke *Amphemerus pseudofelineus* has been reported as occurring in bile ducts of "cat and coyote" from New York to Texas (Krull, 1969). Another liver fluke *Metorchis conjunctus* was reported from 5% of the coyotes examined in Alberta (Holmes and Podesta, 1968).

Alaria mustelae, A. canis, A. oregonensis, and *A. alata* have been reported as occurring in the small intestine of coyotes in Texas (Thornton *et al.*, 1974; Smith, 1976 personal communication), Minnesota (Erickson, 1944), and Saskatchewan (Allen and Mills, 1971). Mesocercaria and metacercaria may be contracted from tadpoles and small frogs by an intermediate predator (paratenic host), such as watersnake or mouse, that eats the secondary host; cercaria penetrate intestinal wall of paratenic host and accumulate in tissues without further development. The definitive host probably has little contact with the intermediate host in which the cercaria develops, but is infected almost entirely by preying on the paratenic host.

Other flukes may be found in coyotes but reports of serious implications have not been found. Of all the flukes, only "salmon sickness" appears to have any real impact on a regional population.

2. Tapeworms

Cestodes (tapeworms) of one or more species occur in 60–95% of the coyotes involved in every report (Table III).

TABLE III

Platyhelminthic Parasites in Coyotes

Parasite	Intermediate host	Habitat in coyote	Presence reported, frequency, area
Alaria americana	Snail to tadpole	Small intestine	79% Alberta[b]; 13/13 Texas[c]
Alaria arisdemoides	Snail to tadpole	Small intestine	10% Alberta[b]; Saskatchewan[d]
Alaria mustelae	Snail to tadpole	Small intestine	2% Minnesota[e]; 1/24 Saskatchewan[d]
Alaria sp.		Upper duodenum	Texas[f]
Amphimurus pseudofelinus	Probably fish	Bile ducts	Texas[g]
Metorchis conjunctus	Snail to sucker	Liver, bile duct	Alberta[b]
Nanophyetus salmincola	Snail to fish (mostly salmon)	Duodenum	Columbia River[h]; Montana[g]; Minnesota[e]; California[g]
Paragonimus kellicoti	Snail to crayfish	Lungs, bronchi	1/31 Ontario[i]
Diphyllobothium sp.	Fishes	Small intestine	4/75 Alberta[b]
Mesocestoides kirbyi	Lizards, rodents	Small intestine	Utah[j]; California[k]; Alaska[l]
Mesocestoides carnivoricolus	*Peromyscus*	Small intestine	Utah[j,m]
M. corti (= variabilis)	Mice, lizards	Small intestine	1% Kansas[n]; California[k]; Utah[j]
Echinococcus granulosus	Ruminants, mostly	Small intestine	18/75 Alberta[b]; 20/239 Ontario[o]; Utah[j]; 7/72, California[p,q]

Echinococcus multilocularis	Rodents	Small intestine	7/171, North Dakota[r]
Taenia hydatigena	Ruminants	Small intestine	1/75 Alberta[b]; 3/339 Ontario[o]; Utah[j]
Taenia krabbei (= *ovis*)	Sheep, deer, moose	Small intestine	1% Alberta[a]; 3.2% Minnesota[e]; Utah[j]
T. laticolis[a]	Unknown	Small intestine	1/309 Ontario[o]
T. lyncis (= *rileyi*)	Rodents, deer	Small intestine	5% Minnesota[e]; 2% Utah[j]
T. multiceps	Sheep, deer, rabbits	Small intestine	3/75 Alberta[b]; 13% Minnesota[e]; California[k]; Utah[j]
T. pisiformes	*Sylvilagus, Lepus*	Small intestine	23/75 Alberta[b]; 66/339 Ontario[o]; 39% Minnesota[e]; 55% Utah[j]; 100% Oklahoma[s]; 95% Kansas[n]
T. twitchelli	Porcupines, rodents	Small intestine	1% Alberta[b]
T. serialis	Lagomorphs	Small intestine	Cosmopolitan; 4 Utah[j]; California[k]
Dipylidium caninum[a]	*Ctenocephalides canis*	Small intestine	1 Utah[j]; 3 Kansas[n]

[a] Probably wrongly identified or at most an incidental or accidental parasite of coyotes.

References: [b] Holmes and Podesta (1968); [c] Thornton *et al.* (1974); [d] Allen and Mills (1971); [e] Erickson (1944); [f] Smith (1976 personal communication); [g] Krull (1969); [h] Schlegel *et al.* (1968); [i] Ramsden and Presidente (1975); [j] Butler and Grundman (1954); [k] Voge (1955a); [l] Voge (1955b); [m] Grundman (1958); [n] Gier and Ameel (1959); [o] Freeman *et al.* (1961); [p] Liu *et al.* (1970); [q] Romano *et al.* (1974); [r] Leiby *et al.*, (1970); [s] Self and McKnight (1950).

The specific tapeworms found in any one coyote reflects directly the food habits of that animal. Larval forms of tapeworms develop in quite specific intermediate hosts, and when ingested by a coyote, may develop into a mature tapeworm in the intestine of the definitive host, i.e., the coyote.

The most commonly found tapeworm of the coyote over most of its range is *Taenia pisiformes* (Fig. 1) which uses the cottontail rabbit as its prime "intermediate host." The larval form of *T. pisiformes* is a "bladder worm" known as a cysticercus, that grows from an egglike embryo with mobile spines, to a cyst possibly 8–10 mm thick and 20–30 mm long, within the liver, abdominal cavity, or mesenteries of the rabbit. If a coyote eats an infected rabbit, the single head (scolex) of the cysticercus remains after the bladder is digested; the scolex extends its hooks and attaches to the wall of the duodenum or jejunum, absorbs the food the coyote has digested, and elongates into a full size tapeworm 100–250 mm long with up to 150 reproductive units (proglottids) in which fertilized eggs develop into infective larvae that are passed with the feces, ready to infect another rabbit. We have found up to 110 adult worms or 500 scoleces in one coyote, with 95% of the coyotes carrying some *T. pisiformes* during years in which 50% or more of the coyote food consisted of rabbit. Other studies, conducted where less rabbit was eaten, showed considerably lower infection rate (Table III). Extremely heavy infections consisting of several hundred *T. pisiformes*, as is frequently found in dogs, has not been reported for coyotes.

Taenia multiceps (*Multiceps multiceps, M. gaigeri*) develops as a water-filled vesicle (coenurus) possibly as large as a hen's egg, within the brain, spinal cord, or other tissues of sheep, deer, and other ungulates. The adult tapeworm occurs in dogs and wolves in many parts of the world but has been reported from coyote only from Minnesota (Erickson, 1944) and Alberta (Holmes and Podesta, 1968). A closely related species, *Taenia serialis* (*Multiceps serialis, M. packii, T. laruei*) has a coenurus stage consisting of a central cyst with many secondary cysts, each with one scolex budding either inward or outward making at times a mass as much as 50 mm across with an overall appearance of a bunch of grapes. *Taenia serialis* coenuri develop within the connective tissue, either subcutaneous or intramuscular, of lagomorphs and possibly in some rodents (Verster, 1969). This species, by its various names has been reported from coyotes infrequently and in small numbers (Table III), not at all in proportion to the utilization of infected rabbits by coyotes. We have not found this species in Kansas, even when coyotes were feeding extensively on a jackrabbit population heavily infested with *T. serialis* coenurus. Smith (1967, 1976 personal communication) and Pence (1976 personal communication) did not find this species in Texas even though both jackrabbits and cottontails of the study areas were carriers of the coenuri. Holmes and Podesta (1968)

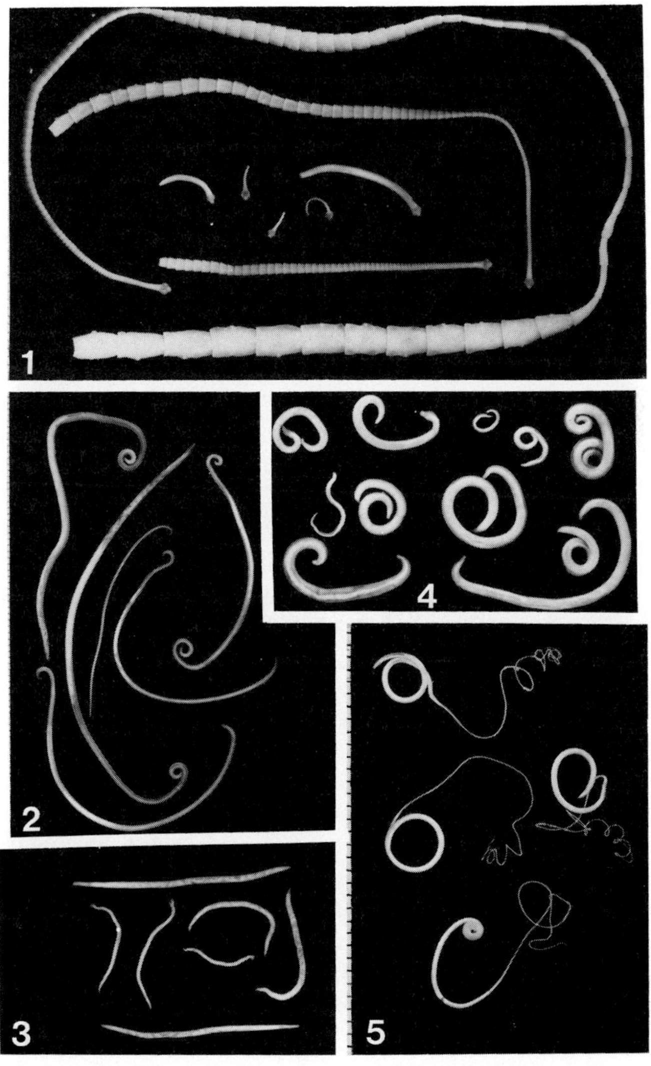

Fig. 1.
Fig. 2.
Fig. 3.
Fig. 4.
Fig. 5.

reported "We follow the suggestion of Esch and Self (1965) and regard our material as *Taenia multiceps* (Leske, 1780). Coenuri of this species have been found in a variety of hares and rabbits; in Alberta we have found them in varying hares (*Lepus americanus* Erxleben) and white-tailed jackrabbits (*Lepus townsendi* Bachman)." We must recommend another look at the members of the former genus *Multiceps* with regard not only for adult morphology but as much for larval morphology and host specificity.

The largest tapeworm parasitic on coyotes is *Taenia hydatigena* (*T. marginata, T. serrata*) reported from 31% of the coyote sample from Minnesota (Erickson, 1944), 3% from Ontario (Freeman *et al.*, 1961), and 2% from Utah (Butler and Grundman, 1954). The adult stage attains a length of 800–4000 mm, with ripe proglottids 10–14 × 4–7 mm. The larva is a coenurus, much larger than the larva of *T. pisiformes,* and develops primarily within muscles or liver of deer or other ungulates. This form is probably of greatest concern to coyotes that are living primarily on deer, elk, moose, or caribou.

Taenia ovis krabbei, T. rileyi, T. twitchelli, T. pseudolaticollis, and *T. laticollis* have each been reported in one or a few occurences in coyotes (Table III). These and possibly other species must be considered as incidental or accidental parasites of coyotes and of no real consequence, until evidence to the contrary is presented.

Mesocestoides spp., primarily *M. corti* (*M. variabilis*), have been found in low to moderate numbers in coyotes in several localities (Table III), but only in Texas (Smith, 1967; Pence, 1976 personal communication) has any considerable infections been found, like 100% infections with some cases of 200+ worms per coyote. Mesocestoides differ from *Taenia* in absence of hooks on the scolex; median, ventral genital pore; relatively small size (50–150 mm long); and larva (tetrathyridium) consisting of a single scolex without a bladder of any sort. Tetrathyridia develop in lizards and mice (Voge, 1955a) and may undergo repeated asexual reproduction by longitudinal splitting of the scolex either in the peritoneal cavity of the secondary host or within the intestine of the definitive host (Eckert *et al.*, 1969; Novak, 1972). Frequent occurrence of only one or two mature *M. corti* in the intestine of a coyote indicates that the coyote is not a favorable host for this parasite and that multiplication of ingested scoleces is severely repressed. The small size of these parasites, absence of hooks that might damage the intestinal wall, and an overall benign action suggest that little damage is done by it to the coyote unless the infection is extreme. Much remains to be learned about this group.

Echinococcus granulosus, the hydatid worm of moose–wolf fame, has been passed to the coyote as coyotes have replaced wolves in the parasite chain. Adults in the carnivore gut are only 1.2 to 8 mm long and have only

2 to 5 proglottids so are easily overlooked during the examination of intestinal contents. The larval stage develops in moose, reindeer, elk, deer, sheep, cow, pig, and man as a large (6 to 150 mm) water-filled cyst in which many protoscoleces may float free, each capable of making a mature tapeworm in a carnivore. *Echinococcus granulosus* is not known to cause ill effects in the coyote (or wolf) but the hydatid cyst may cause severe problems in the secondary host. *Echinococcus granulosus* has been identified in coyotes in Minnesota (Erickson, 1944), California (Romano *et al.*, 1974; Liu *et al.*, 1970), Ontario (Freeman *et al.*, 1961), and Alberta (Holmes, 1961; Holmes and Podesta, 1968) and can be expected in future collections in other areas occupied jointly by wild cervids and coyotes.

Echinococcus multilocularis has a normal cycle of rodent–fox–rodent, and occurs from Alaska, throughout western Canada to Minnesota. Lieby *et al.* (1969) *Echinococcus multilocularis* has been reported from *C. latrans* only in North Dakota (Leiby *et al.*, 1970) but can be expected elsewhere as collections and understanding increase.

Dipylidium caninum has been reported from coyotes only from Utah (Butler and Grundman, 1954) and from Kansas (Gier and Ameel, 1959) in extremely small numbers. Occasional occurrence of this dog–flea–dog tapeworm may be expected, but all identifications of *D. caninum* from coyotes should be viewed with suspicion as this species and *Mesocestoides* have an overall striking similarity and without magnification may be confused. *Dipylidium caninum* utilizes the dog flea *Ctenocephalides canis* as the intermediate host, but the infrequent occurrence of *C. canis* on coyotes directly limits possibility of infection from this source. If *Dipylidium* can be carried by the dog louse *Trichodectes canis* we must consider that *T. canis* on coyotes have never been infected with *Dipylidium* larvae or that coyotes have a strong intolerance for this species.

Adverse effects of tapeworms could result from (1) preempting food that the coyote needs; (2) filling the intestine to the exclusion of normal digestive and absorptive function, thus resulting in malnutrition; (3) causing irritation of the intestinal lining by hook penetration, allowing for bacterial infections and enteritis; or (4) producing some sort of toxin that represses intestinal function—a possibility that has no firm substantiation. Presence of a few tapeworms in the intestine of a coyote probably only increases the coyote's demand for food a little, but a limit of possibly 50 *Taenia pisiformes*, or equivalent of other species, results in a combination of ill effects (1, 2, and 3 as given above) to such extent that the coyote will not be able to provide adequate food for itself and the tapeworms.

Coyotes undoubtedly develop an active immunity against tapeworms. We do not find new infections superimposed upon a sizeable infection of mature worms, nor do we find numbers of immature or mature worms concommitant with the number of scoleces that are known to be ingested. Detailed, specific analyses of these phenomena are needed.

B. Roundworms

Parasites of the nematode–acanthocephala groups are not as common nor as devastating in coyotes as they are in some other wild animals, i.e., ungulates, but nevertheless are a consistent danger to health and life.

1. Ascarids

Intestinal worms of the genus *Toxascaris* have been reported as occurring in various frequencies in every study yet reported (Table IV). *Toxascaris leonina* (Fig. 2) is the persistent ascaroid of coyotes. It is a medium size ascarid, 40 to 100 mm long, that lives in the small intestine, ingesting and utilizing a portion of the food digested by the coyote. Eggs are produced in large numbers, pass out with the feces, and are ready for ingestion and hatching in a new coyote. The infective larvae spend a few days in the intestinal mucosa, then reenter the intestinal lumen where they grow to maturity. No ill effects have been noted except the requirement of extra food. Numbers of *T. leonina* rarely exceed 50 or 60 per coyote, which is not enough to cause intestinal blockage.

Toxacara canis has been infrequently reported from coyotes and probably *never* survive to reproductive condition in a true coyote, but may survive in coyote × dog hybrids. *Toxacara canis* infective larvae pass through the intestinal lining, into the blood stream, to the lungs for a period, then are coughed up and swallowed, to mature in the intestine. There seems to be no consistent morphological characteristic by which *T. canis* can be differentiated from *T. leonina* except the eggs of the former have a sculptured or pitted surface while the eggs of *T. leonina* have a thin, smooth shell.

Various reports of intestinal parasites of coyote prey species, i.e., rabbit, pocket gopher, etc. such as *Protospirura numidica, Mastophorus muris, Molinus patens, Passaluris nonanulatus,* etc., in the stomach or even in the intestine of coyotes probably represent only ingested parasites that survive for a time in the coyote. There is no evidence to date that any of these nematodes actually parasitize coyotes.

2. Ancylostomids

Hookworms of the genus *Ancylostoma* have been consistently reported as found in coyotes in every study of coyote parasites (Table IV). The dog hook worm *A. caninum* (Fig. 3) appears to occur throughout the coyote range, with heavy infections in moist areas, particularly along the Gulf Coast in Texas, where every coyote examined is infected with up to 250 worms each (Mitchell and Beasom, 1974). *Ancylostoma caninum* attaches to the intestinal lining, penetrates the epithelium, and sucks blood, but each worm moves several times each day, leaving the previous wound in a bleeding condition. Eggs are passed with feces, hatch in moist earth, and are ingested by coyotes in contaminated food. Infective larvae migrate through intestinal mucosa, into the bloodstream to the lungs. Larvae may pass through the placenta into developing fetuses where they lie dormant until birth, then complete their migration to the intestine. As few as 25 *A. caninum* in a 10-day-old pup may be fatal. *Ancylostoma caninum* damages the host by (1) tissue penetration, (2) lung congestion, (3) blood loss producing anemia, and (4) a toxic condition further complicating tissue damage and anemia. Animals that survive to 8 months develop partial immunity to hook worms and are rarely hurt by them thereafter.

There seems to be no records of *A. braziliensis* in coyotes but this South American hookworm is found in dogs in Texas and other Gulf states and will surely be found in coyotes.

The European hookworm *Uncinaria stenocephala* was reported from coyotes in Alberta (Holmes and Podesta, 1968) and will almost certainly be found elsewhere as the knowledge of its probability expands. This hookworm occurs in dogs throughout the northern states and the provinces of Canada. It is not as severe in dogs as is *Ancylostoma*; bleeding is less protracted and tissue migration possibly does not occur.

Another Strongyloid species *Filaroides osleri* has been reported from the lungs of coyotes in Texas, Minnesota, and Alberta (Table IV). *Filaroides osleri* is a slender, nearly transparent nematode, 7 to 13 mm long, that lives at the bifurcations of the bronchi, either free or encapsulated. Numbers of these worms per coyote appear to be low, and no ill effects have been reported. More careful examination of coyote lungs will almost certainly reveal a more extensive occurrence of this worm. The life cycle of *F. osleri* probably involves an intermediate stage in a snail or slug, as do most of the other members of the genus, and probably is transferred to coyotes through a paratenic host, or it may have a direct life cycle.

3. Spiruroids

The esophageal worm *Spirocerca lupi* has been reported from coyotes only from Texas (Smith, 1967, 1976 personal communication) but probably occurs more widely. Smith (1967) reported the worm, or evidence of it, in 90% of the adult coyotes examined from southern Texas. The adult worm is 5 to 8 mm long and lives either in the wall of the dorsal aorta or in the wall of the esophagus. In the dorsal aorta, it makes a cyst in the middle layer of the aortic wall; the cyst then expands to appear as an aneurysm up to 15 mm in diameter. These worms may migrate through tissues from aorta to esophagus

TABLE IV

Nematode and Acanthocephalid Parasites in Coyotes

Parasite	Length, mm, thickness	Means of infection	Habitat in coyote	Presence of parasite, reported incidence, area, reference
Toxascaris leonina	20–100	Ingestion	Small intestine	28/75 Utah[b]; 1/10 Texas[c]; Kansas[d]; 52% Alberta[e]; 33% Kansas[f]
Toxacara canis[a]	40–150	Ingestion	Small intestine	1/75 Utah[b]; 1 Texas[c]; 1 Alberta[e]
Ancylostoma caninum	6–11	Ingestion or percutaneous	Small intestine	90% Texas[g]; 1 Alberta[e]; 100% Texas[c]; 25% Kansas[f]
Uncinaria stenocephala	5–12	Ingestion	Small intestine	16% Alberta[e]; northern U.S.[h]; Canada[h]
Filaroides osleri	5–13	Intermediate snail or slug	Nodules at bifurcation of bronchia	12% Texas[i]; 9/13 Texas[j]; 36/65 Minnesota[k]; 15% Alberta[e]
Spirocerci lupi	30–80, 0.7–1.5	Intermediate beetle; orthopteran	Dorsal aorta or esophagus	90% Texas[l]
Physaloptera rara	15–40, 0.6–1.3	Intermediate beetle; orthopteran	Stomach	3/10 Texas[c]; 3/13 Texas[j]; 17% Minnesota[k]; 35% Kansas[f]
Physaloptera preputialis[a]	13–48	Intermediate insect	Stomach (cat)	5% Minnesota[k]; 3% Kansas[d]
Dirofilaria immitis	120–310, 0.1–1.3	Mosquito: *Aedes, Anopheles*	Right ventricle, pulmonary artery	3/13 Texas[j]; 0–40% Texas[m]; 1–8% Kansas[f,n,o]; 8/22 Iowa[p]

Dipetalonema reconditum	100–350, 0.4–0.8	Fleas	Subcutaneous; microfilaria in blood	Frequent in raccoon and skunks, only rumors for coyotes[h]
Thelazia californiensis	8–38 slender	Carried by muscid fly	Tear ducts, conjunctival sac	California[q]; 8/52 California[r]; Arizona[s]; southwest U.S. and Mexico[h]
Capillaria aerophila	15–40, 0.06–0.10	Ingestion	Bloodstream to lungs	5% Alberta[e]
Capillaria hepatica	22–140, 0.08–0.18	Ingestion of infected liver	Liver	1 Saskatchewan[t]
Trichurus vulpis	50–75 (2/3 neck)	Ingestion	Caecum	6% Kansas[f]
Trichinella spiralis	1.4–1.6, 0.05–0.06	Ingestion of infected meat	Alimentary to intramuscular	12.5% Alaska[u]; 4.3% Iowa[v]; 1/193 Colorado[w]
Dioctophyma renale	150–1000, 4–12	Intermediate annelid—bullhead	Right kidney or coelom	4 California[x]; 4 Alberta[e]
Oncicola canis	6–14 (conical)	Arthropod intermediary	Small intestine	4/10 Texas[i]; Texas[y]

[a] Probably misidentified, or at most accidental occurrence.

References: [b] Butler and Grundman (1954); [c] Smith (1967); [d] Ameel (1955); [e] Holmes and Podesta (1968); [f] Gier and Ameel (1959); [g] Mitchell and Beason (1974); [h] Krull (1969); [i] Smith (1976 personal communication); [j] Thornton *et al.* (1974); [k] Erickson (1944); [l] Smith (1971); [m] Knowlton (1976 personal communication); [n] Graham (1974); [o] Graham (1975); [p] Christian *et al.* (1976); [q] Paramelee *et al.* (1956); [r] Burnett and Wagner (1958); [s] Schauffler (1966); [t] Wobeser and Rock (1973); [u] Rausch *et al.* (1956); [v] Zimmerman *et al.* (1959); [w] Olsen (1960); [x] Brunetti (1959); [y] Price (1928).

where they make a comparable cyst that expands into the esophageal lumen with the tail end of the worm extending into the lumen into which eggs are laid. Eggs pass out with the feces, are ingested with contaminated food, and hatch in the stomach. Infective larvae penetrate the stomach mucosa into the bloodstream, then penetrate the wall of the aorta where another phase of the life cycle is passed (Smith, 1971). No evidence has been presented that *S. lupi* is fatal to coyotes, but the presence of a few dozen nodules on the aorta, with blockage of segmental arteries, certainly is detrimental to the well-being of the host.

The stomach worm *Physaloptera rara* (Fig. 4) inhabits the stomach of coyotes and other carnivores, and attaches to the stomach lining. Each worm is a few hundred times the size of *A. caninum* but has no greater effect because it does not leave a bleeding wound. *Physaloptera rara* has an indirect life cycle, with early stages in various insects, probably transferred to coyotes via a paratenic host, such as a rodent. In the laboratory, we found 25 to 50 *P. rara* to be fatal for coyote pups under a month old, but we have no evidence of fatalities from this parasite in nature. Reports of *P. felidis* have all been shown to involve *P. rara,* and *P. felidis* is currently limited to cats. Reports of *P. preputialis,* another felid parasite, should be reexamined. We have serious doubts that they are real. *Physaloptera preputialis* is a distinctly larger worm than is *P. rara,* and the cuticle of the posterior end of *P. preputialis* is protruded over the tail like the foreskin over the penis, from which the name is derived. Investigators should examine specimens closely before reporting such questionable species.

4. Filaroids

The heartworm *Dirofilaria immitis* is a slender worm, up to 300 mm long that lives its adult stage in the right ventricle and pulmonary arteries of coyotes, dogs, and other canids. Eggs hatch either within the uterus or in the blood, microfilaria circulate in the general bloodstream and are taken up by mosquitoes that feed on the host. One to five larvae may develop in a mosquito and be transferred to another host at a later feeding. Various species of mosquitoes of the genera *Aedes, Anopheles,* and *Culex* are capable of serving as intermediate hosts, but all species are not equally capable. Christensen and Andrews (1976) reported *Aedes trivittatis* as being the prime carrier in central Iowa. Occurrence of *D. immitis* in coyotes is extremely variable. We found the first *D. immitis* in a coyote in Kansas in 1954, and established an overall occurrence of less than 1%. In 1976, we determined a 15% infection in the Ft. Riley Military Reservation, and Graham (1975) found 8% occurrence around the Ft. Leavenworth reservation. Knowlton (1976 personal communication) reported occurrence of *D.*

immitis in Texas coyotes to vary from 20% along the Gulf Coast and the Rio Grande River to none in some of the inner counties with over 100 examinations for each of 12 counties. Christian *et al.* (1976) reported *D. immitis* in 8 of 22 (36%) in central Iowa, with 1 to 23 worms per heart. Effects of *D. immitis* on health or livability of coyotes has not been established—we are yet in the process of determining where and how many occur, with effects yet to be studied. We have observed that in areas where coyotes are regularly chased by dogs, the occurrence of heart worms is minimal, indicating to us that even a light infection may mean the difference between survival and death in a chase.

A subcutaneous worm *Dipetalonema reconditum,* common in the axilla and groins of raccoon, skunk, and opossum, has not yet been reported from coyotes. This worm, in adult stage, is 20 to 30 mm long, and can be readily identified in the loose subcutaneous tissue as the skin is being removed. Discussions with numerous professional skinners reveals their knowledge of this worm in other species, but not in coyotes. *Dipetalonema reconditum* has a microfilaria stage similar to that of *Dirofilaria,* but it is transferred by fleas, or possibly lice, not by mosquitoes.

The eye worm *Thelazia californiensis* is transferred from animal to animal by deer flies and other *Tabanidae*. Present reports (Table IV) indicate limitation of this parasite to parts of California and Arizona, (Herman, 1949) although it is known to have a wider range in deer and other wild animals (Krull, 1969).

5. Trichinellids

The lungworm, *Capillaria aerophila,* a very delicate, nearly transparent *Trichuridae,* has been reported from only one group of coyotes: 14% of those examined from Lac la Biche, Alberta (Holmes and Podesta, 1968). It may be more prevalent but overlooked because of its small size (Table IV) and transparency. Effects on coyote are unknown.

The liver worm, *Capillaria hepatica,* a close relative of *C. aerophila,* has been reported from only one coyote, in Saskatchewan (Wobeser and Rock, 1973), and is identified from fine threadlike tracks in the liver, with masses of eggs in the tracks. This parasite normally inhabits livers of rabbits and rodents, and can be acquired only by eating foods contaminated by rotted, infected livers. Alertness for this parasite should produce more records.

The whip worm, *Trichuris vulpis,* (Fig. 5) normally inhabits the cecum of dogs, foxes, and other canids. We have recovered 2 to 12 *T. vulpis* from 6% of over 1200 coyotes examined in Kansas, 1954–1976. Although it has not been reported in other studies, we find it inconceivable that a common dog parasite like *T. vulpis* is limited in coyotes to the state of Kansas. The life cycle of *T. vulpis* is direct; larvae apparently pass through the small intestine into the cecum where they mature and lay eggs. Cecal contents, gummy and stinking as they are, provide the favored habitat for this parasite, and they can be recovered by the use of much water and care. The small numbers recovered indicate a relatively high resistance of coyotes to this infection, and suggest little adverse effects.

The garbage worm, *Trichinella spiralis*, that classically runs a cycle of hog–rat–hog, with dog, human, and other animals that eat either rat or hog being equally susceptible, has been found in coyotes only a few times (Table IV). General inaccessibility of infected hogs for coyote food and the coyote disdain for barn rats probably account for much of the lack of *Trichinella* in coyotes. However, any coyote that has access to garbage dumps where slaughterhouse scrap is discarded, or brown rats are plentiful, have the possibility of infection. Infection occurs by ingestion of infected meat, the worms excyst and produce embryonated eggs in the intestine. The eggs hatch in the intestine, infective larvae penetrate the intestinal wall then encyst in striated muscle, with the diaphragm being the muscle of choice. Cysts in quantity show as granules, but in light infections can be found only by microscopic inspection of strips of muscle pressed between two glass slides. Careful inspection of diaphragm of coyotes that feed on garbage dumps will probably result in more records of *Trichinella spiralis*, but the overall effect of trichina on coyotes is slight. The general occurrence of *T. spiralis* was reviewed by Zimmerman (1971).

6. Dioctophymoides

The giant kidney worm *Dioctyphyma renale* has been reported from coyotes only from California and Alberta (Table IV). This worm is common in mink and their relatives and at times infects canids. The intermediate host, a tiny annelid, is carried by certain fish, principally bullhead, so infection occurs mostly from eating bullhead, which few coyotes have a chance to do. The infective larvae from the annelid penetrate the wall of the duodenum, usually in the bend over the right kidney. One to four larvae may penetrate the kidney, and proceed to devour the kidney parynchema. Adult female worms may be as much as 1 m long. Eggs are passed through the ureter into the bladder, thence out with the urine. Infection with *D. renale* is so obvious that it can hardly be missed, even by an inexperienced observer.

7. Acanthocephalids

Spiny headed worms, *Acanthocephala*, are represented in coyote by a single repoted species, *Oncicola canis*, and only from Texas (Price, 1928;

Smith 1976, personal communication). *Oncicola canis* are short heavy bodied worms with six rows of 6 to 8 hooks each. They inhabit the small intestine, mostly duodenum, with the proboscis embedded in the muscosa, and may occur in numbers up to a few dozen. Little information regarding this parasite was found in the literature but there is probably an anthropod intermediate as occurs with most other acanthocephalids. Effect on the coyote is unknown.

Undoubtedly as studies of coyote parasites are extended, more species will be reported and ranges of those roundworms presently known to parasitize coyotes will be extended. Possibly we will learn of more roundworms that have serious effects on coyote life. At present, the only roundworms that are known to be lethal, either directly or indirectly are hookworms, stomach worms, heart worms, the intestinal worm (*Toxascaris leonina*) and the aortic worm (*Spirocerca lupi*).

IV. DISEASES

Few definitive or discriminative studies have been done on occurrence, severity, or outcome of diseases of coyotes in the wild. Most sick coyotes recover or die without the help of humans, and generally, without humans being aware that any disease condition exists. Recent development of serological techniques for antibody titers has permitted some expansion of knowledge of wildlife diseases in that it is now possible to determine that an animal has had recent exposure to one or more specific diseases and survived. Experimentation on penned coyotes has provided some information about susceptibility of coyotes to certain diseases, but we cannot be sure the results would be the same in the wild as in a pen. Some of the possibilities will be covered with specific diseases.

A. Viral

Rabies continues to be the potential killer of coyotes with the possibility of transmission to man, domestic animals, and wild game animals. There has been no major outbreak of rabies among coyotes in the United States and Canada for over 60 years, although sporadic cases of one to five a year have been recorded. There has been a continued series of rabies outbreaks among dogs and wild mammals in Northwest Mexico that has spilled over into southern California at intervals (Allison, 1963). The endemic areas of fox rabies in the eastern U.S. appears to have little or no effect on coyotes of the area, indicating either that there is little contact between foxes and coyotes or that coyotes are much more resistant to rabies than are foxes. Control of rabies in domestic dogs is probably the greatest safeguard against rabies in coyotes that we can provide, although an epizootic in coyotes could be started from fox, skunk, or bat, either from a bite by the rabid animal or by a coyote eating another animal dead from rabies (Emery, 1969). Any condition which promotes excess contact between coyotes (overpopulation, food shortage, concentration from hunting) increases the possibilities of spread of rabies through that population.

Distemper of coyotes is antigenically the same as the canine distemper that affects dogs. The disease is caused by a myxovirus that is transmitted by aerosol, direct contact, urine, feces, or nasal mucus. The affected animal is listless; develops an elevated temperature; purulent discharge from eyes and nose; hot, dry nose; marked thirst; and maybe diarrhea. In severe cases, the animal becomes emaciated and may die. Although the disease primarily affects the respiratory system, there is involvement of lymphoid tissue, and at times the nervous system is involved to the extent to producing rabies-like symptoms (Budd, 1970). We found canine distemper to be highly lethal for coyote pups and coyote–dog hybrid pups in the laboratory and suspect it takes a high toll of coyote pups in the wild. The only bit of real evidence of distemper in a wild population comes from Texas where 11 of 33 coyotes tested serologically showed a positive titer for distemper, indicating these animals had contracted the disease and survived (Trainer and Knowlton, 1968). Other studies now underway should give some indication of the extent of this disease in coyote populations.

Fox encephalitis (canine infectious hepatitis) was considered by many clinicians until recently to be a part of canine distemper, although Green *et al.* (1934) showed fox encephalitis to be a separate disease that resulted in loss of appetite, muscular twitching, convulsions, paralysis, and death. Necropsy showed severe liver necrosis with congestion and hemorrhage; hemorrhagic areas in lungs, heart, and the central nervous system. Intranuclear inclusion bodies were found in endothelial cells and in hepatic cord cells, but were irregular in other organs. Green *et al.* used five young coyotes as experimental animals, four of which succumbed to the disease. Parry (1951) gave final proof that hepatitis is a disease separate and distinct from distemper. Trainer and Knowlton (1968) reported positive serological reaction to infectious canine hepatitis in 17 of 33 coyotes tested in Texas. We suspect this disease affects coyotes throughout their range, but at present we can only surmise lethality and survival.

Equine encephalitis of Eastern, Western, St. Louis, California, and Venzuelian strains (Table IV) may be moderately pathogenic for coyotes. Lundgren and Smart (1969) inoculated 54 coyote pups with Venzuelan equine encephalitic virus: all but 2 developed viremia, none died. Peak antibody titers were reached within 1 week and were maintained for at least 41 weeks. Trainer and Knowlton (1968) reported 4 of 33 coyotes from west

Texas tested serologically positive for the St. Louis strain and 8 of 33 were positive for the California strain, proving that wild coyotes are exposed and react to equine encephalitis. No information is available to indicate the extent of exposure, duration of the viremia, or effect of the disease on the coyote.

Oral papillamatosis is a viral infection of the skin of lips, tongue, and mouth, resulting in wartlike growths as much as 15 mm long and 5–8 mm thick over part or all of the mouth area. We examined on specimen from Leavenworth County, Kansas, December 1974, that was so afflicted that the lips could not be closed and the tongue, with many warts, protruded from the mouth. Trainer and Knowlton (1968) reported one case from Texas; Broughton and Graeser (1970) reported one from Saskatchewan, two from Alberta; Nellis (1973) reported 5 cases in 277 coyotes from Alberta, and Greig and Charlton (1973) showed that the causative agent was a papovavirus similar to, but not the same, as the virus that similarly afflicts dogs. It is probable that this virus has been recently transferred from dogs to coyotes, and if such transfer has not occurred in several places, oral papillamatosis must be much more common than reports indicate.

B. Bacterial

If viral diseases of coyotes are a puzzle, then bacterial diseases are an enigma. We seem to know only that coyotes are susceptible to certain bacteria but not what transpires between them.

Tularemia is a plaguelike disease of rabbits and some rodents, so coyotes are repeatedly exposed to the causative agent *Franciscella tularense* which may be passed directly from prey to predator or via ticks (*Amblyomma, Dermacentor, Rhipicephalus*). Parker (1926) proved that tularemia is fatal for coyote pups; Lungren *et al.* (1957) reported that heavy doses of *F. tularense,* either by injection or by feeding guinea pigs moribund from tularemia, affected adult coyotes little if at all but usually produced a temporary titer against *P. tularense* that persisted only a few weeks. Knowlton (1976 personal communication) reported that 88% of the coyotes tested from Idaho in 1975 showed positive tularemia titers, some as high as 1:1200. All of this leads us to the conclusion that an epizootic of tularemia in rabbits during the early summer may decimate that year's pup crop, but the mature coyotes will survive for another breeding season.

Sylvatic plague was introduced into North America with rats and oriental rat fleas (*Xenopsylla cheopis*). The disease became established in native mammals and fleas in the San Francisco area about 1920, then spread rapidly eastward, to Colorado by 1941, to West Texas by 1945 (Miles *et al.* 1949). Now several native fleas (most notable, *Orchopeas sexdentatus*) are carriers of the plague organism *Yersinia pestis*. Pocket gophers, ground squirrels, and prairie dogs seem to be the regular targets of *Y. pestis*, and few if any infected animals survive. Dogs and fox squirrels are known to be carriers, without noticeable effects, and a number of human cases have been traced to such carriers (Poland and Barnes, 1970). The first real indictment of coyotes as a carrier of plague was a report by Barnes *et al.* (1976) that 19 of 27 coyotes tested from Larimer County, Colorado (a plague hot-spot) were positive for plague, by passive hemagglutination tests. Four of the coyotes showed titers over 1:1000, indicating an active or very recent infection.

Brucellosis, or Bang's disease, is only a possibility for coyotes. No positive tests were found, but with *Brucella canis*, an organism rather specific for dogs, spreading rapidly among domestic dogs, we must expect it in coyotes, soon.

Listeriosis, caused by *Listeria monocytogenes*, is an infectious, enzooic disease, acquired by eating infected meat, or possibly by ectoparasites. Pups die with bloody stools after considerable emaciation. Necropsy reveals sharply defined whitish-gray foci on liver, spleen, lungs, and heart, with tissues heavily infiltrated with neutrophils (Eveland, 1970). Although listeriosis has not been reported as occurring in coyotes, all workers should be alerted to the possibility that this disease may be the cause of bloody diarrhea and considerable pup loss.

Tyzzer's disease, only recently reported from a coyote (Marler *et al.*, 1976), has been known to be the lethal agent in the stress syndrome of laboratory animals (Ganaway *et al.*, 1971) and now is shown to occur in a population of wild rabbits in New Jersey (Ganaway *et al.*, 1976). This disease has frequently been the lethal agent in animals that have been stressed with cortisone or with immunorepressants. Ganaway *et al.* (1976) proposed that the organism of Tyzzer's disease (*Bacillus piliformes*) could be the real killer in many population crashes, after adrenal exhaustion. *Bacillus piliformes* does not respond to known culture methods, except live chick yolk sac, so must be identified by histological preparations of the liver or by serology (Ganaway *et al.*, 1976).

Leptospirosis (infective jaundice) is a widespread disease of domestic dogs, but to date has been reported only once for coyotes. Trainer and Knowlton (1968) reported one of 33 Texas coyotes tested to give a positive serological test for *Leptospira canicola*. The disease is characterized by hemorrhagic gastroenteritis with bloody vomitus and feces; muscular soreness, particularly in the hind legs; acute nephritis; difficulty of swallowing; and possibly death. The disease is highly contagious, either directly from dog to dog or intermediated by rats. Leptospira may be shed in the urine for weeks after apparent recovery. This disease poses a threat to coyote well-being, and we should know more of its occurrence and effects on coyotes.

C. Fungal

Coccidiomycosis, with its causative agent *Coccidioides immitis* has been recognized in coyotes only by Straub *et al.* (1961) in 3 coyotes in Arizona. Infection foci consist of small nodules in the lungs and enlarged tracheobronchial lymph nodes. Impact of this disease in coyotes in unknown.

Histoplasmosis caused by *Histoplasma capsulatum,* has not been reported for coyotes but almost certainly occurs. Menges *et al.* (1955) reported a severe epizootic of histoplasmosis in raccoon that in 2 years decimated a high population. The disease has many of the features of distemper, with some of the nervous effects of fox encephalitis. A coyote (or fox or raccoon) roaming around the country during daylight hours, oblivious to humans around it, may have rabies, fox encephalitis, or *histoplasmosis.*

Undoubtedly other mycotic diseases, particularly respiratory and dermal, afflict coyotes, but they have not yet been identified or reported.

D. Rickettsial

Rocky mountain spotted fever seems to be the rickettsial disease of greatest concern. The causative agent *Rickettsia rickettsia* is transmitted by ticks, particularly by *Dermacentor andersoni, D. variabilis,* and *D. occidentalis.* Lundgren *et al.* (1957) reported that coyotes infected either by injection or by feeding them with *Microtus montanus* infected with *R. rickettsia* developed rickettsemia and antibodies detectable by complement fixation. Antibody titers ranged from 1:16 to 1:256. *Rickettsia* were recovered from the blood of infected animals for several weeks, allowing adequate time for infection of carrier ticks, thus might be a factor in dissemination. The infected coyotes showed no clinical symptoms of the disease.

Salmon sickness is caused by *Neorickettsia helminthoica,* carried by the salmon fluke *Nanophyetus salmincola,* and is acquired by eating the infected salmon or other fish carrying the encysted metacercaria of the fluke. The disease causes about 90% fatality in dogs and apparently about the same percentage in coyotes. The range of the disease is limited by the range of the carrier (Table V). Effects on the coyote populations have not been determined, but there has been serious consideration given to the use of the disease as a predator control agent, at present unfeasible.

Ehrlichiosis (canine rickettsiosis) caused by *Ehrlichia canis,* is transmitted by ticks, primarily *Rhipicephalus sanguineus. Rickettsia* parasitize monocytes and neutrophils in which they appear as colonies of coccoid bodies. Death rate is high; recovered animals retain a latent infection. This disease can be diagnosed only by microscopic examination of stained blood, and has not yet been reported from coyotes. Ewing *et al.* (1964) showed that coyotes could be infected with *E. canis.*

TABLE V
Diseases of Coyotes, with Recorded Incidence

Disease	Causative agent	Means of infection	Site of action	Effects on coyote	Geographical area, reference
Rabies	Rhabdovirus	Bite of rabid aninal; milk, meat	Nervous system	Abnormal behavior, paralysis, death	Cosmopolitan[a,b,c]
Distemper	Virus of Carre, a paramyxovirus	Saliva, urine, feces	Respiratory, nervous alimentary	Lethargy, diarrhea maybe death	General[d,e]
Infectious hepatitis (fox encephalites)	Adenovirus	Direct: saliva, urine, feces	C.N.S., lungs, kidney, epithelia	Lethargy, convulsions paralysis, death	General over North America[f,g,h]
Oral papillamatosis	Papova virus	Probably direct	Lips, tongue	Sore mouth	Texas[k]; Kansas[j]; Saskatchewan[k]; Alberta[k,l]
Equine encephalitis	Arborviruses A and B	Mosquito bite; biting flies?	Blood, nervous	Viremia then immunity	California[m]; Texas[e]
Tularemia	*Franciscella tularense*	Ticks	Blood, viscera	Fatal to pups, immunity in adults	West U.S.[n]; Utah–Idaho[o]
Sylvatic plague	*Yersinia pestis*	Fleas: *Xenopsylla orchopeas, et al.*	Blood, bone marrow, alimentary tract	No overt symptoms, immunity	West U.S.[p]; Colorado[q,r]; Texas[q]; New Mexico[q]; Oregon[q]
Brucellosis	*Brucella abortus, B. suis, B. canis*	Direct and by ectoparasites	All viscera, uterus, placenta	Unknown; probably abortion	Not recognized[s]
Listeriosis	*Listeria monocytogenes*	Ingestion of infected meat	All viscera	Slight fever to death	Probably general[t]
Tyzzer's disease	*Bacillus piliformes*	Ingestion	All viscera;	Apparently fatal	Experimental[u,v,w]
Leptospirosis	*Leptospira canicola*	Direct, mostly from urine	Kidney, liver; enteritis	May be fatal	1/33 Texas[e]; probably general
Coccidioidomycosis	*Coccidioides immitis*	Ingestion or inhalation	Skin, lungs, spleen	Unknown	Arizona[x]; may be general

Histoplasmosis	*Histoplasma capsulatum*	Inhalation, from musty bedding	Respiratory	Distemperlike; may be fatal	May be general[y]
Rocky Mountain Spotted fever	*Rickettsia rickettsia*	Ticks, mostly *Dermacentor*	Capillary endothelia	Extravasation, temporary immunity	Western North America[z,aa,bb]; not generally recognized
Salmon sickness	*Neorickettsia helminthoeca*	Carried by fluke, *Nanophyetus*	Systemic	Highly fatal; immunity to survivors	Northwest Pacific Coast[cc]; Columbia River[dd]; Minnesota[ee]
Ehrlicheosis	Ehrlichia canis	*Ripicephalis*, maybe other ticks	Monocytes	Cutaneous septicemic, nervous; may be fatal	Experimental[ff]
Babesiosis (piroplasmosis)	*Babesia canis*	Ixodid tick bite	Erythrocytes	Anemia, hemaglobinurea, immunity	Experimental[ff,gg]; nonlethal
Q fever	*Coxiella burnetti*	Ticks: *Ornithodoros, Dermacentor.*	Blood, liver, spleen, kidney	Carrier, then immunity	California[hh,ii]; Idaho[jj]
Coccidiosis	*Isospora rivolta, I. bigemini*	Contaminated food	Intestine	Bloody diarrhea; may be fatal to pups	General; probably common[dd,kk]
Toxoplasmosis	*Toxoplasma gondii*	Transplacental; or by feces and urine	Intracellular in many tissues	May be fatal; immunity to survivors	Cosmopolitan, California[ll]; probably common[kk]
Sarcosporidiosis	*Sarcocystis fusiformes*	Ingestion of contaminated food	Gastrointestinal, tissues, muscle, heart	No overt symptoms	Utah–Idaho[jj]

References: [a] Davis *et al.* (1970); [b] Emery (1969); [c] Gier and Ameel (1959); [d] Budd (1970); [e] Trainer and Knowlton (1968); [f] Cabasso (1970); [g] Green *et al.* (1934); [h] Marler *et al.*(1976); [i] Trainer *et al.* (1968); [j] Gier (1968); [k] Broughton and Graeser (1970); [l] Nellis (1973); [m] Lundgren and Smart (1969); [n] Poland and Barnes (1970); [o] Knowlton (1976 personal communication); [p] Miles *et al.* (1949); [q] Barnes *et al.* (1976); [r] Ecke and Johnson (1952); [s] Witter and O'Meara (1970); [t] Eveland (1970); [u] Ganaway *et al.* (1971); [v] Ganaway *et al.* (1976); [w] Marler and Cook (1976); [x] Straub *et al.* (1961); [y] Menges *et al.* (1955); [z] Cooley and Kohls (1945); [aa] Lundgren *et al.* (1957); [bb] Lundgren *et al.* (1963); [cc] Schlegel *et al.* (1968); [dd] Krull (1969); [ee] Erickson (1944); [ff] Ewing *et al.* (1964); [gg] Howe (1971); [hh] Enright *et al.* (1971a); [ii] Enright *et al.* (1971b); [jj] Fayer and Johnson (1975); [kk] Flynn (1973); [ll] Riemann *et al.* (1975).

Q Fever, caused by the Rickettsia *Coxiella burneti*, is a disease of deer and other ungulates mainly in the Western U.S. *Coxiella burnetti* is transmitted by ticks, mainly *Dermacentor occidentalis*. Infected coyotes show no febrile symptoms but develop distinct antibody reaction against *C. burnetti*. Of 46 coyotes tested, 78% gave serum titers of 1:8 to 1:28, giving positive proof of exposure. Deer, sheep, fox, and lagamorphs of the area tested (Northern California) showed comparable reactions (Enright *et al.*, 1971a,b).

E. Protozoan

Coccidiosis is an enteric disease of many animals. In dogs, a serious to lethal colitis is produced by infection with coccidia of either of the genera *Isospora* or *Eimeria*, and these same organisms are probably as serious for coyote pups. We have positive identification of *Eimeria* infection of 3 penned coyotes and have had several litters of captive coyote pups annihilated by a malady, probably coccidiosis, causing bloody feces. Occurrence of coccidiosis in wild coyotes has not been recorded: diagnosis requires microscopic examination of feces from suspected victims. Loveless and Anderson (1975) demonstrated that coyotes are susceptible to both *Isospora* and *Eimeria*.

Babesiosis (piroplasmosis or red-water disease) is caused by the protozoan *Babesia canis* entering and destroying red blood corpuscles, resulting in anemia and bloody urine. *Rhipicephalus sanguineus* is the regular vector for *B. canis* although *Dermacentor andersoni, D. variabilis, D. albipictus, Amblyomma americana*, and possibly others may carry the disease. Ewing *et al.* (1964) produced tempory infection of *B. canis* in two experimental coyotes. No field diagnosis of babesiosis in coyotes has been found.

Toxoplasmosis caused by infection with *Toxoplasma gondii* apparently is transmitted directly by feces, urine, etc. This coccidium is cosmopolitan and may attack any domestic or wild animal, but the sexual phase takes place only in the intestinal epithelium of the cat family. Trophozoites invade the cytoplasm of any nucleated cell (of any homeothermic animal) and produce serious to fatal illness. Infection usually occurs by the new host eating an infected animal, or the trophozoites may pass through the placenta into developing fetuses. Riemann *et al.* (1975) reported serological evidence of *Toxoplasma* in California coyotes. Other positive reports are lacking.

Sarcocystitis, is apparently another nonlethal coccidianlike protozoan disease of coyotes. The causative agent *Sarcocystis fusiformes* apparently has a direct cycle, from infected host via feces to a new host. Sporozoites concentrate in muscle cells, with preference for heart. Fayer and Johnson (1975) reported *Sarcocystis* sporocytes recovered from 21 of 150 colon samples taken from coyotes killed in Utah–Idaho.

ACKNOWLEDGMENTS

The basic work leading to this report was done under Project 280, Kansas Agriculture Experiment Station with Zoology Department facilities. Much of the detailed preparations of the report were done at, and with the facilities of the Fish and Wildlife Research Center at Denver, Colorado. We greatly appreciate this support, and particularly the encouragement and help of Donald S. Balser, Samuel Linhart, and Dr. Fred Knowlton. We give special credit to Dr. Danny Pence, Texas Tech. University, Lubbock; Dr. J. P. Smith, Texas A & M University, College Station; Dr. William Jellison, Rocky Mountain Laboratory, Hamilton, Montana; and Dr. W. D. Lindquist, Kansas State University for suggestions and unpublished data; Miss Nancy Shepard for special aid in bibliography; and last but not least, to the secretarial staff of the Department of Anatomy and Physiology, particularly Janee Roche and Mary Kemnitz for their extreme patience and proficiency in help with the manuscript. The authors assume full responsibility for all errors, omissions, or unreferenced statements.

REFERENCES

Allen, J. R., and Mills, J. H. D. (1971). *Can. Vet. J.* **12,** 24–28.

Allison, M. N. (1963). *Salud Publica Mex.* **10,** 631–638.

Ameel, D. J. (1955). *Trans. Kans. Acad. Sci.* **58,** 208–210.

Barnes, A. M., Poland, J. D., and Quan, T. J. (1976). "Annual Report," Plague Branch. C.D.C., Fort Collins, Colorado.

Bishopp, F. C., and Trembly, H. L. (1945). *J. Parasit.* **31,** 1–54.

Broughton, E., and Graeser, F. E. (1970). *J. Wildl. Dis.* **6,** 180–181.

Brown, J. H. (1944). *Ann. Am. Entomol. Soc.* **37,** 207–213.

Brunetti, O. A. (1959). *Calif. Fish Game* **45,** 351–352.

Budd, J. (1970). *In* "Infectious Diseases" (J. Davis, L. Karstad, and D. Trainer, eds.), pp. 36–59, Iowa State Univ. Press, Ames.

Burnett, H. S., and Wagner, E. D. (1958). *J. Parasitol.* **44,** 502.

Butler, J. M., and Grundman, A. W. (1954). *J. Parasitol.* **40,** 440–443.

Cabasso, V. J. (1970). *In* "Infectious Diseases" (J. Davis, L. Karstad, and D. Trainer, eds.), pp. 134–139, Iowa State Univ. Press, Ames.

Chandler, A. C. (1944). *J. Parasitol.* **30,** 273.

Christensen, B. M., and Andrews, W. N. (1976). *J. Parasitol.* **62,** 276–280.

Christian, F. J., Jorgensen, R. D., and Bogess, E. K. (1976). *J. Wildl. Dis.* **12,** 165–166.

Cooley, R. A., and Kohls, G. M. (1945). "The Genus Ixodes in North America," NIH Bull. No. 184. U.S. Gov. Printing Office, Washington, D.C.

Davis, J. W., and Anderson, R. C. (1971). "Parasitic Diseases of Wild Mammals." Iowa State Univ. Press, Ames.

Davis, J. W., Karstad, L. H., and Trainer, D. O. (1970). "Infectious Diseases of Wild Animals." Iowa State Univ. Press, Ames.

Dodds, D. G., Martell, A. M., and Yescott, R. E. (1969). *Can. J. Zool.* **47,** 171–182.

Eads, R. B. (1948). *J. Mammal.* **29,** 268–271.

Ecke, D. H., and Johnson, C. W. (1952). *U.S., Public Health Serv., Health Monogr.* No. 6.

Eckert, J., Von Brand, T., and Voge, M. (1969). *J. Parasitol.* **55,** 241–249.

Emery, J. B. (1969). *Practic. Vet.* **41,** 13–16.

Enright, J. B., Behymer, D. E., and Franti, C. E. (1971a). *J. Wildl. Dis.* **7,** 83–90.

Enright, J. B., Franti, C. E., and Behymer, D. E. (1971b). *Am. J. Epidemiol.* **94,** 79–90.

Erickson, A. B. (1944). *Am. Midl. Nat.* **32,** 358–372.

Esch, G. W., and Self, J. T. (1965). *J. Parasitol.* **51,** 932–937.
Eveland, W. C. (1970). *In* "Infectious Diseases" (J. Davis, L. Karstad, and D. Trainer, eds.), pp. 273–292, Iowa State Univ. Press, Ames.
Ewing, S. A., Buckner, R. G., and Stringer, B. G. (1964). *J. Parasitol.* **50,** 704.
Fayer, R., and Johnson, A. J. (1975). *J. Infect. Dis.* **131,** 189–192.
Flynn, R. J. (1973). "Parasites of Laboratory Animals." Iowa State Univ. Press, Ames.
Fox, I. (1940). "Fleas of Eastern United States." Iowa State Univ. Press, Ames.
Freeman, R. S., Adorjan, A., and Pimlott, D. H. (1961). *Can J. Zool.* **39,** 527.
Ganaway, J. R., Allen, A. M., and Moore, T. D. (1971). *Am. J. Pathol.* **64,** 717–731.
Ganaway, J. R., McReynolds, R. S., and Allen, A. M. (1976). *J. Wildl. Dis.* **12,** 545–549.
Gier, H. T. (1968). "Coyotes in Kansas." Kans. Agric. Exp. Stn., Manhattan.
Gier, H. T., and Ameel, D. J. (1959). "Parasites and Diseases of Kansas Coyotes." Kans. Agric. Exp. Stn., Manhattan.
Graham, J. M. (1974). *J. Parasitol.* **60,** 322–326.
Graham, J. M. (1975). *J. Parasitol.* **61,** 513–516.
Green, R. G., Ziegler, N. R., and Carlson, W. E. (1934). *Am. J. Hyg.* **19,** 343–361.
Gregson, J. D. (1956). "The Ixodoidea of Canada." Pub. No. 930, pp. 1–92 Can. Dep. Agric. Ottawa.
Greig, A. S., and Charlton, K. M. (1973). *J. Wildl. Dis.* **9,** 359–361.
Grundman,A. W. (1958). *J. Parasitol.* **44,** 425.
Haas, G. E., Martin, R. P., Swickard, M., and Miller, B. E. (1973). *J. Med. Entomol.* **10,** 281–289.
Hardy, J. L., Reeves, W. C., Scrivani, R. P., and Roberts, D. R. (1974). *Am. J. Trop. Med. Hyg.* **23,** 1165–1177.
Herman, C. M. (1949). *Calif. Fish Game* **35,** 139.
Holmes, J. C. (1961). *J. Parasitol.* **47,** 55.
Holmes, J. C., and Podesta, R. (1968). *Can. J. Zool.* **46,** 1193–1204.
Howe, D. L. (1971). *In* "Parasitic Diseases of Wild Mammals" (J. Davis and R. Anderson, eds.), pp. 335–342, Iowa State Univ. Press, Ames.
Hubbard, C. A. (1947). "Fleas of Western North America." Iowa State Univ. Press, Ames.
Jellison, W. L. (in press). "Tularemia."
Jellison, W. L., and Kohls, G. M. (1943). "Siphonaptera: Species and Host List of Montana Fleas," pp. 1–22. Mont. State Board Entomol., Helena.
Knowles, M. E. (1914). *Breed. Gaz.* **66,** 229–230.
Krull, W. H. (1969). "Veterinary Parasitology." Univ Press of Kans., Lawrence.
Leiby, P. D. (1966). *Proc. N.D. Acad. Sci.* **20,** 133–134.
Leiby, P. D., Lubinsky, G., and Galaugher, W. (1969). *Can. J. Zool.* **47,** 135–139.
Leiby, P. D., Carney, W. P., and Woods, C. E. (1970). *J. Parasitol.* **56,** 1141–1150.
Levine, N. D. (1968). "Nematode Parasites of Domestic Animals and Man." Burgess, Minneapolis, Minnesota.
Liu, I. K. M., Schwabe, C. W., Schantz, P. M., and Allison, M. N. (1970). *J. Parasitol.* **56,** 1135–1137.
Loveless, R. M., and Anderson, F. L. (1975). *J. Parasitol.* **61,** 546–547.
Lundgren, D. L., and Smart, K. L. (1969). *Bull. Wildl. Dis. Assoc.* **5,** 39–42.
Lundgren, D. L., Marchette, W. J., and Smart, K. L. (1957). *J. Infect. Dis.* **101,** 154–157.
Lundgren, D. L., Ushijima, R. N., and Sidwell, R. S. (1963). *Zoonoses Res.* **2,** 125–134.
Marler, R. J., and Cook, J. E. (1976). *J. Am. Vet. Med. Assoc.* **169,** 964–965.
Marler, R. J., Kruckenberg, S. M., and O'Keefe, C. M. (1976). *J. Am. Vet. Med. Assoc.* **169,** 940–941.
Martell, A. M., Yescott, R. E., and Dodds, D. G. (1969). *Can. J. Zool.* **47,** 183–184.

Menges, R. W., Haberman, R. T., and Stains, H. J. (1955). *Trans. Kans. Acad. Sci.* **58,** 58–67.
Miles, V. I., Wilcomb, M. J., and Irons, J. V. (1949). *U.S., Public Health Serv., Public Health Monogr.* No. 6, Pt. 2.
Mitchell, R. L., and Beasom, S. L. (1974). *J. Wildl. Manage.* **38,** 455–458.
Nellis, C. H. (1973). *Can. J. Zool.* **51,** 900.
Novak, M. (1972). *Can. J. Zool.* **50,** 1189–1196.
Olsen, O. W. (1960). *J. Parasitol.* **46**(5), Sect. 2, 22.
Paramelee, W. E., Lee, R. D., Wagner, E. D., and Burnett, H. S. (1956). *J. Am. Vet. Med. Assoc.* **129,** 325–327.
Parker, R. R. (1926). *Public Health Rep.* **41,** 1407–1410.
Parry, H. B. (1951). *Vet. Rec.* **63,** 833–846.
Poland, J. D., and Barnes, A. M. (1970). *Proc. Vertebr. Pest Conf., 4th* pp. 29–33.
Price, E. W. (1928). *J. Parasitol.* **14,** 197.
Ramsden, R. O., and Presidente, P. J. A. (1975). *J. Wildl. Dis.* **11,** 136–141.
Rausch, R., Babero, B. B., Rausch, R. V., and Schiller, E. L. (1956). *J. Parasitol.* **42,** 259–271.
Riemann, H. P., Horvarth, J. A., Ruppanner, R., Franti, C. E., and Behymer, D. E. (1975). *J. Wildl. Dis.* **11,** 272–276.
Romano, M. N., Brunetti, O. A., Schwabe, C. W., and Rosen, M. N. (1974). *J. Wildl. Dis.* **10,** 225–227.
Schauffler, A. F. (1966). *J. Am. Vet. Med. Assoc.* **149,** 521–522.
Schlegel, M. W., Knapp, S. E., and Milleman, R. E. (1968). *J. Parasitol.* **54,** 770–774.
Self, J. T., and McKnight, T. J. (1950). *Am. Midl. Nat.* **43,** 58–61.
Smit, F. G. A. (1958). *J. Parasitol.* **44,** 523–526.
Smith, J. P. (1967). *Southwest. Vet.* **20,** 209–210.
Smith, J. P. (1971). *In* "Pathology of Parasitic Diseases" (S. M. Gaafar, ed.), pp. 259–264, Purdue Univ. Press, Lafayette, Indiana.
Stout, I. J., Clifford, C. M., and Keirans, J. E. (1971). *J. Med. Entomol.* **8,** 143–147.
Straub, M., Trautman, R. J., and Greene, J. W. (1961). *Am. J. Vet. Res.* **22,** 811–813.
Thornton, J. E., Bell, R. R., and Reardon, M. J. (1974). *J. Wildl. Dis.* **10,** 232–236.
Trainer, D. C., and Hale, J. B. (1969). *Bull. Wildl. Dis. Assoc.* **5,** 387–391.
Trainer, D. C., and Knowlton, F. F. (1968). *J. Wildl. Manage.* **32,** 981–983.
Trainer, D. C., Knowlton, F. F., and Kerstad, L. (1968). *Bull. Wildl. Dis. Assoc.* **4,** 52–54.
Verster, A. (1969). *Onderstepoort J. Vet. Res.* **36,** 3–58.
Voge, M. (1955a). *Am. Midl. Nat.* **54,** 413.
Voge, M. (1955b). *Univ. Calif. Berkeley, Publ. Zool.* **59,** 125–155.
Williams, L. A., and Hoff, C. C. (1951). *Proc. U.S. Natl. Mus.* **101,** 305–313.
Witter, J. F., and O'Meara, D. C. (1970). *In* "Infectious Diseases of Wild Animals" (J. Davis, L. Karstad, and D. Trainer, eds.), pp. 249–255, Iowa State Univ. Press, Ames.
Wobeser, G., and Rock, T. W. (1973). *J. Wildl. Dis.* **9,** 225–226.
Young, S. P., and Jackson, H. H. T. (1951). "The Clever Coyote," Stackpole, Harrisburg, Pennsylvania.
Zimmerman, W. J. (1971). *In* "Parasitic Diseases of Wild Mammals" (J. Davis and R. Anderson, eds.), pp. 127–139, Iowa State Univ. Press, Ames.
Zimmerman, W. J., Hubbard, E. D., and Biester, H. E. (1959). *J. Parasitol.* **45,** 88–90.

4

Coyote Reproduction

James J. Kennelly

I. INTRODUCTION

In spite of the long-continued interest in coyotes, particularly with regard to population management, little research has been directed toward understanding the basic mechanisms responsible for observed reproductive patterns. Until recently, only the two extensive reports by Hamlett (1938) and Gier (1968) were available. These have been supplemented by several theses providing a general understanding of coyote biology and behavior (Bowman, 1940; Rogers, 1965; Ogle, 1969; Gipson, 1972; Dunbar, 1973). The recent study by the Cain Committee (Cain, 1972) focused attention on the need for expanded research as a prerequisite for formulating effective and ecologically sound management programs. Accordingly, State and Federal governments increased the availability of research funds resulting in an expansion of existing programs and the initiation of new ones. Reproductive behavior of the coyote will, without doubt, receive increased attention. In view of this anticipated need it is timely to summarize what is known about coyote reproductive patterns.

This chapter will only focus on reproductive studies published during the past 40 years, as many earlier reports were either anecdotal or the conclusions lacked documentation. In addition, unpublished studies I conducted at the Denver Wildlife Research Center, U.S. Fish and Wildlife Service, will be included to provide the most current profile on this subject. Coyotes used in my studies were either born in captivity or captured near San Antonio, Texas and Denver, Colorado and maintained as described by Kennelly and Johns (1976).

II. ANATOMY

Detailed accounts of the gross and microscopic anatomy of coyote reproductive systems are not available for either sex. The published reports as well as my studies suggest, however, that except for the seasonality of breeding and the associated cyclic changes in the reproductive tract, only minor differences, if any, exist between this species and the domestic dog. The reader is advised to consult the excellent review articles on the dog until definitive studies with coyotes are published (Christensen, 1964; Andersen, 1970; Hart, 1970; Andersen and Simpson, 1973).

III. MALE REPRODUCTION

A. Breeding Onset

1. Juveniles

It is well established that males frequently attain sexual maturity during the first breeding season following birth and are capable of impregnating females (Gier, 1968; Kennelly, 1972; Kennelly and Johns, 1976; Dunbar, 1973). The proportion of juvenile males (less than 1 year old) breeding in natural populations each season is unknown, but, because they have successfully bred in pen studies, they probably breed to some extent under favorable conditions in the wild. The onset of breeding condition is much easier to determine than copulation because the former requires only reproductive tracts from known-age males while the latter requires behavioral observations on known-age animals, a combination difficult to obtain. Gier (1968) estimated Kansas coyotes reached breeding condition by late January. The only other information on juvenile breeding patterns is from previously unpublished studies which are reported here.

Eight juvenile males were studied to determine the developmental changes in the reproductive organs the summer following birth. Testes and epididymides weight paralleled body weight increases but specific gravity for both organs remained relatively constant (Table I). The most notable change occurred in the seminiferous tubules. During the first three sampling periods, the ratio between seminiferous tubules and nontubular tissue was nearly 1:1 and tubule diameter about 60 μm. By late September, however, when males were 24 weeks old, gonadotropin stimulation was evident. Tubule diameter enlarged to 70 μm, accounting for 65% of testicular tissue, and spermatogonial proliferation was evident. In another study, coyotes obtained when 3–5 weeks of age from Texas and Colorado were sampled between September and the following April to evaluate onset of spermatogenesis during the first breeding season (Table II). All juveniles showed gonadal stimulation but apparently individuals vary with regard to onset and development. Spermatogonial proliferation started in September, primary spermatocytes were evident by early November, spermiogenesis was ongoing in many tubules in January, and epididymal sperm were recovered in February. Although the gonadal changes of the Texas and Colorado specimens appear similar the small sample size and large sampling intervals preclude making a meaningful comparison.

2. Adults

The onset of breeding condition in adult males varies from year to year both within one geographic region and from one to another (Hamlett, 1938; Gier, 1968). During the nonbreeding season the germinal epithelium is composed of Sertoli cells, spermatogonia, and a reduced number of primary spermatocytes. All postmeiotic developmental phases are absent, probably because androgen levels are insufficient, although this relationship in coyotes has not been examined.

In a series of reproductive tracts collected from 13 western States, the first sign of breeding onset, spermatogonial proliferation, occurred in November (Hamlett, 1938). In January, he observed all developmental stages as well as the start of epididymal sperm storage; the breeding season was in "full-swing" by February. Similarly, Kansas coyotes reach breeding condition in early January (Gier, 1968) which means changes in the seminiferous tubules must begin around November. Studies with coyotes from Arkansas (Gipson, 1972; Gipson *et al.*, 1975), Oklahoma (Dunbar, 1973), and Colorado, however, indicate spermatogenesis begins a month earlier than in Kansas and full breeding condition is attained by December. Gipson *et al.* (1975) reported an increase in testicular weight accompanying

TABLE I

Juvenile Coyotes: Testicular Changes Associated with Onset of Fertility

Tissue collection[a]			Testes					
					Seminiferous tubules			
Date	Age in weeks	Mean body weight (kg)	Weight[b] (gm)	Specific gravity	(%)	Diameter (μm)	Nontubular tissue (gm)	Mean epididymal weight[b] (gm)
July 14	12	2.8	0.129	1.083	49.6	59.2	0.064	0.132
Aug. 27	16	4.8	0.297	1.091	47.7	56.4	0.154	0.271
Aug. 27	21	6.6	0.482	1.065	48.9	61.8	0.246	0.248
Sept. 24	25	7.7	0.580	1.071	65.2	70.2	0.201	0.281

[a] Both sides of two animals in each age group.
[b] Mean per testis/epididymis.

TABLE II

Juvenile Coyotes: Germ Cell Development Stages Associated with Onset of Fertility

	Texas[a]				Colorado			
Date sampled	Animal number	Body weight (kg)	Age[b] (weeks)	Most advanced germ cell development	Animal number	Body weight (kg)	Age[b] (weeks)	Most advanced germ cell development
9-8	30	—	21	Gonocytes	69	—	20	Gonocytes
9-22	30	5.0	23	Spermatogonia	69	4.5	22	Spermatogonia
11-3	45	—	28	Primary spermatocyte	107	—	29	Spermatogonia
11-18	45	7.0	30	Primary spermatocyte	107	6.7	31	Primary spermatocyte
12-1	31	—	33	Primary spermatocyte	70	—	32	Primary spermatocyte
12-16	31	6.4	35	Primary spermatocyte	70	6.7	34	Primary spermatocyte
12-30	35	—	37	Primary spermatocyte	74	—	36	Primary spermatocyte
1-12	35	8.4	39	Spermatids	74	8.4	38	Primary spermatocyte
1-26	60	—	40	Primary spermatocyte	100	—	41	Spermatid
2-9	60	8.7	42	Spermatids	100	8.7	43	Epididymal sperm[c]
3-2	46	—	45	Epididymal sperm				
3-2	61	—	45	Epididymal sperm				
3-9	34	8.4	47	Epididymal sperm				
3-30	46	7.7	49	Epididymal sperm[c]				
4-14	61	9.5	51	Epididymal sperm[c]				

[a] Transferred to Denver, Colorado when 3–5 weeks of age.
[b] Age estimated at capture.
[c] Seminiferous epithelium degenerating.

breeding onset peaks during January and February. One adult in their study was in the early stages of spermatogenesis on October 20 and, considering the kinetics of germ cell development (Kennelly, 1972), spermatogenesis started at least 3 weeks earlier. I observed gonadal stimulation in three Colorado adults sampled in mid-October by unilateral castration (Table III). Between October 14 and December 1, testis weight continually increased with a concomitant increase in both the proportion of the testis composed of seminiferous tubules and tubule diameter, and the estimated weight of intertubular tissue doubled. By December 1 all adults were in full spermatogenesis and sperm numbers sufficiently high in one to consider the animal fertile. The maximum values I observed for both tubular diameter and proportion, 187.5 μm—86.2%, were much greater than the comparable figures Dunbar (1973) reported for Oklahoma coyotes (160 μm—70%). The differences, however, are probably due to sampling bias rather than a real difference between populations.

3. Juvenile vs Adult

To compare the onset of fertility among juveniles and adults, I unilaterally castrated four males in each age class in mid-December with the contralateral testis removed 2 or 4 weeks later (Table IV). The results supported Gier's (1968, 1975) observations that adults reach breeding condition about 3 to 4 weeks earlier than juveniles. On January 10 testis weight, specific gravity, and estimated weight of intertubular tissue of juveniles was similar to adults examined on December 14. Although sperm were recovered from the epididymides of each adult at the first castration, the concentration and motility of only two males were high enough to consider them in breeding condition. Mean body weight at first castration was 10.8 and 10.6 kg for the juveniles and adults, respectively.

B. Spermatogenesis

Upon attaining breeding condition the kinetics of coyote spermatogenesis (Kennelly, 1972) is similar to that reported for the domestic dog (Foote *et al.*, 1972) and, except for the timing of events within, it generally follows the pattern reported for other mammals (Ortavant *et al.*, 1969). The coyote spermatogenic cycle, the time it takes for a germ cell to complete the developmental changes preparatory to passage from the testis as spermatozoa, requires 54.4 days. During this period the germinal epithelium follows a repetitive, well-defined series of eight cellular associations or stages collectively referred to as "the cycle of the seminiferous epithelium" (Leblond and Clermont, 1952); four successive cycles of the seminiferous epithelium constitutes one spermatogenic cycle. At a given point in the

TABLE III

Adult Coyotes: Testicular Changes Associated with the Onset of Breeding

	Testes						
					Seminiferous tubules		
Castration date	Weight (gm)	Specific gravity	Estimated inter-tubular tissue (gm)	(%)	Diameter (μm)	Most advanced germ cell development	Number epididymides with sperm
Oct. 14	1.529	1.078	0.437	71.4	117.5	Zygotene primary spermatocytes abundant; few pachytene	0
Nov. 1	2.710	1.063	0.691	74.5	131.6	Pachytene primary spermatocytes abundant; few round spermatids	0
Nov. 15[a]	3.984	1.048	0.872	78.9	175.7	Round spermatids abundant but a few show elongation	0
Dec. 1[b]	6.556	1.049	0.904	86.2	187.5	All phases of spermiogenesis	1

[a] Alternate side of Oct. 14 animals (N = 3).
[b] Alternate side of Nov. 1 animals (N = 3).

TABLE IV

Comparison of Spermatogenic Activity between Juvenile and Adult Coyotes

			Testes					
						Seminiferous tubule		
Age class	Number of males	Castration date[a]	Weight (gm)	Specific gravity	Estimated inter-tubular tissue (gm)	%	Most advanced germ cell development	Sperm in cauda epidid-ymides[b]
Juvenile	2	Dec. 13	2.804	1.047	0.628	77.6	Pachytene primary spermatocytes	(−)
		Dec. 27	3.728	1.048	0.608	83.7	Spermatids, few differentiated	(−)
Juvenile	2	Dec. 13	3.344	1.050	0.562	83.2	Pachytene primary spermatocytes	(−)
		Jan. 10	6.360	1,047	0.687	89.2	Spermatogenesis in all tubules	(+)
Adult	2	Dec. 14	6.329	1.047	0.608	90.4	Spermatogenesis in all tubules	(+)
		Dec. 28	7.074	1.048	0,736	89.6	Spermatogenesis in all tubules	(+)
Adult	2	Dec. 14	7.852	1.046	1.005	87.2	Spermatogenesis in all tubules	(+)
		Jan. 10	9.648	1.046	0.984	89.8	Spermatogenesis in all tubules	(+)

[a] Unilateral castration (one left–one right) on first date for each age class, alternate testes removed on second date in each age class.

[b] (−) = No sperm; (+) = sperm.

tubule, the germinal epithelium renews the process of sperm formation every 13.6 days, and this cyclic pattern continues until the breeding season ends. The constancy of the duration and morphology of each of the eight stages comprising an epithelial cycle (Kennelly, 1972) provides a basis for determining the start of testicular regression. Spermiogenesis is the first process interrupted followed by other postmeiotic developmental types. Initially, the changes are subtle and difficult to detect without extensive quantitative evaluation of spermatogenesis but as more and more cell types are involved epithelial degeneration becomes obvious (Ogle, 1969).

C. Epididymal Sperm Transit

Kennelly (1972) estimated that spermatozoan transit time in the epididymis was about 14 days. Transit time may be shorter, however, since the estimate was based on first appearance of radioactive sperm in ejaculates obtained by electroejaculation (Christensen and Dougherty, 1955), and sperm numbers at each collection were much less than those of a dog of similar size and testicular development (Foote, 1969).

D. Termination of Breeding

Regression of the adult testis begins in March (Hamlett, 1938; Gier, 1968; Ogle, 1969; Dunbar, 1973; Gipson *et al.*, 1975) and by June sperm production has ceased and epididymal sperm are few or absent. Spermiogenesis is affected first but eventually all postmeiotic developmental phases are interrupted; spermatocytogenesis is reduced and the tubules lose the cellular associations characteristic of spermatogenesis referred to earlier. To monitor the testicular changes during this period I performed unilateral castration on a group of 10 adult males on February 20 and removed the alternate testis from randomly selected pairs at 2 week intervals (Table V).

All males were in full sperm production in February, and the epididymides contained copious quantities of sperm that, upon dilution with physiological saline, were highly motile. This condition prevailed through the first sampling interval, March 4, although both males on that date showed a small decrease in the tubular proportion of the testis. The first indication of the approaching shift in breeding condition occurred on March 19. Testis weight had decreased in both males, and germinal epithelium of one showed some degenerative changes. Specifically, spermatids at various levels of differentiation were missing from some tubules, stage 8 of the epithelial cycle was absent, and many tubules appeared to have an excessive number of primary spermatocytes. Ogle (1969) also noted the absence of developmental types beyond primary spermatocytes in "early

TABLE V

Adult Coyotes: Changes Observed during Testicular and Epididymal Regression

	First castration[a]					Second castration						
	Testes			Epididymides			Testes			Epididymides		
Animal number[b]	Weight (gm)	Specific gravity	Seminiferous tubules (%)	Weight (gm)	Specific gravity	Date	Weight (gm)	Specific gravity	Seminiferous tubules (%)	Weight (gm)	Specific gravity	Sperm concentration[c]
119	6.230	1.046	86.0	1.843	1.063	Mar. 4	6.341	1.046	83.7	1.802	1.060	4
130	7.507	1.045	89.0	1.730	1.066	Mar. 4	6.802	1.047	83.3	1.711	1.067	4
193	11.992	1.044	87.0	1.899	1.063	Mar. 19	8.694	1.048	84.7	1.692	1.070	4
167	8.452	1.043	89.0	1.957	1.064	Mar. 19	7.158	1.044	85.0	1.768	1.071	4
155	7.478	1.046	84.0	2.167	1.068	Apr. 1	6.373	1.048	80.3	2.023	1.065	4
165	5.671	1.046	78.7	2.176	1.066	Apr. 1	2.586	1.056	62.7	1.286	1.073	2
153	8.283	1.044	87.0	2.137	1.061	Apr. 15	4.642	1.048	76.7	2.054	1.063	3
171	8.751	1.045	85.0	1.423	1.072	Apr. 15	3.714	1.054	77.3	0.994	1.074	1
139	6.034	1.045	85.0	1.808	1.074	Apr. 30	1.743	1.065	65.7	0.986	1.078	1
181	11.912	1.043	85.7	2.420	1.065	Apr. 30	6.251	1.048	76.0	1.720	1.059	2

[a] Performed February 20.
[b] Mean body weight = 11.2 kg; no change between 1st and 2nd castration.
[c] Estimated concentration: (4) high; (3) medium; (2) low; (1) few.

postreproductive" coyote testes collected in Washington. The epididymides of both males contained high concentrations of motile sperm suggesting little or no effect on fertility.

Testicular regression was well underway by April 1. Spermatogenesis, interrupted in both males, was more severely affected in one. Although epithelial degeneration, i.e., pycnotic spermatids, aberrant meiotic divisions, absence of expected cell types, and sloughed cells and cellular debris in the tubule lumen, was evident in some seminiferous tubules of the least-affected male, many tubular cross sections appeared normal and examples of all spermatogenic stages were located. Further, the epididymis was sufficiently similar in weight and sperm concentration to the February sample to suggest fertility was unimpaired. Testicular regression was more advanced in the second male; the epithelium within most tubules showed extensive germ cell degeneration, epithelial sloughing together with cells and cellular debris in the lumen was common and, with few exceptions, the orderly cellular associations characteristic of spermatogenesis was absent. I questioned this male's fertility because of reduced epididymal weight and sperm numbers.

As expected, testicular regression was more advanced by April 15 but differences between males are noteworthy. Both showed a reduction in testis weight and tubule proportion, pycnotic cells, missing cell lines, and cellular debris within the tubules. One male (No. 153) had many tubules that appeared normal, and in fact, all stages of the epithelial cycle were located. Further, the epididymis showed only minimal changes from February; weight was relatively unchanged and sperm concentration, though reduced, was sufficiently high to make fertility a distinct possibility. By April 30 all regressive changes noted above were evident in both males and, with few exceptions, the interruption of spermatogenesis complete. Germinal epithelium in many tubules now consisted of mostly Sertoli cells and spermatogonia with a few primary spermatocytes; a condition that will prevail throughout the nonbreeding season. The basement membrane of most tubules appear wavy or scalloped, probably due to a disproportionate loss of tissue within the tubules compared with the rest of the testis.

IV. FEMALE REPRODUCTION

A. Estrous Cycle

The coyote is seasonally monestrous and available data suggest the estrous cycle and associated changes in the reproductive tract are similar to the domestic dog (Gier, 1968; Kennelly and Johns, 1976). Contrary to earlier beliefs, juveniles may cycle and reproduce the first breeding season following birth but the proportion depends upon environmental conditions (Gier, 1968; Nellis and Keith, 1976) and control intensity (Knowlton, 1972).

1. Proestrus

The onset of proestrus in adults is characterized by vulval enlargement and bleeding. These two indicators of sexual maturity are not always evident in juveniles but in those that show them, the changes vary in intensity and duration compared with adults. One captive juvenile showed vulval bleeding beginning February 12, and it persisted for 14 days without accompanying enlargement of the vulva (Whiteman, 1940); another discharged blood for only 3 days beginning February 27, vulval enlargement preceded bleeding, and the organ remained turgid for 6 days (Enders, 1955). We (Kennelly and Johns, 1976) observed both situations in 19 of 22 juveniles studied; three showed no sexual activity. Six were classified as experiencing a false estrus, e.g., vulval bleeding evident, but a typical estrus vaginal smear was never obtained and five showed no appreciable vulval enlargement. The 13 remaining juveniles progressed to an estrus smear and 10 that were checked further all showed vulval enlargement. Although bleeding persisted for up to 4 weeks before estrus, it is difficult to draw comparisons with other reports because our observations were based on the appearance of the vaginal fluid aspirated for smears rather than on gross detection of discharge.

Proestrus is first evident in adult coyotes 2–3 months before estrus onset. Vaginal fluid collected from six of eight 2-year-old coyotes was bloody when first examined on December 1 and within 3 weeks all eight were in this condition; yet estrus onset ranged from early February to early April. Vulval enlargement did not begin until about 2–3 weeks before estrus. The cellular associations of the vaginal smear characteristic of proestrus (Kennelly and Johns, 1976) is similar to that reported for dogs (Evans and Cole, 1931).

2. Estrus

a. Characteristics. Except for the condition of false heat noted in juveniles, estrus indicators were similar in coyotes of different ages. The incidence of false heat in a natural population is unknown but is probably limited to yearlings because only once did we fail to observe a true estrus in more than 50 adults studied. The vulva reaches maximum size about day four of estrus and then begins to recede, taking up to 30 days to return to anestrus (Whiteman, 1940). The aspirated vaginal fluid, a bright red color throughout proestrus, frequently becomes dark brown during estrus. Erythrocytes are usually numerous in the vaginal smear, cornified epithelial cells dominate, and leucocytes, generally absent or scarce, sometimes appear in great numbers. Females readily accept the male at this time, whether pairing occurred several months earlier or at estrus onset. Copulation generally occurred when animals were unattended but on several occasions they bred in view of workers during routine maintenance activities.

b. Estrus Onset and Duration. Date of estrus onset and duration of breeding season varies geographically (Hamlett, 1938) and by season within a particular region (Gier, 1968). Two principle methods have been used to estimate breeding season: (1) evaluation of field specimens, e.g., embryo and placental scar counts and litter recoveries (Hamlett, 1938; Gier, 1968; Gipson *et al.*, 1975) and (2) through studies of captive animals. Field collections are preferable because data are obtained on a natural population and under prevailing environmental conditions. Based on over 2900 records from 13 western States, Hamlett (1938) found breeding generally begins in February and most females bred within a month. Breeding begins about 2 weeks later in Montana and Wyoming, whereas in California, Oregon, and Arizona breeding occurred during a 2-month period. Gier (1968) back-dated embryos obtained from 96 female coyotes over a consecutive 7-year period and estimated February 2 as the earliest ovulation time and March 26 the latest. The mean ovulation dates fluctuated from March 2 in 1949 to February 14 in 1954. Gier, however, feels that ovulation occurs late in estrus, placing breeding onset about one week earlier. February 17 and March 7 were the maximum estimated breeding dates of seven pregnant coyotes trapped in Arkansas (Gipson *et al.*, 1975). The early literature relating to estrus onset, much of it primarily based on trapper's accounts, clearly showed January through March as the general breeding season (Bowman, 1940).

Observations with coyotes in captivity provide more precise estimates of estrus onset and permit an estimate of duration. Gander (1928) observed a 4-day estrus in a female first breeding on January 26. In two Michigan coyotes, Whiteman (1940) described one with a 5-day estrus that began January 27 and the other with a 4-day period beginning on February 25. Based on vaginal smear changes, we found mean onset of estrus for 41 Colorado adults to be March 7, and when 28 of these females were checked for first male acceptance the mean date was March 13. The duration of estrus for the 41 females was 10.2 days (range 4–15 days) with age having no significant effect on either onset or duration. Gier (1968) states "heat" lasts for 10–30 days in coyotes but did not indicate how this estimate was derived.

3. Metestrus–Anestrus

Except for a brief description of the vaginal smear pattern associated with metestrus onset (Kennelly and Johns, 1976), smear patterns characteristic of metestrus and anestrus have not been described. As metestrus proceeds, noncornified epithelial cells and leucocytes become abundant once again and considerable cell debris is evident.

B. Gestation

Gestation, marked from first acceptance of the male or onset of behavioral estrus ranges from 60 to 63 days (Gander, 1928; Brown, 1936; Hamlett, 1938; Whiteman, 1940; Young and Jackson, 1951; Bekoff and Diamond, 1976). Gier (1968) emphasized time of ovulation rather than estrus onset as the beginning of gestation and reported the duration of pregnancy for coyotes to be about 60 days or "56–57 days after the end of receptive heat." There is some evidence in coyotes and substantial evidence in domestic dogs that fetal development varies less among bitches when metestrus rather than estrus onset is used to mark the beginning of gestation (Tietz and Seliger, 1967; Holst and Phemister, 1971). The mean weight and crown–rump measurements of known-age fetuses from 10 female coyotes we (Kennelly *et al.*, 1977) examined at five gestation intervals (Table VI) illustrates the relationship of fetal development with metestrus onset. Note the increased variability among fetuses from each coyote pair sampled at the same time when estrus rather than metestrus onset is the reference base. This is consistent with Gier's (1968) observations; although he used estimated time of ovulation to mark embryogenesis, he associated time of ovulation with the end of receptive heat or onset of metestrus. Apparently embryonic development is synchronized with hormonal changes, specifically progesterone from the corpora lutea, at the onset of metestrus—a hypothesis suggested by Evans and Cole (1931) in their study on the estrous cycle of domestic dogs and sup-

TABLE VI
Weight and Crown–Rump (C–R) Length Measurements of Coyote Fetuses

Female	Days after onset		Litter size	Mean fetal measurements ± S.D.	
	Estrus	Metestrus		Weight (gm)	C–R Length (mm)
1	30	21	8	0.44 ± 0.034	15.6 ± 0.44
2	30	21	5	0.30 ± 0.018	13.6 ± 0.42
3	37	28	6	3.96 ± 0.248	41.8 ± 0.93
4	37	31	6	8.43 ± 0.919	54.2 ± 2.40
5	44	35	8	18.2 ± 0.94	76.9 ± 1.58
6	44	37	6	29.8 ± 2.21	85.3 ± 2.58
7	51	43	8	98.3 ± 5.38	130.5 ± 2.27
8	51	46	3	151.7 ± 6.60	148.0 ± 1.00
9	58	47	7	154.9 ± 10.81	160.4 ± 3.10
10	58	50	5	177.8 ± 6.78	163.6 ± 3.21

ported by recent studies by Tietz and Seliger (1967) and Holst and Phemister (1971).

1. Ovulation

Coyotes are monestrus and produce only one set of ova each breeding season (Hamlett, 1938). Ovulation occurs during estrus and is spontaneous but day of ovulation is uncertain. Gier (1968, 1975) reported ovulation occurred the last 2–3 days before estrus ended but we found evidence for ovulation the first day of estrus and as late as the ninth day but because of small sample size we were unable to determine which, if either, was the predominant situation in coyotes (Kennelly and Johns, 1976). Recent reports indicate that ovulation in domestic dogs occurs early in estrus, usually by day 2 or 3 (Holst and Phemister, 1971; Andersen and Simpson, 1973).

The mean number of ovulations, usually estimated from counts of corpora lutea, is about equally divided between left and right ovaries (Kennelly and Johns, 1976) but varies among individuals within and among seasons. Some variability is caused by nutritional factors because Gier (1975) reported changes in food availability directly affected corpora lutea counts. He observed a mean of 6.5 corpora per female with over 80% ovulating in abundant food periods but in times of food scarcity the count dropped to 4.5 corpora with only 50% ovulating. Moreover, Gier (1968) and Nellis and Keith (1976) observed the proportion of juveniles that reproduce each year depends upon favorable environmental conditions including food availability. Clark (1972) provided indirect evidence for a possible effect of food availability on ovulation when he showed coyote reproductive rate was correlated with jackrabbit density, a major food item. In our studies with captive coyotes (Kennelly and Johns, 1976), we found age significantly affected ovulation rate; females were 2, 3, and 4 years old with mean corpora lutea counts of 5.6, 6.2, and 7.1, respectively. Field specimens Gier (1968) evaluated did not show differences between juveniles and older females in number of ova produced and Gipson *et al.* (1975) reported no "appreciable difference" in ova production between 2 year olds and older females. One report provides indirect evidence for a density effect on ovulation. Knowlton (1972) found that the number of "uterine swellings" per female and litter size, both indicators of ovulation rate, varied inversely with density in several Texas populations.

The freshly ovulated coyote ovum is covered with a dense layer of coronal cells and the diameter of the complex is about 272 μm (S.D. $\pm$ 9.5). Initially only the outline of the opaque vitellus, diameter 126 μm, is visible; the perivitelline space is absent and the zona is hidden by coronal cells. As the ovum ages the coronal cells disperse revealing a 37 μm thick zona pellucida. Following the two maturation divisions, polar bodies are visible in the small (5–6 μm) perivitelline space now present. The uniform appearance of the ova and development of associated follicles (corpora lutea) suggest ovulation occurs over a short period of time if not simultaneously; the domestic dog is similar (Andersen and Simpson, 1973).

2. Fertilization and Oviduct Transport

Reports concerning the interval between ovulation and passage of ova or zygotes to the uterus are lacking. Ova remain in the dog oviduct about a week (Bischoff, 1845; Evans and Cole, 1931) and if fertilization occurs, they persist until at least the 16-cell stage before entering the uterus (Andersen, 1927; Holst and Phemister, 1971). Our studies suggest the coyote is similar. We recovered ova from the left oviduct of three estrus females and 2, 4, and 5 days later, respectively, while the animals were still in estrus, ova were recovered from the other oviduct. Two of the females had bred, and sperm were present in the flushing media from oviducts and uteri at both sampling periods; however, the ova were not cleaved. Doak and associates (1967) reported motile sperm persisted throughout estrus in the uteri and oviducts of dogs bred early in estrus. We observed motile sperm in oviduct and uterine flushings of 10 females bred during estrus and subsequently examined at varying intervals before metestrus onset. Generally, fertilized ova distribution followed the pattern observed in dogs; with one exception, all zygotes beyond the 16-cell stage were in uterine flushings. Further, the zona pellucida persisted until after passage to the uterus and always contained numerous sperm head remnants in the outer region.

3. Uterus and Implantation

The coyote, like the dog, compensates for unequal production of ova between ovaries through transuterine embryo migration; we observed this in 8 of 11 bitches used in a study of fetal development (Kennelly *et al.*, 1977). Implantation sites, indicated by the beginning of uterine swelling, is evident in the dog 16–21 days after breeding (Tietz and Seliger, 1967; Holst and Phemister, 1971). Gier's (1968) data indicates uterine swelling occurs about 11 days after estrus ends, and based on a 10-day estrus period (Kennelly and Johns, 1976) coyote implantation sites should be grossly visible 21 days after breeding. The site of each successful embryo implant that proceeds to term is marked by a pigmented band in the uterine wall—"placental scar"—that persists for 2 years (Gier, 1968). Scars from the most recent pregnancy may be distinguished from the previous year's by size, color, and spacing. Recent scars are larger, more intensely pigmented and implantation sites each year are uniformly spaced according to the number of fetuses. Further, corpora lutea counts will provide an indication of the maximum number of scars to expect for that season since normally each corpus luteum is associated with one fetus. The same criteria will distinguish sites of postimplantation embryo death or resorptions, particularly if only a single set of scars exist; however, when scars from 2 years are present resorptions may be confused with full-term scars of the preceding year. The minimum interval between implantation and the formation of a grossly detectable scar is unknown.

Gier (1968) provides the only description of the temporal relationships of coyote embryogenesis but he used ovulation time, estimated to occur about 3 days before the end of estrus, as a reference point to date embryos. His results must be adjusted accordingly when specimens are aged by a different method, e.g., from onset of estrus or metestrus. He considered the process similar in coyotes and dogs and combined data from six sets of known-age coyote fetuses with over 60 sets from dogs to develop growth curves based on (a) fetal weight, (b) crown–rump length, and (c) hind foot length. He noted one exception; after 40 days gestation fetuses from dogs weighing 25–35 pounds tended to be heavier than coyote fetuses. His data indicate crown–rump length may be determined by 16–17 days gestation, hind foot differentiates on the limb bud at 27–28 days, weight exceeds 1 gm at 28–29 days, and parturition occurs at 59–60 days.

Since there is uncertainty about time of ovulation and coyotes vary in duration of estrus and hence metestrus onset, we (Kennelly *et al.*, 1977) measured the same parameters (weight, crown–rump length, and hind foot length) in 10 sets of known-age fetuses and calculated regression equations to estimate age of unknown fetuses. Each fetus was dated from estrus and metestrus onset and analyzed separately; the former is easier to determine and more meaningful to the field biologist and the latter, because it is more precise, is useful for intensive studies with captive animals. Also, it is frequently necessary to preserve field-collected specimens, and each fetus was measured before and after fixing in 10% formalin. Crown–rump measurements provided the most reliable equations (Table VII) and were the only values significantly ($P < 0.05$) affected by formalin. Two other facts are worth noting: male fetuses were heavier than females, and location in the uterus did not significantly affect fetal weight.

C. Fecundity

Population fecundity, the number of young born annually, is a function of the proportion of females that breed and the frequency and size of litters. The report by Dixon (1920) notwithstanding, coyotes produce but one litter each year. Hamlett (1938) was the first to call attention to the morphological changes in the ovary each breeding season and the improbability of two litters in one year. The number of females breeding each year, particularly the proportion of juveniles that become sexually mature,

TABLE VII

Predicting Coyote Fetal Age from Crown–Rump Length Measurements[a]

Specimen condition	Fetal age reference point			
	Estrus onset		Metestrus onset	
	Prediction equation[b]	Correlation coeffieicnt	Prediction equation	Correlation coefficient
Fresh	$X = \frac{Y + 148.821}{5.354}$	0.988	$X = \frac{Y + 106.786}{5.455}$	0.991
Formalin preserved	$X = \frac{Y + 132.948}{4.878}$	0.988	$X = \frac{Y + 93.956}{4.932}$	0.997

[a] Ten sets of known-age fetuses.

[b] Based on linear regression equation $Y = a + bX$; X = estimated fetal age, Y = crown–rump length in mm.

depends on environmental conditions and the intensity of coyote control practices (Gier, 1968; Knowlton, 1972). Various estimates for the adult class are available and range between 74–94% (Rogers, 1965; Gier, 1968; Gipson *et al.*, 1975; Nellis and Keith, 1976). Juveniles, however, fluctuate more widely; the proportion that contributes to the breeding population ranges from none (Gipson *et al.*, 1975; Gier, 1968) to as high as 80% (Rogers, 1965; Gier, 1968; Clark, 1972; Gipson *et al.*, 1975; Nellis and Keith, 1976). Since juveniles represent from 35–45% of the female population (Gier, 1968), most of the annual variation in numbers of breeding females is due to the number of juveniles that become sexually mature. Gier (1968) provides some interesting calculations that illustrate how productivity may fluctuate in good and poor reproductive years and suggests about 48–50% of all females produce an average litter of 5.6 pups.

Litter-size estimates are generally derived from examination of the reproductive tract, e.g., ovulation rate, fetal and placental scar counts, or pup counts at the den site. Both methods may provide inaccurate estimates if potential sources of error are not considered. Ovulation rate requires correction for unfertilized ova and prenatal mortality. Approximately 20% of ova and embryos are lost between ovulation and parturition (Gier, 1975). Preimplantation losses range from 8–14% (Knowlton, 1972; Gier, 1975) but estimates as great as 27% have been reported (Gipson *et al.*, 1975). There is less information available on postimplantation loss, perhaps due to difficulties noted earlier in distinguishing between resorption and term placental scars. The reports by Gier (1968, 1975) indicate 10–15% may be lost in this period. Early postnatal mortality, estimated at 10–15% (Gier, 1975), is one of several sources of error associated with counts of pups. Hamlett (1938) compared mean number of fetuses per pregnant female, 6.2, with mean litter size at dens, 5.7, and estimated prenatal mortality at 8.5%; in the report by Nellis and Keith (1976) the comparable values were 5.8 and 5.3, respectively, indicating a loss of 8.6%. Double litters and single litters divided between two dens are additional sources of error (Gier, 1968; Knowlton, 1972). Gier (1975) reported 10% of Kansas litters are double and states that more than 12 pups at a den indicates two litters. However, Bowman (1940) captured a bitch with 17 pups and subsequent examination of the uterus showed 17 placental scars.

V. HYBRIDIZATION

Coyotes hybridize with the domestic dog and produce fertile progeny (Seton, 1929; Silver and Silver, 1969; Kennelly and Roberts, 1969; Mengel, 1971; Gipson, this volume; Hilton, this volume). Coyote × wolf crosses occur (Kolenosky, 1971), and the hybrids produced are probably fertile (Mengel, 1971; Gipson, 1972). Since the karotypes for the three species are identical ($2N = 78$) it is not surprising the F_1 progeny are fertile. The coyote × dog hybrids appear to be aseasonal breeders following more the pattern of the domestic parent (Kennelly and Roberts, 1969). In that study the testes of two hybrid males did not regress during the second summer after birth but instead appeared, by palpation, to be typical of the sexually active condition. This was confirmed in September of that year when a high quality semen sample was collected through electroejaculation procedures, when testicular recrudesence is normally beginning in the coyote. Three hybrid females in the same study showed a shift in time of estrus onset compared with the wild parent. In December, at 7 months of age, each hybrid came into estrus but failed to conceive when artificially inseminated with dog semen. The following year (September–October) all three hybrids again showed signs of estrus, and two conceived after artificial insemination. It is noteworthy that not only was there a shift in time of breeding but it occurred at a different time each year. Mengel (1971) observed a similar phase-shift in the coyote–dog hybrid breeding season, but both sexes retained an annual breeding cycle; males showed testicular regression between breeding seasons and females cycled annually. The results of Gipson *et al.* (1975) agree with Mengel's (1971) findings on the seasonality of hybrid breeding but they indicated the period of sexual activity was much longer than Mengel observed; males about 5 months and females 7.

ACKNOWLEDGMENTS

The author gratefully acknowledges all assistance from personnel at the Denver Wildlife Research Center, Denver, Colorado, especially B. E. Johns, J. D. Roberts, and C. P. Breidenstein.

REFERENCES

Andersen, A. C. (1970). *In* "The Beagle as an Experimental Dog" (A. C. Andersen and L. S. Good, eds.), pp. 312–326. Iowa State Univ. Press, Ames.

Andersen, A. C., and Simpson, M. E. (1973). "The Ovary and Reproductive Cycle of the Dog (Beagle)," 290 pp. Geron-X Inc., Los Altos, California.

Andersen, D. (1927). *Am. J. Physiol.* **82,** 557–569.

Bekoff, M., and Diamond, J. (1976). *J. Mammal.* **57,** 372–375.

Bischoff, T. L. W. (1845). "Entwicklungsgeschichte des Hunde-Eies," 134 pp. Druck and Verlag von Friedrich Vieweg und Sohn, Braunschweig.

Bowman, S. W. (1940). M.S. Thesis, 110 pp. Univ. of New Mexico, Albuquerque.

Brown, E. C. (1936). *J. Mammal.* **17,** 10–13.

Cain, S. A., chn. (1972). "Predator Control—1971," 207 pp. Inst. Environ. Qual., Univ. of Michigan, Ann Arbor.

Christensen, G. C. (1964). *In* "Anatomy of the Dog" (M. E. Miller, G. C. Christensen, and H. E. Evans, eds.), pp. 741–806. Saunders, Philadelphia, Pennsylvania.

Christensen, G. C., and Dougherty, R. W. (1955). *J. Am. Vet. Med. Assoc.* **127,** 50–52.

Clark, F. W. (1972). *J. Wildl. Manage.* **36,** 343–356.

Dixon, J. (1920). *Calif. Agric. Exp. Stn., Bull.* **320,** 379–397.

Doak, R. L., Hall, A., and Dale, H. E. (1967). *J. Reprod. Fertil.* **13,** 51–58.

Dunbar, M. R. (1973). M.S. Thesis, 24 pp. Oklahoma State Univ., Stillwater.

Enders, R. K. (1955). *J. Mammal.* **36,** 133.

Evans, H. M., and Cole, H. H. (1931). *Mem. Univ. Calif.* **9,** 65–103.

Foote, R. H. (1969). *In* "Reproduction in Domestic Animals" (H. H. Cole and P. T. Cupps, eds.), 2nd ed., pp. 313–353. Academic Press, New York.

Foote, R. H., Swierstra, E. E., and Hunt, W. L. (1972). *Anat. Rec.* **173,** 341–352.

Gander, F. F. (1928). *J. Mammal.* **9,** 75.

Gier, H. T. (1968). *Kans. Agric. Exp. Stn. Bull.* **393,** 118 pp.

Gier, H. T. (1975). *In* "The Wild Canids; Their Systematics, Behavioral Ecology and Evolution" (M. W. Fox, ed.), pp. 247–262. Van Nostrand-Reinhold, New York.

Gipson, P. S. (1972). Ph.D. Thesis, 188 pp. Univ. of Arkansas, Fayetteville.

Gipson, P. S., Gipson, I. K., and Sealander, J. A. (1975). *J. Mammal.* **56,** 605–611.

Hamlett, G. W. D. (1938). *U.S. Dep. Agric. Tech. Bull.* **616,** 12 pp.

Hart, B. L. (1970). *In* "The Beagle as an Experimental Dog" (A. C. Andersen and L. S. Good, eds.), pp. 296–312. Iowa State Univ. Press, Ames.

Holst, P. A., and Phemister, R. D. (1971). *Biol. Reprod.* **5,** 194–206.

Kennelly, J. J. (1972). *J. Reprod. Fertil.* **31,** 163–170.

Kennelly, J. J., and Johns, B. E. (1976). *J. Wildl. Manage.* **40,** 272–277.

Kennelly, J. J., Johns, B. E., Breidenstein, C. P., and Roberts, J. D. (1977). *J. Wildl. Manage.* **41** (in press).

Kennelly, J. J., and Roberts, J. D. (1969). *J. Mammal.* **50,** 830–831.

Knowlton, F. F. (1972). *J. Wildl. Manage.* **36,** 369–382.

Kolenosky, G. (1971). *J. Mammal.* **52,** 446–449.

Leblond, C. P., and Clermont, Y. (1952). *Am. J. Anat.* **90,** 167–215.

Mengel, R. M. (1971). *J. Mammal.* **52,** 316–336.

Nellis, C. H., and Keith, L. B. (1976). *J. Wildl. Manage.* **40,** 389–399.

Ogle, T. F. (1969). M.S. Thesis, 85 pp. Washington State Univ., Pullman.

Ortavant, R., Courot, M., and Hochereau, M. T. (1969). *In* "Reproduction in Domestic Animals" (H. H. Cole and P. T. Cupps, eds.), 2nd ed., pp. 251–276. Academic Press, New York.

Rogers, J. G. (1965). M.S. Thesis, 36 pp. New Mexico State Univ., University Park.

Seton, E. T. (1929). "Lives of Game Animals," Vol. I, Part II, p. 401. Charles T. Branford Co., Boston, Massachusetts.

Silver, H., and Silver, W. T. (1969). *Wildl. Monogr.* **17,** 41 pp.

Tietz, W. J., and Seliger, W. G. (1967). *Anat. Rec.* **157,** 333–334.

Whiteman, E. E. (1940). *J. Mammal.* **21,** 435–438.

Young, S. P., and Jackson, H. H. T. (1951). "The Clever Coyote." The Stackpole Co., Harrisburg, Pennsylvania, and Wildlife Management Institute, Washington, D.C.

Section II

BEHAVIOR

5

Behavioral Development in Coyotes and Eastern Coyotes

Marc Bekoff

I. INTRODUCTION

In the last decade or so, there has been an increase in the appearance of well-documented studies of the social behavior of canids (Mech, 1970; Kleiman and Eisenberg, 1973; Fox, 1975; Zimen, 1976; Lehner, Chapter 6, this volume Kleiman and Brady, Chapter 7, this volume); as well as of other carnivores (e.g., Ewer, 1968, 1973; Herrero, 1972; Kruuk, 1972; Schaller, 1972; Leyhausen, 1973; Rasa, 1973). Interspecific, as well as intraspecific, differences in behavior have been sufficiently demonstrated. Among members of the genus *Canis*, recent studies (Eisfeld, 1966; van Lawick and van Lawick-Goodall, 1971; Bekoff, 1972, 1974, 1977a; Bekoff *et al.*, 1975; Wandrey, 1975; Zimen, 1976) have shown that even among these closely related species there are marked differences in the ontogeny of behavior, as well as in adult social organization. Furthermore, individual differences among littermates have been detected (Bekoff, 1977a), and it is possible that these intralitter differences may play some role in the development of social systems and in control programs (see Section VII).

In this chapter I shall discuss the behavioral development of coyotes (*Canis latrans*) and Eastern coyotes (*C. latrans*, var.). It is of interest to compare these two canids because the latter group appears to have a mixed ancestry (Silver and Silver, 1969; Lawrence and Bossert, 1969, 1975; Hilton, Chapter 9, this volume) in which the "coyote phenotype" currently predominates and also because there are no detailed comparative behavioral studies available. I am using the term "Eastern coyote" rather than "New England canid" because recent results have justified this change in nomenclature (see Section IV,E and Fig. 3). "Now, why, study development?" First, during very early life, the extent to which environmental variables can have an effect is lessened, although not absolutely removed). In addition, by rearing different species in a similar manner (Bekoff, 1974), one can study the gradual emergence of behavioral similarities and more importantly, behavioral differences, that may have a strong genetic component. For example, the behavioral differences that have been discovered among various members of the genus *Canis* have been found in animals reared in a wide variety of situations, ranging from hand-reared individuals who have been removed from the mother within 1–2 days after parturition to animals that have been observed in seminatural conditions and raised by their parents. By studying behavioral development, one can also answer questions related to the immediate adaptive significance of the infant's behavior to the infant itself, as well to the ways in which species differences in the time-course of behavioral ontogeny may be related to differences in the behavior and social organization of adults.

II. PHYSICAL DEVELOPMENT

Data on physical development in coyotes and other canids have recently been reported by Bekoff and Jamieson (1975). There are few data available for Eastern coyotes. The average day of eye-opening for both coyotes and

Eastern Coyotes is 14. Coyote pups at birth weigh approximately 250–300 gm (25% of adult weight: Gier, 1968; Bekoff and Jamieson, 1975). Eastern coyotes weigh slightly more at birth. Silver and Silver (1969) reported an average birth weight of 349 gm for males and 360 gm for females. A comparison of the weights of two similarly hand-reared litters of coyotes and Eastern coyotes (Bekoff and Hill, unpublished data) showed that by 35 days of age, the Eastern coyote pups weighed an average of 1590 gm ($n = 5$) while the coyote pups weighed 1390 gm ($n = 4$).

There are also differences in dental development. Eastern coyotes show later eruption of teeth and a different order of emergence from that observed in coyotes. The order of eruption of canines and incisors in coyotes is: upper canines (day 14), lower canines and upper incisors (14–15), and lower incisors (16). Silver and Silver (1969) reported for Eastern coyotes that canines and incisors frequently erupted on the same day but that canines never preceded incisors. They first observed upper incisors on day 17, lower incisors on day 18, upper canines on day 17, and lower incisors on day 21. The delay in tooth eruption may be due to the mixed ancestry of the Eastern coyote. Domestic dogs, for example, show later eruption of teeth than coyotes (Scott, 1958; Scott and Fuller, 1965; Bekoff and Jamieson, 1975).

Skeletal differences are also detectable early in life. Eastern coyote pups are more "leggy" than coyote pups of the same age. The hindfoot length of five 30-day-old Eastern coyote pups from one litter ranged from 8.2–9.0 cm. Gier (1968, p. 50) reported the average hindfoot length for 30-day-old coyotes to be 7.5 cm. At 30 days of age, both coyote and Eastern coyote pups are approximately 38–40 cm in length (middle of head to tail–base).

III. PARENTAL BEHAVIOR

There are no detailed data concerning parental (maternal or paternal) care in coyotes or Eastern coyotes. We have been able to collect some data on a litter of captive coyotes that were mother-reared and remained with her until they were 10 months of age (Bekoff and Lampert, unpublished data). The father was removed when the pups were born and introduced to his offspring when they were 4 months of age. Until the pups were 33 days of age, no "disciplining" by the mother was observed. When she did not want to interact with the pups she simply avoided them. During nursing, there was no apparent nursing order (hierarchy) or detectable teat preference by the pups. Weaning began at approximately 28–30 days and was essentially completed by the time the pups were 37 days of age. Snow (1967) reported that weaning was a gradual process occurring between 3–5

Fig. 1. A litter of 35-day-old coyote pups playing with their mother. (A) A pup bites his mother's scruff; she attempts to lick another pup. (B) The pup biting his mother's scruff performs a head-shake (blur). (C) He then bites her muzzle. (D) She threatens him and he releases his grip.

Fig. 1c and d

weeks. In our pups, there were brief periods of nursing on days 42, 44, and 53, and on day 57, five of the six pups nursed for 3 minutes. Returning to the nipple is a phenomenon that has been observed in a wide variety of mammals (Horwich, 1974). Perhaps the behavior is important in reinforcing mother–infant bonds just before the mother's milk supply dries up. Regurgitation was first observed on day 35. After eating a mouse, the mother circled about the enclosure. The pups rushed toward her and began nudging her muzzle with their snouts, licking her mouth, and whining. She immediately regurgitated a partially chewed bolus of food. Although we have not had the opportunity to observe females other than the mother engage in care-giving to pups, Snow (1967) and Camenzind (Chapter 12, this volume) reported that this does occur in coyotes.

With respect to interactions other than feeding, the mother allowed her pups to bite and wrestle with her. Most attention was given to her tail and face (Figs. 1a–c). If a pup bit too hard she responded by threatening it (Fig. 1d). Only rarely was she observed to attack a pup and/or pin it to the ground. In response to maternal discipline, the pup(s) either would run away in a low crouched posture with the tail tucked under the body or simply roll-over and whine (and frequently urinate). A number of interesting observations were consistently noted in 3 litters of coyotes [S. Knight (personal communication) has observed similar patterns in 1 coyote litter]. (1) The mother showed no preferential treatment of any pup. (2) The mother was never observed to initiate interaction with any of the pups. This included play-soliciting and aggression. (3) She never interfered with an infant–infant interaction. On numerous occasions 2 pups would engage in serious fights within a few centimeters of the mother. Not once did she attempt to break up the squabbles, some of which were serious enough to draw blood. The amount of discipline that a pup received appeared to be a simple function of the number of times it attempted to interact with its mother. This was also true when the mother came into heat. Beginning in early September (pups approximately 4 months old) the mother showed increased intolerance of her young. During September she responded aggressively 56 times to attempts made by the young to interact with her. (Before this time, aggressive responses by the mother were very infrequent.) The frequency of maternal aggression increased to 75 in October, 95 in November, and dropped sharply to 26 in December (based on 20 hours of observation per month). An aggressive reaction was *not* sufficient to drive a juvenile off. Frequently an individual would approach its mother, be rebuffed, and immediately approach once again. Although our observations require field confirmation, they suggest that aggression by the mother is not sufficient to produce juvenile dispersal. The same holds for father–young interactions. In fact, after being introduced to his offspring in early September, he was the target of significantly more aggression through late December (615 occurrences; next highest was 92) than any other animal. The young were more likely to respond aggressively to the male's aggression than they were to the female's aggression. It is possible that this was due to the fact that he had been separated from the pups during early life. Finally, it is of interest to note that from September to December, fewer than 10 playful parent–young interactions were observed.

In summary, agonistic (fighting, threatening) interactions between parents and young occurred almost to the total exclusion of playful interactions. However, the result of this high level of agonism did not appear to be sufficient to result in active avoidance of the parents by the young. Rather, patterns of avoidance *among pups* that were based upon earlier interactions appeared to be a major factor controlling both spatial arrangements and who interacted with whom. Recent observations by Storm *et al.* (1976) indicate that in red foxes (*Vulpes vulpes*), *avoidance* between individuals and *not* aggression by dominant adults, is important in initiating dispersal by juveniles (see Bekoff, 1977a).

IV. SOCIAL BEHAVIOR AMONG INFANTS

General information concerning social development in canids is presented in Scott and Fuller (1965), Fox (1971), Bekoff (1972, 1974), and Fox and Bekoff (1975). Briefly, Scott and Marston (1950) divided the development of the domestic dog into 4 periods: *neonatal* period, birth until 2 weeks of age; *transition* period, 2–3 weeks of age during which rudiments of adult social behavior appear; *socialization* period, 3–12 weeks of age, during which social relationships are established among conspecifics and possibly with other species; *juvenile* period, 12 weeks to sexual maturity, during which social independence is achieved. The time course of development varies from species to species. For example, the period of socialization in coyotes ends at approximately 6–9 weeks while for some domestic dogs it can be extended to 14 weeks.

A. Ethogram (Behavioral Repertoire) Analyses

One of the most important first steps in any behavioral study involves the compilation of an ethogram, or behavioral repertoire, for the animals under study. Careful observation and objective description of motor actions are necessary to ensure both interobserver and intergroup consistency in terminology. A "working" ethogram for coyotes wolves, and beagles is presented in Fig. 2 and Table I. All of these acts have been observed in wild popula-

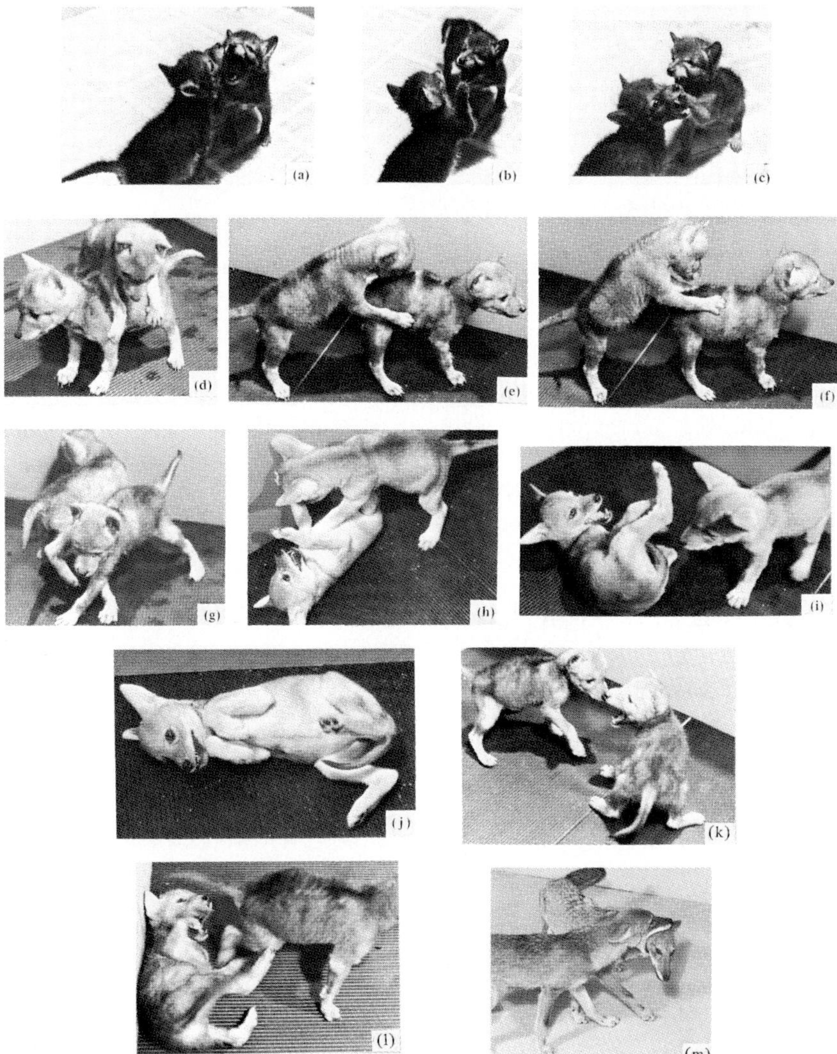

Fig. 2. (a–c) Aggressive display by two 23-day-old coyotes consisting of aggressive vocalizations (AV) and face-slapping (FSl). (d–e) Incomplete stand-overs (ISO) during which both forepaws are placed on another animal's back but not extended. (f) Complete stand-over (SO), during which both forepaws are placed on another animal's back and extended fully. (g) Inguinal response (IR) by coyote on the left; light contact to the inguinal region results in lifting of the limb off the ground (not pushed) or slight lateral rotation of the hindleg: during inguinal present (InP) one animal approaches another and then turns away (TA) and rotates one of its hindlegs out. (h–j) Passive-submission (PSub), during which the animal typically rolls-over (RO) on its back and then either

tions of these and other canids (Mech, 1970; van Lawick and van Lawick-Goodall, 1971; Fox, 1975; Henry, 1976; Bekoff, Hill, and Doran, unpublished data), and with few exceptions the behavioral repertoires of many canids (infants and adults) and their hybrids (Bekoff, 1972) are markedly similar. It should be stressed that in some cases the presumed "function" and "motivation" that is suggested by the descriptive term has not been conclusively demonstrated (see also Lehner, Chapter 6, this volume).

Most of the acts listed in Table I are observed before 30 days of age. In general, the less social canids (e.g., jackals and coyotes) show more rapid motor development than do wolves (Wandrey, 1975) and domestic dogs. Acts such as chin-resting, contactual circling, face-pawing, face-licking, and biting are observed prior to day 21 but actions requiring considerable motor coordination such as hip-slamming and leaping occur later (days 25–28). Infant canids usually are able to urinate and defecate without maternal assistance by 18–20 days of age. There are very few data concerning the development of marking behavior. And, in fact, it is very difficult to determine whether the young animals are merely urinating or actually "marking" (see Kleiman, 1966). Simpson (1975) first observed ground-scratching after defecation at 23 weeks and leg-lifting by males at 44 weeks. Allander and Balph (personal communication) observed leg-lifting by a male at 94 days of age, and I have observed 2 males perform leg-lifting at 105 days of age. Females have been observed to "mark" at 26 weeks (Simpson, 1975). Knight (personal communication) observed the top-ranking female in one of her litters defecate, scratch the ground, and then urinate at 22 weeks of age. With respect to sexual behavior, coyotes engage in much less "sexual play" than do domestic dogs or wolves (Bekoff, 1974). Mounting with pelvic thrusting has been observed in infant dogs (mostly males) and wolves as early as 4–5 weeks of age. However, in coyotes, pelvic thrusting rarely is observed before 14–15 weeks (Simpson, 1975; Bekoff, unpublished data). With respect to the occurrence of other actions, there do not appear to be any sex differences.

It must be stressed that although the basic repertoire appears to be almost identical for most species of canids that have been studied, the rela-

---

performs face-pawing (FP) as in (h) or simply retracts the front legs (i,j); in addition, a submissive grin (SG: lips drawn back horizontally and teeth usually not bared) frequently accompanies passive-submission and high-pitched distress (defensive) vocalizations (DV) often are heard. Tail tucking is very common. (k) Defensive threat (DTh) by coyote on the right; its back is slightly arched (BA) and it is defensively gaping (DG): the lips are drawn back horizontally and slightly vertically and the teeth may be bared. (See Fox, 1970, for more complete discussion of facial expressions in a variety of canids.) (l) Coyote on the right is completing a hip-slam (HS). (m) Inhibited face-bite (FB) during play by two 4-month-old coyotes.

tive frequency of occurrence of various acts varies from species to species (Table II). For example, the relative frequency of occurrence of aggressive vocalizations (AV), defensive gapes (DG), and passive-submission (PSub) is significantly higher in coyote pups than in beagles or wolves. This is a reflection of the fact that infant coyotes are significantly more aggressive than are same-aged wolves or beagles (see Section IV,C). In addition, there are also a few acts that are typically performed by one species but not by others. Two examples are the inguinal response (IR) [see Section IV,C,1) and leap–leaps (LL) Table II].

After detailing the specific actions, one can also ask, "How complete are the behavioral repertoires that have been compiled?" The results of a completeness analysis are presented in Table III. Based on an analysis of 24,275 acts, it was found that the observed repertory and the expected repertory size were identical. The results strongly support the idea that few (if any) acts have been omitted and that the most "significant" motor

TABLE I

The Observed Repertory (and Code) of Motor Patterns in Infant Canids[a]

Approach (A)
Play-soliciting (PS)[b]
Approach/withdrawal (A/W)
Tail-wag (TW)
Chin-rest (CR): one animal rests its chin on the back or shoulder of another individual (Fig. 2a)
Incomplete stand-over (ISO) (Fig. 2d,e)
Stand-over (SO) (Fig. 2f)
Face-bump (FBp)
Face-bite intention (FBI)
Face-bite (FB)
Scruff-bite intention (SBI)
Scruff-bite (SB)
General body-bite intention (flank, tail, legs, back) (GBI)
General body-bite (GB)
Head-shake (HsH): shaking of the head from side-to-side while delivering a bite
Mount (M)
Clasp (Cl)
Pelvic thrust (PT)
Jaw-wrestling (JW)
Wrestling (Wr)
Turns away (TA)
Turns toward (TT)
Chase (Ch)
Hip-slam (HS) (Fig. 2l)
Aggressive vocalization (AV): Threat/growl (Fig. 2a–c)

TABLE I ***(Continued)***

Distress vocalization (DV): high-pitched squealing or whining
Submissive grin (SG) (Fig. 2i,j)
Bark (bk)
Leap (L)
Leap–leap (LL): two successive high amplitude leaps in which the fore-paws are lifted off the ground together[c]
Inguinal response (IR) (Fig. 2g; see text, Section IV,C)[d]
Inguinal present (InP)
Contactual-circling (CC): two animals perform reciprocal chin-rests on the rear end of the partner and circle together
Passive-submission (PSub) (Fig. 2h,i,j,l)
Active-submission (ASub): approach followed by face-licking and muzzle -nudging
Defensive threat (DTh) (Fig. 2k)
Defensive gape (DG) (Fig. 2k)
Roll-over on back (RO)
Self-directed play (SP): tail-chasing, limb-biting
Face-paw (FP) (Fig. 2h)
Face-slap (FSL((Fig. 2a,b,c)
Back-arch (BA)
Face-lick (FL)
Body-lean (BL)

[a] See Bekoff (1972, 1974) and Fox *et al.* (1976) for further details.
[b] Based on 5–7 actions including play bows, exaggerated "gamboling" approaches, approach/withdrawals, exaggerated head movements, leap–leaps, and barking. (See Bekoff, 1974, for descriptions.)
[c] Rarely observed in coyotes; observed mainly in domestic dogs.
[d] See Section IV,C.

patterns have been accounted for (note also that 23 acts account for over 85% of the total number of acts observed; Table II).

B. Contactual and Locomotor Behaviors

Behaviors that involve a lot of body contact such as group sleeping, prolonged chin-resting, and contactual circling decrease between 4 to 5 weeks of age (Bekoff, 1972; Fox *et al.*, 1976). Chin-resting, contactual circling, and group sleeping may enable the infant to keep warm during the first weeks of life, since the pup relies on thermal conductance from an external source to provide heat. During the third and fourth weeks of life, the temperature regulation system of canids becomes functional (Solarz, 1970; Fox, 1971) and the pups spend more time apart. However, even older (4–8 months old) pups will huddle together in cold weather (R. Jamieson, personal communication).

TABLE II

Relative Frequencies of Behavioral Acts by Three Infant Canids Observed between 21–50 Days of Age[a]

Act	Wolves	Coyotes	Beagles
A	571 (8.00)	698 (9.02)	1164 (12.37)
CR	1155 (15.19)	700 (9.05)	879 (9.34)
ISO	461 (6.46)	314 (4.06)	651 (6.91)
SO	214 (2.99)	500 (6.46)	520 (5.52)
FB + FBI	544 (7.62)	323 (4.17)	1182 (12.56)
SB + SBI	502 (7.03)	237 (3.06)	193 (2.05)
GB	881 (12.34)	713 (9.22)	1141 (12.21)
Hsh	319 (4.97)	237 (3.06)	126 (1.33)
HS	123 (1.72)	28 (0.36)	2 (0.02)
AV	419 (5.87)	916 (11.84)	322 (3.42)
DV	146 (2.04)	317 (4.09)	118 (1.25)
LL	36 (0.50)	0 (0)	658 (6.99)
IR	55 (0.77)	380 (4.91)	54 (0.57)
PS	146 (2.04)	196 (2.53)	337 (3.58)
FP	158 (2.22)	61 (0.79)	389 (4.13)
L	131 (1.83)	283 (3.65)	97 (1.03)
DG	2 (0.02)	187 (2.41)	0 (0)
SP	134 (1.87)	319 (4.12)	496 (5.27)
FL	41 (0.57)	27 (0.34)	81 (0.86)
CC	50 (0.70)	16 (0.20)	21 (0.22)
PSub	3 (0.04)	351 (4.53)	0 (0)
Total	6091 (85.38)	6803 (87.97)	8431 (89.62)

[a] Number in parentheses represents % of total number of acts observed; see Table III. See Table I for code.

During the fourth week of life (the early part of the socialization period) there is an increase in activity (e.g., chase and running interactions). This increase in activity coincides with the period in neural development characterized by rapid development of reflexes, increased myelinization of the spinal cord and cerebral cortex, and the development of a differentiated electroencephalogram (Fuller and Fox, 1969; Fox, 1971).

C. Agonistic Behavior

Agonistic behavior (Scott and Fredericson, 1951) refers to the cluster of behaviors including aggression (fighting, threatening) and submission (e.g., flight, immobility, and passivity). It is important to stress that aggression cannot be studied apart from the response that it evokes (Eibl-Eibesfeldt, 1967; Rowell, 1966, 1974; Lockwood, 1976). That is, the interacting animals must be viewed as a social unit, the results of an agonistic interaction having its effects on all of the interactants. Behaviors associated with aggression and submission may be communicated by body postures, gestures, facial expressions, tail position, vocalizations, and changes in orientation and spatial distribution (see Chapters 6 and 7).

Comparative studies of canids have shown that there is a relationship between the development of agonistic (and play) behavior and the social organization that is characteristic of a given species. Specifically, the less social canids fight more and play less earlier in life than do the more social canids (Fox and Clark, 1971; Bekoff, 1972, 1974; Bekoff *et al.*, 1975; Wandrey, 1975; Zimen, 1976). The most conclusive data exist for members of the genus *Canis*. For example, infant coyotes are significantly more aggressive than are same-aged wolves or beagles (and most domestic dogs) and infant coyote–dog hybrids are more aggressive than are infants of the parental dog breed (Silver and Silver, 1969; Mengel, 1971; Bekoff, 1972). The differential development of behavior may be used to assess taxonomic affinities (see Section IV,E).

1. The Development of Agonistic Behavior

With respect to the method of fighting and threatening and the ways in which submission are expressed, there are no differences between coyotes and Eastern coyotes (and minor although possibly significant differences when other *Canis* are considered; Kleiman, 1967; Bekoff, 1975). Fighting consists of bites directed to the face, scruff, and body, and threat generally involves vertical retraction of the lips and baring of the front teeth (see Chapter 6). During agonistic interactions, dominant pups and adults approach one another with a stiff-legged gait, ears forward and erect, the

TABLE III

A Completeness Analysis on the Behavior Repertory of Three Canids

Species	Total number of acts observed	Observed repertory size	Estimated repertory size[a]	Estimated 95% confidence intervals, total repertory size (Chi square; df[b])
Wolves	7134	50	50	50,51 (8.7; 6)
Coyotes	7733	49	49	49,49 (8.9; 6)
Beagles	9408	47	47	47,48 (6.1; 5)
Total	24,275			

[a] Based on goodness-of-fit to the log normal Poisson distribution. (For details, see Fagen and Goldman, 1977.)

[b] df = Degrees of freedom.

tail at about 45° angle from the vertical, and frequently snarling and exposing the teeth (see Chapter 6, Fig. 4c). The fur on the back may also be erect (piloerection). This is referred to as *offensive threat.* During *defensive threat,* an individual bares its teeth and may display a piloerection. However, its ears are laid back against its head and its tail is tucked between its hindlegs. Submission may take the form of flight, active avoidance, or passive or active submission (see Schenkel, 1967). During *passive submission* the animal rolls over on its back, usually flattens its ears against its head, retracts the lips horizontally into a "submissive grin," and may urinate and whine. Passive submission appears to develop from one of the positions that the pups assume when they are stimulated to excrete by their mother or other adults. During *active submission* one individual(s) approaches another animals(s) in a low crouch-walk with the tail either tucked under the body or held low. Face-pawing, face-licking, and whining often occur, and the ears typically are laid back against the head. Active submission probably develops from food-begging. Active submission has only rarely been observed in captive coyote pups or adults (J. Brown, personal communication; Simpson, 1975; Bekoff, personal observations). Lehner (personal communication) has observed it infrequently among pups and adults in the wild. In contrast, it occurs with a high frequency in other *Canis* for which there are data (wolves and domestic dogs). In coyotes, a behavior pattern that resembles active submission frequently occurs when two (or more) individuals are separated by more than a "paw's length" (and may occur when the animals are as far apart as 20 m) and are not moving. An individual will look at another animal and then cock its head slightly to one side, lay its ears back against its head, perform "exaggerated" paw-raising directed toward the other individual(s), and frequently bare its teeth (Chapter 6, Fig. 4D). This behavior actually appears to be a combination of defensive threat and active submission. In some instances, paw-raising is not incorporated into this display (Knight, personal communication).

As mentioned above, there are marked species differences in the ontogeny of social interaction in *Canis*. In coyotes, Eastern coyotes, and golden jackals (*C. aureus:* van Lawick and van Lawick-Goodall, 1971; Wandrey, 1975) serious rank-related fighting occurs during the fourth to fifth weeks of life (Wandrey reports fighting as early as 12 days of age in jackals). In contrast, wolves do not show rank-related aggression until during the latter part of the first year of life or later (Zimen, 1976). When comparing Eastern coyotes to coyotes, fighting was more intense in the coyotes and began at an earlier age (as early as 22 days). Early fights frequently lasted 2–3 minutes in duration and usually involved a pair of animals. Fighting soon became ritualized and decreased in duration as signals of threat and submission were "honored." Fighting also occurred in a significantly higher relative frequency in coyotes than in Eastern coyotes (Bekoff *et al.*, 1975; see Table VI below).

In both coyotes and Eastern coyotes, fighting and threat decreased in frequency within 3–5 days after the first rank-related agonistic encounter was observed. In Eastern coyotes, for example, on day 27 there were 54 agonistic encounters, of which 53 resulted in submission (4 hours of observation). On day 28 there were only 28 agonistic encounters (3 hours and 20 minutes of observation) and on day 30 there were only 9 such encounters (5 hours and 15 minutes of observation). As the frequency of fighting decreased the frequency of social play increased.

a. Standing-over. Standing-over (Fig. 2f), an action observed in a wide variety of canids (Mech, 1970, p. 129 refers to it as "riding up") is observed in a very high frequency among infant coyotes, Eastern coyotes, wolves, and dogs (up to a rate of 20 per minute). It occurs almost reflexively, usually following a chin-rest and may last up to 30–40 seconds in duration. After about 25 days, stand-overs may directly follow an approach. Although standing-over is observed during both play and agonistic interactions, in infant coyotes it occurs in its highest frequency both preceeding and during agonistic encounters; *initially* it *appears* to be an expression of dominance. In coyotes, stand-overs that occur during agonistic interactions last longer than stand-overs that occur during play. In the Eastern coyotes, stand-overs occurred in only 2% of the agonistic interactions and in 21% of the play interactions. As in coyotes, stand-overs performed during agonistic encounters lasted significantly longer than did stand-overs performed during play ($\bar{X}$ = 6.10 and 3.36 seconds, respectively; Hill and Bekoff, 1977).

The suggested relationship between standing-over and dominance early in life is not very clear-cut in infant wolves, domestic dogs, or Eastern coyotes. Let us briefly further consider coyotes. In two pairs of coyotes that were studied by this author (Bekoff, 1972), the dominant animals performed significantly more stand-overs (107 and 187) than did their subordinate partners (29 and 101; $p < 0.05$, sign test) between days 21–35. Other data collected on pairs of animals indicated that there was a strong positive correlation between the frequency of occurrence of standing-over and dominance. That is, the individuals who perform the highest frequency of standing-over prior to and during initial agonistic interactions are those who eventually become dominant as a result of these interactions. This same relationship was found in a full, mother-reared litter of coyotes, with one very notable exception. For the six animals that comprised the litter, the frequency of occurrence of standing-over up until the time that dominance relationships were established (litter 1, Table IV) was as follows (in order of decreasing rank): 109, 62, 64, 56, 53, 114. (For 11 of the 15 possible paired

TABLE IV

Hierarchy Formation in Infant Coyotes and Eastern Coyotes

	Days of age	No. of fights	h^a
Coyotes, litter 1[b]	25–31	220	0.77
(n = 6)	32–35	59	0.88
	36–50	50	1.00
Coyotes, litter 2	23–25	40	1.00
(n = 4)	26–29	38	1.00
	30–32	36	1.00
Eastern coyotes	21–25	65	0
(n = 5)	26–29	178	0.80
	30–35	137	1.00

[a] h = Landau's index for the measurement of the degree of linearity of a social hierarchy; h may vary between 0 and 1. A low value of h indicates a weak, or nonlinear hierarchy; a value of 0 indicates that each animal dominates an equal number of group members while a value of 1 means that the hierarchy is perfectly linear. That is, A dominates B, C, and D; B dominates C and D but not A, etc. (For details concerning the application of Landau's method, see Chase, 1974; Wilson, 1975; Lockwood, 1976; Bekoff, 1977b.)

[b] Coyote litter 1 was mother-reared, coyote litter 2 was hand-reared.

interactions, the relationship noted above was suggested.) The top-ranking animal was clearly separated from the next four animals, however, the bottom-ranking female performed more stand-overs than did any of her sibs! A more detailed analysis showed that her stand-overs tended to be of a shorter duration and that her forelegs were not as rigidly extended as those of her sibs. Also, she wore a submissive face and never growled while standing-over. Although the bottom-ranking animal did perform a high frequency of stand-overs that differed qualitatively from those performed by other littermates, observation of her interaction patterns with her sibs indicated clearly that she was low-ranking. She continually was dominated by all other animals and behaved submissively upon the approach of another individual.

So, in coyotes at least, standing-over during which the body and legs of the "top" individual are rigid, *may* be used as a predictor of dominance, but alone, does not constitute a sufficient measure. Observations of the interaction patterns of individuals must be also used (see Sections VII,A).

b. Inguinal responses. The inguinal response (Fig. 2g) is an action that occurs almost exclusively in coyotes, hybrids with coyote ancestry, and Eastern coyotes (Bekoff, 1972; Fox *et al.*, 1976). While performing this behavior, the animal remains immobile. The inguinal response has also been observed in a less ritualized form and in a lower frequency in the golden jackal and gray fox (*Urocyon cinereoargenteus*) (Fox, personal communication), both of whom fight early in life. Interestingly, it has not been observed in the red fox (*Vulpes vulpes*), which also forms early dominance relations and whose agonistic interactions are less ritualized than those of the coyote. It has been suggested that the inguinal response develops from the pups remaining passive in response to light inguinal stimulation given by the mother as she stimulates them to urinate and defecate (Fox, 1971). However, it is virtually absent from the behavioral repertoire of other canids (see Table II) in which agonistic behavior develops later in life, even though they too are given inguinal stimulation to induce elimination of body wastes.

The relationship between the occurrence of the inguinal response and the development of agonistic behavior is interesting. Briefly, the inguinal response occurs in its highest frequency in coyotes during the time period in which agonistic interactions and stand-overs also are predominant. It also is performed in a higher frequency by dominant individuals in paired interactions (Bekoff, 1972). Data from one pair of coyotes suggest that subordinate coyotes may attempt to elicit an inguinal response from a more dominant individual in an attempt to terminate an interaction that may develop into a fight. In this pair of coyotes, 71% of all inguinal responses performed by the dominant individual occurred immediately after a stand-over (or incomplete stand-over). When the dominant female dismounted from a stand-over, the subordinate male would lean his body into hers, making light inguinal contact with either his tail or hindend, eliciting an inguinal response and terminating the behavioral interaction. Whether or not inguinal stimulation remotivates the aggressor is still an open question, but the effect of inhibiting continued aggression and ongoing behavior, in general, is evident. The generality of this finding to other coyotes (and canids) remains speculative, but the fact that many canids that show high levels of aggression as infants also have a low threshold for the elicitation of the inguinal response, is intriguing.

2. The Formation of Dominance Relationships

Fighting both in coyotes and Eastern coyotes resulted in the formation of dominance hierarchies. In most cases, it was not difficult to determine who dominated whom, in that fighting and threat resulted in clear submission by the recipient. Changes in spatial relationships, e.g., avoidance or "displacement," also were obvious. Individuals who were considered to dominate other individuals based on the results of agonistic interactions could "control" the movement of their subordinates. It should be pointed out that both before and after the initial fights occurred, dominant individuals were not necessarily the most aggressive (in terms of frequency of initiation of agonistic encounters). Their mere presence was frequently sufficient to elicit submission. However, fighting did continue to occur between animals in which dominance relations were not clear-cut (at least to the observer).

In order to assess whether or not the hierarchies formed were linear, we analyzed data collected on 2 litters of coyotes (1 mother-reared and 1 hand-reared) and 1 litter of Eastern coyotes. We calculated a quantitative measure of linearity known as Landau's index (for reviews of the application of this procedure, see Chase, 1974; Wilson, 1975; Lockwood, 1976; Bekoff, 1977b). The results are presented in Table IV. A large number of rank-related fights were observed. Note that in coyote litter 2, after only 3 days of fighting, a linear hierarchy was established. Linearity was progressively achieved in the other litter of coyotes and in the Eastern coyotes. It should be stressed that a linear hierarchy may retain its integrity even if some animals shift in rank. This occurred in both groups of animals. Knight (1976) reported that in the 4 coyote litters she observed, there were shifts in rank during the first 6 months, with smaller litters tending to have more stable hierarchies. In one coyote litter for which we have observations throughout the first 9 months of life (litter 1, Table IV), linearity was maintained throughout the observation period and there were no shifts in rank after the animals were 135 days of age. Whether or not linearity is the "rule" rather than the exception in these canids will require further study.

D. Play Behavior

Play behavior in canids and other mammals has been reviewed recently by Bekoff (1974, 1976) and Fagen (1976). In both coyotes and Eastern coyotes (and other canids) the same actions are used to solicit play (Bekoff, 1974). In addition, during early ontogeny, as the frequency of agonistic interactions decreased, the frequency of play increased. In both groups of animals, middle-ranking individuals were the most playful (as has been observed in wolves; Lockwood, 1976). Nonetheless, there were some very interesting differences between coyotes and Eastern coyotes concerning this category of behavior.

1. While coyotes typically do not engage in social play until dominance relations are fairly well established, the Eastern coyotes played before fighting.

2. Overall, the Eastern coyotes were more playful than were coyotes of the same age. For example, from days 21–28, 9.6% of all interactions

involved reciprocal social play while for same-aged coyotes, only 0.61% of all interactions involved social play. The same trend was obvious between 29–35 days of age (see Section IV,E and Table VI).

3. As reported by Bekoff (1974), coyotes precede play bouts with play intention signals 90% of the time. Vincent (unpublished data) found that play signals preceded play bouts in a full litter of coyotes 88% of the time. It was suggested (Bekoff, 1974) that coyotes "need" to signal play because of the prevailing aggressive atmosphere. In Eastern coyotes, in which there is less aggression and more play, play signals preceded play bouts only 31.7% of the time.

4. In coyotes, there appear to be rank-related differences in the ability to solicit play from littermates. Higher ranking individuals are generally less successful in initiating play than are lower-ranking individuals (Table V). This trend was not evident in the Eastern coyotes.

TABLE V

The Success (Successful Play-Solicits/Total Number of Play-Solicits) in Soliciting Play by Individual Coyote Littermates[a]

Social Rank[b]	Successful play-solicits	Unsuccessful play-solicits	Success (%)[c]
1 (male)	13	21	38.2
2 (female)	10	10	50.0
3 (male)	9	10	47.4
4 (male)	20	22	47.6
5 (male)	13	10	56.5
6 (female)	2	1	66.7

[a] Note that the highest ranking male attempted to solicit play more frequently than did four of his littermates and that the lowest ranking female was virtually noninteractive. (From Bekoff, 1977.)

[b] Mother-reared; results are from approximately 100 hours of observations between 35–50 days of age; in this litter, severe dominance fights beginning on day 28 resulted in a linear hierarchy by day 37 (confirmed using Landau's measure of linearity) (Chase, 1974; Lockwood, 1976; Bekoff, 1977b). Although linearity occurs quite frequently in coyote litters, even in situations when nonlinearity is the case, "top" and "bottom" individuals are clearly distinguishable.

[c] Spearman's rho = −0.79 (correlation between rank and success). From days 52–70, the success rate of male 1 fell to 17%, a decrease of 21.2%. The success rates of all of the other animals also fell during this time period (female 6 did not attempt to solicit play at all), but not greater than 9% in any case. Excluding female 6 still results in a negative correlation between rank and success. It is important to note that she was noninteractive for reasons other than those that applied to 1 male. Namely, she had been the "scapegoat" of her litter. (See Bekoff, 1977.)

E. A Behavioral Taxonomy of Infant Coyotes, Eastern Coyotes, and Wolves

Since young *Canis* show distinct and significant differences in behavioral ontogeny, we decided to use behavioral phenotypes as analyzable characters to assess the taxonomic relationships among infant coyotes, Eastern coyotes, and wolves (Bekoff *et al.*, 1975). One advantage of the comparative approach is that it allows an investigator to analyze, in detail, the similarities and differences among a number of different species. Specifically, we analyzed the time course of development of agonistic behavior and social play. The techniques of linear discriminant function analysis was used so that we could directly compare our results to those of Lawrence and Bossert (1969, 1975) who analyzed skull and dental characteristics of a variety of canids (for details concerning the method, see Sneath and Sokal, 1973). The results are presented in Table VI and Fig. 3. Coyotes, when compared to both wolves and Eastern coyotes, were more aggressive, while the Eastern coyotes and wolves were more playful than the coyotes. Also,

TABLE VI

Discriminant Functions Differentiating Species of Canids on the Basis of Four Behavioral Characters[a]

	Agonistic behavior		Play behavior	
Combination	Character 1 (days 21–28)	Character 2 (days 29–35)	Character 3 (days 21–28)	Character 4 (days 29–35)
Coyote/wolf	46.61 (0.47, 0.25/ 0,0)	0 (0.36, 0.27/ 0.11, 0.09)	312.99 (0.01, 0/ 0.21, 0.16)	0 (0.14,0.09/ 0.34, 0.30)
Coyote/ Eastern coyote	9.60 (0.47, 0.25/ 0.09–0.32)	35.09 (0.36, 0.27/ 0.07–0.23)	110.31 (0.01, 0/ 0.03–0.10)	65.88 (0.14, 0.09/ 0.11–0.20)
Wolf/Eastern coyote	63.75 (0, 0/ 0.09–0.32)	56.92 (0.11, 0.09/ 0.07–0.23)	116.56 (0.21, 0.16/ 0.03–0.10)	297.20 (0.34, 0.30/ 0.11–0.20)

[a] The top numbers are weights for the characters, and define the axis that discriminates to the greatest degree between the species. The higher the number, the better the discrimination. The numbers in parentheses indicate the observed proportion of the behavior in relation to the total number of interactions observed in the stated time period for each species pair. Ranges of proportions are reported for the ten pairs of Eastern coyotes. For example, 0.47 and 0.25 are the proportions of observed agonistic behavior (character 1) for the two pairs of coyotes, and 0 and 0 are the corresponding proportions of agonistic behavior for the two pairs of wolves. (From Bekoff *et al.*, 1975; see text.)

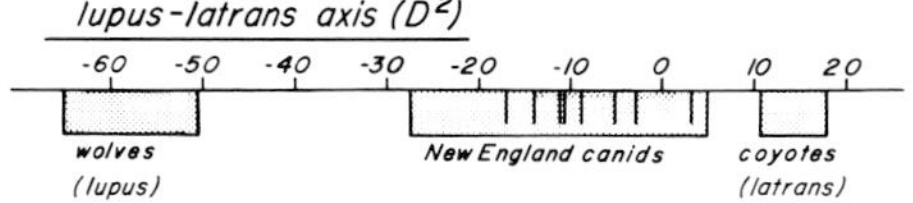

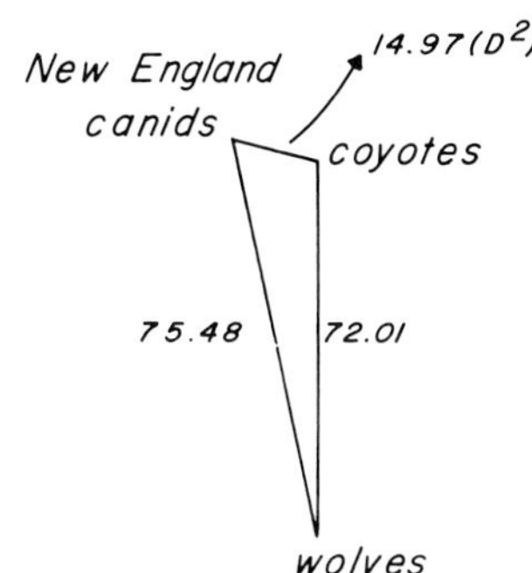

Fig. 3. The results of a behavior taxonomy study on infant coyotes, wolves, and New England canids (= Eastern coyotes; see text). The relative frequencies of occurrence of social play and agonistic behavior were used as behavioral characters. (See Section IV,E; see also Bekoff *et al.*, 1975.) Top: Linear discriminant values of known *lupus* (wolf) and *latrans* (coyote) litters cast on a *lupus–latrans* discriminant axis onto which New England canids are projected. Note that the New England canids fall between *lupus* and *latrans*, but closer to *latrans*. Bottom: Distances (D^2) in discriminant function units based on pairwise analyses of *lupus, latrans,* and New England canids. Note the close relationship between coyotes and New England canids and also that both fall approximately the same distance from wolves. Because of the close relationship between coyotes and New England canids, the latter group is now referred to as "Eastern coyotes." (See Lawrence and Bossert, 1969, 1975; Silver and Silver, 1969; Bekoff *et al.*, 1975.)

wolves were more playful and less aggressive than Eastern coyotes (Table VI). When all of the data were combined and plotted on a linear discriminant function axis (Fig. 3, top) the Eastern coyotes fell intermediate to the wolves and coyotes and closer to the coyotes (the mean positions for the wolves, Eastern coyotes, and coyotes were −57.88, −8.90, and +14.14, respectively). A pair-wise analysis in which each group was matched against one another (Fig. 3, bottom) showed that the coyotes and Eastern coyotes were more closely related to one another than either was to the wolves. Lawrence and Bossert (1969, 1975) showed a similar relationship using skull and dental characters. The use of term "Eastern coyote" for animals previously referred to as New England canids (Silver and Silver, 1969; see Hilton, Chapter 9, this volume) is justified both on behavioral and morphological grounds.

V. PREDATORY BEHAVIOR

Coyotes and other canids are adapted for a cursorial existence to hunt mainly by pursuit (Pocock, 1914; Eisenberg, 1966; Mech, 1970; Hildebrand, 1974; Bekoff, 1975). Coyotes are well adapted to hunt diurnally using visual cues (Horn and Lehner, 1975). Wells and Lehner (1977) reported the relative priority of senses used in locating rabbits to be (in order of decreasing importance) vision, audition, and olfaction. Movement is a key stimulus for eliciting orientation and attack (Lehner, 1976). Coyotes and other canids (Radinsky, 1969; Atkins, Chapter 2, this volume) possess large olfactory bulbs and input from all three of the above-mentioned senses probably is important during predation.

Although it is an unquestioned fact that coyotes do kill a wide variety of other animals (Bekoff, 1977c), surprisingly few data are available concerning their predatory behavior in the field—the ways in which they sense, pursue, kill, and eat their prey. Accordingly, it often is very difficult, if not impossible, to distinguish a "coyote kill" from that other predators or domestic dogs (Ogle, 1971; Davenport *et al.*, 1973). Attacks oriented to the head, neck, and throat are frequently used on deer and sheep (Ozoga and Harger, 1966; White, 1973; Janzen, 1974; Connolly *et al.*, 1976) as are belly and rump attacks (Ogle, 1971). A shearing bite (Young, 1951) and bite-and-tear sequences are common. For smaller mammals, a stalk-and-pounce sequence usually is used. Rapid shaking of the head from side-to-side is used on a wide variety of mammals.

Although there is a lot of interest in coyote predation on domestic livestock, there are very few systematic studies in this area (Janzen, 1974; Connolly, *et al.*, 1976). When captive coyotes do attack sheep, latencies to attack plus killing time average approximately 1 hour, and there is an enormous amount of individual variability ($\bar{X}$ = 47 minutes, S.D. = 48 and $\bar{X}$ = 13 minutes, S.D. = 13, respectively; Connolly *et al.*, 1976). Although one might expect a more rapid predatory sequence, when one considers the behavior of the sheep, the long time periods reported by Connolly and his colleagues are understandable. Defensive behavior by the sheep deterred coyotes only 31.6% of the time. Antipredatory behavioral responses have been selected against in favor of increased productivity. Clearly, more work is needed in this area of coyote biology.

A. The Predatory Repertoire and the Development of Predatory Behavior

Actions used to take down prey vary with the size of the prey and the defensive acts with which the prey reacts. Infant coyotes, wolves, and

Eastern coyotes use similar actions during predation. An ethogram of predatory actions observed in infant and adult canids in the field and in captivity is presented in Table VII. A sequence of predation involving a 32-day-old coyote and a 2-day-old chicken is shown in Fig. 4, and a composite predatory sequence from 15 individual trials of coyotes aged 35–45 days of age (with mice as the prey) is presented in Fig. 5.

The results of detailed developmental studies of predatory behavior in young coyotes using small prey species (chickens, mice, and rats) may be summarized as follows:

1. There were marked individual differences in the reaction of young coyotes to prey. Not all individuals were "killers" nor did all individuals even

TABLE VII
Actions Performed in Canid Prey-Killing Sequences by Infants and Adults

Action code	Description
OR	Orient
AP	Approach: directed movement toward the prey animal—walk, trot, or gallop
AW	Approach/withdraw: approach followed immediately by withdraw; hesitant AP
SA	Stalking approach
FC	Follow
CH	Chase: high intensity follow
SN	Sniff: sniffing prey animal
NS	Nose stab: prodding prey with nose
Lk	Lick: licking prey animal
LI	Lick intention: licking without contact with prey
PW	Paw, paw stab, and paw intention
PL	Paw lift
PO	Pounce: low leap directed at prey, hind legs remain on ground, forelimbs in rigid extension
PN	Pin: immobilizing prey with one or both forelimbs
AB	Attempted bite: bite intention
BI	Bite
LF	Lift: lifting prey off substrate
CR	Carry: carrying prey in mouth
HS	Headshake: vigorous side-to-side head movement
TS	Toss: jerking head to one side and releasing prey
LP	Leap: all four legs leave substrate
DR	Drop: dropping prey to substrate
CL	Circle: moving in tight circles, usually with prey in mouth
WD	Withdraw: backing or moving away from prey animal
ET	Eat: eating prey animal

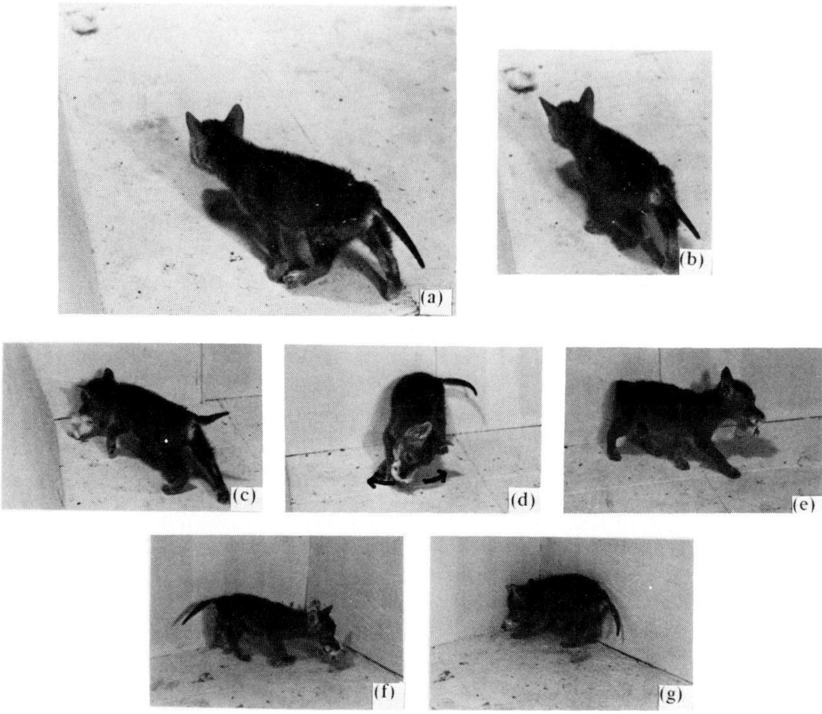

Fig. 4. A sequence of predation by a 32-day-old coyote pup with a 2-day-old chicken. The pup approaches the chicken in a slow stalking manner—slightly crouched posture (A,B) and then bites (C) the chicken and lifts and head-shakes it (D). The pup then carries the dead chicken (E) to a corner where it eats it (F,G).

show interest in the prey. It seems likely, however, that all individuals are potential "killers."

2. There was no relationship between an individual's social rank and its prey-killing success [contrary to what has been found occasionally for captive coyotes preying on sheep (Horn, 1976) and for other carnivores (Leyhausen, 1965; Rasa, 1973)].

3. Early social experience was not related to later predatory success (Vincent and Bekoff, 1977).

4. When two individual infants were placed together, the latency to kill mice and chickens was significantly shorter.

5. During initial interactions with prey, animals appeared to be using "lie-of-the-hair" as a directional cue for orientation to the head region.

As mentioned above, there are data that indicate that less social canids show more rapid motor development than do more social canids. Certainly, motor development and coordination are related to the time-course of the development of adaptive skills. Rasa (1973) has suggested that the slow maturity of predatory behavior favors sociality. Comparative data presented by Fox (1969) do not support this contention for Canidae. Among different species of young canids [with the exception of domestic dogs (Vauk, 1953)], there appear to be few differences in the success with which same-aged animals kill prey, although detailed comparative data from well-controlled studies still remain to be collected.

VI. VOCALIZATIONS

There are very few data available for vocalizations in infant canids (see Tembrock, 1976). I was able to record vocalizations of a litter of Eastern coyotes between 21–35 days of age using a Sony 800B reel-to-reel tape recorder. The tapes were analyzed by D. Rothenmaier (unpublished data).

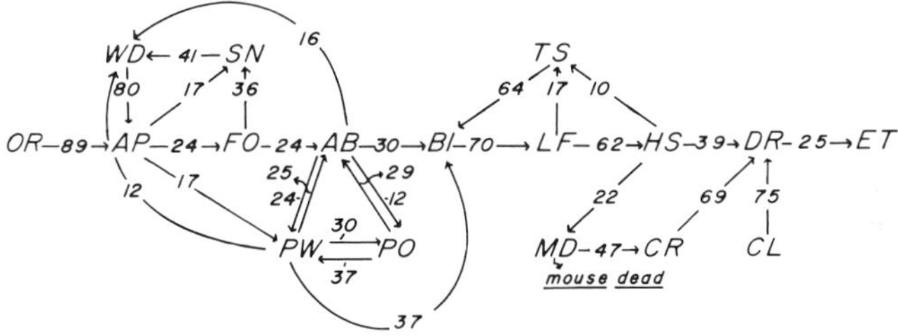

Fig. 5. A composite predatory sequence from observations of 15 successful individual trials (with mice) by 4 coyotes aged 35–45 days. The numbers represent transition probabilities in percent. All of the listed behaviors (see Table VII for code) occurred more than ten times with the exception of CL (four times). Sequences in which prey were killed began with an almost immediate orientation (OR) to the mouse followed by an approach (AP). A cycle of follow (FO), sniff (SN), withdraw (WD), and approach (AP) may precede the first attempted bite (AB). AB's led to a cycle of paw (PW) and pounce (PO) or directly to a bite (BI). A cycle of bite, lift (LF), headshake (HS), and toss (TS) usually was repeated several times before a bite and headshake lead to death (MD). The dead mouse was then usually carried (CR) to a corner (see also Fig. 4E,F,G) where it was dropped (DR) and eaten (ET). After two trials all the coyote pups immediately began eating at the anterior end of the mouse. Those coyotes that did not begin anterior eating on the first trial appeared to be using lie-of-hair as a directional cue. Pounce and paw-stabbing have been observed in coyote pups in the field (Bekoff, Hill, and Doran, in preparation).

Based on sonogram analyses, Rothenmaier found 5 distinct vocalizations. They were as follows:

1. *Yelps* (n = 7): Yelps were characterized by a series of rapid pulses ranging from 0.14 ± 0.05 to 0.28 ± 0.06 seconds. The frequency range of the fundamental was 1250 ± 300 to 2050 ± 300 Hz, and the interval between successive yelps ranged from 0.12 ± 0.02 to 0.15 ± 0.01 seconds. Yelps occurred primarily during situations in which a pup was submitting to an attack by a more dominant pup.

2. *Yelp-Howls* (n = 4): Yelp-howls were very similar to yelps. There were no differences in the pulse duration, in the interpulse interval, or in the upper frequency limit. The lower frequency limit for yelp-howls was 900 + 400 Hz. Yelp-howls unlike yelps were never recorded during submission and frequently graded into howls.

3. *Howls:* We were able to record only 2 instances of howling by the pups. One of the howls contained 2 flat pulses of about 1 second each ranging from 500–1500 Hz. They looked similar to what McCarley (1975) called the "flat howl" for coyotes.

The other 2 distinct vocalizations that were recorded were growling and huffing. Growling occurred during offensive threat and is a "noisy" sound containing a wide spectrum of frequencies between 1000 and 3000 Hz. Huffing was recorded only once. It is a short, breathy sound with a frequency of highest intensity between 4000 and 5300 Hz, consisting of 3 pulses of approximately 0.13 seconds each. It matches very closely the huff described by Lehner (Chapter 6) for adult coyotes.

Clearly, more work is needed on the ontogeny of vocal behavior in canids. Perhaps physical analyses of vocalizations will be good phenotypes on which to do taxonomic work.

VII. ONTOGENY AND THE ORGANIZATION OF SOCIAL SYSTEMS: POSSIBLE BEHAVIORAL MECHANISMS OF DISPERSAL

A. The Development of Individual Differences

In addition to the existence of species differences in the time-course of the ontogeny of agonistic and play behaviors, *intralitter* individual differences also have been detected. Specifically, it appears that the early development of dominance hierarchies in coyotes (and possibly other canids) affects the way in which individuals interact with littermates. For example, it was mentioned above (see Section IV,D and Table V) that high-ranking individuals have difficulty in initiating play with sibs. These and possibly other behavioral differences may predispose a given individual(s) to disperse from its natal group prior to or around the time that sexual maturity is attained. That is, it is not unlikely that individuals who have interacted least with littermates (either because they cannot or simply do not; see Table V; see also Bekoff, 1977a) and have not formed strong social bonds may leave their natal group during the first year of life without necessarily being forced to do so. A delay in the appearance of potentially divisive aggression combined with high frequencies of intralitter social play such as observed in wolf litters, would increase the likelihood of littermates remaining together. In contrast, the early ontogeny or rank-related aggression in the less social canids may result in weaker ties between littermates.

The above idea is developed more fully in Bekoff (1977a), and in addition, a critical evaluation of the relationship between behavior and dispersal is attempted. Suffice it to say, behavioral mechanisms underlying dispersal still are relatively unknown and the relationship between aggression and dispersal (e.g., Christian, 1970) is not clear-cut. That is, in many mammals, aggression at the time of dispersal does not provide the adequate stimulus for dispersal of some individuals because patterns of *avoidance* and not increases in aggression characterize the social environment (Storm *et al.*, 1976). It is suggested (Bekoff, 1977a) that *behavioral antecedents* of dispersal must be investigated systematically to determine the significance of both the early ontogeny of rank-related aggression in coyotes, Eastern coyotes, golden jackals, and various fox species, and the delay in the appearance of rank-related aggression in wolves. The final analysis must account for the ways in which individual behavioral types interact with their environment and also the flexibility of the organization under study (Goss-Custard *et al.*, 1972). For example, "packs" of coyotes have been reported in the literature (Kropotkin, 1914; Camenzind, Chapter 12, this volume; Bekoff, 1977c), and lone wolves also have been observed by a number of researchers (Mech, 1970).

B. Dispersal and Management

Knowlton (1972) has suggested that it would be useful to have knowledge of which individuals in a coyote litter are most likely to disperse from their natal site. Certainly, if it does become possible to predict with a high degree of accuracy which individuals will leave their litter, then selective control programs could be initiated, if dispersers are, in fact, the "problem" animals. *However,* in terms of predator control which would be of interest and of economic use to ranchers, one would have to demonstrate that the dispersing individuals *are* the ones that are taking domestic livestock. On the other hand, it remains just as likely that nondispersers are doing more damage to livestock. At the moment, *we just do not know* the relationship between dispersal, coyote movements, and livestock predation. Indeed, more critical attention must be given to these factors *and* others so that the relationship between individual differences in behavior and "predatory potential" may be better understood.

VIII. CONCLUSIONS

Species differences in the ontogeny of social behavior have been documented in many canids. Among *Canis,* species that show less social organization and group coordination as adults show an earlier ontogeny of rank-related agonistic behavior. It is suggested that the ontogeny of agonistic behavior may predispose certain individuals to disperse from their natal group during their first year of life. With respect to predatory behavior, very little actually is known about coyotes and Eastern coyotes, with the exception of the compilation of exhaustive lists of food items taken. The dearth of field data on the behavior of coyotes appears to be one obstacle in the way of initiating efficient control programs.

ACKNOWLEDGMENTS

The research reported herein was supported in part by PHS Grant Nos. GM-01900 and ES-00139 and by a faculty research initiation fellowship and biomedical grant support from the University of Colorado. To all of the fine people (too numerous to list) who helped with the collection of data, the procuring of animals, animal care, moral support, and in the formulation of ideas I am grateful. Three people who must be singled out for their unrelenting support are Suzanne King, Robert Jamieson, and Harriet Hill. Michael Fox's support during my graduate career is also appreciated. Robert Fagen performed the "completeness" analysis. I would like to thank Philip Lehner, Sandra Knight, Harriet Hill, Joel Berger, Robert Jamieson, Dennis Rothenmaier, and Devra Kleiman for reading an earlier draft of this chapter.

REFERENCES

Bekoff, M. (1972). Ph.D. Thesis, Washington Univ., St. Louis, Missouri.

Bekoff, M. (1974). *Am. Zool.* **14,** 323–340.

Bekoff, M. (1975). *In* "The Wild Canids" (M. W. Fox, ed.), pp. 120–142. Van Nostrand-Reinhold, New York.

Bekoff, M. (1976). *In* "Perspectives in Ethology" (P. P. G. Bateson and P. H. Klopfer, eds.), Vol. 2, pp. 165–188. Plenum, New York.

Bekoff, M. (1977a). *Am. Nat.* **111,** 715–732.
Bekoff, M. (1977b). *In* "Quantitative Methods in the Study of Animal Behavior" (B. A. Hazlett, ed.), pp. 1–46. Academic Press, New York.
Bekoff, M. (1977c). *Mammal. Species* No. 79, 1–9.
Bekoff, M., Hill, H. L., and Mitton, J. B. (1975). *Science* **190,** 1223–1225.
Bekoff, M., and Jamieson, R. (1975). *J. Mammal.* **56,** 685–692.
Chase, I. D. (1974). *Behav. Sci.* **19,** 374–382.
Christian, J. J. (1970). *Science* **168,** 84–90.
Connolly, G. E., Timm, R. M., Howard, W. E., and Longhurst, W. M. (1976). *J. Wildl. Manage.* **40,** 400–407.
Davenport, J. W., Bowns, J. E., and Workman, J. P. (1973). *Agric. Exp. Stn., Utah State Univ.* pp. 1–17.
Eibl-Eibesfeldt, I. (1967). *In* "Aggression and Defense: Neural Mechanisms and Social Patterns" (C. D. Clemente and D. B. Lindsley, eds.), pp. 57–94. Univ. of California Press. Los Angeles.
Eisenberg, J. F. (1966). *Handb. Zool.* **10,** 1–92.
Eisfeld, D. (1966). *Z. Wiss. Zool.* **174,** 226–289.
Ewer, R. F. (1968). "Ethology of Mammals." Plenum, New York.
Ewer, R. F. (1973). "The Carnivores." Cornell Univ. Press, Ithaca, New York.
Fagen, R. (1976). *In* "Perspectives in Ethology" (P. P. G. Bateson and P. H. Klopfer, eds.), Vol. 2, pp. 189–219. Plenum, New York.
Fagen, R., and Goldman, R. (1977). *Anim. Behav.* **25,** 261–274.
Fox, M. W. (1969). *Behaviour* **35,** 259–272.
Fox, M. W. (1970). *Behaviour* **36,** 49–73.
Fox, M. W. (1971). "Integrative Development of Brain and Behavior in the Dog." Univ. of Chicago Press, Chicago, Illinois.
Fox, M. W., ed. (1975). "The Wild Canids." Van Nostrand-Reinhold, New York.
Fox, M. W., and Bekoff, M. (1975). *In* "The Behaviour of Domestic Animals" (E. S. E. Hafez, ed.), 3rd Ed., pp. 370–409. Baillière, London.
Fox, M. W., and Clark, A. (1971). *Z. Tierpsychol.* **28,** 262–278.
Fox, M. W., Halperin, S., Wise, A., and Kohn, E. (1976). *Z. Tierpsychol.* **40,** 194–209.
Fuller, J. L., and Fox, M. W. (1969). *In* "The Behaviour of Domestic Animals" (E. S. E. Hafez, ed.), 2nd Ed., pp. 438–481. Baillère, London.
Gier, H. T. (1968). *Agric. Exp. Stn., Kans. State Coll. Agric. Appl. Sci.* pp. 1–118.
Goss-Custard, J. D., Dunbar, R. M. I., and Aldrich-Blake, F. P. G. (1972). *Folia Primatol.* **17,** 1–19.
Henry, J. D. (1976). Ph.D. Thesis, Univ. of Calgary, Calgary, Alberta.
Herrero, S. M., ed. (1972). "Bears—Their Biology and Management," IUCN Publ. No. 23. Int. Union Conserv. Nat. Nat. Resour., Morges, Switzerland.
Hildebrand, M. (1974). "Analysis of Vertebrate Structure." Wiley, New York.
Hill, H. L., and Bekoff, M. (1977). *Anim. Behav.* **25,** 907–909.
Horn, S. W. (1976). *Anim. Behav. Soc., Meet., Boulder, Colo.*
Horn, S. W., and Lehner, P. N. (1975). *J. Comp. Physiol. Psychol.* **89,** 1070–1076.
Horwich, R. H. (1974). *Primates* **15,** 141–149.
Janzen, C. D. (1974). M.S. Thesis, Colorado State Univ., Fort Collins.
Kleiman, D. G. (1966). *Symp. Zool. Soc. London* **18,** 167–177.
Kleiman, D. G. (1967). *Am. Zool.* **7,** 365–372.
Kleiman, D. G., and Eisenberg, J. F. (1973). *Anim. Behav.* **21,** 637–659.
Knight, S. W. (1976). *Anim. Behav. Soc., Meet., Boulder, Colo.*
Knowlton, F. F. (1972). *J. Wildl. Manage.* **36,** 369–382.

Kropotkin, P. (1914). "Mutual Aid." Knopf, New York.

Kruuk, H. (1972). "The Spotted Hyena." Univ. of Chicago Press, Chicago, Illinois.

Lawrence, B., and Bossert, W. H. (1969). *Breviora* **330,** 1–13.

Lawrence, B., and Bossert, W. H. (1975). *In* "The Wild Canids" (M. W. Fox, ed.), pp. 73–86. Van Nostrand-Reinhold, New York.

Lehner, P. N. (1976). *Wildl. Soc. Bull.* 120–126.

Leyhausen, P. (1965). *Z. Tierpsychol.* **22,** 412–494.

Leyhausen, P. (1973). *Z. Tierpsychol., Suppl.* **2,** 3rd Ed.

Lockwood, R. (1976). Ph.D. Thesis, Washington Univ., St. Louis, Missouri.

McCarley, H. (1975). *J. Mammal.* **56,** 847–856.

Mech, L. D. (1970). "The Wolf." Nat. Hist. Press, Garden City, New York.

Mengel, R. M. (1971). *J. Mammal.* **52,** 316–336.

Ogle, T. F. (1971). *Northwest Sci.* **45,** 213–218.

Ozoga, J. J., and Harger, E. M. (1966). *J. Wildl. Manage.* **30,** 809–818.

Pocock, R. I. (1914). *Proc. Zool. Soc. London* pp. 913–941.

Radinsky, L. B. (1969). *Ann. N.Y. Acad. Sci.* **167,** 277–288.

Rasa, O. A. E. (1973). *Z. Tierpsychol.* **32,** 449–498.

Rowell, T. E. (1966). *Anim. Behav.* **14,** 430–443.

Rowell, T. E. (1974). *Behav. Biol.* **11,** 131–154.

Schaller, G. B. (1972). "The Serengeti Lion." Univ. of Chicago Press, Chicago, Illinois.

Schenkel, R. (1967). *Am. Zool.* **7,** 319–329.

Scott, J. P. (1958). *Psychosom. Med.* **20,** 42–54.

Scott, J. P., and Fredericson, E. (1951). *Physiol. Zool.* **24,** 273–309.

Scott, J. P., and Fuller, J. L. (1965). "Genetics and the Social Behavior of the Dog." Univ. of Chicago Press, Chicago, Illinois.

Scott, J. P., and Marston, M. W. (1950). *J. Genet. Psychol.* **77,** 25–60.

Silver, H., and Silver, W. T. (1969). *Wildl. Monogr.* **17,** 1–42.

Simpson, T. R. (1975). M.S. Thesis, Texas A & M Univ., College Station.

Sneath, P. H., and Sokal, R. (1973). "Numerical Taxonomy." Freeman, San Francisco, California.

Snow, C. (1967). *Am. Zool.* **7,** 353–355.

Solarz, A. K. (1970). *In* "The Beagle as an Experimental Dog" (A. C. Andersen, ed.), pp. 453–468. Iowa State Univ. Press, Ames.

Storm, G. L., Andrews, R. D., Phillips, R. L., Bishop, R. A., Siniff, D., and Tester, J. R. (1976). *Wildl. Monogr.* **49,** 1–82.

Tembrock, G. (1976). *Behav. Proc.* **1,** 57–75.

van Lawick, H., and van Lawick-Goodall, J. (1971). "Innocent Killers." Houghton, Boston, Massachusetts.

Vauk, G. (1953). *Zool. Anz., Suppl.* **17,** 180–184.

Vincent, L., and Bekoff, M. (1977). *Anim. Behav.* (in press).

Wandrey, R. (1975). *Z. Tierpsychol.* **39,** 365–402.

Wells, M., and Lehner, P. N. (1977). *Anim. Behav.* (in press).

White, M. (1973). *J. Mammal.* **54,** 291–293.

Wilson, E. O. (1975). "Sociobiology: The New Synthesis." Harvard Univ. Press, Cambridge, Massachusetts.

Young, S. P. (1951). "The Clever Coyote" (S. P. Young and H. H. T. Jackson), pp. 1–226. Stackpole, Pennsylvania.

Zimen, E. (1976). *Z. Tierpsychol.* **40,** 300–341.

6

Coyote Communication

Philip N. Lehner

I. INTRODUCTION

The coyote has traditionally been considered a moderately social canid (Type II of Fox, 1975) which lives in temporary pairs or small labile groups. Recent studies (e.g., Camenzind's, Chapter 11) have demonstrated the coyote's capacity to exist in fairly stable, permanently territorial groups containing as many as seven individuals. An integral part of the coyote's capacity for long-term social relationships is their highly developed communication system which utilizes several channels and incorporates characteristics which provide for selective and extensive information transfer. This chapter discusses the channels, signals, and signal characteristics which comprise this complex communication system.

A complete and conclusive determination of the function of animal communication is extremely difficult. Hence, we are left, in many instances, with only "educated guesses" as to the function of a particular signal or the underlying motivation of an individual that transmits a particular signal. These "educated guesses" are often incorporated into functional terms which are applied to displays (e.g., facial displays). These functional terms add color to an ethological discourse but are potentially dangerous if the reader assumes that they reflect proven functions and motivations—in most cases they do not. I have incorporated many functional terms from the literature into this chapter in order to make it somewhat more readable. However, the reader is cautioned not to read too much into those terms.

Communication, as discussed in this chapter, will be restricted to action on the part of one (or more) coyotes that affects the behavior of one (or more) other coyotes in a predictable manner. Emphasis will be placed on those signals which produce immediate effects although possible primer effects will also be mentioned. Knowledge of communication in coyotes ranges from pure conjecture to hard data from experimental research; both are included in this chapter. Conjecture in the form of hypotheses has been included as a point of departure for future research.

II. OVERVIEW OF COYOTE SENSORY RECEPTORS

Illustrative of our lack of knowledge of coyote communication is the paucity of information available on receptor systems. We can make inferences from what is known about receptors in the domestic dog, but this is poor practice and potentially misleading. Much more research on coyote sensory receptors needs to be completed before we can answer the important "how questions" concerning coyote communication.

A. Visual

The coyote eye appears to be a compromise designed for crepuscular activity. The eyeball is relatively circular with intermediately sized anterior and posterior chambers and a moderately curved lens. The retina is duplex (contains both rods and cones) with a slight preponderance of rods (Horn and Lehner, 1975). The coyote apparently lacks color vision (Eisfeld, 1966a). Both the coyote's scotopic sensitivity (Horn and Lehner, 1975) and activity patterns in the laboratory (Kavanau and Ramos, 1975) suggest a crepuscular proclivity. Field studies have shown the coyote to be active both at night and during the day (Gipson and Sealander, 1972; Ozoga and Harger, 1960).

B. Auditory

Coyotes have been shown to be receptive to sounds as high as 80 kHz (Peterson *et al.*, 1969) based on cochlear microphonics. However, Ewer (1973) believes that their upper "useful limit" is 30 kHz. Although the ability to perceive ultrasonic sounds is still unconfirmed it might be related to detection of rodents and/or intraspecific communication (Lehner, 1977a).

C. Olfactory and Gustatory

Although olfaction is generally believed to be one of the coyote's most important senses it has been shown to have a relatively low priority in predation on rabbits (Wells and Lehner, 1977). The coyote has a vomeronasal (Jacobson's) organ lying ventral to the nasal fossae, connecting with the buccal cavity via the nasopalatine canal. The function of this accessory olfactory organ in coyotes is unknown, but it may be important in detecting odoriferous substances brought to the palatine fissures by the tongue during a flehmenlike response (Fig. 2i). Gier (personal communication) was unable to find neural connections between the vomeronasal organ and the brain in coyotes and believes that the organ may be merely vestigial and inoperative.

D. Tactile

The hair follicles are divided into a bundle of hairs which are isolated into groups of two to four bundles on the well-furred parts of the body (Hildebrand, 1952). Each bundle contains several underhairs and a single guard hair. Tactile stimulation received through the bending of body hair may be important in communication. Cranial vibrissae may also play a role in both transmitting and receiving tactile communication during such displays as food begging and greeting. The length of the coyote's mystactial, superciliary, genal, and interramal vibrissae are intermediate in length between those of the gray wolf (*Canis lupus*) and the foxes (kit *Vulpes velox*, red *V. vulpes*, and gray *Urocyon cinereoargenteus*) (Hildebrand, 1952). Carpal vibrissae may be useful during pawing displays, but Hildebrand (1952) found them on only nine front feet of ten tanned coyote skins.

III. VISUAL COMMUNICATION

Several parts of the body provide important sources of visual signals. Of most importance are the mouth (including teeth, lips, and tongue), eyes, ears, hackles, and tail (Fig. 1a,b,c,d,g). Many signals have undoubtably evolved from other behaviors into displays with communicatory value; a few of these will be discussed later (Section VII).

Various displays take on different meanings according to the context in which they occur. In some instances the meanings seem quite obvious while in play, "metacommunicative" signals may be used to inform prospective participants that what is about to occur is "play-fighting," not real aggression (Bekoff, 1972a).

Visual displays will be discussed according to their behavioral contexts and the separate parts of the body involved.

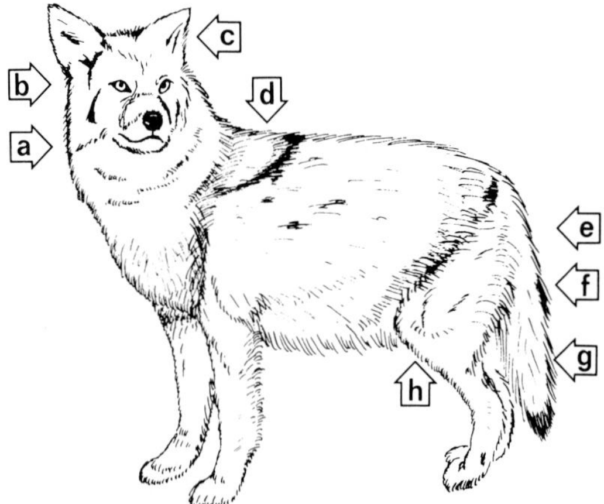

Fig. 1. Some of the most important sources of signals used in coyote communication. a, Mouth; b, eyes; c, ears; d, shoulder hackles; e, anus and anal glands; f, supracaudal tail gland; g, tail; h, genitals. (Drawn from a photograph of an adult male *Canis latrans* ssp. from Alberta, Canada.)

Fig. 2. Expressions of a coyote. a, Small mouth threat face; b, aggressive threat gape; c, defensive threat gape; d and e, defensive threat combined with submissive "grin", f, submissive, avoiding eye contact; g, defensive aggressive threat gape; h, open mouth submissive greeting or "play face"; i, "Flehmen" face (upper lip elevated); j, low-intensity threat face. (From The Wild Canids by M. Fox © 1975 by Litton Educational Publishing, Inc. Reprinted by permission of Van Nostrand Reinhold Company.)

A. Agonistic

1. Facial Displays

The coyote's face is marked with contrasting colors which accentuate particular facial expressions (Fig. 2). The lips are black which contrasts with the white fur bordering the mouth. The eyes are bordered by black tissue and fur which accentuate the shape of the eyelids, as well as focus attention on them. The black border around the eye is often further highlighted by a contrasting border of white. The white hair in the auditory meatus may enhance the visual impact of ear position (Fox, 1970), as may the black fur on the outer edges of the ears. The terms used to designate the following facial displays are from Brown (1973) and Fox (1971a, 1975). It should be emphasized that the implied functions and motivations inherent in these terms have not, as yet, been documented by intensive, quantitative studies.

a. *Neutral face* (Fig. 1)—the position of most of the signal sources indicate neutrality. The eyes are open, the ears erect and the lips relaxed. The neutral face often grades into a relaxed open-mouth face (Fox, 1971a).

b. *Alert face*—the ears and eyes directed strongly forward suggest that the coyote is alert to some source of stimulation. The lips also appear more tensed than in the neutral face (Brown, 1973).

c. *Low intensity threat face* (Fig. 2j)—the corners of the mouth are brought forward and the lips may be retracted vertically slightly to expose the canines and some of the other teeth. The eyes are closed slightly or narrowed as the threat becomes more intense.

d. *Small mouth threat face* (Fig. 2a)—the ears are erect and directed forward and the eyes are closed slightly. The mouth is closed with the lips covering the teeth and the corners of the mouth are brought forward into a "pucker" (Fox, 1970).

e. *Aggressive threat face* (Fig. 2b)—the mouth is opened wide into a gape (Fox, 1971a) with the corners of the mouth brought forward and the lips retracted vertically to expose the canines and incisors (Brown, 1973). The eyes are narrowed.

f. *Defensive threat face* (Fig. 2c)—the mouth is opened wide but the corners of the mouth are pulled back and the lips are retracted to expose most of the teeth. This jaw gape emerges first as a startle response in coyote pups (Fox, 1971a). The ears are laid back on the head and the eyes are open. The defensive threat face may incorporate the *submissive grin* (Fig. 2d,e). The mouth is opened only slightly and the corners are pulled back with the lips retracted to expose most of the teeth (see Chapter 5). The ears vary in position from erect to laid back.

g. *Defensive aggressive threat face* (Fig. 2g)—the mouth is opened wide with the lips drawn back to expose the teeth. The ears are laid back and eyes are open or narrowed.

h. *Submissive play face* (Fig. 2h)—the mouth is opened slightly with the lips moderately retracted to expose the tips of the teeth. The eyes are wide open and the ears are back. It is given not only in play but also agonistic contexts.

These facial expressions have been described at rather arbitrary points along a finely graded agonistic continuum incorporating various levels of aggression and fear (see Fig. 7). The ears generally provide a good indication of the position of the animal along the agonistic continuum from aggression (ears erect) to submission (ears laid back) (Figs. 3, 7). However, the ears often rapidly oscillate between intermediate positions reflecting not only oscillations in motivation, but probably also response to auditory stimuli from the environment. When the coyote is extremely submissive with its ears laid back tightly (Figs. 2c,g) auditory stimuli are probably at a low priority.

The eyes are not consistent barometers of agonistic intent. They may be wide open or narrowed during either aggression or submission. However, line of sight is important since a direct stare constitutes a threat. The submissive antithesis of the stare is to look away (Fig. 2f).

Position of the head is a fairly reliable indicator of agonistic motivation. Aggression is indicated by the head held high with the neck arched (Fig. 3D), and submission is reflected by a lowered head with the neck extended horizontally and twisted to expose the white throat area. The white throat may also provide a visual signal during howling and especially during howling intentions which often precede a bout (S. Horn, personal communication).

The tongue may be extruded as a submissive gesture (Fig. 4D) and

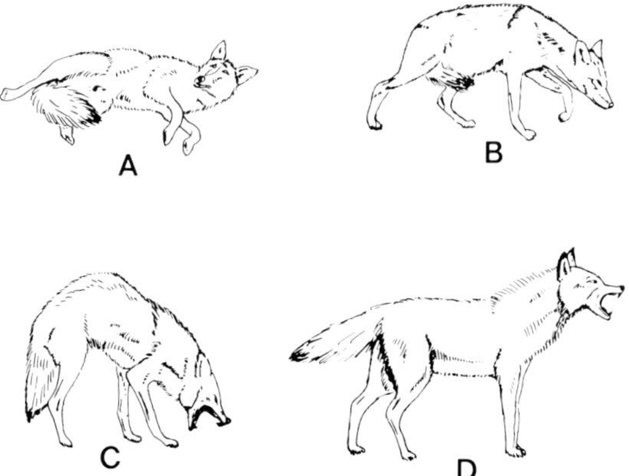

Fig. 3. Coyote postures reflecting motivational states along the agonistic continuum. A, Passive-submission; B, submission with tail tucked, head and body low, neck extended, and ears back; C, defensive threat with tail low but not tucked, and defensive threat face; D, aggressive threat with tail raised, shoulder and neck hairs piloerected, ears in forward position, legs stiff, and mouth in an aggressive threat gape.

Fig. 4. Agonistic displays near elk carcasses on the National Elk Refuge, Jackson, Wyoming. A, Coyote approaching other coyotes on elk carcass and showing visual signs of submission: tail tucked, body compressed lengthwise with back arched, ears laid back, and submissive grin. B, Coyote approaching other coyotes on an elk carcass and showing less submission than individual in A including more piloerection (a threat signal). C, Individual aggressively approaching coyotes on an elk carcass: tail out, stiff-legged, extensive piloerection, ears more forward, aggressive threat face. D, Interactions on an elk carcass; individual on left is showing signs of submission: ears back, face-licking intentions (note tongue protruded), face-pawing intentions (note elevated foreleg). E, Alpha males from adjoining territories culminate threats at an elk carcass on their territorial boundary: aggressive threat gapes, stiff-legged foreleg stabs, ears erect. F, Individual approaching coyotes on an elk carcass has just defecated while maintaining a submissive posture: tail low, body compressed lengthwise, ears back, eyes mostly closed, submissive grin with mouth almost closed. (Photos by F. Camenzind.)

apparently serves to inhibit further aggression by a dominant individual (Fox, 1970).

2. Tail

a. Color Markings. The tail is generally a buff color with a black marking on the dorsal surface about one-third of the distance from the base and over the supracaudal tail gland (Fig. 1f). The tip of the tail is usually black (Merriam, 1897). The black spot over the tail gland may serve as a target for conspecific sniffing of the tail gland (Fox, 1971a) or the anal gland (Wickler, 1967), or it may provide an additional visual signal which enhances tail-wagging and tail-position displays (see Section VII). The black tip on the tail probably serves this latter function.

b. Position. The elevation of the tail appears to reflect the relative agonistic intent of the coyote from submission (held low or tucked, Figs. 3B,C) to aggression (held high, Fig. 3D). This is only true when the coyote is relatively immobile since tail position changes with different gaits and speeds of locomotion. The male generally carries its tail erect during precopulatory behavior (Bekoff and Diamond, 1976), perhaps a reflection of the close relationship between courtship and aggression.

c. Movement. Tail movement is another signal of motivation and intent. A submissive coyote often wags its tail with high frequency and low amplitude. Low frequency, high amplitude tail-wagging is shown by coyotes that are soliciting play or stalking prey.

3. Piloerection

The hair on the neck, shoulder, rump, and tail may be piloerected during heightened aggression (Figs. 3D, 4C) or during a display in which the coyote is in conflict between being aggressive and submissive (Fig. 4B). The long black-tipped guard hairs which form the saddleback (Fig. 1) may enhance the visual signal when these shoulder hairs are piloerected.

4. Inguinal Presentation

Inguinal presentation is the rotation outward of a hind leg to expose the inguinal area. It may occur during active submission when the subordinate bends its body into the "C posture" (Fox, 1971b) as it approaches a dominant. It is also a component of passive submission in which the coyote lies on its side with the uppermost hindleg raised to expose the genital area (Fig. 3A). Passive submission is first seen in coyote pups at approximately 21 days of age (Bekoff, 1972b). Bekoff (Chapter 5) discusses the role of inguinal presentation in the development and termination of behavior in pups.

5. Foreleg Raising

Sustained raising of one foreleg in the bent position signals submission (Fig. 4D) while foreleg-stabbing is used by a dominant to intimidate a subordinate.

B. Play

Both adult and young coyotes play. Young coyotes play in bouts throughout the day with the adults occasionally joining in. This is generally when the more immediate physiological drives of the adult have been satisfied (Bekoff, 1972a).

Play bouts contain many behavior patterns which are also used in agonistic or predatory contexts (e.g., biting and stalking, respectively). Hence, young coyotes not only develop and sharpen these communicative skills for later life, but they also inform potential playmates that: (1) they want to play (play-soliciting), and (2) that what is about to occur is play (metacommunication). The displays discussed below are all seen in adult coyotes. For a discussion of play and play-soliciting in pups see Bekoff (1972a, 1974a, and Chapter 5).

1. Play-Bow and Play-Dance

These visual displays are used to solicit play. In the play-bow the coyote lowers the forepart of its body with its forelegs extended straight out and its hindquarters elevated. The tail generally wags with low frequency but high amplitude. This later frequently grades into the play-dance (Fox, 1970) in which the coyote moves laterally back and forth in front of the potential playmate. It will sometimes dive at, and in front of the playmate (Bekoff, 1974b).

2. Exaggerated Approach and Approach–Withdrawal

A play soliciting coyote will often approach a potential playmate in an exaggerated manner with a stiff-legged, high-stepping gait. This approach is often followed by a rapid withdrawal for a short distance in an apparent attempt to elicit chase from the other animal.

3. Face-Pawing and Face-Licking

A foreleg is often raised and extended toward a potential playmate by a play-soliciting coyote (see Chapter 5, Fig. 2f). It may actually touch the other coyote (generally on the head) or merely appear as an intention to make contact. Likewise, the face-licking intentions are often seen with actual contact being made only infrequently (Bekoff, 1972a). Face-pawing may be accompanied by tail-wagging and growling (Fox and Clark, 1971). Both face-pawing and face-licking are apparently signals of submission in adult coyotes.

All of these play-soliciting and metacommunicative signals are generally given in concert with a play-face (Fig. 2h), which provides an additional metacommunicative signal. Coyote pups also recognize the individual which is play-soliciting and are less apt to join in play with high-ranking littermates (Bekoff, 1974b, 1977).

4. Play Behavior in Other Contexts

The play-dance and approach–withdrawal were both directed toward sheep in a large enclosure during studies of sheep-killing behavior by coyotes (Jansen, 1974 and personal observation).

Play behavior has also been reported to occur extensively during courtship (Ozaga and Harger, 1966); however, Bekoff and Diamond (1976) observed very little during their study.

C. Greeting

Greeting is a complex behavior which generally involves visual, auditory, and tactile signals, as well as, probably olfactory signals. Coyotes can apparently recognize individuals at several hundred meters based on visual characteristics alone (Lehner, personal observation). They may also recognize the sex of a strange individual on sight since in Ryden's (1975) study an intruder was always chased off by a coyote of the same sex. Visual cues used in individual identification probably include not only body conformation and coloration, but also carriage and other behavioral characteristics which may be individually specific. Dominant individuals are generally approached and greeted by subordinates which first show active submission (muzzle-nibbling and wow-oo-wow vocalization) then often lay down and roll over into a passive-submission posture (Fig. 3A). This may last only briefly after which they again stand and engage in active submission greeting. It may oscillate back and forth between active and passive submission several times before the dominant either walks away or threatens (growl and/or bite intention) the subordinate and inhibits further displays. During greeting the tail is held low or tucked between the hind legs and may be wagged with low amplitude and varying frequency.

All of the visual displays discussed above occur in gradations rather than in a stereotyped pattern. This appears to provide for more resolution of meaning and when combined with signals from other channels also reduces potential ambiguity (see Section VIII).

IV. AUDITORY COMMUNICATION

Vocalizations are the primary means of auditory communication in the coyote ". . . the most vocal of all North American wild mammals . . ." (Gier, 1975, p. 258). Taxonomists recognized the coyote's vocal proclivity in assigning its scientific name, *Canis latrans,* which means "barking dog."

TABLE I
Coyote Vocalizations Listed in Order along a Physical Continuum

Vocalization	Description
Growl	"gr-r-r-r" Sound; low–medium amplitude
Huff	Rapid expulsion of air through mouth and nose
Woof	Low amplitude bark
Bark	Burst of high-amplitude and short duration; appear as wide frequency range noise or concentration of energy into narrow frequency bands
Bark-howl	Frequency modulated short howl; interspersed with a series of barks and generally immediately preceded by a bark; high amplitude
Whine	Spectrographically resembles a low-frequency howl with several harmonics; low amplitude
Woo-oo-wow	Howl of low amplitude and frequency which modulates in both frequency and amplitude
Yelp	"Yelp" portion resembles a high-frequency bark; "yi-e-e-e" portion resembles a short howl broken into segments
Lone howl	High amplitude; slight–moderate frequency modulation; relatively long duration
Group howl	Same as lone howl but given by two or more coyotes antiphonally; generally with different dominant frequencies
Group yip-howl	High amplitude; rapid yipping sounds interspersed with howls of generally shorter duration than the lone howl or group howl

The only nonvocal sound with obvious signal value is occasional teeth-snapping as an aggressive threat.

The vocal repertoire of the adult coyote contains eleven vocalizations (Table I), several of which are also given by pups (see Bekoff, Chapter 5). These vocalizations grade into one another such that their separation into eleven types is somewhat arbitrary based on their different sounds, behavioral context (Table II), and physical characteristics (Fig. 5). The vocalizations in Fig. 5 are arranged along a physical continuum from the growl to the group yip-howl. They grade into one another so that intermediates can be demonstrated for most adjacent vocalizations. For example, the bark (Fig. 5D) grades into the bark-howl (Fig. 5E) as shown in Fig. 6. The gradations between vocalizations may have different signal value as can be shown for variations within a vocalization, as well as for different vocalizations.

The behavioral contexts in which the eleven vocalizations are known to occur are listed in Table II. Quantitative differences in the signal value of the different vocalizations have been indicated by *intensity of communica-*

TABLE II
Coyote Vocalizations in Their Behavioral Context

Vocalization	Behavioral context	Distance	Intensity of communication
Woof	Agonistic (threat) ; alarm	Short	Low
Growl	Agonistic (threat)	Short	Low–high
Huff	Agonistic (threat)	Short	High
Bark	Agonistic (threat); alarm	Long	Low–medium
Bark-howl	Agonistic (threat); alarm	Long	High
Yelp	Agonistic (submissive); startle	Short	High
Whine (high freq.)	Agonistic (submissive)	Short	Low
Whine (low freq.)	Greeting	Short	Low
Wow-oo-wow	Greeting	Short	High
Group yip-howl	Greeting; contact; reunion of group members; response to distant howling	Long	High
Lone howl	Contact; separated group members; response to distant howling	Long	Low–high
Group howl	Contact; separated group members; response to distant howling	Long	Low–medium

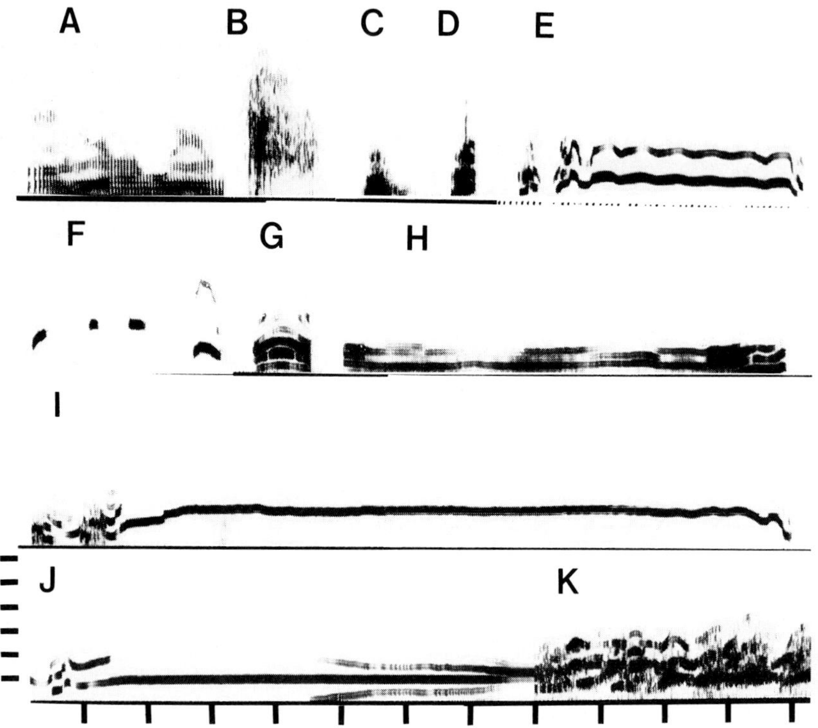

Fig. 5. Sound spectrograms of the eleven coyote vocalizations. A, Growl; B, huff; C, woof; D, bark; E, bark-howl; F, yelp; G, whine; H, wow-oo-wow; I, lone howl; J, group howl; K, group yip-howl. The vertical scale is marked in 1-kHz intervals. The horizontal scale is marked in 0.25-sec intervals.

tion (Table II). An increase in intensity of communication reflects an increase in "urgency" and the probability that the signaler will follow through (Smith, 1969), that is, the credibility of the signal increases. An increase in intensity of communication within a particular vocalization can be altered through increases in amplitude and frequency (vocalizations/unit time, and in some cases hertz), as well as by combining the vocalization with another type of display (visual, olfactory, or tactile). For example, a growl takes on an increased intensity of communication if it becomes louder, of higher frequency (Hz) and is combined with the aggressive threat face (Fig. 2b).

A. Agonistic and Alarm

1. Woof

The woof is used as a low-intensity threat and alarm. It sounds like a muffled bark and resembles the bark in physical characteristics (Fig. 5C). A woof given near the den generally causes the pups to go into the den (Camenzind, 1974); if the disturbance continues, the adult(s) moves off some distance from the den before barking loudly.

2. Growl

The growl sounds phonetically like "gr-r-r-r." It is used as a short-distance threat but can vary in intensity of communication from low to high (see above). Coyote pups growl during play fighting at about 18 days of age (Bekoff, 1972a; Fox, 1969). Bekoff and Diamond (1976) reported that a male emitted low growls during precopulatory behavior.

3. Huff

The huff is produced by a rapid and forceful expulsion of air through the mouth and nose. This often results in the expulsion of phlegm from the nose and saliva from the mouth. Hence, spitting is often recognized as a part of this display. It is a high-intensity threat vocalization which is used only over very short distances, for obvious reasons. Silver and Silver (1969, p. 25) reported that their captive New England canids (Eastern coyotes) (*Canis latrans* var.) made a ". . . chuffing sound like a series of rapid exhalations . . ." Both Brown (1973) and Bekoff (personal communication) reported that their captive coyotes gave a vocalization made by a rapid expiration of air.

4. Bark

The bark is a long-distance threat vocalization which can vary in intensity of communication from low to medium. It is also used as a low to medium intensity alarm vocalization but, as mentioned above, is rarely used near the den. Its physical characteristics (Fig. 5D) can generally be described as a burst of high amplitude, relatively short duration, and relatively low frequency. However, its frequency characteristics vary from wide frequency range noise to relatively narrow and discrete frequencies with accompanying harmonics. Fox (1971a) stated that coyotes bark to coordinate hunting movements; however, I know of no evidence to support his statement, including observations from more than 100 hunts (Bekoff and Hill, unpublished data).

The source of a bark is generally easily localized although Ryden (1975) and Bekoff (personal communication) have expressed difficulty in determining the location of a barking coyote. The bark's physical characteristics (wide frequency range and short duration) should provide for easy localization.

Tembrock (1965) hypothesized that the frequency, duration, and repetition of canid barks determine the information transmitted, and amplitude and frequency may also be important. Measurements of the frequency and duration of barks taken from six individual free-ranging coyotes showed no significant differences between individuals (Lehner, 1977). This suggests that the variation may represent differential information content, and individual recognition may be based on other characteristics such as formant shape (Kiley, 1972; Theberge and Falls, 1967).

5. Bark-Howl

The bark-howl appears to function as a long-distance, high-intensity threat and/or alarm. It begins with a bark which immediately blends into a short, frequency modulated howl (Figs. 5E, 6E). In a bark, bark-howl bout, the bark-howl is always preceded by a separate bark. The howl portion may increase the localization features (Kiley, 1972) of the bark-howl as well as increase the potential for transmitting information.

6. Yelp

The yelp occurs primarily in high-intensity submission but also occurs as a startle response. A "yi-e-e-e" often precedes or follows the yelp portion which (Fig. 5F) resembles a high-frequency bark both phonically and

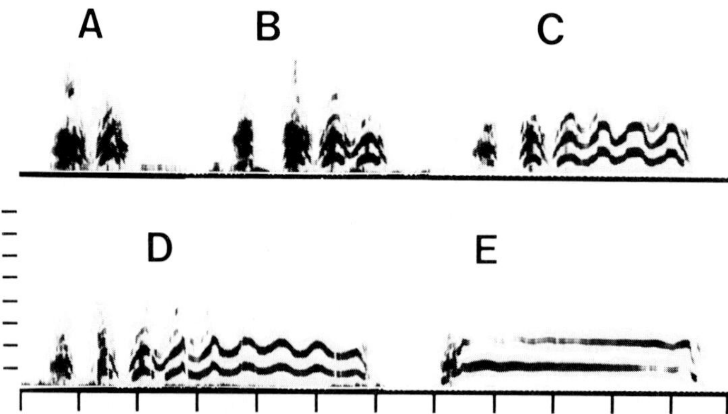

Fig. 6. Development of the bark-howl (C,D,E) from the bark (A,B). These were selected from a single bout by an individual coyote. The vertical scale is marked in 1-kHz intervals. The horizontal scale is marked in 0.25-sec intervals.

spectrographically. The "yi-e-e-e" appears on a sonogram like a short howl chopped into segments.

7. Whine (High-Frequency)

The high-frequency whine is often given by a subordinate during passive-submission. It is a short-range, low-amplitude vocalization which spectrographically resembles a low-frequency howl with several harmonics (Fig. 5G). Joslin (1966) reported that the gray wolf's "whimper" was used to express submission.

B. Greeting

1. Whine (Low-Frequency)

The low-frequency whine is given by a subordinate individual to a more dominant during low-intensity greeting (active submission). It is generally accompanied by muzzle-nibbling and tail-wagging with the tail held low or tucked between the hind legs.

2. Wow-Oo-Wow

This vocalization slowly modulates in both frequency and amplitude (Fig. 5H). It is of low amplitude but occurs during high-intensity greeting displays and has been referred to elsewhere as the "greeting song" (Camenzind and Lehner, 1975). It is a mixed sound (Tembrock, 1968) which apparently results from an oscillation between motivations. The result is a vocalization which grades back and forth between a low-frequency whine (low-intensity submission) and a growl (low-intensity threat).

3. Group Yip-Howl

Often two or more members of a social group will reunite, greet, and then give a group yip-howl. The group yip-howl may also be the finale of a greeting ceremony which preceeds separation and dispersal for hunting (Ryden, 1975).

This vocalization involves two or more individuals howling and yipping simultaneously in seemingly disjunct patterns (Fig. 5K). It develops from one individual howling, generally the dominant individual (Brown, 1973; A. Olsen, personal communication), being gradually joined by the others in the group as the vocalization increases in intensity (Lehner, 1977). As the other individuals join, the howls become more frequency and amplitude modulated and yips become more frequent. The group yip-howl includes vocalizations which McCarley (1975) has called "screams," "gargles," and "laughs." References in the literature to unison howling in canids are numerous and have been tabulated by Lehner (1976a).

The group yip-howl probably strengthens social bonds in the group and may also help to synchronize their mood (Ewer, 1968). Yawning, which may have evolved as a ritualized intention to howl, is a contagious behavior which Ewer (1968) suggests may synchronize the group's initiation of activity following a rest.

Males appear to be more aggressive immediately following a group yip-howl bout (S. Horn, personal communication). They often walk with a stiff-legged gait with their tails elevated, become piloerected, urinate, scratch, and are seemingly less tolerant of subordinates. This suggests that the group yip-howl may also be used to reaffirm social status within the group.

C. Contact: Intra- and Intergroup

1. Lone Howl

This is the vocalization most often associated with coyotes. It is of relatively long duration (Table III), high amplitude, and varies from slight to moderate frequency modulation. The lone howl in Fig. 5I is only slightly frequency modulated and is typical of what McCarley (1975) has called a "flat howl." Lone howls are often preceded by a short series of barks, called "herald barks" by Mengel (1971).

There is a large amount of variability in lone howls both between (McCarley, 1975) and within individual coyotes, and elsewhere (Lehner, 1977), I have indicated that this would make it difficult to demonstrate significant interindividual differences. However, the results of recent field studies using playback (Lehner, 1976a) strongly suggest that coyotes can distinguish lone howls of group members from those of nongroup coyotes. Kolenosky and Johnston (1967) reported that it was almost impossible for them to distinguish individual wild gray wolves by their voices, but Theberge and Falls (1967) learned to distinguish the howls of their three captive gray wolves.

The lone howl appears to announce the location of individuals separated from their social group. It is often reciprocated by a lone howl from another individual which then generally leads to a reunion. Preliminary field observations indicate that the subordinate individual generally approaches the more dominant.

2. Group Howl

A group howl is sometimes given following the reunion of two or more coyotes, or may be given in response to distant lone howls, group howls, or group yip-howls. Playback studies (Lehner, 1976a) demonstrated that it is responded to (vocally) by coyotes in a qualitatively different way than is the

TABLE III
The Duration and Dominant Frequency of Coyote Vocalizations

		Duration (sec)			Dominant frequency (Hz)[a]		
Vocalization	N	Mean	S.D.	Range	Mean	S.D.	Range
Growl	15	3.0	±3.0	0.3–10.4	658	±279	300–1600
Huff	14	0.2	0.1	0.1–0.5	1236	752	500–3000
Woof	47	0.2	0.1	0.1–0.3	552	87	200–700
Bark	150	0.1	0.1	0.1–0.2	1528	333	600–2150
Bark-howl	102	1.2	0.4	0.5–2.6	609	248	250–1500
					1465	526	750–3000
Whine	19	0.5	0.5	0.1–1.9	1022	889	250–3000
Wow-oo-wow	10	2.0	0.2	1.8–2.2	340	212	250–900
					1064	278	600–1250
Yelp	10	0.9	0.5	0.2–1.3	1235	420	700–2100
					2125	302	1400–2450
Lone howl	74	1.8	0.9	0.6–3.8	1106	241	400–1600
					1252	278	600–2000
Group howl	75	50.7	43.8	4.5–246.0	706	170	400–1000
					1359	395	750–2300
Group yip-howl	54	35.3	33.5	4.0–198.0	590	177	250–1000
					1817	452	950–3000

[a] Midpoint of the blackest part of the spectrogram of the vocalization (Marler, 1973). For those vocalizations which have two sets of measurements, they refer to the lowest and highest dominant frequencies, respectively.

group yip-howl. Although the message may be similar, a group howl is not simply a low-intensity group yip-howl.

The group howl is essentially two or more coyotes giving lone howls successively or simultaneously. When the howls overlap the coyotes appear to avoid howling at the same dominant frequency (Fig. 5J; Ryden, 1975), a phenomenon also reported for gray wolves (Crisler, 1958). Its primary function appears to be similar to the lone howl; that is, announcement of location of group members. In addition, it may serve to reinforce group bonds (Camenzind, 1974; Ewer, 1968).

3. Group Yip-Howl

The group yip-howl (discussed previously) may be most important in announcing territorial occupancy and preventing visual contact between groups of coyotes.

In addition, the group yip-howl may help to regulate density in populations of coyotes (Brown, 1973), as I have proposed elsewhere (Lehner, 1976a,b) in a *population regulation hypothesis*. The group yip-howl may assist in regulating population density in two ways. First, as a means of indirectly defending a group's territory, the group yip-howl would serve to space coyotes throughout the habitat. Second, the group yip-howl may provide a means by which the coyotes assess their density ("epideictic display" of Wynne-Edwards, 1962) relative to the food supply and regulate their density (Wynne-Edwards, 1962) through reproductive rate. It is not necessary to invoke group selection in this hypothesis (see Dawkins, 1976, p. 129ff) however, kin selection may be operating if members of rather stable groups (Chapter 12, this volume) are shown to be related.

Coyote population densities have been positively correlated with rodent (Gier, 1968), and lagamorph (Clark, 1972) population densities. Clark (1972, p. 343) concluded that in his study area the jackrabbit (*Lepus californicus*) food base ". . . is a partial determinant of coyote density. The physiological or behavioral links, or both, are unknown at present." Connolly and Longhurst (1975, p. 1) state that "According to a model developed to simulate coyote population dynamics, the primary effect of killing coyotes is to reduce the density of the population thereby stimulating density-dependent changes in birth and natural mortality rates." Knowlton (1972) demonstrated that in Texas average litter size in coyotes was inversely correlated with population density. If the group yip-howl does assist in regulating coyote population density through spacing and/or reproductive rate, then it will provide the potential to artificially (and nonlethally) reduce coyote densities in areas where their activities are not compatible with man's. J. Flinders (personal communication) is presently testing the hypothesis that both strange urine and excess howling reduces reproduction and encourages dispersal.

TABLE IV

The Distriburtion of Similar Vocalizations in Diverse Canid Species.[a,b]

Canid species	Vocalizations										
	Growl	Huff	Woof	Bark	Bark-howl	Whine	Woo-oo-wow	Yelp	Lone howl	Group howl	Group yip-howl
Coyote (*Canis latrans*)	4,7, 10,37, 40,57, 58	7	7,10	7,9, 10,12, 25,37, 45,70	2,5, 19,37, 63	7,12, 22,37, 58,69	11	10,12, 24,37, 58	12,17, 19,37, 45	10,45	2,7,10, 11,25, 32,37, 45,54, 55,61
Eastern Coyote (*Canis latrans var.*)	42,57	57				57		57	57		57
Coyote × Dog hybrid				39							39,57
Domestic dog (*Canis familiaris*)	6,12, 19	6		6,12, 15,43, 48,50, 51		6,12, 26,51		6,12, 26,48	12		32,51
Gray Wolf (*Canis Lupus*)	12,30, 38	12	19,21	12,19, 28,38, 49,65, 68	12,38, 59	12,19, 30,38, 47	14,20	12	12,14, 19,21, 29,34, 38,49, 64,65, 66	14,19	17,25, 32,38, 51,55
Red Wolf (*Canis rufus*)				44							
Golden Jackal (*Canis aureus*)	53	53	19	53	19,63	61,67		53	19,66	27,67	61
Black-backed Jackal (*Canis mesomelas*)	23,68	18	68	18	63			68	68		61

TABLE IV (Continued)

The Distriburtion of Similar Vocalizations in Diverse Canid Species [a,b]

Canid species	Vocalizations										
	Growl	Huff	Woof	Bark	Bark-howl	Whine	Woo-oo-wow	Yelp	Lone howl	Group howl	Group yip-howl
Dingo (*Canis dingo*)				12,62	13				13		32,36
Red Fox (*Vulpes vulpes*)	12,62	28	60,62	1,8, 12,62	60	12,62		62			
Corsac Fox (*Vulpes corsac*)						62					
Arctic Fox (*Alopex lagopus*)	12,62			12,62		12		62			
Fennec (*Fennecus zerda*)								62			
Maned Wolf (*Chrysocyon brachyurus*)	33			33		32					
Culpeo (*Dusicyon culpaeus*)	12										
African Hunting Dog (*Lycaon pictus*)				20,35, 46			20,62		20		
Dhole (*Cuon alphinus*)						62					16

Bush Dog (*Speothos venaticus*)	33	3	3,33	62
Gray Fox (*Urocyon cinereoargenteus*)	12	12,62	12	62
Raccoon Dog (*Nyctereutes procyonoides*)			52,62	62

[a] Categorization of the vocalizations was based primarily on the authors' written descriptions, but was in some cases somewhat arbitrary. The species are separated into four groups according to the hypothetical evolutionary relationships suggested by Fox (1975).

[b] Key to number citations: 1:Ables (1975); 2: Alcorn (1946); 3: Bates (1944); 4: Bekoff (1972b); 5: Benson (1948); 6: Bleicher (1963); 7: Brown (1973); 8; Burrows (1968); 9: Cahalane (1961); 10: Camenzind (1974); 11: Camenzind and Lehner, (1975); 12: Cohen, Fox (1976); 13: Corbett, Newsome (1975); 14: Crisler (1958); 15: Darwin, (1872); 16: Davidar (1975); 17: Dobie (1949); 18: Eaton (1969); 19: Eisfled (1966b); 20: Estes and Goddard (1967); 21: Fentress (1967); 22: Fichter (1950); 23: FitzSimons (1919); 24: Fox (1969); 25: Fox (1971a); 26: Fuller, and Fox (1969); 27: Golani, and Keller (1975); 28: Huxley, and Koch (1938); 29: Jordan *et al.* (1967); 30: Joslin (1966); 31: Joslin (1967); 32: Kleinman (1967); 33: Kleinman (1972); 34: Kolenosky, and Kohnston (1967); 35: Kuhme (1965); 36: MacIntosh (1975); 37: McCarley (1975); 38: Mech (1970); 39: Mengel (1971); 40: Murie (1940); 41: Pimlott (1960); 42: Pringle (1960); 43: Pulliainen (1967); 44: Riley, and McBride (1975); 45: Ryden (1975); 46: Schaller (1973); 47: Scott (1950); 48: Scott (1961); 49: Scott (1967); 50: Scott (1968); 51: Scott, and DeGhett (1972); 52: Seitz (1955); 53: Seitz (1959); 54: Seton (1909); 55: Seton (1929); 56: Shortridge (1934); 57: Silver, and Silver (1969); 58: Snow (1967); 59: Stephenson, and Ahgook (1975); 60: Tembrock (1958a); 61: Tembrock (1959b); 62: Tembrock (1963); 63: Tembrock (1965); 64: Theberge (1971); 65: Theberge and Falls (1967); 66: Theberge, and Pimlott (1969); 67: Van Lawick-Goodall and Van Lawick (1970); 68: Van Der Merwe (1953); 69: Van Wormer (1964); 70: Young, and Jackson (1951).

D. Comparisons with Other Canids

Similar vocalizations are found in many canid species (Table IV), but their evolutionary relationships are difficult to establish. The categorization of vocalizations in Table IV can be considered only tentative since they were based primarily on the authors' written descriptions and in some cases were somewhat arbitrary.

E. Nonvocal Sounds

Teeth-snapping is a mechanical sound produced by rapidly opening and closing the mouth with small amplitude of movement and with the teeth meeting upon closing. The lips are held vertically retracted which allows greater amplification of the sound. It is a threat sound which often accompanies a bite intention or a growl and a small mouth threat face (Fig. 2a). Teeth-snapping may be directed at a dominant by a subordinate pup before it rolls over in passive submission, a seemingly ambivalent component of play (Fox and Clark, 1971).

V. OLFACTORY AND GUSTATORY COMMUNICATION

A. Scent Glands

Scent glands in coyotes are relatively unstudied even though the coyote has long been credited with outstanding olfactory abilities. However, although their sense of smell is undoubtedly acute, they appear to be a primarily visually oriented predator (Grinnell *et al.*, 1937; Wells and Lehner, 1977).

1. Anal Glands, Feces, and Urine

The paired anal sacs lie laterally on either side of the anal sphincter, and their ducts open externally into the anus. These sacs serve as reservoirs for secretions from the anal glands which lie in the wall of the sacs and open into them. The secretion is a strong-smelling, pasty liquid which may in itself have signal value. However, the position of their duct openings suggests that their secretion is also deposited on feces. Domestic dogs (*Canis familiaris*), and perhaps coyotes, are able to voluntarily control the flow of anal sac secretions (Donovan, 1967). Ryden (1975) suggests that anal gland scent may be used to repel other coyotes. The anal area is investigated during greeting, and the anal gland secretion may provide for individual identification as in mongooses (*Herpestes auropunctatus*) (Gorman, 1976). Anal gland secretions contain short-chain aliphatic acids, trimethylamine, ethanol, and acetone, all of which may arise via microbial action on proteins, carbohydrates, and lipids in the anal sacs (Preti *et al.*, 1976). These secretions are essentially the same as those of the red fox (Albone and Fox, 1971) and domestic dog (Preti *et al.*, 1976).

Fecal piles are investigated by other coyotes and may serve to identify individuals and/or groups; that is, territorial marking based on familiar versus unfamiliar odors.

Likewise urine is used to mark territorial boundaries (Lehner, personal observation). Regularly established scent posts are visited periodically, investigated, and urinated upon. Camenzind (personal communication) believes that urination for the purpose of scent-marking is always followed by scratching, a behavior which probably provides an additional visual signal to the spot, in contrast to the belief that it is used to cover the deposit (Young and Jackson, 1951). Scent-marking with urine may only be indirectly related to territorial defense, and its primary function may be to provide the resident with familiar odor and a feeling of security (Ewer, 1968; Kleiman, 1966; Ralls, 1971). Ewer (1968) and Kleiman (1966) state that female coyotes mark only during or around the time of estrus; however, I have observed female coyotes marking vigorously following an apparent territorial intrusion by other coyotes.

Males investigate the urine, feces, and vulva of females in estrus (Bekoff and Diamond, 1976), and through odors and taste they determine the reproductive state of the female. They may give a "flehman"-like response (Fig. 2i) with an upturned nose and curled lip after smelling and tasting the females' urine. This may aid in the transfer of odor through the palatine fissures to the vomeronasal organ (Knappe, 1964) or may restrict the nasal apertures so that odors already inhaled may be retained on the olfactory epithelium for an extended period of time (Dagg and Taub, 1970).

Both males and females may raise a hind leg while urinating, although the female seldom raises it as high or as often as the male. Ewer (1968) suggested that leg cocking may have originated as a movement to ensure that the urine did not soil the animal's own coat. However, the apparent correlation of leg-lifting with sex of the individual and behavioral context argues against Ewer's hypothesis. Also, the leg-lifted posture is sometimes assumed by coyotes without any obvious urination occurring. This suggests that the visual component of the behavior may by itself possess signal value, as has been reported for the domestic dog (Fox and Bekoff, 1975). A male coyote may leave a sign of his size when he urinates on a vertical object since a larger individual is more apt to leave a higher mark (Lorenz, 1954).

Urination often occurs during passive-submission (Fig. 3a) and may be derived from neonatal mother–infant interactions in which the mother stimulates urination in the neonate by licking its genitals (Fox, 1971b).

Coyotes often urinate on their food before eating it (Young and Jackson, 1951) and occasionally in the water supply. The function of this behavior is unknown, although Young and Jackson (1951) suggest that this may serve as proclamation of ownership.

2. Supracaudal Tail Gland

The supracaudal tail gland, a collection of apocrine sweat glands and modified sebaceous glands (Lehner, unpublished data; Gier, personal communication), lies on the dorsal surface of the tail at a point approximately one-third of the distance from the base to the tip of the tail. Its position is marked by an oblong patch of dark guard hairs (Fig. 1f) which may be somewhat shorter and stiffer than the hairs of adjacent areas (Young and Jackson, 1951). The gland is approximately 10×40 mm and is covered by sparse underfur (Hildebrand, 1952).

The size, shape, and activity of the gland varies in different canid species (Hildebrand, 1952) but its function is unknown. It has been suggested that its odor is used in species (Lovell *et al.,* 1957) and individual recognition (Van Wormer, 1964; Seton, 1923). The latter does not seem likely since the strength of the odor decreases from fox to coyote to gray wolf (Fox, 1971a); that is, from the least sociable (red fox) to the most sociable (gray wolf) of the three canids.

Ewer (1968) suggested that the position of the gland may be such that the secretion is rubbed off on the roof of the entrance to the den. Odor dispersion may have originally been the primary function of tail-wagging with the visual signal function becoming ritualized and taking on more importance in the more social canids (see Section VII).

3. Pedal Glands

Merocrine sweat glands are found in the foot pads of both eastern and western coyotes (Sands and Coppinger, 1975). While their primary function is probably temperature regulation, they may also produce an odor with communicatory value. In addition, the coyote may have interdigital glands similar to those found in the red fox (Fox, 1971a), but their presence has not been documented. Coyotes consistently investigate the footprints of conspecifics which suggests that they do receive some olfactory information from the impressions.

B. Other Potential Sources of Odor Signals

The muzzle area of coyotes is investigated and licked by pups when food soliciting and by adults during greeting. Schaffer (1940) reports that the fox has glands around the lips, but none have been reported in the coyote. Coyotes often initiate rolling on an object (e.g., meat) by lowering their head and rubbing the side of their muzzles across the object. It is generally assumed that this transfers odor from the object to the coyote; however, the reverse may also be important.

Coyotes may roll over onto their backs on an object and twist back and forth with their legs thrashing in the air. The apex of the saddle-back marking (Fig. 1) on their backs is generally positioned on the object as they rub back and forth. Odor from the object (e.g., rabbit fur) is rubbed onto the coyote and may be of some communicatory significance. I have observed coyotes sniffing the area at the apex of the saddleback (approximately the middle of the back) during the initiation of the "T-position" (Golani and Mendelssohn, 1971) in agonistic encounters and during social investigation as a part of greeting.

Ears are occasionally probed and sniffed during social investigation. The external auditory meatus contains ceruminous glands which produce a secretion commonly referred to as ear wax. Odors from the ear wax and/or other secretions in and around the ears may provide information (e.g., individual identification) to investigating coyotes.

Sebaceous glands and apocrine sweat glands are both found in association with the hair follicles in domestic dogs (Lovell *et al.*, 1957), and we can infer that the same arrangement probably exists in coyotes. This tends to produce a general body odor which is reportedly very strong in African wild dogs (R. Taylor, personal communication). This odor may provide important information regarding individual identification, social status, and group affiliation, although none of these possibilities have been investigated. Grinnell *et al.* (1937) stated that pups use odor to maintain close physical contact, and it may be the general body odor that provides the cue for their chemotaxic behavior.

IV. TACTILE COMMUNICATION

Coyotes are often in physical contact as pups (Chapter 5), but they tend to maintain increasingly inviolable individual distances as they mature. However, tactile communication remains important in certain contexts, especially agonistic encounters and greeting. The behaviors discussed below are seen in pups but are retained into adulthood and serve communicatory functions. Face pawing and foreleg stabbing which may become tactile are discussed in Section III,B,3.

A. Biting

The muzzle-bite and scruff-bite, accompanied by head-shaking, are seen as agonistic behaviors in adults (Fox and Clark, 1971) and occur in a play context in pups. Bites are often oriented to various parts of the head (e.g., Chapter 5, Fig. 2m) but muzzle- and scruff-biting is most common. Muzzle-biting often develops into jaw-wrestling in which the two individuals twist and pull while varying the pressure of the bite. Severe bites are inhibited except in extreme agonistic encounters.

B. Chin-Resting and Contactual-Circling

These two behaviors are seen in pups (see Chapter 5). Contact by one pup on another elicits rooting and "auriculonasocephalic responses" (Fox and Clark, 1971) in the first and results in it circling around and over the other. Contactual-circling is occasionally interrupted by a period of chin-resting during which one pup rests its chin on the shoulder of the other pup. Contactual-circling is a component of precopulatory behavior (Bekoff and Diamond, 1976).

C. Standing-Over

Chin-resting frequently precedes standing-over (Bekoff, 1972a) in which one pup stands with its forelegs on the back of a conspecific (for further discussion see Bekoff, Chapter 5). It is seen first at about 21 days of age (Fox and Clark, 1971). In adults, a dominant may stand over a subordinate and growl.

D. Hip-Slam and Bumping

Hip-slams are seen during play-fighting in pups and agonistic encounters in adults. Hip-slamming is simply the elevation of the hindquarters and rapid movement laterally so that the hips slam into another individual. It occurs in both play and agonistic contexts. Bumping, in which one pup will run at and bump into its playmate with its chest, is a component of play (Fox and Clark, 1971).

E. Face-Licking

This behavior is a submissive signal given by pups in a play-fighting context. It may have evolved from the neonatal food-begging response (Fox, 1971b) and is often seen as only an intention. In adults, licking and licking-intention is sometimes seen as a component of active submission (Fig. 4D).

F. Inguinal Response

Probing with the nose in the inguinal area during social investigation often causes rotation of the hind leg, or leg lifting and immobility in the recipient (see Bekoff, Chapter 5). During mounting and copulation the male's forelegs are clasped around the female's inguinal area and may inhibit the female from moving, thereby improving the chances of a successful copulation (Fox, 1971b).

VII. ORIGINS OF SELECTED SIGNALS

Signals often arise through a process called ritualization. That is, a behavior, or behavioral component, takes on signal value and becomes incorporated into the communication repertoire of the individual. It may then spread through the population, genetically or culturally, and ultimately may become a characteristic of the species. Ritualization generally occurs through the exaggeration, repetition, or change in relative timing of movements or postures. These new signals are then often strengthened by incorporating other movements or postures, or altering the morphology (e.g., shape, color) to enhance the signal. For example, white hair in the external auditory meatus increases the visual impact of erect ears.

Neonatal behaviors may be retained into adulthood and become important signals. By studying the development of behavior (see Chapter 5) it is often possible to recognize the neonatal precursors of adult displays. Some examples follow.

Passive-submission (Fig. 3A) in adults is similar to a response given by pups in response to maternal discipline. Submissive adult males raise the uppermost hind leg, expose the penis and often urinate, a submissive signal which also occurs in pups but may have been derived from the mother licking the genitals to stimulate urination.

Muzzle-licking and muzzle-nibbling which occurs during active submission and greeting is probably derived from neonatal food-begging behavior. This behavior is widespread in the family Canidae.

Sustained *paw-raising* may have originated from the intention to roll over into the passive-submission position (Fox, 1971a). *Face-pawing* and *face-stabbing* are given by pups in an attempt to solicit play from littermates or food from adults. In adults sustained *paw-raising* is given in a submissive context (Fig. 4D) but *face-pawing* and *face-stabbing* is exaggerated and is used as a threat signal (Fig. 4E).

Tail position is an important visual signal in coyotes (see Section II,A,2). Kiley-Worthington (1976) suggests that the origin of this signal was from the normal high postural tonus of the tail which is an antigravity tonus in preparation for locomotion. In contrast to the high tail position which signals confidence and/or threat, low tail position denotes fear and submission. This low postural tonus is associated with a protective withdrawal of the tail and ears, and hence becomes characteristic of fear and indicative of submission (Kiley-Worthington, 1976). The black patch over the supracaudal tail gland may have given morphological support (i.e., increased visual impact) to the tail display (Kleiman, 1967), or it may have evolved as a target for olfactory investigation of the tail gland or the perineum (Wickler, 1967) by other individuals.

Tail-wagging has apparent signal value in coyotes, but Kiley-Worthington (1976) believes that the primary cause of tail-wagging in dogs is "frustrated locomotion." She agrees that some tail movements have become ritualized, but states that they have not become emancipated from their original cause (frustrated locomotion) nor are they of typical intensity (Morris, 1957). Like the majority of coyote communication signals, tail-wagging is graded in intensity but can be divided into two general categories: (1) low frequency and high amplitude, and (2) high frequency and low amplitude (Section III,2,C). I agree with Kleiman's (1967) suggestion that tail movements are probably associated with anal and supracaudal tail-gland secretions, although there is no experimental evidence for this. The black tip on the tail (Fig. 1) of most coyotes may enhance the visual impact of signals associated with tail movement and position.

The *lone howl* of coyotes is probably derived from the *bark-howl* which is derived from *barks*. Figure 6 shows *barks* and *bark-howls* selected from a single bout by an adult coyote. It can be seen that the howl portion of the bark-howl (E) can be systematically formed by bringing barks very close together (A), then stringing them together with increased tonal purity (i.e., more separation of frequency bands) (B), then further increasing the tonal purity and extending the duration (C) until it becomes a wavering howl (D) and finally a howl with only slight frequency modulation (E). Although the lone howl was seemingly derived from the bark-howl, its message is much different than the bark-howl (see Table II).

VIII. CONCLUSIONS

Coyote communication can best be characterized as being *graded, combined,* and *dynamic*. These three characteristics suggest that it can also be considered relatively *complex*.

Both visual and auditory signals are obviously *graded,* and olfactory, gustatory, and tactile signals may be likewise, but there is less known about them. Visual signals are graded by posture (e.g., ears and mouth, Fig. 7) and movement (e.g., rate and amplitude of tail-wagging). Vocalizations are graded by type, frequency, and amplitude. No visual or auditory signal has been stereotyped into a "typical intensity" (Morris, 1957). The gradations provide for more resolution in the message, including intensity of communi-

Fig. 7. Gradation and simultaneous combination of visual signals, especially ears and mouth, along an agonistic continuum. (Drawing by F. Jacobs, based on a figure in Fox, 1971a.)

cation (see Section II), at the possible expense of increased ambiguity. However, ambiguity appears to be offset by the combination of signals through various communication channels. For example, a subordinate may bend its body into the "C position" (Fox, 1971b) when approaching a dominant. It keeps its head and rump low with its tail-tucked (visual), licks the muzzle of the dominant (tactile), while giving low-amplitude, high-frequency whines (auditory). It often adds an olfactory component by urinating as it assumes the passive-submission posture (Fig. 3A).

The simultaneous and/or successive *combination* of signals has one of two effects. First, it may have a synergistic effect and increase the intensity of communication of the entire display (Section II). Second, it may not heighten the intensity of communication but rather produce redundancy which decreases ambiguity. These two effects often differ only slightly and discrimination between the two demands intensive and repeated observations on the part of the researcher. Many displays which appear ambiguous to the human observer are probably distinct to coyotes. This apparent ambiguity is often the result of two factors. First, we recognize that several signals from different channels are being transmitted simultaneously and that some of them are apparently contradictory. Second, we often analyze communication at a point in time (e.g., photograph) or over a very short time period (e.g., during a growl). Both of these fail to take into account that the coyote apparently receives and responds to these signals as a gestalt (i.e., all signals taken together as a whole) both across signals and throughout time. The coyote's displays are generally in a dynamic flux reflecting the flow from one motivational state to another (see Section II,B,2). This characteristic led Van Wormer (1964, p. 98) to conclude that tail position has little or no signal value and that ". . . a coyote carries his tail in whatever manner is natural or necessary to help do what he wants to do at the moment."

Ambivalence is not synonymous with ambiguity. The *dynamic* nature (i.e., lability) of most coyote displays suggests that the oscillation itself may carry as important a message as any of the constituent signals themselves. For example, in active greeting, a subordinate coyote generally oscillates between aggression and submission (visual, auditory, and tactile signals), and the oscillation itself is perhaps more meaningful to the recipient than either the aggressive or submissive components alone. This is suggested by the recipient's response to the entire display rather than the individual components as they occur. Communication of "emotional state" (communication of affect) is fairly common in animals (Griffin, 1976), but among canids it has been discussed only in relation to domestic dogs (Scott and DeGhett, 1972) and gray wolves (Theberge, 1971). Some signals (or components of displays) appear to be more labile and more often in flux. These signals may, therefore, more closely reflect instantaneous changes in "emotional state" while others are less dynamic.

Intimately tied together are the coyote's adaptability and its complex behavior. The complexity of its total communication system seems rivaled by only a few other mammals. For these reasons alone, the further study of coyote communication promises to be very rewarding.

ACKNOWLEDGMENTS

This chapter is, in part, the result of many long discussions with individuals too numerous to mention. I have benefited especially from knowledge shared by Marc Bekoff, Franz Camenzind, Steve Horn, and Mike Wells. Devra Kleiman and Becky Field provided valuable comments on an earlier draft of this chapter. Valuable assistance in the production of sonagrams was provided by Ingrid Belan.

REFERENCES

Ables, E. D. (1975). *In* "The Wild Canids" (M. Fox, ed.), pp. 216–236. Van Nostrand-Reinhold, New York.

Albone, E. S., and Fox, M. W. (1971). *Nature* (*London*) **233**, 569–570.

Alcorn, J. R. (1946). *J. Mammal.* **27**, 122–126.

Bates, M. (1944). *J. Mammal.* **25**, 152–154.

Bekoff, M. (1972a). *Q. Rev. Biol.* **47**, 412–434.

Bekoff, M. (1972b). Ph.D. Thesis, Washington Univ., St. Louis, Missouri.

Bekoff, M. (1974a). *Am. Zool.* **14**, 323–340.

Bekoff, M. (1974b). *BioScience* **24**, 225–229.

Bekoff, M. (1977). *Am. Nat.* (in press).

Bekoff, M., and Diamond, J. (1976). *J. Mammal.* **57**, 372–375.

Benson, S. B. (1948). *J. Mammal.* **29**, 406–409.

Bleicher, N. (1963). *Am. J. Vet. Res.* **24**, 415–427.

Brown, J. B. (1973). M.S. Thesis, Purdue Univ., Lafayette, Indiana.

Burrows, R. (1968) "Wild Foxes." David & Charles, Newton Abbot, Devon.

Cahalane, V. H. (1961). "Mammals of North America." Macmillan, New York.

Camenzind, F. (1974). *Teton Mag.* **7**, 10–13, 40–42.

Camenzind, F., and Lehner, P. N. (1975). *Coyote Res. Newsl.* **3**, 14–15. Abstr.

Clark, F. (1972). *J. Wildl. Manage.* **36**, 343–356.

Cohen, J. A., and Fox, M. W. (1976). *Behav. Processes* **1**, 77–92.

Connolly, G. E., and Longhurst, W. M. (1975). Univ. Calif. Bull. 1872.

Corbett, L., and Newsome, A. (1975). *In* "The Wild Canids" (M. Fox, ed.), pp. 369–379. Van Nostrand-Reinhold, New York.

Crisler, L. (1958). "Arctic Wild." Harper, New York.

Dagg, A. I., and Taub, A. (1970). *Mammalia* **34**, 686–695.

Darwin, C. (1872). "The Expression of the Emotions in Man and Animals." Univ. of Chicago Press, Chicago, Illinois.

Davidar, E. R. C. (1975). *In* "The Wild Canids" (M. Fox, ed.), pp. 109–119. Van Nostrand-Reinhold, New York.

Dawkins, R. (1976). "The Selfish Gene." Cambridge Univ. Press, London and New York.

Dobie, J. F. (1949). "The Voice of the Coyote," Little, Brown, Boston, Massachusetts.

Donovan, C. A. (1967). *Pract. Noteb.* **62**, 1047–1048.

Eaton, R. (1969). *Mammalia* **33**, 87–92.

Eisfeld, D. (1966a). *Z. Wiss. Zool.* **174**, 177–225.

Eisfeld, D. (1966b). *Z. Wiss. Zool.* **174**, 227–289.

Estes, R. D., and Goddard, J. (1967). *J. Wildl. Manage.* **31**, 52–70.

Ewer, R. F. (1968). "Ethology of Mammals." Logos Press, London.

Ewer, R. F. (1973). "The Carnivores." Cornell Univ. Press, Ithaca, New York.

Fentress, J. C. (1967). *Am. Zool.* **7**, 339–351.

Fichter, E. (1950). *J. Mammal.* **31**, 66–73.

FitzSimons, F. W. (1919). "The Natural History of South Africa." Longmans Green, London.

Fox, M. W. (1969). *Behaviour* **35**, 242–258.

Fox, M. W. (1970). *Behaviour* **36**, 49–73.

Fox, M. W. (1971a). "Behavior of Wolves, Dogs and Related Canids." Harper, New York.

Fox, M. W. (1971b). *Z. Tierpsychol.* **28**, 185–210.

Fox, M. W. (1975). *In* "The Wild Canids" (M. W. Fox, ed.), pp. 429–460. Van Nostrand-Reinhold, New York.

Fox, M. W., and Bekoff, M. (1975). "The Behavior of Domestic Animals," 3rd Ed. Williams & Wilkins, Baltimore, Maryland.
Fox, M. W., and Clark, A. L. (1971). *Z. Tierpsychol.* **28,** 262–278.
Fuller, J. L., and Fox, M. W. (1969). "The Behaviour of Domestic Animals," 2nd Ed. Williams & Wilkins, Baltimore, Maryland.
Gier, H. T. (1968). "Coyotes in Kansas." Agric. Exp. Stn., Kansas State Coll., Manhattan.
Gier, H. T. (1975). *In* "The Wild Canids" (M. W. Fox, ed.), pp. 247–262. Van Nostrand-Reinhold, New York.
Gipson, P. S., and Sealander, J. A. (1972). *Proc. South East Assoc. Game Fish. Comm.* pp. 82–94.
Golani, I., and Keller, A. (1975). *In* "The Wild Canids" (M. W. Fox, ed.), pp. 303–335. Van Nostrand-Reinhold, New York.
Golani, I., and Mendelssohn, H. (1971). *Behaviour* **38,** 169–192.
Gorman, M. L. (1976). *Anim. Behav.* **24,** 141–145.
Griffin, D. S. (1976). *Am. Sci.* **64,** 530–535.
Grinnell, J., Dixon, J. S., and Linsdale, J. M. (1937). "Fur-Bearing Mammals of California." Univ. of Calif. Press, Berkeley.
Hildebrand, M. (1952). *J. Mammal.* **33,** 419–428.
Horn, S. W., and Lehner, P. N. (1975). *J. Comp. Physiol. Psychol.* **89,** 1070–1076.
Huxley, J., and Koch, L. (1938). "Animal Language." Grosset, New York.
Jansen, C. (1974). M.S. Thesis, Colorado State Univ., Fort Collins.
Jordan, P. A., Shelton, P. C., and Allen, D. L. (1967). *Am. Zool.* **7,** 233–252.
Joslin, P. W. B. (1966). M.S. Thesis, Univ. of Toronto, Toronto.
Joslin, P. W. B. (1967). *Am. Zool.* **7,** 279–288.
Kavanau, J. L., and Ramos, J. (1975). *Am. Nat.* **109,** 391–418.
Kiley, M. (1972). *Z. Tierpsychol.* **31,** 171–222.
Kiley-Worthington, M. (1976). *Behaviour* **56,** 69–115.
Kleiman, D. (1966). *Sym. Zool. Soc. London* **18,** 167–117.
Kleiman, D. (1967). *Am. Zool.* **7,** 365–372.
Kleiman, D. (1972). *J. Mammal.* **53,** 719–806.
Knappe, H. (1964). *Zool. Gart.* **28,** 188–194.
Knowlton, F. F. (1972). *J. Wildl. Manage.* **36,** 369–382.
Kolenosky, G. B., and Johnston, D. H. (1967). *Am. Zool.* **7,** 289–303.
Kuhme, W. (1965). *Z. Tierpsychol.* **22,** 495–541.
Lehner, P. N. (1977a). *Anim. Behav.* (in press).
Lehner, P. N. (1976a). *Anim. Behav. Soc., Meet., Boulder, Colo.*
Lehner, P. N. (1976b) *Wildl. Soc. Bull.* **4,** 120–126.
Lorenz, K. (1954). "Man Meets Dog." Methuen, London.
Lovell, J. E., and Getty, R. (1954). *Am. J. Vet. Res.* **18,** 873–885.
McCarley, H. (1975). *J. Mammal.* **56,** 847–856.
McIntosh, N. W. G. (1975). *In* "The Wild Canids" (M. Fox, ed.), pp. 87–106. Van Nostrand-Reinhold, New York.
Marler, P. (1973). *Z. Tierpsychol.* **33,** 223–247.
Mech, L. D. (1970). "The Wolf." Nat. Hist. Press, Garden City, New York.
Mengel, R. M. (1971). *J. Mammal.* **52,** 316–336.
Merriam, C. H. (1897). Proc. Biol. Soc. Wash. Vol. 11.
Morris, D. (1957). *Behaviour* **11,** 1–12.
Murie, A. (1940). "Ecology of the Coyote in the Yellowstone." U.S. Gov. Printing Office, Washington, D.C.

Ozoga, J. J., and Harger, E. M. (1966). *J. Wildl. Manage.* **30,** 809–818.

Peterson, E. A., Heaton, W. C., and Wruble, S. D. (1969). *J. Mammal.* **50,** 566–578.

Pimlott, D. H. (1960). *Midwest Wildl. Conf., 22nd,* Toronto, Can.

Preti, G., Muetterties, E. L., Furman, J. M., Kennelly, J. J., and Johns, B. E. (1976). *J. Chem. Ecol.* **2,** 177–186.

Pringle, L. P. (1960). *J. Mammal.* **41,** 278.

Pulliainen, E. (1967). *Am. Zool.* **7,** 313–317.

Ralls, K. (1971). *Science* **171,** 443–449.

Riley, G. A., and McBride, R. T. (1975). *In* "The Wild Canids" (M. Fox, ed.), pp. 263–277. Van Nostrand-Reinhold, New York.

Ryden, H. (1975). "God's Dog." Coward, McCann, Geohagen, New York.

Sands, M., and Coppinger, R. P. (1975). *Coyote Res. Newsl.* **3,** 38. Abstr.

Schaffer, J. (1940). "Die Hautdrüsenorgane der Säugetiere." Urban & Schwarzenberg, Berlin.

Schaller, G. B. (1973). "Golden Shadows, Flying Hooves." Knopf, New York.

Scott, J. P. (1950). *Ann. N.Y. Acad. Sci.* **51,** 1009–1021.

Scott, J. P. (1961). *Am. Zool.* **1,** 387. Abstr.

Scott, J. P. (1967). *Am. Zool.* **7,** 373–381.

Scott, J. P. (1968). *In* "Animal Communication" (T. A. Sebeok, ed.), pp. 17–30. Indiana Univ. Press, Bloomington.

Scott, J. P., and DeGhett, V. J. (1972). *In* "Communication and Affect" (T. Alloway, L. Krames, and P. Pliner, eds.), pp. 129–150. Academic Press, New York.

Seitz, A. (1955). *Z. Tierpsychol.* **12,** 463–489.

Seitz, A. (1959). *Z. Tierpsychol.* **16,** 747–771.

Seton, E. T. (1909). "Life-Histories of Northern Animals, an Account of the Mammals of Manitoba. Vol. II: Flesh Eaters." Scribners, New York.

Seton, E. T. (1923). *J. Mammal.* **4,** 180–182.

Seton, E. T. (1929). "Wild Animals at Home." Doubleday, Doran, Garden City, New York.

Shortridge, G. C. (1934). "The Mammals of Southwest Africa." Heinemann, London.

Silver, H., and Silver, W. T. (1969). *Wildl. Monogr.* **17.** 41 pp.

Smith, W. J. (1969). *Science* **165,** 145–150.

Snow, C. J. (1967). *Am. Zool.* **7,** 353–355.

Stephenson, R. O., and Ahgook, R. T. (1975). *In* "The Wild Canids" (M. Fox, ed.), pp. 286–291. Van Nostrand-Reinhold, New York.

Tembrock, G. (1959a). *Z. Tierpsychol.* **16,** 351–368.

Tembrock, G. (1959b). "Tierstimmen: Eine Einfuhrung in die Bioakustic." Ziemsen Verlag, Wittenburg.

Tembrock, G. (1963). *In* "Acoustic Behaviour of Animals" (R. G. Busnel, ed.), pp. 751–786. Elsevier, Amsterdam.

Tembrock, G. (1965). *Z. Säeugetierk.* **30,** 257–273.

Tembrock, G. (1968). *In* "Animal Communication" (T. A. Sebeok, ed.), pp. 338–404. Indiana Univ. Press, Bloomington.

Theberge, J. B. (1971). *Nat. Hist.* **80,** 37–42.

Theberge, J. B., and Falls, J. B. (1967). *Am. Zool.* **7,** 331–338.

Theberge, J. B., and Pimlott, D. H. (1969). *Can. Field Nat.* **83,** 122–128.

Van Der Merwe, N. J. (1953). *Fauna Flora* **4,** 1–51.

Van Lawick-Goodall, J., and Van Lawick, H. (1970). "Innocent Killers." Houghton, New York.

Van Wormer, J. (1964). "The World of the Coyote." Lippincott, Philadelphia, Pennsylvania.

Wells, M. C., and Lehner, P. N. (1976). *Anim. Behav.* (in press).

Wickler, W. (1967). *In* "Primate Ethology" (D. Morris, ed.), pp. 89–189. Aldine, Chicago, Illinois.

Wynne-Edwards, V. C. (1962). "Animal Dispersion in Relation to Social Behaviour." Oliver & Boyd, Edinburgh.

Young, S. P., and Jackson, H. H. T. (1951). "The Clever Coyote." Stackpole, Harrisburg, Pennsylvania.

7

Coyote Behavior in the Context of Recent Canid Research: Problems and Perspectives

D. G. Kleiman and C. A. Brady

I. INTRODUCTION

The study of canid behavior and ecology has advanced significantly during the past decade. Yet the data base available for comparisons is heavily biased toward particular areas of research with only meager information existing about some of the most elemental aspects of canid biology. Obviously this sets limits on the validity of certain types of species comparisons. A short history of canid studies would perhaps indicate what emphases and biases exist.

Early behavioral studies by ethologists concentrated on comparisons of the fixed action patterns exhibited by different species or on developing a complete ethogram for single species. A classic example of this approach was Tembrock's comprehensive observations of red fox (*Vulpes vulpes*) behavior (Tembrock, 1957a,b, 1958, 1959, 1962a,b) with later comparisons of red and arctic foxes (*Alopex lagopus*) (Tembrock, 1960). Other examples of single species captive studies include those on the wolf *Canis lupus* (Schenkel, 1947, 1967; Rabb *et al.*, 1967; Zimen, 1971, 1975, 1976), the golden jackal *Canis aureus* (Seitz, 1959; Golani, 1966, 1973; Wandrey, 1975), the fennec fox *Fennecus zerda* (Gauthier-Pilters, 1962; Koenig, 1970), the maned wolf *Chrysocyon brachyurus* (Encke *et al.*, 1970; Altmann, 1972; Lippert, 1973; Hämmerling and Lippert, 1976), and the raccon dog *Nyctereutes procyonoides* (Seitz, 1955). Less comprehensive but more broadly comparative descriptive studies include those of Heimburger (1959, 1961), Scott (1950, 1967), Kleiman (1966, 1967, 1972), Fox (1969a,b, 1970, 1971), and Eisfeld (1966) on a variety of species.

In the majority of the comparative studies, the form or structure of behavior patterns was used to suggest taxonomic relationships, however, the earliest hypotheses concerning the relationship between social behavior and social structure also developed from these investigations.

A major criticism of captive studies has been that captivity distorts the frequencies of occurrence of behavior patterns to such a degree that few valid hypotheses may be generated. Of course, the degree of distortion will be greater the more unnatural the physical and social environment. This criticism has been less frequently applied to comparisons of fixed action patterns since it appears less likely that the captive condition will distort the form of a behavior, although in captivity animals may show behavior patterns not observed in the wild (Kummer and Kurt, 1965).

The earliest field studies of either single or several species included both original observations and anecdotal accounts or summaries of other work. Examples include those of Young and Goldman (1944) on the wolf, Murie (1940, 1944) on the wolf and coyote *Canis latrans*, Seton (1925) on various North American canids, and van der Merwe (1953) on the black-backed jackal *Canis mesomelas*. Some of these studies, because they were semipopular, often did not distinguish between original research and anecdotal accounts, (e.g., Dobie (1949) on the coyote) thus restricting their use fo later biologist. Such problems exist even more so with books on the fauna of particular geographic regions where life history information on canid species is presented. This has resulted in statements whose origins are obscure and validity are questionable being repeated time and again in the canid literature.

Following such early accounts, two types of field studies emerged. Firstly, ecologists began broad investigations of feeding ecology, reproduction, and population dynamics in single species, often depending for the data on material obtained from trapping or hunting. Examples include Rausch (1967) on wolves, Crespo and De Carlo (1963) on the culpeo *Dusicyon culpaeus*, Macpherson (1969) on arctic foxes, and Gier (1968) on coyotes. Such investigations produced little information on social structure and individual behaviors. As the technique of radiotelemetry became more common, studies of movements, home range, and activity patterns of individuals were initiated, but these also provided limited information on social behavior (e.g., Storm *et al.*, 1976, on red foxes; Mech *et al.*, 1971, on wolves).

Recognition of the limitations of such studies led to the second type of field study in which the social behavior of known individuals was investigated in detail. Observations of coyotes (Ryden, 1974; Camenzind, this volume), golden jackals (Golani and Keller, 1975; van Lawick, 1971), and Cape hunting dogs *Lycaon pictus* (Kühme, 1965; van Lawick, 1971, 1973) were some of the first modern studies to define canid social structure in the wild but, because of the small sample size in each study, these investigations possess the same inherent limitations as the older single species accounts, i.e., they may be anecdotal and generalizations may be made from observations on individuals or groups whose behavior is idiosyncratic. Obviously for each species, this type of study must be replicated in different habitats and be conducted over several annual cycles before a complete picture of social structure emerges. Yet, such studies are essential for an understanding of the evolutionary relationship between social behavior, social structure, and ecology, as has been shown from investigations of other carnivores (e.g., lion *Panthera leo*, Schaller, 1972; spotted hyena *Crocuta crocuta*, Kruuk, 1972).

In general, the dearth of adequate observations of the behavior in the wild of identifiable individuals in the canids, as compared with the primates where numerous studies exist, derives from the secretive nature of many canid species, their primarily nocturnal or crepuscular activity, and their ability to range widely in movements. The return on such studies as measured by the information gained per hour of field work is relatively small. It is encouraging, however, that more biologists are now engaged in long-term studies of canids where the behavior and ecology of small numbers of known individuals are being investigated.

Although our knowledge of canids has increased dramatically during the past 25 years, we are still ignorant of most aspects of species-typical reproductive behavior, parental care, behavioral ontogeny, and social structure, and we have not defined the quantitative differences in behavior. Kleiman and Eisenberg (1973) suggested that ultimately differences in social behavior might become more apparent when actual frequencies of occurrence of different behaviors were compared rather than just the form or presence or absence of a behavior pattern. Quantitative methods for comparing species differences in social behavior are now being used, although not commonly (e.g., see Chapter 5; Bekoff, 1974; Bekoff *et al.*, 1975). Thus, the types of synthesis of social structure, social behavior, and ecology which are possible in primate studies (Eisenberg *et al.*, 1972) should not be extended to canids despite recent attempts (Fox, 1975). The data base simply does not exist. Moreover, there are canid species about which we know little, but which are important because of their presumed phylogeny and/or social structure; for example, the dhole (*Cuon alpinus*), bat-eared fox (*Otocyon megalotis*), and bush dog (*Speothos venaticus*).

Another major problem with canid studies has been the choice of species investigated, both in captivity and the field. The four best-studied canids are the domestic dog (*Canis familiaris*), the wolf, the coyote, and the red fox. The origin of the domestic dog is obscure; it is not known whether it is a domesticated form of the wolf or is descended from a now extinct canid. Regardless, it has been selectively bred by man for thousands of years and now exhibits certain behavioral traits which differ from other species in the genus *Canis*. For example, insofar as we understand the social organization of dogs from studies in urban and nonurban environments, affiliative bonds do exist between certain individuals but long-term pair bonds, paternal care, and the maintenance of a cohesive family group are seen rarely (Beck, 1973; Scott and Causey, 1973; Fox *et al.*, 1975; Nesbitt, 1975). These behavioral traits appear to be among the oldest and most enduring characteristics of the genus *Canis* (Kleiman and Eisenberg, 1973; Kleiman, 1977). Moreover, dogs, in general, are more tolerant of unfamiliar conspecifics than wild *Canis* (King, 1954; Fox *et al.*, 1974; Scott and Causey, 1973). Thus, when social groups exist, they seem to be more loosely organized and to split and coalesce more frequently than wild *Canis*. Bitches usually rear young alone since the mate rarely remains in the female's company. It is not clear whether such social behavior is "phylogenetically old," results from the intense selection to which they have been subjected, or arises from intense persecution by man of feral dogs. In any case, results from studies of domestic dog social behavior should not be compared with related *Canis* species, if the intent of the comparison is to develop broad generalizations concerning the evolution of social behavior and social structure in wild canids.

At least in some areas of research, similar caution should be exercised when comparing wolves, coyotes, and red foxes. Field studies of population structure and density, home range size, social structure, natality, and mortality are all going to be biased severely by human interference and persecution of these species (as with feral domestic dogs). Storm *et al.* (1976) report that a large majority of all red fox deaths each year are due to human activities, e.g., hunting, trapping, and road deaths. The effects of human-induced mortality on the social structure of red fox populations have not been examined, but are likely to be disruptive. For example, Ables (1975) has noted a disproportionate sex ratio in favor of females during the breeding season in adult red foxes that are subjected to hunting or trapping, and questions whether strict monogamy could exist since such populations are highly productive, i.e., most females breed. Both coyotes and wolves are also subjected to similar persecution and in wolves reproductive rates differ depending upon the level of exploitation. Only 60% of adult females breed annually in unexploited wolf populations (Pimlott *et al.*, 1969), while 90% of females may breed where wolves are being persecuted by man (Rausch, 1967). Pimlott *et al.* (1969) suggest that the high percentage of breeding females in Rausch's (1967) study is a compensation for high mortality incurred by man.

In addition to reproduction and sex ratios of adults, the age structure of populations that are persecuted may differ from those that are not (see Mech, 1970), another factor which is likely to affect social structure and therefore behavior. It is possible that our inability to clearly characterize the social structure of both red foxes (Ables, 1975) and coyotes (Gier, 1975) in recent years (when compared with older accounts, e.g., Seton, 1925) and some of the variability in observed social structure are due in part to heavy human exploitation. Clearly, generalizations about social systems and social evolution based on captive observations are unwise unless we have supportive field observations on social structure from canid populations in undisturbed habitats.

II. ECOLOGY

Canid species do not show the extremes of size that are seen in some other carnivore families, and the coyote falls somewhere in the middle to upper range of canids. Species within the same size range as the coyote include the golden jackal, the culpeo, the black-backed jackal, and the Simien jackal *Canis simensis*. The foxes (*Vulpes* sp.) are generally smaller in size than wild dogs and jackals (*Canis* sp.). Some individual species (e.g., the golden jackal) may be highly variable in size (Kleiman and Eisenberg,

1973). Canid species do not show extremes of sexual dimorphism, like some felids or mustelids, although males tend to be slightly larger than females.

A. Habitat Preference

Canids are primarily terrestrial predators and mainly exploit wet and dry savanna and grassland, tundra, and montane, mixed or deciduous forest. They are underrepresented in tropical rain forests when compared with felids (Kleiman and Eisenberg, 1973), probably because they are adapted to hunting in open or semi-open country.

B. Feeding Habits

Both the preferred habitat and the size of the species affect food habits as do seasonal changes in food availability. Canids typically alter their natural diet to exploit foods introduced by humans, especially domestic livestock and poultry. The canid species that take advantage of domestic animals are thought to do considerable damage. Gier (1968), as well as others, has provided estimates of the financial loss apparently caused by coyotes feeding on livestock. Unfortunately since most studies of coyote food habits have been conducted in areas where there is concern about coyote damage, there are few studies of coyote feeding ecology under conditions where man has not interfered. Thus, we do not have a particularly good understanding of coyote feeding ecology even though we do know that the species is opportunistic.

Similar statements may be applied to other canid species. In the study area of Crespo and De Carlo (1963), culpeos relied heavily on meat from livestock; of 96 stomachs examined, 40 had remains from sheep, cattle, or horses. In 201 black-backed jackal stomachs, Grafton (1965) reports that livestock remains were present 17.3% by occurrence and 18.5% by volume. The stomach samples were both from farming areas and nature reserves, thus domestic livestock were not available to all animals.

Of course, where livestock are part of the diet of a canid species, it is difficult to determine the degree to which the canid actually hunts and kills the prey animal. Grafton (1965) concluded that most livestock or antelope remains in black-backed jackal stomachs were carrion obtained by scavenging because of the presence of maggots and fly larvae and because of the jackal's size and hunting habits.

Canid species of coyote size and smaller exist well in areas where human activities, such as farming, predominate, since the smaller species forage individually, can scavenge, eat many small food items, and rapidly exploit new food sources. Humans have not been as concerned with their presence when compared with larger predators, such as the wolf, which hunt socially and are more conspicuous. The smaller species may be persecuted, but they have not been hunted to extinction.

Excluding the eating of carrion from livestock, small to medium-sized canids mainly feed on a variety of small mammals ranging in size from hares to mice as well as on other small vertebrates and vegetable matter, such as fruits and grass. Gipson (1974) reviewed some studies of coyote food habits which indicated that 41.1% of stomachs and scats contained lagomorph remains and 36.2% small rodents and shrews; 15% of the specimens had wild bird, and 6.7% fruits and other vegetable matter. At certain seasons or in certain areas, fruits may play a large role in the diet, e.g., 23% of coyote stomachs in Arkansas contained persimmons. Finally, there was usually a small percentage of reptiles (lizards and snakes) and invertebrates (crayfish, grasshoppers, and beetles) in coyote stomachs and scats. Recent observations by Nellis and Keith (1976) support this basic diet. Major differences between results of numerous studies are in the percent carrion from livestock and percent of lagomorphs in the diet. Both of these food items are a large percent of coyote diet where they are available.

There have been few comparable studies on similarly sized species. The studies of Grafton (1965) on black-backed jackals have already been mentioned and indicate a reliance on animal foods, such as small rodents, lagomorphs, small birds, and insects (excluding carrion and hoofstock). Vegetable food such as wild berries and fruits were found in many stomachs but were of less importance by volumetric analysis.

A recent study by Stuart (1976) on the composition of black-backed jackal scats in the Central Namib Desert indicated clearly the opportunistic nature of jackal feeding habits in that jackal scats in a location where large numbers of birds were present consisted in large part of bird remains, while in another study area plant food was the major item found.

There have been no definitive studies of golden jackal feeding ecology, but observations by Kruuk (1972) and van Lawick (1971) in the Serengeti suggest a mixed diet of small rodents, lagomorphs, insects, snakes, vegetable foods, and the occasional gazelle fawn, usually killed during hunts by at least a pair of jackals. Animals also fed on carrion and placentae during the short synchronized birth season of wildebeest (van Lawick, 1971).

Two South American canids which resemble the coyote in their size and probably their ecology are the crab-eating fox (*Cerdocyon thous*) and the culpeo. Crespo and De Carlo (1963), in their analysis of culpeo feeding habits, indicated a heavy reliance on European hare (*Lepus europaeus*) and small rodents, above and beyond domestic hoofstock. The smaller crab-eating fox has been less studied, but Mondolfi (in Walker, 1968) reports that 19 stomachs contained in order of abundance, field mice, rats, insects, fruits, lizards, frogs, and crabs. Observations by one of us (C. B.) on free-roaming crab-eating foxes on the Venezuelan llanos indicated a reliance on small vertebrates (rodents) and invertebrates. Of 110 predation attempts, 43 resulted in invertebrate captures and 10 in vertebrate captures; the remainder were unsuccessful.

In summary, medium-sized canids, in the absence of domestic hoofstock, tend to feed opportunistically on small mammals ranging from the fawns of small ungulates, to hares and rabbits, to mice-sized rodents. Other vertebrates may be taken if available, such as wild birds, lizards, and snakes. All species feed on fruits, berries, and other vegetation, including grass. Such catholic tastes allow these species to survive in numerous habitats and in close association with man. By and large, such species forage alone, unlike the larger canids, wolf, Cape hunting dog, and dhole, which typically hunt cooperatively in packs.

C. Population Dynamics

There are few available population studies of coyotes from areas where there is no human persecution. Therefore, most existing data on the age structure of coyotes in the wild are probably distorted. Table I presents a summary of the reported age structures of canid species under conditions of varying levels of human persecution. It is clear that in populations which are heavily exploited by man, the proportion of juveniles is high. This suggests that adult females are reproducing at near maximum capability where persecution is common. The effects of human exploitation on wolf population dynamics have already been mentioned and are discussed in more detail by Pimlott *et al.* (1969) and Mech (1970).

From the information in Table I, one would predict that in a stable population of a canid species, juveniles would account for less than 50% of the total animals. This is less than expected if a population were reproducing and young were surviving at maximum capability. High infant mortality may occur in utero or neonatally, if the nutritional condition of the breeding female is poor. Egoscue (1975) documents an annual decrease in litter size of kit foxes, *Vulpes macrotis* (from 5.0 to 2.75), during a 3-year population decline where the main prey species, the black-tailed jack rabbit (*Lepus californicus*) had been declining. Since pups were not trapped at birth, a small litter size could have resulted from fewer ova being shed or mortality occurring at any time prior to the initial trapping. Van Ballenberghe and Mech (1975) suggest for wolves that poor nutrition in juveniles, as indicated by low weights, may be a factor in juvenile mortality.

A low percentage of juveniles could also arise because fewer females

TABLE I

Age Structure of Canid Species in Relation to Human Persecution[a]

Species	Adult weight (kg)	Persecution level	% Juveniles (<12 mo)	% Yearlings (13–24 mo)	% Adults (>25 mo)	No. animals in sample	Remarks	Reference
Canis lupus	27–79	1	13	87		?		Kelsall (1968)
		1	31	17	52	106	60% ♀♀ breed	Pimlott *et al.* (1969)
		4	73	27		136		Kelsall (1968)
		4	45	56		4150	90% ♀♀ breed	Rausch (1967)
Canis latrans	9–12.7	4	68	15	17	548	1:1 sex ratio; 14% yearlings; 94% adult ♀♀ breed	Nellis and Keith (1976)
		1	49.5	50.5		556		Knowlton (1972)
Dusicyon culpaeus	7.35	4	78	13	9	254	59.2% ♂♂	Crespo and De Carlo (1963); Crespo (1975)
Dusicyon gymnocerus	4.4	2	52.8	34.3	12.9	324		Crespo (1975)
Urocyon cinereoargenteus	4.2 ♂	3	58	28	15	780	sex ratio favors ♂♂; 92.3% ♀♀ breed first year	Wood (1958)
Vulpes vulpes	4.5–5.4 ♂ 4.1–4.5 ♀	4	59	24	16	600	56% ♂♂	Lloyd (1975)
		5	82	15	3	786	54% ♂♂, except before breeding season; 95% all ♀♀ breed	Storm *et al.* (1976)
Vulpes macrotis[b]	2.1 ♂ 1.9 ♀	1	47	53		20–52	sex ratio favors ♂♂; 59% adult ♀♀ breed	Egoscue (1975)
Alopex lagopus	2.5–9.0	4	73	16	11	2891	1:1 sex ratio	MacPherson (1969)

[a] Persecution level has been scaled from low (1) to high (5).

[b] Data from foxes trapped over 4 year period during population decline.

breed in a population. During a population decline, Egoscue (1975) for the first time noticed nonbreeding females among the kit foxes in his study area. Other authors, studying apparently stable populations, also report the presence of nonbreeding adult females (e.g., wolf, Pimlott *et al.*, 1969; coyote, Ryden, 1974; Camenzind, Chapter 12; golden jackal and Cape hunting dog, van Lawick, 1971). The tendency for nonreproductive adult females to be present in canid populations seems most pronounced in the genera *Canis* and *Lycaon* (see Section III,A), but probably also occurs in *Cuon*, although there are no confirmatory data.

It is difficult to compare longevity in the wild in canid species because of the problem of aging animals correctly. From Table I, it appears as though in wolves there may be a greater proportion of older animals in the population than in other canid species. This could be predicted since the specialized hunting and feeding habits, pack structure, and large body size of wolves (as well as *Lycaon* and *Cuon*) would tend to make them a *K*-selected species relative to other canids. However, Egoscue (1975) reports ages of 4 to 6 years in his kit fox population, based on retrapping marked adults over several years, which is quite old considering kit fox size. Knowlton (1972) has examined wild coyotes that were up to 13 years old.

The question of sex ratios is interesting and deserves further study. Sex ratios biased heavily in favor of males have been found in the wolf (Kleiman and Eisenberg, 1973; Mech, 1975), Cape hunting dog (Kleiman and Eisenberg, 1973), culpeo (Crespo and De Carlo, 1963; Crespo, 1975), and kit fox (Egoscue, 1975). In the grey fox *Urocyon cinereoargenteus* (Trapp and Hallberg, 1975) and red fox (Lloyd, 1975; Ables, 1975; Storm *et al.*, 1976), sex ratios vary but still tend to favor males. This is true for all age classes, although Ables (1975) suggests that the red fox sex ratio tends to change seasonally due to hunting pressure, with females being favored at the time of breeding.

In the wolf, the sex ratio favors males most strongly in populations declining in numbers in a saturated habitat (Mech, 1975). Egoscue (1975) has shown the same trend for the kit fox. In these cases, the sex ratio is biased at birth, as well as in adults, which suggests a physiological cause for the difference and not just differential trappability or postnatal mortality (both of which may also have an effect).

Mech (1975) has pointed out that the wolf sex ratio does not conform with the predictions made by Trivers and Willard (1973), i.e., a lower ratio of males to females should occur when maternal condition declines. However, the Trivers–Willard hypothesis is based on the assumption that a male will out-reproduce a female under normal conditions. In monogamous mammals like canids, the males and females produce offspring equally and there is considerable parental investment by males and older nonreproductive offspring (Kleiman, 1977). Under these conditions, it would seem more advantageous for females to produce males when they are in poor condition since they will be creating potential helpers who will be less competitive with them for food, denning sites, and other resources in short supply.

D. Home Range Size and Territoriality

Canid home range size depends on several factors including the species' size, social organization, food distribution and abundance, adequate denning sites, and over-all habitat. Food abundance probably has the greatest effect on home range size; where prey density is low, as in the Arctic, home range size increases (Kleiman and Eisenberg, 1973). Species that follow migratory prey may exhibit seasonal changes in home range, e.g., Cape hunting dog. Although calculations of home range size or density are useful, direct comparisons are not since so many factors may influence such calculations.

The degree to which most canids are territorial can only be established by long-term observations of small, known populations. Territoriality can be assumed if animals have a stable limited home range and are aggressive to strangers that are encountered within the home range. Although there are only limited data to confirm or deny territoriality for most species, it is generally believed that canids are territorial, especially within the breeding season. Obviously, at certain seasons and with differing population densities, individuals may not inhabit a stable home range or exhibit territoriality.

III. SOCIAL STRUCTURE

A. The Pair Bond and Family Group

The basis of canid social organization in an evolutionary sense is the pair bond (Eisenberg, 1966; Kleiman, 1977; Kleiman and Eisenberg, 1973), i.e., the most enduring affiliation is between a single heterosexual pair. Variations on the monogamous theme lead to the differences which are observed in group sizes, both between and within species. Species which are observed in groups of 3 to 7 animals may be nuclear family units composed of parents and recent young. Larger group sizes are probably composed of parents and young of successive litters with the occasional presence of one or two siblings of one of the breeding pair. Polygamy may be common in persecuted canid populations, but is occasionally observed in species that are undisturbed (e.g., kit foxes, Egoscue, 1962).

Fox (1975) has divided canid social structure into three types, based on hunting strategy, i.e., whether individuals hunt alone or cooperatively. The red fox is used as an example of a Type I or solitary hunter, the coyote as a Type II or solitary–social hunter (transitional type), and the wolf as a Type III or social hunter (pack type). Fox (1975) then goes on to classify canid social systems in the same manner, thus implying that a species exhibiting a solitary hunting strategy would also exhibit a solitary social organization, except during the breeding season. Although the correlation between hunting strategy and social system may be suitable for understanding the evolution of group size in wolves, dholes, and Cape hunting dogs, it is misleading when broadly applied to other canid species. For example, there are several canids which hunt individualistically, but which probably live in stable pairs year round, e.g., kit foxes (Egoscue, 1962, 1975), swift foxes *Vulpes velox* (Kilgore, 1969), bat-eared foxes (Hendrichs, 1972), and crab-eating foxes (C. Brady, personal observation). For bat-eared foxes, it is likely that small family groups persist throughout the year since Hendrichs (1972) observed them in pairs 35%, but in groups of three to five 42% of the time. In observational field studies, the degree of association of individuals is probably underestimated (especially if individuals hunt alone), since one animal of a pair may be sighted while the second remains undetected. We have certainly found this to be true in our observations of crab-eating fox pairs.

The point is that the stability and persistence of the family need not correlate with hunting strategy. The degree to which the red fox (Fox's example of the Type I canid) is only seasonally bonded to a mate is not really understood due to the extreme persecution suffered by this species (see above); since several other *Vulpes* species are permanently paired, red fox as an example may in fact be a red herring.

A generalized scheme of the annual social cycle of the Canidae will help to illustrate where variations in social organization might occur. Canids are for the most part annual breeders (see Section V,A). If it is assumed that the adult male is necessary to provide for or at least to protect the lactating female and young, the pair will persist for at least 18 to 20 weeks. That is 3 to 5 weeks for courtship and mating, 9 weeks for gestation, and 6 to 8 weeks until the young are weaned. If the male is not necessary as a provider or protector, he will probably leave directly after mating. There appear to be few canids of this type, but the maned wolf might fit into this category. Maned wolf pairs at our facilities have been relatively hostile and incompatible outside of the short mating season. It is likely that in the wild they also forage alone since they depend on small vertebrates and vegetable matter for food (Kleiman, 1972). Thus, the maned wolf may be a solitary hunter that does not form a long-term pair bond characterized by a heterosexual association outside the breeding season. This does not exclude the possibility that animals in overlapping or adjacent territories may mate with each other in successive years or that pair bonds do exist since some zoos successfully maintain pairs together year round.

Canid pups are weaned at six to eight weeks of age, but are still dependent on the parents for food. The length of this period of dependency is where much of the variation in social structure occurs in species that exhibit a prolonged pair association. In the red fox (Storm *et al.*, 1976), the grey fox (Trapp and Hallberg, 1975), the arctic fox (Chesemore, 1975), and the crab-eating fox (C. Brady, unpublished data), the young disperse at 5–8 months. Subadults become disassociated from the adult pair a month or so before dispersing, but remain within the home area while refining their hunting skills on familiar terrain.

The adult pair have two options at the time the young disperse. They may remain together, defending a common home area and mate again during the following season, or they may separate. In the crab-eating fox (unpublished data), the black-backed jackal (van der Merwe, 1953), swift and kit foxes (Kilgore, 1969; Egoscue, 1962), pairs are sighted together throughout the year. Among these pair-bonded forms, there may be seasonal variation in interaction frequencies, but little data are available on this topic. Among more "solitary" forms, periodic interactions may occur outside the breeding season.

In other canid species, some of the young may not disperse and will remain with the parents through the birth of a subsequent litter. In golden jackals, young have been observed in the parents' home range after a birth the following year (van Lawick, 1971). The family had several rendezvous sites near the natal site, but individuals usually hunted alone. Moehlman (1976) has observed nonbreeding black-backed jackals acting as "helpers" at dens who were probably older young or perhaps siblings of the breeding pair, suggesting the maintenance of a family group. The coyote might have a similar social structure since one-year-old females often do not breed (Gier, 1968; Knowlton, 1972). Tagging studies indicate that some young coyotes disperse at about 9 months and may wander extensively (Robinson and Grand, 1958). However, coyote families under stable conditions may remain intact for much longer (Ryden, 1974; Camenzind, Chapter 12).

The wolf, the Cape hunting dog, and the dhole are organized in a pack social structure. The pack is an extended family unit in wolves (Mech, 1970) and the Cape hunting dog (van Lawick, 1971), including the nuclear family and possibly nonreproductive siblings of the adult breeding pair. Little is known about the relationships among members of a dhole pack. Pack size in wolves is regulated by many factors including food availability and social stress which increases as pack size increases beyond eight (Zimen, 1976).

Wolf pups do not usually breed until 22 months and during their first year obtain food from all pack members (Mech, 1970). Both wolves and hunting dogs have separate hierarchies for males and females and aggression is typically sex-specific. Generally, only the dominant female breeds and raises a litter. Zimen (1976) feels that subdominant female wolves rarely breed because of the lack of courtship and pair-bond formation, however, direct aggression towards subdominant females is also seen. Pack members (especially the alpha female) obstruct copulations between subordinate wolves (Rabb *et al.*, 1967). In addition, subordinate wolf females which give birth often neglect their litters in favor of those of the dominant pair (Altmann, 1974) or, as in hunting dogs, cannot rear their young because pack members will only feed the dominant female and her cubs (van Lawick, 1973). Observations on hunting dogs even include a case where an alpha female killed most of the offspring of a subordinate female (van Lawick, 1973).

This form of social structure is not in its essence much more complex than that described for the golden jackal (van Lawick, 1971) or coyote (Ryden, 1974), except that the group size is larger and siblings of the adult pair may be incorporated into the family group.

B. Dispersal Mechanisms and Puberty

The age and mechanisms of dispersal have an important effect on the social systems observed in the various canid species. Bekoff (1977) has proposed that intralitter differences in behavior that develop during early ontogeny may determine which pups of a litter disperse first, and suggested, based on observations of a mother-reared coyote litter, that the pups which interacted with littermates the least would be the first to disperse since they formed weaker social bonds with other littermates. In his study, the noninteractive individuals were the most dominant or most subordinate individuals of the litter. Fox (1972) observed a wide range of behavioral temperaments in wolf litters (based mainly on reactions to a variety of non-social stimuli), and felt that this variability enabled the pups to later integrate into the pack. Fox (1972, 1975) contrasted the above with observations on nonpack canids, such as the red fox and coyote, which may have a narrower range of intralitter temperaments (see Bekoff, 1977). Both Fox and Bekoff's hypotheses are interesting, but need testing, especially by obtaining data on the range of intralitter behavioral differences in a variety of species, especially social behavior.

Dispersal often corresponds with the onset of sexual maturity in canids. Storm *et al.* (1976) found that young red fox males disperse before females; they suggested that the difference might be due to the fact that males reach sexual maturity earlier than females. At our facility, members of a litter of crab-eating foxes avoided each other between 3 and 5 months of age when suddenly one male attacked and severely wounded his brother. The attacks corresponded to the onset of leg-lift urinations, and probable sexual maturity in the males. However, the father was not present and in a subsequent litter where the father was left with the litter, attacks were not seen at this time.

Storm *et al.* (1976) and Bekoff (1977) also found that red fox and coyote juveniles tended to avoid both the parents and littermates before the age of normal dispersal. This suggests that dispersal may not be initiated because of aggressive interactions with parents. By contrast, in wolves and hunting dogs, where an alpha pair may have siblings as well as young present in the group, the alpha pair (and especially the alpha female) are aggressive and may be responsible for the dispersal of individuals over 2 years old (Zimen, 1976; van Lawick, 1973). Recent observations by Frame and Frame (1976) suggest that in Cape hunting dogs, mainly the females disperse. Thus, the core of a hunting dog pack may be a group of related males. There are insufficient data to indicate whether wolves exhibit the same trait although Zimen (1976) does suggest that females are more likely to be driven out of a wolf pack than males.

C. Flexibility in Social Structure

A species' social structure is an abstract concept. Short-term field observations of canid species in a single habitat provide only a partial picture of social structure since local populations never achieve stability or homeostasis; the environment is in a state of flux and animals are being born, reach sexual maturity, disperse, reproduce, and die. With such changes occurring continuously, individuals and groups are always altering their spatial and social relationships.

Observed deviations from the abstract norm of social structure may be greater in species like the wolf and hunting dog where the social group is composed of animals of several age classes and both sexes. But even in species like the kit fox, where the annual cycle in social relationships is apparently more rigid in that all young do disperse at 5 to 8 months of age, the over-all picture of social structure may vary. Under conditions of a decreasing food supply and population decline, Egoscue (1975) noted the sudden presence of nonbreeding adult females in a population after 14 years of research. Previously every adult female had bred. Our knowledge of coyote social structure is limited because of the great variation in group size observed by different authors at different times.

For an accurate definition of modal social organization and the range of variation, the following questions must be answered for each canid species in different habitats: (1) What is the major food supply and how is it distributed in space? (2) What is the distribution and density of other limiting resources, such as denning sites? (3) What is the population density and age structure and is the population increasing, decreasing, or stable? (4) What other competitors coexist in the same habitat and what is their influence? (5) What kinds of human-induced disturbances are present and what are their effects?

IV. SOCIAL BEHAVIOR

A. Interactions between Pairs

Since the basis of canid social structure is the pair bond, variation in species typical group size and organization results in differences in three characteristics: variation in (1) pair-bond strength, (2) distribution of parental care activities, and (3) age and mechanism of dispersal of juveniles. Since species typical social behavior is likely to reflect the species typical modal social structure, comparisons between canid species should emphasize differences in the behavior repertoire and frequency distribution of behaviors within the above three characteristics. Thus, comparative studies of social behavior should concentrate on the formation and maintenance of the pair bond, parental care, and ontogeny. Pair-bond strength can be measured not only by the relative frequencies of aggressive and affiliative behaviors in heterosexual pairs, but also by the distribution of behaviors associated with territorial maintenance and the level of sex-specific aggression (see Kleiman, 1977).

Comparisons of canid behavioral patterns alone have yielded insufficient information to characterize canid social structures with any degree of precision (Kleiman, 1967, 1972; Fox, 1971), although they have suggested phylogenetic relationships. Except for Bekoff's studies (Chapter 5; Bekoff *et al.*, 1975) of ontogeny and play, quantitative comparisons are unavailable although such comparisons are essential for a real understanding of species differences.

We are currently attempting to undertake such comparisons with three species of South American canids, the crab-eating fox, the bush dog, and the maned wolf. Comparative behavioral data have been collected on the interactions of heterosexual pairs with respect to the length of pair association and season. Since the crab-eating fox may be closest to the coyote in terms of ecology and social structure, the data in Table II may provide an example of the type of information on pair-bond behavior which could be collected for comparative purposes.

TABLE II
Hourly Frequency of Social Interactions in *Cerdocyon thous* Pairs as a Function of Pair-Bond Duration

	Pair A			Average	Pair B
Time since pairing	1–14 days	15–29 days	30–45 days		1 year
Number of observation hours	5	5	5		15
Aggressive interactions	8.4	2.8	1.8	4.3	0.2
Attempts to stand on	7.0	0.6	1.4	3.0	0
Nonaggressive interactions	10.4	10.4	5.4	8.7	3.9
Sniffing and licking					
Face	1.8	2.8	6.6	3.7	2.9
Body	0	0.8	2.2	1.0	0.4
Anogenital region	2.6	2.8	1.6	2.3	1.9
Sequence urinations					
Completed	3.0	3.8	5.2	4.0	3.3
Incompleted	6.0	1.0	1.6	2.9	0.5
Ratio	0.33	0.79	0.76	0.58	0.87

Unfamiliar male and female crab-eating foxes were paired and their interactions recorded during 1-hour observation periods while they cohabited. Table II contains data from two pairs during a single 45-day period. In the newly formed Pair A, the shift from aggressive to affiliative behaviors as the pair bond forms is evident while the long-established Pair B exhibits generally low interaction frequencies. Early interactions of a newly formed pair are intense and characterized by aggressive acts including attacks with biting, many of which result from resistance to attempts to stand on the partner's back or sniff the anogenital region. Little facial sniffing and licking is seen, but such affiliative behaviors increase as aggression decreases.

Pair-bond duration and strength may also be measured by urination patterns. Established pairs of crab-eating foxes tend to urinate in sequence at the same site; the sequence may be initiated by male or female. During pair-bond formation, such sequences are infrequent (see Table II). Although an individual may sniff the urine mark of a partner, the site is less frequently covered than after the pair bond is established. Golani and Keller (1975) made similar observations on free-ranging golden jackal pairs, as did van Lawick (1971) on hunting dogs, and we have observed this in a range of canid species in captivity, including bush dogs, raccoon dogs, coyotes, and maned wolves.

Once the pair bond is established, crab-eating fox pairs exhibit little aggression towards one another and have decreased numbers of interactions. This trend has been noted for other monogamous mammals (Kleiman, 1977). At the same time, the duration of certain behavior patterns increases. For example, mutual grooming of cheeks, muzzle, and ears increases dramatically. Pairs exchange grooming roles frequently, and the recipient will sit still, raising its muzzle or turning its head as the mate licks and nibbles its face. Mutual facial grooming has also been described for pairs of golden jackals, raccoon dogs, and bat-eared foxes (Kleiman, 1967; van Lawick, 1971), but its role and frequency in other pair-bonded canids is not clear.

At the approach of estrus in crab-eating foxes, interactions more common to pair formation reappear. Both partners attempt to stand on the other's back and the female rejects anogenital sniffing attempts by moving in tight circles and biting the male's muzzle. The courtship behavior of golden jackals and coyotes contains similar behavior elements (see Section V,A).

The captive observations of pair-bond behavior in crab-eating foxes have been confirmed by field observations in Venezuela in llanos habitat. Crab-eating fox pairs associate with each other all year round. Each day at dusk, the foxes begin to move through the home range, and pairs are usually separated by less than 10 m even when foraging individually. Either the male or female may lead. Should one partner fall behind, e.g., after locating a food item, the other typically will halt and wait. As the pair slowly progresses through the home range, one partner will urinate on prominent clumps of grass and the pair mate will cover the site with its own urine as it passes. Table III presents observations on urination behavior in three free-

TABLE III

Distribution of Urination Frequencies in Three Free-Ranging Crab-Eating Fox Pairs in the Venezuelan llanos

	Pair I		Pair II		Pair III	
	♂	♀	♂	♀	♂	♀
Initiates sequence urination	20	9	11	12	22	21
Complites sequence urination	2	11	9	8	20	10
% Completed sequence urinations	22%	55%	75%	73%	95%	45%
Urinates while trailing partner	12	4	4	2	20	16
Urinates while alone	18	6	25	8	32	6
Total urination	52	30	49	30	94	53

ranging crab-eating fox pairs. Nearly 70% of all observed urinations were seen while pairs were traveling together. Males urinated more than females, but there was little sexual difference in the initiation of sequence urinations. Males tended to cover female urine more often than the reverse and to urinate while alone more often than females. The rate of successful completion of sequence urinations was probably underestimated since a failure was scored if a partner did not respond to a urine mark when passing within 10 m of it. It is not known whether crab-eating foxes can easily detect urine odor at that distance.

Members of pairs regularly come together while progressing through the home range and lick and sniff the facial region or sit together like established captive pairs. The majority of contacts are affiliative. In an observed trio of two adults and a juvenile, the adults' behavior towards the subadult comprised more aggressive patterns, such as biting, standing on the back, or standing-over, even though frequent affiliative interactions were also observed. The subadult's age was estimated to be about 5 months.

B. Communication Mechanisms

Lehner (Chapter 6) has summarized the available information on coyote communication, and numerous other publications have compared the behavioral repertoires of canid species. Although there appear to be some striking differences in behavioral repertoires, the phylogenesis of these differences is unknown. Kleiman (1967) first proposed that the communication systems of more social species were more complex. This hypothesis has yet to be proven and now appears to be an oversimplification. The vocal, olfactory, tactile, and visual signals of the coyote are at least as complex as those of the wolf, despite clear-cut differences in group size and coordinated hunting behavior. This may be because most canid species are social, at least insofar as heterosexual bonding is the norm.

Since differences in the form or structure of visual and tactile signals may be phylogenetic in origin, species comparisons between broader categories of behavior are essential, as stated above. This is especially important since visual and tactile communication always involves at least two interacting animals. Thus, distances between pairs in different contexts and seasons must be examined. The frequencies of agonistic behavior between heterosexual pairs, such as opened mouth gapes, ears laid back, growls, lunges, biting, and withdrawal, must be measured as Bekoff (Chapter 5) has done for young animals. The relative frequency of ritualized versus nonritualized agonistic behavior must be compared for different species. Affiliative behaviors involving tactile contact, such as allogrooming and resting in contact, should also be examined. Similar data must be collected for same-sexed pairs to determine the degree of cohesion or aggression between adults of the same sex. In each case the species comparisons must be made taking into account that social interactions may vary with season, and that such seasonal changes may be the basis of species differences.

In the case of olfactory and vocal communication, both of which may occur in the presence or absence of a conspecific, slightly different comparisons should be made. Do the rates of urine-marking in both sexes differ among species? Are there differences in the rate of sequential urination in heterosexual pairs of different species? Do the vocal repertoires differ with respect to call structure, and also is there a differential emphasis on close-contact affiliative calls (e.g., whimpers), aggressive calls (e.g., growls) and long-distance calls (e.g., howls)? Such information is more relevant to species comparisons than signal structure.

V. REPRODUCTION

A. Reproductive Cycle and Mating

Most temperate-zone canids like coyotes are monoestrus (except the domestic dog) and bear only a single litter annually during a short season (Kleiman, 1968; Ewer, 1973). Although it had been assumed that even tropical species were strictly monoestrus, apparently this is not the case (see Ewer, 1973). The bush dog may have two breeding seasons each year (Kleiman, 1972; Jantschke, 1973), and we have recorded births in the spring and late summer in crab-eating foxes (Kleiman and Brady, unpublished data). One *Cerdocyon* female bore and reared two litters within a year. Some tropical canid species may also have a prolonged breeding season, although only producing young annually, e.g., the Cape hunting dog (Ewer, 1973). Thus, the reproductive cycle of canids is more flexible than had been assumed.

Within the genus *Canis* the onset of reproductive activity is characterized by the discharge of a blood-tinged fluid from the vagina, beginning 2–3 weeks before estrus or receptivity (Kleiman, 1968; Mech, 1970). Kennelly and Johns (1976) report that the bloody fluid was present in captive coyotes 2–3 months before full estrus, but these data are based on vaginal smears from captive coyotes, while other observations have depended on blood being visible around the vulva. To date, the discharge has not been reported from other genera; it has been observed in the black-backed jackal (van der Merwe, 1953), but not in the other three jackal species (*C. aureus, C. adustus*, and *C. simensis*).

Before the onset of full receptivity, coyote pairs, like most canids, increase interaction frequencies including both aggressive and affiliative behaviors. Some descriptions of these changes can be found in Ewer (1973), Kleiman (1968), Golani and Mendelssohn (1971), Golani and Keller (1975), Bekoff and Diamond (1976), Tembrock (1957b), and Mech (1970). In addition to increased interaction frequencies, the members of a pair exhibit more frequent urine marking, especially in alternation.

Female canids are not passive during precopulatory interactions, but may actively solicit male mounting by sniffing and licking the male's genitalia, mounting the male, and presenting the anogenital region to him with the tail twisted to one side (Kleiman, 1968). Wandrey (1975) describes a female golden jackal urinating over a male when receptive. The factors influencing the degree of female solicitation behavior have not been investigated in canids.

The receptive posture of the female includes standing immobile with the tail twisted to one side at its base. Bush dogs (Kleiman, 1972) and perhaps dholes (Davidar, 1974) may lie in a prone position with the hindquarters partly raised and the base of the tail averted.

The copulatory tie or lock of canids is a phylogenetically old trait within the family, having been described for every species in which copulations have been observed. A tie is rare among mammals and its origin and function are unknown (Dewsbury, 1972). Table IV presents data on the length of the copulatory tie in canids. There is considerable variability both within

TABLE IV

Length of the Copulatory Tie (in minutes) in Canid Species

Species	Time	Source
Canis familiaris	14.3 (n = 18)	Hart (1967)
Canis lupus	15 to 36	Mech (1970)
Canis aureus	4.5; 4.4	Golani and Keller (1975)
Canis latrans	18 (n = 4)	Bekoff and Diamond (1976)
	5 to 15	Kleiman (1968)
Vulpes vulpes	20–35	Tembrock (1957b)
Alopex lagopus	8	Kleiman (1968)
Nyctereutes procyonoides	10	Kleiman (1968)
Cerdocyon thous	8.2; 6	Brady (unpublished)
Chrysocyon brachyurus	12	Da Silveira (1968)
	9.0 (n = 6)	Lippert (1973)
Speothos venaticus	10, 15	Kleiman (1968)
	2.7	Brady (unpublished)
Lycaon pictus	1–5	van Lawick (1971)
Cuon alpinus	15–20	Sosnovskii (1967)
	7	Davidar (1974)

and among species. Cade (1967) reported that the Cape hunting dogs he observed did not tie.

During a lock, the pair typically assumes a back-to-back position. Species in which this has not been observed include the bush dog (Kleiman, 1972; Kitchener, 1971), dhole (Davidar, 1974), and raccoon dog (Kleiman, 1968). Lippert (1973) presents photographs indicating that maned wolves lie recumbent or stand back-to-back while tied.

B. Parental Care

The litter size in canids averages 2 to 7 pups although litters as large as 16 have been reported for Cape hunting dogs (Ewer, 1973). Litter sizes in canids are the largest among the carnivores, except for some genera in the Mustelidae (Ewer, 1973). Since most canids are also monoestrus, a terrific reproductive burden is imposed upon a single female. It seems clear that the evolution of monogamy and paternal care in canids is directly attributable to the large single litter that must be reared each year (Kleiman, 1977). The maned wolf which may not pair bond has the smallest litter size of any canid (Ewer, 1973).

Responsibility for digging or choosing a burrow prepartum mainly rests with the female, and the initiation of this behavior may occur at any time from estrus to parturition in coyotes and other canids (Bekoff and Diamond, 1976; van Lawick, 1971). After the birth, the major burrow is used for several weeks, but young are typically moved to a second or third burrow at some point; in coyotes, disturbance of the female may cause the move to be made prematurely (Ryden, 1974; Gier, 1975), a trait probably shared by most canids.

The role of the canid female in the rearing of young is reasonably clear. She must nurse the young until they are capable of feeding on more solid food. In canids, young are slowly weaned, first by being fed partially digested food which the parents regurgitate, and then by having small intact prey brought to them. The role of the male in parental care has been disputed, yet it is predicted that paternal care will be well developed in monogamous mammals (Kleiman, 1977). Paternal care, involving aggression towards intruders near the den area, feeding the young by regurgitating or carrying small prey to the den, and interacting socially with young, has been described for the following genera in captivity or the wild: *Canis* (Mech, 1970; van Lawick, 1971; Wandrey, 1975; Ryden, 1974; Moehlman, 1976), *Vulpes* (Tembrock, 1957b), *Alopex* (Macpherson, 1969), *Fennecus* (Gauthier-Pilters, 1962; Koenig, 1970), *Nyctereutes* (Novikov, 1956), *Otocyon* (Wemmer, personal communication), *Lycaon* (Kühme, 1965; van Lawick, 1971), *Cuon* (Davidar, 1975), and *Cerdocyon* (C. Brady, personal observation). Since these descriptions vary in accuracy and quality, a major effort to define the distribution and elements of canid paternal care is needed.

The involvement of older juveniles from previous litters in rearing young has mainly been described for the genera *Canis* and *Lycaon* (van Lawick, 1971; Mech, 1970; Ryden, 1974; Moehlman, 1976). It probably occurs in *Cuon* as well and possibly *Otocyon*. Further investigation of this characteristic, which is usually associated with delayed puberty and dispersal of only some or no young in the previous year's litter (Kleiman, 1977) is required.

Data are also needed on the frequency with which same-sexed kin maintain relationships after dispersal and/or reproductive maturity. It may well be that the essential difference between the pack hunting canids and those species living in nuclear family groups is the persistence of a same-sexed kin group, such that the alpha male or female are helped by their own brothers or sisters in rearing offspring, at least through one or two litters. The observations of Frame and Frame (1976), indicating that hunting dog sisters migrate from their natal pack and join unrelated groups of males who are themselves kin, supports this notion.

VI. SUMMARY AND CONCLUSIONS

In this paper, previous and current canid research is reviewed, and the effects of biases in approach are discussed with reference to the interpretation of results. It is apparent that we are still ignorant of many aspects of canid social biology and that more observational field and captive studies are necessary before a synthesis of canid social evolution can be attempted.

Since the coyote is of economic importance, funds should be available to launch a series of studies that would encompass all aspects of coyote ecology and behavior. With an organized research program, coyote studies could provide a model for investigations of other canids. Such a cooperative venture would seem to be possible at the moment because of interest in coyote control programs.

ACKNOWLEDGMENTS

Our studies of South American canids have been supported by the Smithsonian Research Foundation. Observations in Venezuela were conducted on the ranch of Sr. Tomas Blohm, Hato Masaguaral, to whom we are grateful. We are grateful to J. F. Eisenberg for his support and critical reading of the manuscript.

REFERENCES

Ables, E. D. (1975). *In* "The Wild Canids" (M. W. Fox, ed.), pp. 216–236. Van Nostrand Reinhold-New York.
Altmann, D. (1972). *Zool. Gart.* **41,** 278–298.
Altmann, D. (1974). *Zool. Gart.* **44,** 235–236.
Beck, A. M. (1973). "The Ecology of Stray Dogs." York Press, Baltimore, Maryland.
Bekoff, M. (1974). *Am. Zool.* **14,** 323–340.
Bekoff, M. (1977). *Am. Nat.* **111,** 715–732.
Bekoff, M., and Diamond, J. (1976). *J. Mammal.* **57,** 372–375.
Bekoff, M., Hill, H. L., and Mitton, J. B. (1975). *Science* **190,** 1223–1225.
Cade, C. E. (1967). *Int. Zoo Yearb.* **7,** 122–123.
Chesemore, D. L. (1975). *In* "The Wild Canids" (M. W. Fox, ed.), pp. 143–163. Van Nostrand-Reinhold, New York.
Crespo, J. A. (1975). *In* "The Wild Canids" (M. W. Fox, ed.), pp. 179–191. Van Nostrand-Reinhold, New York.
Crespo, J. A., and De Carlo, J. M. (1963). *Rev. Mus. Argent. Cienc. Nat. "Bernardino Rivadavia"* **1,** 1–55.
Da Silveira, E. K. P. (1968). *Int. Zoo Yearb.* **8,** 21–23.
Davidar, E. R. C. (1974). *J. Bombay Nat. Hist. Soc.* **70**(2), 373–374.
Davidar, E. R. C. (1975). *J. Bombay Nat. Hist. Soc.* **71,** 183–187.
Dewsbury, D. A. (1972). *Q. Rev. Biol.* **47,** 1–33.
Dobie, J. F. (1949). "The Voice of the Coyote." Bison Book, University Nebraska Press, Lincoln.
Egoscue, H. J. (1962). *Ecology* **43,** 481–497.
Egoscue, H. J. (1975). *Bull. South. Calif. Acad. Sci.* **74**(3), 122–127.
Eisenberg, J. F. (1966). *Handb. Zool.* **VIII** 10(7), 1–92.
Eisenberg, J. F., Muckenhirn, N. A., and Rudran, R. (1972). *Science* **176,** 863–874.
Eisfeld, D. (1966). *Z. Wiss. Zool. Abt. A* **174,** 226–289.
Encke, W., Gandras, R., and Bieniek, H.-J. (1970). *Zool. Gart.* **38,** 47–67.
Ewer, R. F. (1973). "The Carnivores." Cornell, Univ. Press, Ithaca, New York.
Fox, M. W. (1969a). *Behaviour* **35,** 242–258.
Fox, M. W. (1969b). *Behaviour* **35,** 259–272.
Fox, M. W. (1970). *Behaviour* **36,** 49–73.
Fox, M. W. (1971). "Behaviour of Wolves, Dogs and Related Canids." Cape, London.
Fox, M. W. (1972). *Behaviour* **41,** 298–313.
Fox, M. W. (1975). *In* "The Wild Canids" (M. W. Fox, ed.), pp. 429–460. Van Nostrand-Reinhold, New York.
Fox, M. W., Lockwood, R., and Shideler, R. (1974). *Z. Tierpsychol.* **35,** 39–48.
Fox, M. W., Beck, A. M., and Blackman, E. (1975). *Appl. Anim. Ethol.* **1,** 119–138.
Frame, L. H., and Frame, G. W. (1976). *Nature* (*London*) **263,** 227–229.
Gauthier-Pilters, H. (1962). *Z. Tierpsychol.* **19,** 440–464.
Gier, H. T. (1968). "Coyotes in Kansas." Agric. Exp. Stn., Kans. State Coll. Agric. Appl. Sci., Manhattan.
Gier, H. T. (1975). *In* "The Wild Canids" (M. W. Fox, ed.), pp. 247–262. Van Nostrand-Reinhold, New York.
Gipson, P. S. (1974). *J. Wildl. Manage.* **38**(4), 848–853.
Golani, I. (1966). *Isr. J. Zool.* **15,** 27–32.
Golani, I. (1973). *Behaviour* **44,** 89–112.

Golani, I., and Keller, A. (1975). *In* "The Wild Canids" (M. W. Fox, ed.), pp. 303–335. Van Nostrand-Reinhold, New York.
Golani, I., and Mendelssohn, H. (1971). *Behaviour* **38,** 169–192.
Grafton, R. N. (1965). *Zool. Afr.* **1**(1), 41–53.
Hämmerling, F., and Lippert, W. (1975). *Zool. Gart.* **45,** 393–415.
Hart, B. L. (1967). *J. Comp. Physiol. Psychol.* **64,** 388–399.
Heimburger, N. (1959). *Z. Tierpsychol.* **16,** 104–113.
Heimburger, N. (1961). *Z. Tierpsychol.* **18,** 265–284.
Hendrichs, H. (1972). *Z. Tierpsychol.* **30,** 146–189.
Jantschke, F. (1973). *Int. Zoo Yearb.* **13,** 141–143.
Kelsall, J. P. (1968). "The Migratory Barren Ground Caribou of Canada." Can. Wildl. Serv., Ottawa.
Kennelly, J. J., and Johns, B. E. (1976). *J. Wildl. Manage.* **40,** 272–277.
Kilgore, D. L. (1969). *Am. Midl. Nat.* **81,** 512–534.
King, J. A. (1954). *Proc. Am. Philos. Soc.* **98,** 327–336.
Kitchener, S. (1971). *Int. Zoo Yearb.* **11,** 99–101.
Kleiman, D. G. (1966). *Symp. Zool. Soc. London* **18,** 167–177.
Kleiman, D. G. (1967). *Am. Zool.* **7,** 365–372.
Kleiman, D. G. (1968). *Int. Zoo Yearb.* **8,** 3–8.
Kleiman, D. G. (1972). *J. Mammal.* **53,** 791–806.
Kleiman, D. G. (1977). *Q. Rev. Biol.* **52,** 39–69.
Kleiman, D. G., and Eisenberg, J. F. (1973). *Anim. Behav.* **21,** 637–659.
Knowlton, F. F. (1972). *J. Wildl. Manage.* **36,** 369–382.
Koenig, L. (1970). *Z. Tierpsychol.* **27,** 205–246.
Kruuk, H. (1972). "The Spotted Hyena." Univ. of Chicago Press, Chicago, Illinois.
Kühme, W. (1965). *Z. Tierpsychol.* **22,** 495–541.
Kummer, H., and Kurt, F. (1965). *In* "The Baboon in Medical Research" (H. Vagtborg, ed.), pp. 65–80. Univ. of Texas Press, Austin.
Lippert, W. (1973). *Zool. Gart.* **43,** 225–247.
Lloyd, H. G. (1975). *In* "The Wild Canids" (M. W. Fox, ed.), pp. 207–215. Van Nostrand-Reinhold, New York.
Macpherson, A. H. (1969). "The Dynamics of Canadian Arctic Fox Populations," Rep. Ser. No. 8. Can. Wildl. Serv., Ottawa.
Mech, L. D. (1970). "The Wolf: The Ecology and Behavior of an Endangered Species." Nat. Hist. Press, Garden City, New York.
Mech, L. D. (1975). *J. Wildl. Manage.* **39,** 737–740.
Mech, L. D., Frenzel, L. D., Ream, R. R., and Winship, J. W. (1971). *In* "Ecological Studies of the Timber Wolf in Northeastern Minnesota" (L. D. Mech and L. D. Frenzel, Jr., eds.), Res. Rep. NC-52, pp. 1–34. U.S. For. Serv., St. Paul, Minnesota.
Moehlman, P. D. (1976). *Annu. Meet. Anim. Behav. Soc., Boulder, Colorado.*
Murie, A. (1940). "The Ecology of the Coyote in the Yellowstone," Fauna Ser. No. 4. U.S. Natl. Park Serv., Washington, D.C.
Murie, A. (1944). "The Wolves of Mount McKinley," Fauna Ser. No. 5. U.S. Natl. Park Serv., Washington, D.C.
Nellis, C. H., and Keith, L. B. (1976). *J. Wildl. Manage.* **40**(3), 389–399.
Nesbitt, W. H. (1975). *In* "The Wild Canids" (M. W. Fox, ed.), pp. 391–395. Van Nostrand-Reinhold, New York.
Novikov, G. A. (1956). "Fauna of the U.S.S.R., Carnivorous Mammals," No. 62. Zool. Inst. Acad. Sci. USSR. [Isr. Program Sci. Transl., Jerusalem, 1962.]

Pimlott, D. H., Shannon, J. A., and Kolenosky, G. B. (1969). "The Ecology of the Timber Wolf in Algonquin Provincial Park," Res. Rep. (Wildl.) No. 87. Ont. Dep. Lands For., Toronto.

Rabb, G. B., Woolpy, J. H., and Ginsburg, B. E. (1967). *Am. Zool.* **7,** 305–312.

Rausch, R. A. (1967). *Am. Zool.***7,** 253–266.

Robinson, W. B., and Grand, E. F. (1958). *J. Wildl. Manage.* **22,** 117–122.

Ryden, H. (1974). *Natl. Geogr.* **146**(2), 278–294.

Schaller, G. B. (1972). "The Serengeti Lion." Univ. of Chicago Press, Chicago, Illinois.

Schenkel, R. (1947). *Behaviour* **1,** 81–129.

Schenkel, R. (1967). *Am. Zool.* **7,** 319–330.

Scott, J. P. (1950). *Ann. N.Y. Acad. Sci.* **51,** 1009–1021.

Scott, J. P. (1967). *Am. Zool.* **7,** 373–381.

Scott, M. D., and Causey, K. (1973). *J. Wildl. Manage.* **37,** 253–265.

Seitz, A. (1955). *Z. Tierpsychol.* **12,** 463–489.

Seitz, A. (1959). *Z. Tierpsychol.* **16,** 747–771.

Seton, E. T. (1925). "Lives of Game Animals." Charles T. Branford Co., Boston, Massachusetts. [Reissue: 1953.]

Sosnovskii, I. P. (1967). *Int. Zoo Yearb.* **7,** 120–122.

Storm, G. L., Andrews, R. D., Phillips, R. L., Bishop, R. A., Siniff, D. G., and Tester, J. R. (1976). *Wildl. Monogr.* **49,** 1–82.

Stuart, G. T. (1976). *Zool. Afr.* **11**(1), 193–205.

Tembrock, G. (1957a). *Zool. Gart.* **23,** 289–532.

Tembrock, G. (1957b). *Handb. Zool.* **10**(15), 1–20.

Tembrock, G. (1958). *Zool. Beitr.* **3,** 423–496.

Tembrock, G. (1959). *Z. Tierpsychol.* **16,** 351–368.

Tembrock, G. (1960). *Z. Säeugetierkd.* **25,** 1–14.

Tembrock, G. (1962a). *Z. Tierpsychol.* **19,** 577–585.

Tembrock, G. (1962b). *Behaviour* **19,** 261–282.

Trapp, G., and Hallberg, D. L. (1975). *In* "The Wild Canids" (M. W. Fox, ed.), pp. 164–178. Van Nostrand-Reinhold, New York.

Trivers, R. L., and Willard, D. E. (1973). *Science* **179,** 90–92.

Van Ballenberghe, V., and Mech, L. D. (1975). *J. Mammal.* **56,** 44–63.

van der Merwe, N. J. (1953). *Fauna Flora* **4,** 1–83.

van Lawick, H. (1971). *In* "Innocent Killers" (H. van Lawick and J. van Lawick-Goodall), pp. 49–148. Houghton, Boston, Massachusetts.

van Lawick, H. (1973). "Solo." Houghton, Boston, Massachusetts.

Walker, E. P. (1968). "Mammals of the World." Johns Hopkins Press, Baltimore, Maryland.

Wandrey, R. (1975). *Z. Tierpsychol.* **39,** 365–402.

Wood, J. E. (1958). *J. Mammal.* **39,** 74–86.

Young, S. P., and Goldman, E. A. (1944). "The Wolves of North America." Dover, New York.

Zimen, E. (1971). "Wölfe und Königspudel." R. Piper, Munich.

Zimen, E. (1975). *In* "The Wild Canids" (M. W. Fox, ed.), pp. 336–362. Van Nostrand-Reinhold, New York.

Zimen, E. (1976). *Z. Tierpsychol.* **40,** 300–341.

Section III

ECOLOGY AND SYSTEMATICS

8

Coyotes and Related *Canis* in the Southeastern United States with A Comment on Mexican and Central American *Canis*

P. S. Gipson

I. Introduction

Southeastern North America has been inhabited by a unique complex of *Canis* species during the past 10,000 years. Coyotes (*C. latrans*) and dogs (*C. familiaris*) and at least three species of wolves, dire wolves (*C. dirus*), gray wolves (*C. lupus*), and red wolves (*C. rufus*), have been present, at times simultaneously. The presence of so many closely related and potentially interbreeding canids is unparalled in the world. This raises questions about the fate of dire wolves, interactions among red wolves, gray wolves, and coyotes, the role of the Indian dog, and the effects of modern man and his dogs, both feral and domestic, on canids of the region. This paper treats these questions and other topics relating to *Canis* in the Southeast. The status of canids south of the United States is also discussed.

The southeastern region of North America is considered as a zoogeographic unit that approximates the Texan, Carolinian, and Louisianian mammal provinces defined by Hagmeir (1966). This region approximates the former range of the red wolf (Paradiso and Nowak, 1972).

II. STATUS AND SYSTEMATICS

A. Early History

The post-Pleistocene history of *Canis* in southeastern North America is difficult to trace because of a shortage of fossil material and because of disagreement regarding identification and relationships of fossil *Canis*. Hay (1923, 1924) reviewed the early literature and theories about Pleistocene mammals including *Canis* in central and eastern North America. The pre-1925 literature contains a confusing group of proposed *Canis* species. Matthew (1930), Young and Goldman (1944), and Young and Jackson (1951) helped clarify evolution and systematics of the genus. In 1973, Nowak examined nearly 500 specimens and reviewed paleontological history of the genus. Nowak (1973) concluded the genus *Canis* evolved by the middle Pliocene, and that the wolf line has been distinct at least since the early Pleistocene. Nowak recognized five species of North American wolves: *C. rufus, C. edwardii, C. armbusteri, C. lupus,* and *C. dirus*. He considered *C. ayersi* to be a synonym of *C. dirus* and *C. milleri* a synonym of *C. lupus furlongi*. The following year Webb (1974 pp. 71–77) reviewed the systematics of Pleistocene *Canis* and concluded that there were only two wolves *C. dirus* and *C. lupus,* common in Middle and Late Pleistocene deposits in North America. Webb (1974, pp. 77, 126) noted that the red wolf *C. rufus* was also present during the Pleistocene. Kurten (1974) surveyed coyotelike canids and concluded that living coyotes were derived from *C. lepophagus,* a Blancan species in North America. He noted that *C. priscolatrans* may have bridged from early *C. lepophagus* to living coyotes. Nowak (Chapter 1) treats the early history of the family Canidae.

The absence of *Canis* museum specimens collected from eastern states during historic times is another problem in tracing changes that have occurred. Wolves were extripated from most eastern states before specimens were preserved.

The open plains of North America were probably the chief center for evolution and dispersal of the canids (Stains, 1975). Range shifts of the respective species probably occurred between southeastern forests and the plains, as forests and grasslands alternately advanced west and east in response to climatic change. At least four major dry periods have occurred in North America since the end of the Pleistocene (Antevs, 1955). The Altithermal drought referred to as the Long Drought lasted from about 4000 to 7000 years ago. Three additional droughts of much shorter durations have been noted: The Fairbank Drought occurred about 500 BC, the Whitewater Drought occurred about AD 300, and the Great Drought occurred AD 1276–1299. Evidence for these droughts came primarily from western North America. However, it is likely the past droughts extended into the Southeast since most modern droughts of the West spread across the continent. Quinn (1958) has shown that desert conditions existed as far southeast as Arkansas one or more times in the past. Relatively moist conditions existed prior to and following the Long Drought and following subsequent droughts.

The present treatment considers three wolves, dire wolves, gray wolves, and red wolves, as well as coyotes and dogs as inhabitants of the Southeast since the Pleistocene.

1. Dire Wolves

Dire wolves appeared and spread over much of North America during the late Pleistocene. They ranged from Alaska to Mexico and from California to Indiana, Florida, southern Missouri, and Arkansas (Young and Goldman, 1944; Easterla and Jackson, 1961; Galbreath, 1964; Quinn, 1972; Webb, 1974; Gipson and Quinn, 1977). These wolves were generally larger and more massive than modern gray wolves, although some northern gray wolves exceed small dire wolves in general dimensions. Most researchers now agree that dire wolves were not ancestral to modern *Canis*. Webb (1974, p. 76) hypothesized that dire wolves were derived from early gray wolves.

Dire wolves probably became extinct in most areas 8000 to 11,000 years ago (Martin and Wright, 1967), but recently discovered fossils from sites in the Ozark Mountains of northwestern Arkansas indicate dire wolves may have existed in that area 4000 to 7000 years ago (Davis, 1969; Gipson and Quinn, 1977) and possibly as recent as 3000 years ago (Quinn, 1972). One jaw fragment from this area examined by Gipson and Quinn (1977) was particularly interesting. The lower third and fourth premolars in the jaw fragment were intermediate in size to lower premolars examined from dire wolves and gray wolves. This suggests that hybridization possibly occurred between dire and gray wolves. Comparative dire wolf teeth were from

Rancho La Brae tar pits, California, and Peccary Cave, Arkansas; gray wolves were from Michigan. As a rule the teeth of dire wolves are distinctly larger than those of gray and red wolves, although Webb (1977, p. 77) examined some large skulls of Recent gray wolves with lower fourth premolars that approached dire wolf lower premolars in length and equaled them in width.

According to Webb (1974) skulls referred to *C. armbrusteri* from Cumberland Cave, Maryland, range in size from typical gray wolves to dire wolves. Webb examined one skull from the cave that had characteristics intermediate between the two wolf species. Limited hybridization may have occurred between dire wolves and gray wolves or possibly even red wolves. Hybridization has occurred in historical times among red wolves and coyotes, gray wolves and coyotes, coyotes and dogs, and gray wolves and dogs (Young and Goldman, 1944; McCarley, 1962; Standfield, 1970; Paradiso and Nowak, 1971; Gipson *et al.*, 1974).

In one Indian burial site excavated in northwestern Arkansas, dire wolf teeth were present along with projectile points and an artifact made from a beaver incisor (Quinn, 1976 personal communication). It is possible that Indians and their dogs, red wolves, gray wolves, and coyotes occurred contemporaneously with dire wolves in the Ozark Mountains.

2. Gray Wolves

Fossils indicate gray wolves occurred in and adjacent to the Southeast during and probably following the Pleistocene. Remains similar to both red and gray wolves were found in Cumberland Cave, Maryland (Young and Goldman, 1944). Hay (1923, pp. 365–366) reported a wolf jaw fragment from Pleistocene deposits in South Carolina that contained teeth similar to those of modern gray wolves. The teeth were significantly larger than red wolf teeth, yet too small to be from a dire wolf. I examined gray wolf bones and teeth during 1973 reportedly taken from a northeastern Oklahoma bluff shelter. Gray wolf teeth were recently recovered from a bluff shelter in northwestern Arkansas (Gipson and Quinn, 1977).

Authorities generally agree that red wolves and gray wolves occurred in the eastern United States at the time of settlement (Young and Goldman, 1944; Hall and Kelson, 1959; Paradiso and Nowak, 1972). Hall and Kelson (1959) indicated that gray wolves occurred from southeast Tennessee to northeast Florida. According to Paradiso (1969), gray wolves were found throughout Maryland in historic times. Gray wolves were common in northwestern Missouri, Kansas, Oklahoma as far east as the Wichita Mountains, and throughout western Texas during the early 1800's (Young and Goldman, 1944).

3. Red Wolves

The fossil record for red wolves is sparse, but newly discovered bones and teeth indicate that red wolves have been present in the Southeast for thousands of years. Webb (1974, p. 126) assigned a 7000–8000-year-old *Canis* mandible from Devil's Den, Florida, to *C. rufus*; Hirschfield (1968) recovered red wolf remains in a sub-Recent sinkhole deposit of the Florida Everglades. Remains of a wolf similar to modern red wolves were found in Pleistocene deposits in Cumberland Cave, Maryland (Young and Goldman, 1944, p. 399). Teeth from northwestern Arkansas, estimated to be 2900 years old or older, were identical to teeth from red wolves taken in the same area during the early 1920's (Gipson and Quinn, 1977). Cleland (1965) reported finding red wolf remains 500 to 1500 years old in four of 57 bluff shelters excavated in northwest Arkansas. Paradiso and Nowak (1973) described a skelton of an early red wolf from Alabama. The location and condition of bones indicated the wolf lived in Recent times, but long before the area was disturbed by man.

It is possible that red wolves occurred over a large portion of North America during the Pleistocene. Paradiso and Nowak (1972) discussed fossils morphologically similar to modern red wolves from Pleistocene deposits in Arizona and Mexico. Some wolves from the Rancho La Brea tar pits, southern California, had cranial characters similar to red wolves (Young and Goldman, 1944).

A newly excavated *Canis* carnassial from northwestern Arkansas relates to early red wolf and coyote interactions (Gipson and Quinn, 1977). Length and width measurements of this tooth were almost exactly midway between measurements of the same tooth from modern red wolves and coyotes. Measurements of carnassials from coyote × red wolf hybrids taken in Arkansas during the 1960's (Gipson *et al.*, 1974) clustered closely around this tooth. Nowak (1970, p. 84) referred to a Late Pleistocene fossil from Florida that appeared to be intermediate between coyote and red wolf. Interbreeding may have occurred between coyotes and red wolves in the Southeast before white man altered the environment. Coyotes may have periodically invaded the region during dry periods coming into contact with red wolves.

Red wolves occurred throughout southeastern North America when Europeans arrived (Paradiso and Nowak, 1972). These wolves were extirpated over much of the eastern portion of their range by 1900 (Young and Goldman, 1944). Massive hybridization has apparently occurred among coyotes and red wolves in eastern Texas and sections of Arkansas and Louisana (McCarley, 1962; Paradiso, 1968; Nowak, 1970; Paradiso and Nowak, 1971; Gipson *et al.*, 1974). Populations of red wolves presently occur in a pure form only on the southeastern Texas and Louisiana coastal prairies and marshes (Paradiso and Nowak, 1971, 1972; Goertz *et al.*, 1975).

4. Coyotes

Coyotes are generally considered recent invaders of the southeastern states, but fossils indicate they occurred in the region several hundred to several thousand years ago. Coyote remains estimated to be 500 to 1500 years old were recovered in three of 57 bluff shelters excavated in northwestern Arkansas (Cleland, 1965). Additional coyote fossils have been found in the same areas since 1965 along with red wolf, dire wolf, and Indian dog remains (Davis, 1969; Gipson and Quinn, 1977). Remains of a canid similar to modern coyotes were found in Pleistocene deposits in Cumberland Cave, Maryland (Gidley and Gazin, 1938). As noted above, coyotes may have periodically inhabited the Southeast during dry periods.

Coyotes began to expand their range during the late 1800's apparently in response to habitat alterations and possibly reduction of red and gray wolf populations. Today coyotes occur throughout the contiguous states, Alaska, Canada, and Mexico. There are several areas where coyotes have hybridized with red wolves (Paradiso, 1968; Nowak, 1970; Paradiso and Nowak, 1971; Gipson *et al.*, 1974), dogs (Gipson *et al.*, 1974; Mahan and Gipson, 1977), and even gray wolves (Standfield, 1970; Nowak, 1973).

5. Dogs

Domestic dogs have been present in North America for 10,000 years or longer (Lawrence, 1966, 1968). The early dogs ranged from about the size of a modern fox terrier to almost as large as a small gray wolf. Dogs have probably been present in the Southeast since Indians arrived. Webb (1974, pp. 127–128) described several dog bones and teeth from Florida estimated to be 7000 to 8000 years old. A dog skeleton unearthed in Benton County, Missouri, suggests that the practice of burying dogs in a prepared grave had been initiated by 5500 BC (McMillian, 1970). Later sedentary Archaic groups who occupied the shell mound sites of Kentucky, Tennessee, and Alabama commonly buried dogs (Haag, 1948; McMillan, 1970).

It is likely that feral Indian dogs were common where dogs were free ranging and camps were often moved. Indian dogs frequently encountered wolves and coyotes and some hybridization probably occurred. According to numerous accounts presented by Young and Goldman (1944) hybridization between Indian dogs and wolves was common. Both dog × wolf and dog × coyote crosses are well documented (Young and Goldman, 1944; Gier, 1968; Gipson *et al.*, 1974) and such hybridization may be common locally. Nowak (1973) found dog hybridization had no significant influence on coyote and wolf populations he studied.

Dogs used for hunting and strays have been numerous throughout the southeastern states since settlement (Gipson and Sealander, 1977; Perry and Giles, 1970). There are populations of feral dogs that exist independent of man is some areas of the southeast today (Scott and Causey, 1973; Gipson *et al.*, 1974; Barick, 1969).

B. Recent History

1. General

The status and systematics of *Canis* in the southeastern states appeared to be well understood during the 1940's (Young and Goldman, 1944) and 1950's (Young and Jackson, 1951). Biologists generally agreed that red wolves had been extirpated east of the Mississippi, but as late as 1964 reports indicated that a sizable breeding population of red wolves occurred from the Texas Gulf Coast north through eastern Oklahoma and east across Arkansas and northern Louisiana (Cahalane, 1964; Nowak 1967). The only other *Canis* species considered common in the southeastern states was the domestic dog, and although occasional matings between dogs and red wolves (Young and Goldman, 1944) and dogs and coyotes (Young and Jackson, 1951) had been noted, dog hybridization was not considered important. Coyotes were known to occur west from western Arkansas (Sealander, 1956) and eastern Texas (Young and Jackson, 1951). Limited hybridization between red wolves and coyotes was suspected (Young and Goldman, 1944; Young and Jackson, 1951).

2. West of the Mississippi River

A number of biologists became concerned about the status of the red wolf during the late 1950's and early 1960's. McCarley reported in 1962 that red wolves had been replaced by coyotes over much of their former range west of the Mississippi River. Other research verified that pure populations of red wolves existed only along the Texas Gulf Coast and in Louisiana (Paradiso, 1965; Nowak, 1967; Pimlott and Joslin, 1968). The red wolf was placed on the list of rare and endangered species by the U. S. Fish and Wildlife Service in 1965.

There was considerable disagreement about the status and identity of canids in the southcentral states after publication of McCarley's paper and the subsequent listing of the red wolf as endangered. Numerous canids ranging in size from typical coyotes to small red wolves were taken by predator control agents in areas recently invaded by coyotes where red wolves had formerly occurred. Extensive hybridization between coyotes and red wolves was hypothesized to explain the intermediate-sized canids. Paradiso (1968) indicated that interbreeding among coyotes and red wolves suggested that they were the same species. Other researchers questioned whether or not the red wolf should be considered a distinct species from gray wolves (Lawrence and Bossert, 1967). Mech (1970) attempted to reconcile the two views by suggesting that red wolves might turn out to be fertile gray wolf × coyote hybrids, with eastern forms more closely resembling gray wolves and western forms more similar to coyotes.

Research reported after 1969 supported recognition of the red wolf as a distinct species and further clarified *Canis* range and taxonomic changes that occurred in southcentral states (Nowak, 1970; Paradiso and Nowak, 1971; Atkins and Dillon, 1971; Gipson *et al.*, 1974; Goertz *et al.*, 1975). Many canids collected around the turn of the century from the Edwards Plateau of central Texas showed intermediate characters between red wolves and coyotes. Nowak (1970) examined these specimens and postulated that a hybrid swarm started there. Nowak suggested that this hybrid swarm moved eastward into areas where red wolf numbers had been drastically reduced. Intermediate-sized animals, apparently resulting from red wolf and coyote hybridization, were located in east Texas and Louisiana (Paradiso and Nowak, 1972; Goertz *et al.*, 1975) and in remote areas of Arkansas (Gipson *et al.*, 1974). A strong red wolf influence was noted on the southwestern Coastal Plain of Arkansas north and east of the Red River. I examined five canids taken in this area from 1968 through 1970 that weighed 46 to 53 pounds (20.9–24 kg). All appeared to be coyote × red wolf hybrids or possibly red wolves.

The role of dogs in *Canis* species changes was questioned. Documented crosses between dogs and coyotes (Young and Jackson, 1951; Gier, 1968, 1975; Kennelly and Roberts, 1969; Mengel, 1971) and dogs and gray wolves (Young and Goldman, 1944; Iljin, 1941) resulting in fertile hybrids showed that dog crosses were possible. However, most researchers felt that the breeding season of dog hybrids was always shifted to autumn or early winter, before coyotes or wolves were capable of mating (Mengel, 1971). Published accounts of the reproductive biology of dog hybrids were based on a limited number of captive animals (Gier, 1968; Mengel, 1971). Gipson *et al.* (1975) examined a number of reproductive tracts from wild caught dog hybrids and wild dogs, as well as coyotes and coyote × red wolf hybrids. The reproductive seasons of all these canids overlapped, indicating that interbreeding is possible among the various forms. Apparently hybridization has occurred in the Southeast between coyotes and red wolves and to some extent between coyotes and dogs, and between red wolves and dogs.

In Arkansas a strong dog influence was detected in the wild *Canis* population (Gipson *et al.*, 1974). A multivariate statistical analysis of skulls from

254 Arkansas canids collected 1968 through 1971 was made to identify each specimen. The analysis showed that wild canid population was composed primarily of coyotes (73%) with admixtures of wild dogs (3%), coyote × dog hybrids (13%), coyotes × red wolf hybrids (10%), and and dog × red wolf hybrids (1%). Pockets of coyote × dog and coyote × red wolf hybrids occurred over the state. Similar results were obtained in a taxonomic study of 138 recently collected Oklahoma *Canis* (Freeman, 1976): 81% coyotes, 13% coyote × dog hybrids, and 5% coyote × red wolf hybrids.

Goertz *et al.* (1975) examined 155 wild *Canis* skulls collected in Louisiana from 1963 to 1973. They found that most specimens closely resembled coyotes, but some were larger and apparently were part red wolf. A single specimen shot as it ran with two coyotelike canids appeared to be a coyote × dog cross. In 1969 I examined two coyote × dog hybrids killed near the Red River in northwestern Louisiana.

The mixture of *Canis* species is reflected in the size and appearance of wild canids in the southeastern states. Typical male coyotes weigh about 30 pounds (13.6 kg) and females are slightly smaller (Gier, 1968); 23 male red wolves collected prior to 1930 in Arkansas averaged 60.9 pounds (27.6 kg) and 34 females averaged 47.6 pounds (21.6 kg) (Paradiso and Nowak, 1972). I examined a large series of wild canids taken in Arkansas from 1968 through 1972. The average weight of 113 adult males was 34.4 pounds (15.6 kg). Weights ranged from 25 to 53 pounds (11.3–24 kg). Two males weighed 53 pounds, one was identified as a coyote × red wolf hybrid and the other as a red wolf × dog hybrid. Total lengths and tail lengths ranged from 42.2 inches and 12 inches to 54.1 inches and 15.0 inches (1078 mm and 304 mm to 1373 mm and 383 mm), respectively. The male of greatest length was identified as a coyote × red wolf hybrid.

Weights of 62 adult females from Arkansas ranged from 20 to 37 pounds (9.1 to 16.8 kg) and averaged 28.4 pounds (12.9 kg). The 37-pound female was identified as a coyote × red wolf hybrid. Total and tail lengths for females ranged from 40.5 inches and 11.5 inches to 49.8 inches and 13.9 inches (1029 mm and 293 mm to 1265 mm and 352 mm), respectively. The female of greatest length was identified as a coyote × red wolf hybrid.

Coats of most of the wild canids taken during the Arkansas study were typical salt-and-pepper gray. Pelt coloration varied from spotted, to rufous to almost pure black. All coyotes and coyote × red wolf hybrids examined (even black specimens) had the agouti banding on guard hairs. Dogs and some dog hybrids did not. Pale, golden-brown eye color was typical of animals identified as coyotes or coyote × red wolf hybrids. The eye color of other canids ranged from golden-green to blue and deep brown. Brown eye color was associated with dog or part dog specimens.

Black canids occur over much of the former range of the red wolf, west of the Mississippi River. Most of the black canids are coyote sized, but some individuals weigh 45 to 50 pounds and appear wolflike. Black pelage, often accompanied by a white pectoral spot and white on the feet, occurred among red wolves (Arthur, 1928; Young and Goldman, 1944; Sealander, 1956; Riley and McBride, 1972). Black (1936) estimated that roughly 25% of the red wolves taken in the western Ozark Mountains of Arkansas during the early 1930's were melanistic. Melanism has been considered a diagnostic feature of red wolves, useful in distinguishing red wolves from coyotes (Halloran, 1958, 1959; Pimlott and Joslin, 1968). Only one case of melanism was reported by Young and Jackson (1951) in their treatment of coloration in western coyotes. Other reports of black coyotes (Halloran, 1959, 1963; Pimlott and Joslin, 1968) are from, or adjacent to, areas known to have been inhabited by melanistic red wolves (Halloran, 1958, 1960) and/or dogs in recent times. Black pelage is common among domestic dogs and has been observed in coyote × dog hybrids (Gier, 1968; Mengel, 1971).

Forty-three black canids were collected or observed in Arkansas from 1968 through 1971 (Gipson, 1976). Skulls from 24 of these were identified using a multivariate statistical analysis. Twelve of the black canids were considered coyotes, six coyote × dog hybrids, five coyote × red wolf hybrids, and one wild dog. Lawrence (1970 personal communication) felt that another black specimen she examined was probably a coyote × dog hybrid. Freeman (1976) identified 12 black canids recently collected in Oklahoma as eight coyotes, two coyotes × dog hybrids, and two coyote × red wolf hybrids.

There are at least two possible sources of melanism in coyotes and coyotelike canids in southern states today. Genes for melanism may have been present in eastern coyote populations in Texas, Oklahoma, and Missouri before coyotes from these areas extended their range eastward. Environmental factors in the Southeast could have provided some selective advantage for melanism permitting an increase in black pelage among coyotes. This hypothesis is supported by the fact that 12 of the 24 black canids from Arkansas could not be differentiated from coyotes. The second possibility is that melanism was derived from red wolves and/or dogs through hybridization which occurred as coyotes extended their range across the western edge of the Southeast (Gipson *et al.*, 1974). Genes for melanism were probably passed to some hybrid offspring which, in turn, became a part of the gene pool of the present interbreeding canid population. The presence of black canids, some apparently intermediate between coyotes and red wolves, supports Nowak's (1970) concept of a hybrid swarm in the region.

During the 1950's predator control agents realized wolves were becoming rare in Arkansas and Louisiana because most canids trapped were coyote sized and few were black. An effort was apparently made to preserve wolves by control agents in the two states. According to the 1957 annual report of the Branch of Predator and Rodent Control prepared by H. F. Sessums: "Since the population of black timber wolves is rapidly diminishing a refuge along the Arkansas and Louisiana line has been set aside for their protection." The refuge was located in Ashley County, Arkansas and Morehouse Parish, Louisiana. Four black wolflike canids from Arkansas were released in the area in 1958 and four in 1959 (Sessums, 1958, 1959). Apparently this was not an official refuge since no additional record of it has been located. It may be significant that there is a red wolf influence in the present canid population of this area.

The coyote × red wolf hybrid swarm appears to have gradually dissipated during the 1950's and 1960's in eastern Arkansas and Louisiana where red wolves had been extirpated before the arrival of coyotes. Pockets of red wolves may have continued to exist along the Mississippi River in Louisiana through the 1960's (Nowak, 1967, 1970). Coyotes were reported in the most southeastern county of Arkansas in 1966 (Paradiso, 1966). During the late 1960's coyotes were often trapped on islands in the Mississippi River between Arkansas and Tennessee by animal damage control agents.

3. East of the Mississippi River

No wild *Canis*, other than occasional feral dogs and extremely isolated pockets of red wolves, occurred in southern states east of the Mississippi River from 1900 until about 1965. Coyotes moved eastward through Tennessee, Mississippi, and other eastern states during the 1960's and early 1970's. In addition to true range expansion, coyotes have been released in southeastern states by man (Cunningham and Danford, 1970; Bekoff, 1976), often for sport hunting. Released coyotes may be responsible for some local populations. Today coyotes occur in all the southeastern states.

Canis populations east of the Mississippi River are undergoing rapid change. Expanding coyote populations often encounter dogs. Free-ranging hunting and farm dogs are found in abundance (Barick, 1969; Perry and Giles, 1970) and feral dogs occur in the region (McKnight, 1964; Scott and Causey, 1973). Feral dogs have been able to survive along with red wolves, coyotes, and *Canis* hybrids in Arkansas (Gipson, 1972; Gipson *et al.*, 1974).

Coyotes, feral dogs, and some free-ranging domestic dogs probably occupy similar ecological niches in the Southeast. Feral dogs are often about the size of coyotes (Gipson, 1972; Scott and Causey, 1973; Nesbitt, 1975) and their diets are similar (Gipson, 1972, 1974; Scott and Causey, 1973; Gipson and Sealander, 1976). One factor that has apparently helped feral dogs to survive in Arkansas has been the presence of abundant poultry carrion at dumps scattered through the state (Gipson, 1972). Coyotes and hybrid canids also frequent poultry dumps, and there is social interaction among the various canids at these common feeding stations. Scott and Causey (1973) and Nesbitt (1975) reported that some feral dogs they studied fed at dumps, but one pack observed by Scott and Causey appeared to obtain food from the wild.

It is likely that an easy source of food such as carrion dumps is necessary for feral dog populations to exist in the presence of coyotes or wolves. Dogs appear to be relatively inefficient predators as compared with wolves and coyotes. Mech (1966) obtained data on the efficiency of gray wolves as predators of moose (*Alces alces*) on Isle Royale. Six of 77 moose tested by wolves were killed, resulting in an efficiency rating of 7.8%. No figures are available for the kill rate of coyotes, but Cook *et al.* (1971) and others consider coyote predation to be a major cause of mortality among white-tailed deer fawns in Texas. Calculations of the efficiency of dogs in catching deer, based on 175 monitored chases of radio-tagged deer in southeastern states (Sweeny *et al.*, 1971; Corbett *et al.*, 1971; Gavitt *et al.*, 1974; Gipson and Sealander, 1977), indicate that dogs have an efficiency rating of only 1.1%. It is not likely that a predator with such a low degree of hunting success would be able to compete with coyotes or wolves for limited prey. It should be noted that most of the dogs used in the deer harassment investigations were hounds or hound crosses that barked on the trail. Silent trailing dogs might be more efficient.

4. Reasons for Population Changes

At least four factors have been responsible for changes in *Canis* populations in the Southeast. One of the most important has been removal of forests by lumbering and clearing for crops and pastures. The timber harvest practice of clear-cutting large blocks, often several square miles or more in size, has created ideal habitat for coyotes in areas of dense forest.

A factor in the decline of red wolves and the subsequent increase in coyotes, free-ranging dogs, and hybrids has been food supply. During the past 50 years, land-use patterns in the Southeast have shifted from small-scale farming with free-ranging livestock to large-scale farming with controlled livestock and confined poultry (Gipson and Sealander, 1976). The increase in coyotes in Arkansas and neighboring states appears to be associated with development of the poultry industry and the availability of poultry carrion.

Predator control was probably an important factor in reducing red wolf populations. Red wolves appear to have more sterotyped behavior and seem to be less wary than coyotes (Knowlton, 1971). According to Nowak (1970) the decline of red wolves was primarily due to killing by man. He concluded that the marked reduction of red wolf populations permitted coyotes to invade the Southeast.

A fourth factor influencing canid populations was availability of mates. Russell and Shaw (1971) have shown that the number of red wolves in Texas was greatly reduced before coyotes began to expand their range eastward. The same situation existed in Arkansas (Gipson, 1972). As the red wolf population was reduced individuals were at times isolated and unable to find mates of their own species. In such cases coyotes and occasionally dogs were available and some hybridization occurred.

C. Present and Future Trends

Coyote populations are likely to expand in the Southeast, particulary east of the Mississippi River. States east of the River are similar to Arkansas and Louisiana where large coyote populations have developed in the past 40 years. There are many areas suitable for coyotes east of the Mississippi River where large blocks of timber have been clear-cut.

There is an abundant food supply for coyotes in eastern states. The poultry industry is concentrated in the Southeast and coyotes adapt readily to a diet of poultry (Gipson, 1974; Gipson and Sealander, 1976). Turkeys, produced in large open-range pens, are particulary attractive prey for coyotes. Open dumps where coyotes and other scavengers can obtain dead chickens and turkeys are found throughout the region. Small domestic mammals, particularly hogs, goats, sheep, and calves, are abundant, and animal husbandry is lax in some areas. There is a rich supply of native wildlife ranging from insects, song birds, and rodents to white-tailed deer that should prove attractive to coyotes.

Little is known about the social structure of coyote populations. Ryden's (1975) and Camenzind's observations of coyote families in protected areas suggests that coyotes form packs and that associations between family members continue for long periods. However, coyotes at the Rocky Mountain National Park (Estes Park, Colorado) do not form "packs" although they too are protected (Bekoff and Hill, unpublished data). One of my graduate students has initiated a study of coyote social interactions in an intensely farmed and hunted area of eastern Nebraska to determine social organization among coyotes that are not protected. Studies are needed in southeastern states to determine social organization among invading coyotes.

The red wolf influence will probably become more diluted as coyotes expand. This trend could possibly be reversed by releasing red wolves in areas where a red wolf influence still exists in Arkansas, Louisiana, and eastern Texas. A controlled release would be an exciting experiment to conduct with surplus red wolves produced in zoos or possibly wolves captured along the Texas Gulf Coast. Zoo wolves would have to be taught to kill prey and care for themselves before release. This could possibly be accomplished by maintaining red wolves in large, isolated enclosures where prey animals could be introduced. Coyotes and/or feral dogs should be removed from the release area prior to release of wolves if there is not a strong red wolf influence in the local population. Removal of coyotes and dogs would reduce chances of hybridization. The Ozark and Ouachita National Forests in Arkansas and National Forests east of the Mississippi River offer several potential red wolf release sites.

The future role of dogs in the wild canid population should prove interesting. Unconfined dogs are more common in the Southeast than in any other part of the United States. Hybridization between coyotes and dogs is likely to continue west of the Mississippi due to the abundance of dogs. Coyotes will often encounter dogs east of the Mississippi River as they invade new areas. There will be opportunities to study expanding coyote populations in the presence of feral and/or free-ranging dogs. Studies are needed to determine interactions among and between coyotes and dogs in this region.

III. *CANIS* SOUTH OF THE UNITED STATES

A. General

A survey of *Canis* in Mexico and Central American countries is needed. Leopold (1959) reviewed coyotes and gray wolves (*C. lupus baileyi*) in Mexico through the 1950's. Cahalane (1964) and Mech (1970) briefly discussed the status of wolves in Mexico. Several scientists that have worked in Mexico since 1970 advised me that coyotes are abundant and that wolves still exist. The wolf in Mexico is now classified as endangered by the U. S. Fish and Wildlife Service. Free-ranging and occasionally wild dogs occur, but the size of the dog population and the extent of interactions between dogs and native *Canis* have not been investigated. The present status of *Canis* is unknown in southern Mexico and Central American countries.

B. Coyotes

According to Young and Jackson (1951) coyotes probably existed in large numbers in what is now Mexico prior to the arrival of Spaniards. They indicated that coyotes may have extended their range southward into Central American countries during the sixteenth century as Spaniards introduced livestock. In the early 1950's coyotes occurred on the open plains of Mexico and along the west coast in some desert or semidesert areas (Young and Jackson, 1951, p. 11). The southernmost limit of the coyote's range was Costa Rica adjacent to the Peninsula of Nicoys.

Leopold (1959) reported that coyotes were abundant on the open plains and scrublands of Mexico, but they were absent in the southern rain forests and cloud forests. There were few or no coyotes in the virgin pine forests of the Sierra Madre Occidental where wolves were still plentiful. Leopold noted that coyotes were moving into former wolf ranges where logging, grazing, and wolf control had been initiated. Coyotes ranged as far south in Mexico as the Isthmus of Tehuantepec and the Chiapas Highlands (Leopold, 1959).

C. Wolves

Wolves occurred throughout the temperate uplands of Mexico from Sonora and Tamaulipas south to Michoacan and Puebla until 60–90 years ago (Leopold, 1959). Leopold indicated that wolves had been exterminated in the central uplands and along the eastern escarpment by 1959. He noted two extensive areas where wolves occurred: (1) the Sierra Madre Occidental, and (2) the arid mountains of western Coahuila and eastern Chihuahua. Dalquest (1953) reported a population of wolves in western San Luis Potosi. Leopold noted that wolves were declining in abundance and that their distribution was being reduced.

Mech indicated in 1970 that wolves were still present in the three areas listed above. He also noted that the taking of wolves was prohibited in all Mexican states except Sonora and Chihuahua. Villa (cited in Mech, 1970) indicated wolves were in danger of extinction.

REFERENCES

Antevs, E. (1955). *Am. Antiq.* **20,** 317–335.

Arthur, S. C. (1928). "The Fur Animals of Louisiana," 433 pp. La. Dep. Conserv., New Orleans.

Atkins, D. L., and Dillon, L. S. (1971). *J. Mammal.* **52,** 96–107.

Barick, F. B. (1969). *White-Tailed Deer South. For. Habitat; Symp., South. For. Exp. Stn., Nacogdoches, Tex.* pp. 25–31.

Bekoff, M. (1976). *Mamm. Species* No. 79.

Black, J. D. (1936). *J. Mammal.* **17,** 24–35.

Cahalane, V. H. (1964). "A Preliminary Study of Distribution and Numbers of Cougar, Grizzly and Wolf in North America," 12 pp. N.Y. Zool. Soc., New York.

Cleland, C. E. (1965). *Arkansas Archeol.* **6,** 39–63.

Cook, R. S., White, M., Trainer, D. O., and Glazener, W. C. (1971). *J. Wildl. Manage.* **35,** 47–56.
Corbett, R. L., Marchinton, R. L., and Hill, C. E. (1971). *Proc. Southeast. Assoc. Game Fish Comm.* **25,** 69–77.
Cunningham, V. D., and Danford, R. D. (1970). *J. Fla. Acad. Sci.* **38,** 279–280.
Dalquest, W. W. (1953). *La. State Univ. Stud. Biol. Sci. Ser.* No. 1, 229 pp.
Davis, L. C. (1969). *Proc. Arkansas Acad. Sci.* **23,** 192–196.
Easterla, D. and Jackson, G. (1961). *Bluebird (St. Louis)* **28,** 3–4.
Freeman, R. C. (1976). Coyote × Dog Hybridization and Red Wolf Influence in the Wild *Canis* of Oklahoma. M.S. Thesis, 62 pp. Oklahoma State Univ., Stillwater.
Galbreath, E. C. (1964). *Trans. Ill. State Acad. Sci.* **57,** 229–242.
Gavitt, J. D., Downing, R. L., and McGinnes, B. S. (1974). *Proc. Southeast. Assoc. Game Fish Comm.* **28,** 532–539.
Gidley, J. W., and Gazin, C. L. (1938). *U.S. Natl. Mus., Bull.* **171,** 1–99.
Gier, H. T. (1968). *Kans. Agric. Exp. Stn. Bull.* No. 393, 118 pp.
Gier, H. T. (1975). *In* "The Wild Canids: Their Systematics, Behavioral Ecology and Evolution" (M. W. Fox, ed.), pp. 247–262. Van Nostrand-Reinhold, New York.
Gipson, P. S. (1972). The Taxonomy, Reproductive Biology, Food Habits, and Range of Wild *Canis* (Canidae) in Arkansas. Ph.D. Thesis, 188 pp. Univ. of Arkansas, Fayetteville.
Gipson, P. S. (1974). *J. Wildl. Manage.* **38,** 848–853.
Gipson, P. S. (1976). *Southwest. Nat.* **21,** 124–126.
Gipson, P. S., and Quinn, J. H. (1977). Early *Canis* in the Ozark Highlands. In preparation.
Gipson, P. S., and Sealander, J. A. (1976). *Am. Midl. Nat.* **95,** 249–252.
Gipson, P. S., and Sealander, J. A. (1977). *Predator Symp., Univ. Montana, Missoula* (in press).
Gipson, P. S., Sealander, J. A., and Dunn, J. E. (1974). *Syst. Zool.* **23,** 1–11.
Gipson, P. S., Gipson, I. K., and Sealander, J. A. (1975). *J. Mammal.* **53,** 605–612.
Goertz, J. W., Fitzgerald, L. V., and Nowak, R. M. (1975). *Am. Midl. Nat.* **93,** 215–218.
Haag, W. G. (1948). *Rep. Anthropol.* **7,** 107–264.
Hagmeier, E. M. (1966). *Syst. Zool.* **15,** 279–299.
Hall, E. R., and Kelson, K. R. (1959). "The Mammals of North America," 2 Vols., 1083 pp. Ronald Press, New York.
Halloran, A. F. (1958). *Okla. Wildl.* **14,** 6–8.
Halloran, A. F. (1959). *Tex. Game Fish* **17,** 10–11.
Halloran, A. F. (1960). *Tex. Game Fish* **17,** 2–5.
Halloran, A. F. (1963). *Southwest. Nat.* **8,** 48–49.
Hay, O. P. (1923). The Pleistocene of North America and its Vertebrated Animals from the States East of the Mississippi River and from the Canadian provinces East of Longitude 95°," 499 pp. Carnegie Inst. Washington, Washington, D.C.
Hay, O. P. (1924). "The Pleistocene of the Middle Region of North America and its Vertebrated Animals," 385 pp. Carnegie Inst. Washington, Washington, D.C.
Hirschfield, S. E. (1968). *Q. J. Fla. Acad. Sci.* **31,** 177–189.
Iljin, N. A. (1941). *J. Genet.* **42,** 359–414.
Kennelly, J. J., and Roberts, J. O. (1969). *J. Mammal.* **50,** 830–831.
Knowlton, F. (1971). "Scent posts of *Canis rufus,*" 13 pp. Newsl. Bur. Sport Fish. Wildl., San Antonio, Texas.
Kurten, B. (1974). *Acta Zool. Fenn.,* No. 140, 38 pp.
Lawrence, B. (1966). *Z. Saeugetierk.* **1,** 44–59.
Lawrence, B. (1968). *Tebiwa* **11,** 43–49.
Lawrence, B., and Bossert, W. H. (1967). *Amer. Zool.* **7,** 223–232.

Leopold, A. S. (1959). "Wildlife in Mexico: The Game Birds and Mammals," 568 pp. Univ. of California Press, Berkeley.

McCarley, H. (1962). *Southwest. Nat.* **7,** 227–235.

McKnight, T. (1964). "Feral Livestock in Anglo-America," 87 pp. Univ. of California Press, Berkeley.

McMillan, R. B. (1970). *Science* **167,** 1246–1247.

Mahan, B. R., and Gipson, P. S. (1977). Distribution and characteristics of coyote × dog hybrids collected in Nebraska with comments on hybrid ecology and behavior. *Am. Midl. Nat.* (in press).

Martin, P. S., and Wright, H. E., Jr., eds. (1967) "Pleistocene Extinctions—The Search for a Cause, 453 pp. Yale Univ. Press, New Haven, Connecticut.

Matthew, W. D. (1930). *J. Mammal.* **11,** 117–138.

Mech, L. D. (1966). "The Wolves of Isle Royale," No. 7, 210 pp. U.S. Natl. Park Serv., Fauna Surv., Washington, D.C.

Mech, L. D. (1970). "The Wolf: The Ecology and Behavior of an Endangered Species," 384 pp. Nat. Hist. Press, Garden City, New York.

Mengel, R. M. (1971). *J. Mammal.* **52,** 316–336.

Nesbitt, W. H. (1975). *In* "The wild Canids: Their Systematics, Behavioral Ecology and Evolution" (M. W. Fox, ed.), pp. 391–396. Van Nostrand-Reinhold, New York.

Nowak, R. M. (1967). *Defenders Wildl. News* **42,** 60–70.

Nowak, R. M. (1970). *Defenders Wildl. News* **45,** 82–94.

Nowak, R. M. (1973). North American Quaternary *Canis*. Ph.D. Thesis, 555 pp. Univ. of Kansas, Lawrence.

Paradiso, J. L. (1965). *Southwest. Nat.* **10,** 318–319.

Paradiso, J. L. (1966). *Southwest. Nat.* **11,** 500–501.

Paradiso, J. L. (1968). *Am. Mild. Nat.* **80,** 529–534.

Paradiso, J. L. (1969). "Mammals of Maryland." North American Fauna, No. 66, 193 pp. Bur. Sport Fish. Wildl.

Paradiso, J. L., and Nowak, R. M. (1971). *U.S. Bur. Sport Fish. Wildl., Spec. Sci. Rep.—Wildl.* No. 145, 36 pp.

Paradiso, J. L., and Nowak, R. M. (1972). *Mamm. Species* **22,** 1–4.

Paradiso, J. L., and Nowak, R. M. (1973). *J. Mammal.* **54,** 506–509.

Perry, M. C., and Giles, R. H., Jr. (1970). *Proc. Southeast. Assoc. Fish Game Comm.* **24,** 64–73.

Pimlott, D. H., and Joslin, P. W. (1968). *Trans. North Amer. Wildl. Nat. Resour. Conf.* **33,** 373–389.

Quinn, J. H. (1958). *Bull. Geol. Soc. Amer.* **69,** 1632.

Quinn, J. H. (1972). *IGC* **24,** 89–96.

Riley, G. A., and McBride, R. T. (1972). *U.S. Bur. Sport Fish. Wildl., Spec. Sci. Rep.—Wildl.* No. 162, 15 pp.

Russell, D. H., and Shaw, J. H. (1971). *Proc. Tex. Acad. Sci.* 5 pp.

Ryden, H. (1975). "God's Dog," 285 pp. Coward, McCann, Geoghegan, New York.

Scott, M. D., and Causey, K. (1973). *J. Wildl. Manage.* **37,** 253–263.

Sealander, J. A., Jr. (1956). *Am. Midl. Nat.* **56,** 257–296.

Sessums, H. F. (1957). "Annual Report," 22 pp. U.S. Fish Wildl. Serv., Branch Predator Rodent Control, State College, Mississippi.

Sessums, H. F. (1958). "Annual Report," 17 pp. U.S. Fish Wildl. Serv., Branch Predator Rodent Control, State College, Mississippi.

Sessums, H. F. (1959). "Annual Report," 22 pp. U.S. Fish Wildl. Serv., Branch Predator Rodent Control, State College, Mississippi.

Stains, H. J. (1975). *In* "The Wild Canids: Their Systematics, Behavioral Ecology and Evolution" (M. W. Fox, ed.), pp. 3–26. Van Nostrand-Reinhold, New York.

Standfield, R. O. (1970). *Proc. Symp. Wolf Manage. Selected Areas North Am.; U.S. Fish Wildl. Serv., Twin Cities, Minn.* pp. 32–38. (Mimeo.)

Sweeney, J. R., Marchinton, R. L., and Seeeney, J. M. (1971). *J. Wildl. Manage.* **35**, 707–716.

Webb, D. S. (1974). "Pleistocene Mammals of Florida," 270 pp. Univ. of Florida Press, Gainesville.

Young, S. P., and Goldman, E. A. (1944). "The Wolves of North America," 636 pp. Am. Wildl. Inst., Washington, D.C.

Young, S. P., and Jackson, H. H. T. (1951). "The Clever Coyote," 411 pp. Stackpole, Harrisburg, Pennsylvania.

9

Systematics and Ecology of the Eastern Coyote

Henry Hilton

Knowledge of the eastern coyote (*Canis latrans* var.) is limited by the comparatively recent occurrence and recognition of the animal and by the somewhat adolescent phase of the investigations *in toto*. This is not to say that investigations to date have not been fruitful, for indeed they have shown that (1) the coyote as a species has or is occupying most of the former wolf (*Canis lupus lycaon*) range in the east; (2) traditional wild *Canis* isolating mechanisms are apparently being broken down; (3) the eastern coyote has a unique taxonomic position among the *Canis* species; (4) growth and behavior of the eastern form are different than that of previously classified *Canis latrans;* and (5) the feeding strategy of the coyote may be expanding from the traditional role as an opportunistic scavenger and predator of small mammals to more frequently include larger prey where it is available.

It is the purpose of this chapter to bring together current theories and assessments of the status of the eastern coyote as a basis for future investigations and impending management decisions.

I. DISTRIBUTION

The eastern coyote has invaded much of eastern Canada, New England, and New York in variable, but for the most part, undetermined numbers. The precise easterly movement of coyotes is difficult to trace, however, because (1) sparse human populations have precluded a complete and

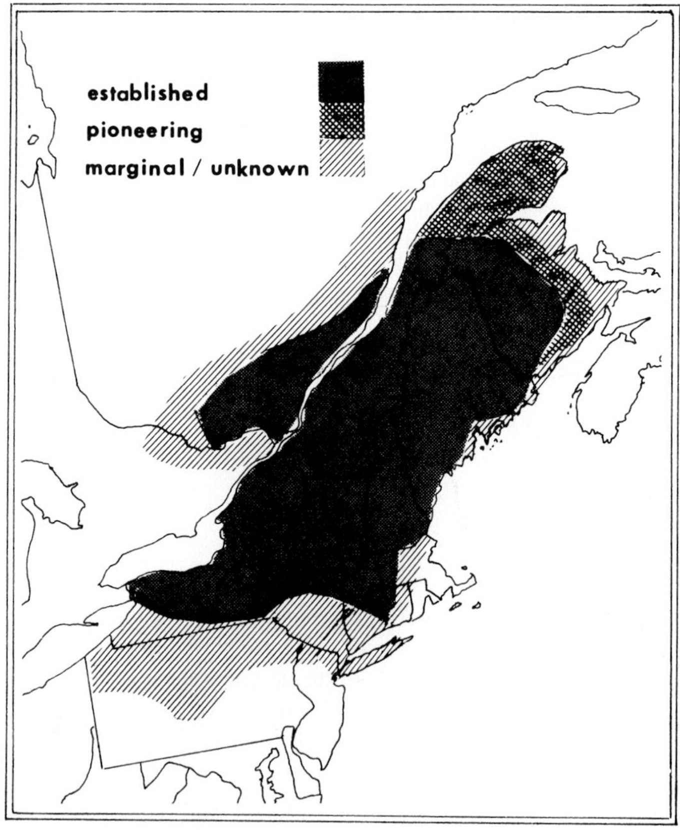

Fig. 1. Approximate distribution of eastern coyotes based on published reports (see Table I) and personal communication by the author with authorities in the respective regions. The occurrence of eastern coyotes does not preclude the existence of other wild *Canis*, feral dogs, and various hybrids.

accurate documentation; (2) there has often been little or no attempt to distinguish between coyotes and wolves; (3) hybridization between coyotes, dogs (*Canis familiaris*) and wolves inhibited accurate identification of many early specimens obtained in pioneering stages (see Standfield, 1970; Severinghaus, 1974); and (4) expansion was sporadic and in pioneering

TABLE I

Records of Coyote Occurrence and Establishment in Eastern United States and Canada

Date	Records[a]/Region	No. Specimens	Authority and Reference
1919	(R) S.W. Ontario	1	Ontario Department of Lands and Forests (1974)
1920–28	(E) S.E. Ontario	—	Ontario Department of Lands and Forests (1974)
1934–36	(R) N.W. New York	8[b]	Amer. Mus. Nat. Hist.; Severinghaus (1974)
1936–38	(R) Central Maine	12[c]	Biol. Surv. Team[d]; Aldous (1939)
1942	(R) Vermont	1	W. J. Hamilton, Jr.; Pringle (1960)
1944	(R) S. Quebec	1	S. Young; Young and Jackson (1951)
1944	(R) New Hampshire	1	S. Young; Young and Jackson (1951)
1946	(R) Pennsylvania	1	??; Smithson. Inst. Collect.
1955	(R) Connecticut	1	B. Lawrence; Glatz (1976)
1957	(R) Massachusetts	1	B. Lawrence; Pringle (1960)
1958–61	(E) New York	—	Bounty records; Chambers *et al.* (1974)
1961	(R) Maine	1[e]	R. H. Manville; Carson (1962)
1961	(R) Islet Cty, P.Q.	1	R. Ouellet; Georges (1976)
1966	(R) New Brunswick	1	??; Cartwright (1975)
1971–73	(E) W. Maine	—[f]	Richens; Richens and Hugie (1974)
1972–74	(R) Gaspe Region, P.Q.	3	van Zyll de Jong, Georges; Georges (1976)
1973–75	(E) Maine	—[f]	Hilton, Richens; unit records
1973–75	(E) New Brunswick	—	Cartwright; Cartwright (1975)

[a] First recorded specimen (R); period during which population first became established (E).

[b] Notwithstanding considerable disagreement at the time regarding the identity of these specimens, they now appear to be the first recorded evidence of eastern coyotelike animals in New York.

[c] Several were identified as coyote–dog hybrids; all probably descended from introduced animals. See text.

[d] C. M. Aldous, W. B. Bell, H. H. T. Jackson, L. K. Couch.

[e] Identified as *C. latrans thamnos*, it likely represents the first reliable record of an indigenous coyote in Maine.

[f] Maine Cooperative Wildlife Research Unit, Univ. of Maine, Orono.

stages consisted of relatively few individuals. In short, dispersal of coyotes into the East was, and to some degree still is, obscure.

Existing chronological records of coyote occurrence and establishment in various regions of the East can only serve as an approximation; but empirical and anecdotal evidence cumulatively suggest that coyotes dispersed east from Ontario into New York in the late 1920's and thence north to Quebec Province, New England, and the Maritimes (Table I). Also, reports suggest that throughout the East it was not uncommon for captive western coyotes to escape or be released. These animals may have been the progenitors of small localized populations of alien coyotes which then died out, were killed, or were genetically assimilated into existing populations. This would account for the seemingly spontaneous occurrence of local "pockets" of coyotes in Maine (Aldous, 1939), New York (Severinghaus, 1974), and Pennsylvania (H. McGinnis, personal communication). Such groups of animals, for the most part, cannot be considered part of the principal coyote dispersal into the East.

II. SYSTEMATICS

When the first "wild canids" appeared in the Northeast, there was considerable disagreement among both laymen and taxonomists as to their collective identity. Individuals were often named by the former group without regard to scientific accuracy, especially when depredation or bounty payments were restricted to a specific *Canis* species. Also, the prestige of wolves in a hunter's or trapper's bag often transcended the application of objective identification criteria. To taxonomists working with cranial features and superficial characteristics of color, size, and proportions, the new coyote form was an enigma. Howard's ratio of the palatal width to the upper molar tooth-row length (Howard, 1949), which had been commonly used in the West to separate dogs and coyotes, often placed eastern coyotelike animals in the dog category, erroneously implicating domestic dogs in the genetic development of the current eastern coyote form. It was not until 1969 that biologists suggested the introgression of wolf genes into the coyote gene pool, and 1971 before it was verified that such an introgression could occur through fertile crossbreeding.

A. Adult Physical Characteristics

The most distinctive physical characteristic of the eastern coyote is its large size which is nonetheless, often overestimated in the field. Erroneous reports of 60–80 pound (27.2–36.3 kg) coyotes are not uncommon. On

Fig. 2. Typical male eastern coyote (A) and atypical cream or "blond" female (B) both from the Maine Seven Islands Litter. Maine coyotes typically, are similar to (A), but the occurrence of the latter type is worth noting. (Photos by H. Hilton.)

several occasions I have weighed animals reputed to exceed 70 pounds (31 kg), and found them to weigh only 35–40 pounds (15.8–18.1 kg). The average weight of coyotes throughout the East is less than 18 kg, and authenticated reports of coyotes exceeding 22 kg are uncommon.

The external appearance of eastern coyotes, basically, is not unlike that of western coyotes and wolves, while external characteristics of domestic dogs (e.g., curled tail, irregular markings, tipped-over ears) are absent. The ears are erect, the tail is full and straight, the black tail-gland spot is conspicuous, and the chest is narrow. In addition, a broad (8–10 cm), black tail tip, and a prominent V-shaped shoulder harness are characteristic (Fig. 2).

Four color phases can be distinguished (Hilton, 1976; Hilton and Kutscha, 1978) which range from dark brown to blond or reddish blond, but the most common (typical) is an overall gray-brown, with tan legs, rufous flanks, rich rufous ears, and grizzled gray frontals. A light eye ring was particularly evident on several blond-colored (cream) specimens.

B. Origin and Identity

1. The Question of Hybridization

On the basis of external appearance, the eastern coyote might represent the rapid evolution of *latrans* to meet new environmental demands. The multiple character analyses (see Section II,D) could be interpreted similarly. Lawrence and Bossert (1969, p. 10) concluded, however, that "the combinations of non-homogeneous [morphological] characters strongly suggest multiple ancestry." Furthermore, the variability of characters, and the comparatively rapid acquisition of characters considered diagnostic of wolves and/or dogs, and the absence of such modifications where coyote range has expanded elsewhere, lend support to a hypothesis that the eastern coyote evolved, at least in part, by hybridization.

Almost from the beginning of the coyote expansion eastward, the concept of coyote–dog hybridization was promulgated both popularly and scientifically. For example, coyote–dog crosses were reported as early as 1885 (Seton, 1929), and more recently by others including Bee and Hall (1951), McCarley (1962), Carson (1962), and Gipson (Chapter 8). The implications of such crosses occurring in the Northeast often were exaggerated, and in some cases erroneously derived (see Cook, 1952). In retrospect, the belief that dogs and coyotes were interfertile was, of course, correct. But it was not until the last decade that the compatibility of dog and coyote karyotypes was corroberated by experimentation. However, Mengel (1971) questioned the importance of this fact because of doubt concerning the compatibility of other physiological and behavioral traits of dogs and coyotes, and in 1969 the idea that wolves, as well as dogs, were implicated in the origin of the eastern coyote was brought to the fore by Silver and Silver (1969) and Lawrence and Bossert (1969). At that time there was still no conclusive evidence that coyotes and wolves could (or would) hybridize. But Standfield (1970) presented a hypothesis that direct coyote–wolf crossbreeding was responsible for *C. lupus lycaon,* Tweed type occurring in Ontario. In 1971, Kolenosky (1971) added support to that hypothesis by reporting a successful mating of a coyote and wolf which produced offspring having phenotypes similar to those of eastern coyotes. In view of Mengel's credible arguments against extensive coyote–dog hybridization and the apparent absence of singularly doglike characteristics in eastern coyote specimens examined (Hilton, 1976), the coyote–wolf hybrid theory is most attractive.

2. Supporting Evidence for Coyote–Wolf Hybridization

Mengel (1971) suggested that a phase shift in the breeding cycle of offspring from dog and wild *Canis* parents (Ilgin, 1941; Gier, 1968; Silver and Silver, 1969; Kennelly and Roberts, 1969) was sufficient to prevent coyote–dog hybrids (coydogs) from back crossing with coyotes, thus blocking the infusion of dog genes into the gene pool of wild *Canis* populations. First-generation coyote–dog hybrids generally would result when an ovulating coyote female accepts a male dog (which unlike male wild *Canis,* is constantly in breeding condition). Theoretically, populations of such hybrids could freely intrabreed; however, at least three factors would act to prevent coydog populations from becoming established and reproducing, at least in northern latitudes: (1) the phase shift in breeding period would cause subsequent generations to be born in the middle of winter; (2) unlike wild *Canis* the male parent does not usually assist in the care of the young (Mengel, 1971, p. 323); and (3) successive generations would continually lose the adaptive characteristics of wild *Canis*, particularly coyotes, and would not be so competitive in the wild. Successive generations produced by backcrosses with dogs would resemble domestic dogs so much that it is unlikely that they would be called "coydogs" (Gier, 1968; Silver and Silver, 1969; Mengel, 1971).

The rarity of wolves in southeastern Canada, and the frequent interspersion of coyote and wolf habitats along the margins of their respective ranges (Kolenosky and Standfield, 1975) is probably sufficient to break down the behavioral isolating mechanisms which normally exist.* Coyote–wolf hybrids would not suffer the liabilities of dog–coyote hybrids since coyotes and wolves are similarly adapted for breeding conditions in the wild.

3. Expansion and Evolution: A Theory

This theory of the evolution and development of coyotes in the East is based on existing information, and while the ideas are by no means mine alone, I must accept responsibility for the conclusions. The reader is directed to the paper by Mengel (1971) for further details of the physiological aspects of the theory.

Large coyotes of the subspecies *thamnos* probably began to emigrate from the Plains States and the Canadian Prairies soon after the turn of the century in response to poisoning campaigns of the late 1800's. The first of two main migration routes believed used by coyotes brought them into Ontario from Manitoba and northeastern Minnesota; the second brought them into southern and southeastern Ontario at Sault Ste. Marie and the vicinity of Lake St. Clare (Ontario Department of Lands and Forests, 1974). The first expansion was extensive but short lived and resulted in established populations primarily in agricultural lands north of Lake Superior and Lake Huron. The second route brought coyotes into contact with the then declining numbers of *C. lupus lycaon*, Algonquin type† in

* Kolenosky and Standfield (1975, p. 71) state: "We can only speculate that in areas where [wolf] types are sympatric, highly developed social and behavioral characteristics and adaptations to their prey have maintained an effective barrier against hybridization." They further state that the existence of the Tweed type ". . . lead[s] us to question the origin and identity of *C. l. lycaon*."

† For a review of variation among gray wolves in Ontario see Kolenosky and Standfield (1975).

southern Ontario. Direct hybridization with this particularly small race of wolf likely resulted in what is now classified as *C. lupus lycaon,* Tweed type. Such a cross produced phenotypes which were, to the untrained eye, indistinguishable from those of large coyotes or small wolves. These animals may have occupied remote areas of eastern Quebec and even Vermont and Maine in low numbers before wolves were completely exterminated in the northeast.* As the true wolves continued to be pushed out of southern and eastern Canada the more adaptable and resistant coyotelike animals continued to maintain breeding populations which, in the absence of wolves and pure western coyotes, and through natural selection of the most beneficial traits, rapidly evolved to become a true breeding animal similar to the eastern coyote of today.

Habitat conditions, normal cyclic trends in prey abundance, agricultural trends, and other factors probably influenced the size and distribution of the evolving coyote populations in the early years. Periodically, pioneering individuals spilled into various inhabited areas of Quebec, New York, and parts of New England and bred with domestic dogs. The resulting first-generation hybrids (coydogs) proceeded to confuse taxonomists and then died out (e.g., see Severinghaus, 1974). A well-ensconced coydog legacy persists to this day largely because of the writings at the time.

Following periodic amenable environmental conditions (e.g., severe winters of the 1950's and late 1960's provided an abundance of winter-killed deer; see Chambers *et al.*, 1974), coyotes continued to disperse northeastward, and by the mid-1970's, they were well established in all areas but extreme northeast Canada.

C. Cranial and Dental Morphology

Eastern coyote specimens for which morphological descriptions are available are largely from New Hampshire and Massachusetts (Lawrence and Bossert, 1969) and Maine (Richens and Hugie, 1974; Hilton, 1976, 1977). In addition, I was fortunate to obtain on loan a series of coyote skulls from southern Quebec.

Individual skulls from New Hampshire, Maine, and Quebec vary from being coyotelike in narrowness of the rostrum, in inflation and elevation of the braincase, and in relative size of teeth, to being uncoyotelike in the shortened rostrum, in the elevated frontals, and in the disproportionate dental characters. Lawrence and Bossert (1969) found that most skulls of

* Published reports supporting this hypothesis are lacking, but the continuous occurrence of animals irrespectively referred to as "les loups" (wolves) to this day suggests that the transition from wolf to coyote occupation in certain areas was sufficiently inapparent that local people were not aware of the change.

the Boscawen Series* and of several wild specimens exhibited incompatibility of size of teeth in relation to length of jaw. Relatively few of the Maine skulls exhibited overlapping premolars, and less than a third were badly crowded. In general, however, a typical eastern coyote skull exhibits a combination of coyote and wolf characteristics.† Maine coyote skulls averaged 6 and 11% larger than those of western coyotes in total length and breadth, respectively. Unlike western coyotes, the Maine skulls invariably lacked the round protuberance of the occiput and the accessory cusp on P/4. Like wolves, the braincase was positioned low, the postorbital region was well separated from the anterior constriction of the braincase, and the frontal shield was moderately elevated (see Fig. 3).

The Quebec skull series exhibited dichotomy: one group was coyotelike in having a short postorbital region, a typical round protuberance of the occiput, a small size (within one standard deviation of the mean skull length for western coyotes), and light dentition and cranial proportions. The second group was indistinguishable from the typical Maine skulls.

The proportions and sizes of cranial and dental features, although sometimes visually distinctive individually, overlap to such a degree that conventional diagnostic techniques (e.g., Young and Jackson, 1951) are not sufficient to separate satisfactorily many *Canis* species taxonomically, especially when overall size is not considered as a factor. Thus, a new approach was required.

D. Discriminant Function Analyses

Lawrence and Bossert (1967, 1969) applied the numerical technique of linear discriminant function analysis to *Canis* taxonomy and developed "target" discriminant function coefficients for domestic dogs, wolves, and coyotes. They found that the discriminant function values for various possible hybrids were intermediate to the values of their respective parental types. The New Hampshire coyotes (Silver and Silver, 1969) subjected to this analysis were the first eastern coyotes to be analyzed using this technique, and the shift away from coyoteness towards wolf- and/or dogness was described. A review of that work is presented by Lawrence and Bossert (1975) and need not be repeated here.

* The Boscawen series were offspring of a sibling pair of adults taken from a den as whelps and raised by Silver and Silver (1969). These were thereby subject to the genetic liabilities of inbreeding.

† Wolflike could also be interpreted as doglike; however, several specific characteristics of dogs described by Lawrence and Bossert (1967) are notably absent in Maine and Quebec skulls that I have examined. These include relatively small teeth, elongated interorbital region and palate, and heavily ossified braincase and bullae. Thus, together with corresponding considerations contained in this chapter, I have excluded dogs from general comparative discussion.

In a recent application of the discriminant function technique (Fig. 4), I found that of the available canid skulls collected in Maine from 1968 to 1976, all but three were positioned intermediate to coyotes and wolves in the same general range as the New Hampshire animals. The remainder were unmistakably dogs, and no coyote–dog hybrids were recognized. Thirty coyote skulls from Quebec were collectively positioned higher than the Maine skulls but overlapped considerably, largely due to the marked dichotomy described earlier (Section II,C). The difference in mean discriminant function values was consistent with the trend noted by Lawrence and Bossert (1969). The values of eastern coyote specimens from

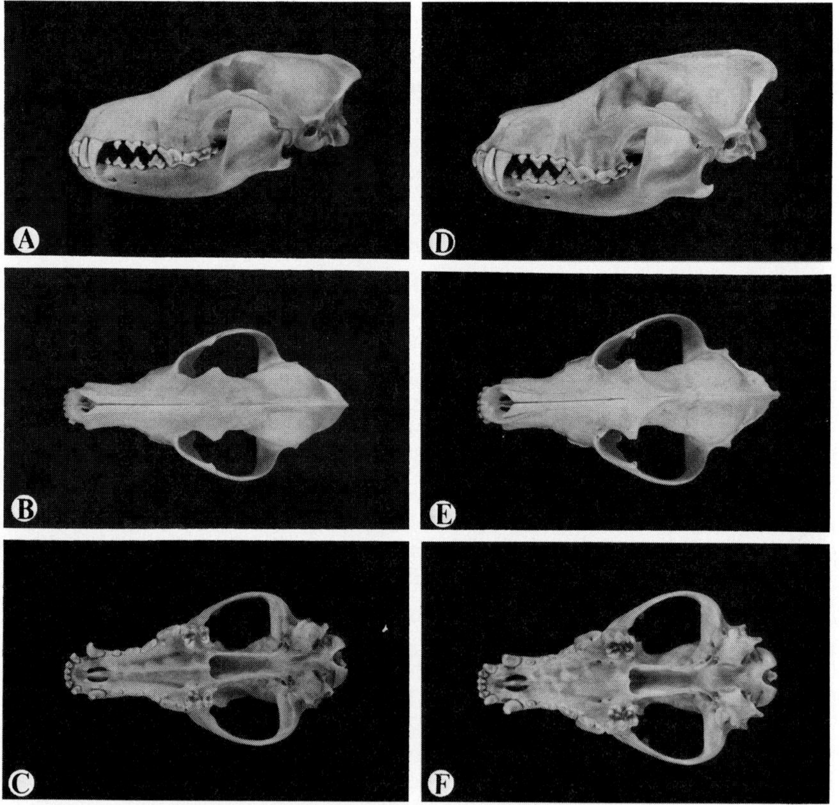

Fig. 3. The variation in eastern coyote skulls is shown by two male skulls in the Maine collection: C-42-74 (A–C), and C-45-74 (D–F). Note the comparative massiveness of the latter. The former is positioned near the mean, the latter near the right margin of the value range for Maine specimens shown in Fig. 4. (Photos by H. Hilton.)

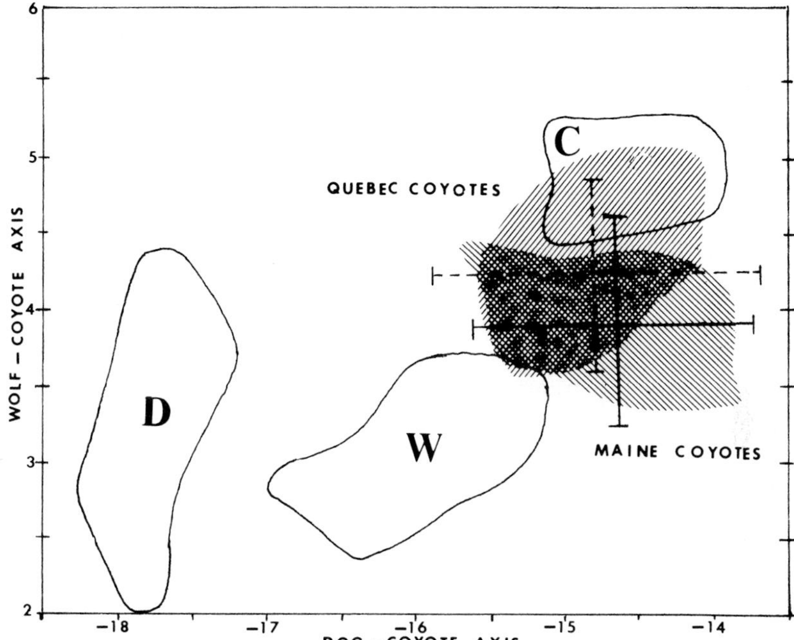

Fig. 4. Comparison of results of discriminant function analyses of Maine and Quebec coyotes. The solid and dashed coordinates represent the mean and 2 standard deviations of the discriminant function values for Maine and Quebec coyotes, respectively. The dog (D), wolf (W), and western coyote (C) ranges and the coordinate axes are identical to those of Lawrence and Bossert (1967, 1969).

throughout their range were situated similarly to those of the Maine and New Hampshire animals. But the values of several specimens from Pennsylvania (H. McGinnis, personal communication) and New York (R. Chambers, personal communication) were more extremely varied suggesting that in areas where access to a variety of *Canis* stock exists, or where introductions may occur, coyote populations consist of a "mixed bag" of phenotypes. Elsewhere, as in Maine, coyote populations may still be evolving towards a more homogeneous state.

III. REPRODUCTION AND GROWTH

The reproduction, growth, and development of eastern coyotes was first documented by Silver and Silver (1969) during a 6-year study of New

Hampshire Wild Canids.* I raised 5 Maine coyotes (Seven Islands Litter) which, together with two other siblings, provided additional data on growth and development. Field data were collected in connection with other work (Hilton, 1976) in remote western Aroostook County, Maine. The behavioral development of the Seven Islands coyotes was studied by Bekoff (Chapter 5).

Tracking data from Maine indicated that females became sexually active near the end of the first week of February. Traces of blood appeared in the urine, and sets of two coyote tracks became more common than single tracks. The patterns of travel appeared not to change perceptibly, but there was more activity suggestive of den hunting. By the first week of March, dens were being prepared but also abandoned; by mid-March dens appeared to be maintained periodically. Coyotes apparently prepared more than one den and subsequently transferred young from one to the other, immediately if disturbed, and periodically even when not disturbed (R. Sirois, personal communication). Many of the dens were of a temporary nature. Several which I found in March were virtually nonexistent later in the spring after snow-melt revealed them to be unprotective brushpiles and tree roots. Fox dens which had been abandoned or from which the inhabitants had been evicted by coyotes, were often used. Still, the coyote is capable of digging its own dens in the absence of existing facilities. Dens were generally within a few hundred yards of a stream or other early-opening water.

The young are born about mid-April, but dates may range from early April to the first week in May after a gestation period of 61–66 days (Silver and Silver, 1969). The Seven Islands Litter was 12 to 15 days old on April 29 when the pups were taken from a den near the St. John River by wardens. These birth dates are essentially the same as those reported for western coyotes (Gier, 1975), even though at northern latitudes they are born in the final throes of winter.

Examination of the uterine scars of five mature Maine coyotes showed an average of 7.0 full-term uterine scars (Hilton, 1976); six females from Massachusetts and Vermont showed 6.8 (J. Lorenz, personal communication). Silver and Silver (1969) reported captive litter sizes of 5–10 (average 7.8). In the New Hampshire study sex ratios at birth were in favor of females, 1 : 1.4; in the Maine litter of 7, 1.3 : 1.

At birth, pups are dark gray, but by 2 weeks the head is distinctly reddish brown with white marks becoming distinct on the chest. By 6 weeks, individual variation is apparent (Fig. 5), and by the third month, adult markings are conspicuous. Weights of New Hampshire coyotes at birth averaged 440 gm (Silver and Silver, 1969). Pups in the Seven Islands Litter (not weighed

* In their report, the Silvers referred to eastern coyotes as New Hampshire Wild Canids, to distinguish them from subsequent hybrids, western coyotes and other *Canis* in the study.

Fig. 5 Two of the Seven Islands Litter at 6 weeks. Reneé, on left, exhibits light coloration and eye rings; Dominique, on right, is darker and heavier. (Same individuals as in Fig. 2). (Photo by H. Hilton.)

at birth) averaged 0.8 kg by 2 weeks, 1.9 kg by 6 weeks, 5.9 kg by 3 months, and 13.2 kg by 6 months. At 8 months, the weights of females began to stabilize, but males continued to gain weight well into the second year.

Unlike many western coyotes (see Silver and Silver, 1969, p. 27), eastern coyotes do not appear to breed until the second year. None of the yearling female specimens examined in Maine were pregnant or had produced litters, nor did any of the captives breed in the first year. Vaginal smears taken from New Hampshire coyotes at 10 months showed that estrogen levels were low, indicating that ovulation did not occur. Testicles remained undeveloped until 19–20 months. A male examined during the breeding season by Dr. E. D. Colby at Dartmouth Medical School did not naturally produce sperm in the first year of age. Only after 7 weeks of gonadotropin injections did sperm production begin (Silver and Silver, 1969, p. 11).

IV. HABITAT

In their expansion eastward coyotes have occupied farmland, timberland, wilderness parks, rural, and even suburban habitats. They occur in the heavily forested regions of northern New York (Chambers *et al.*, 1974) where there is little or no agriculture and in the more highly agricultural regions from New York to Quebec (Georges, 1976) and New Brunswick (Cartwright, 1975). While there is insufficient data available to precisely relate habitat productivity to coyote densities in the Northeast, it seems likely that semiagricultural areas support higher densities of coyotes than heavily forested areas or extensively cleared agricultural regions. Chambers *et al.* (1974) concluded that "within its established range, coyote populations are more dense in areas containing a mixture of agricultural and forested lands." Most coyotes taken in Maine are from areas containing both mixed-growth third and fourth generation timber and small farms, many of which have been abandoned or neglected. These areas provide abundant edge for a variety of prey species.

As in New York, however, coyotes do occur in the more heavily forested areas of western and northern Maine and parts of New Hampshire, generally concentrating along the major watersheds. In New Hampshire the recorded observations and collections of coyotes appeared closely associated with water systems (Silver and Silver, 1969, p. 38). In the winter in northern Maine I found that most hunting, travel, and denning activities were associated with the Big Black, St. John, and Allagash rivers and their tributaries (Hilton, 1976). Especially in the winter, whitetailed deer (*Odocoileus virginianus*), snowshoe hare (*Lepus americanus*), and other potential prey thrived in the edge areas provided by these streams.

Where the distribution and extent of human populations varies widely, coyote observations and kills are, at best, unreliable indices to coyote density. Such records are more likely related to the extent of the human activity than to the number of coyotes. While actual coyote densities will vary by habitat, geographical region, and time, Richens and Hugie (1974) have concluded that there is no barrier to coyote expansion into areas where there is adequate food available.

V. FOOD HABITS

The coyote has been shown by a number of researchers (e.g., Murie, 1939; Sperry, 1941; Gier, 1975) to be an extremely versatile scavenger and predator. Unlike the wolf, which is a predator almost exclusively of ungulates (Mech, 1970; Pimlott, 1975), the opportunistic character of coyote feeding is likely most responsible for its great success in the face of habitat manipulation and destruction by man. The loss of that versatility through hybridization with wolves might operate against the survival of coyotes. On the other hand, if wolf hybridizations increased the capability of the coyote as a predator through greater physical strength and/or aggressive behavior, then that versatility may be enhanced. These and other behavioral considerations make food habits and prey relationships a critically important aspect of research on canid ecology and taxonomy.

Unfortunately there is limited information regarding the comparative predatory behavior of wolves and eastern coyotes. Stomach and scat contents from New York (Hamilton, 1974; Chambers *et al.*, 1974) and Maine (Hilton, 1976) have shown whitetailed deer in some form to be an important component of the coyote diet in the east, but the opportunistic tendency for feeding on any available food is still apparent.

A. Opportunistic Food Selection

In the lower third of Maine where human habitations are sparse but well distributed, habitat is a generous mix of active and abandoned farmland providing an abundance and variety of food sources. Here the diet of coyotes is typically diverse and consisting of small mammals, vegetation (apples, berries, grasses), dump refuse, deer, and domestic livestock, and smaller amounts of virtually every conceivable food item available (Richens and Hugie, 1974; Hilton and Richens, 1975; Hilton, 1976). Deer remains were considered by the former authors to be generally of nonpredation sources. Over 1500 scats collected in the central Adirondacks (N.Y.) suggested that snowshoe hare was the primary prey species. Remains of whitetailed deer were found in large proportion, but it was concluded by Hamilton (1974) that most of those remains were carrion resulting from hunter-killed and winter-killed deer. The remainder of items were typically diverse: overall 78% mammal and 36% vegetation by frequency of occurrence. Fruit and insects comprised nearly one-third of the items in summer scats. Of 56 scats collected in northern Onondaga County, New York, mice (including *Peromyscus, Microtus*), cottontail rabbits (*Sylvalagus floridanus*), woodchucks (*Marmota monax*), muskrats (*Ondatra zibethica*), and berries were the most frequent items (Chambers *et al.*, 1974). J. Lorenz (personal communication) found the diet of coyotes in Massachusetts and Vermont to be equally diverse. Of 414 scats collected in northern Maine (Hilton, 1976), where spruce–fir forests are broken only by waterways, logging roads, and timber cuttings, the diet appeared to be less diverse, but included most available prey items: whitetailed deer, snowshoe hare, muskrat, beaver (*Castor canadensis*), and birds. The diet included other items in trace amounts such as insects, amphibians, and field mice. No dump refuse was found, although active dumps at logging camps were accessible to coyotes. In winter, whitetailed deer and snowshoe hare almost exclusively comprised the mammal portion of the diet, with field mice, muskrat, and beaver each comprising less than 5% frequency. In summer, mice were more important (38%) than deer (20%). The diminished diversity in diet is related to the lower diversity of prey in deep-woods habitats. Clearly, the opportunistic feeding habits of *Canis latrans* has not been lost in the eastern coyote.

B. Relationship with Prey

Coyotes of most subspecies are less than half the size of wolves and hve evolved as relatively unspecialized predators. Unlike the coyote, the wolf has historically fared best where large prey satisfied a high-energy budget. The western coyote being smaller and less social must satisfy a lower energy requirement, and can survive well on small mammals, perhaps approaching an energy imbalance when relying on larger or more difficult prey. However, in the absence of other food, whitetailed deer, and perhaps beaver may be effectively utilized by the physically and behaviorally well-equipped eastern coyote.

1. Deer Hunting Success

In the remote northwestern region of Maine, I followed 109 sets of coyote tracks a total of 206 km (Hilton, 1976). In December, all track sets consisted of single animals. From January to late February, over 80% of the track sets were of two coyotes, and in March (essentially late winter at that latitude) groups of 3 to 4 animals were not uncommon. Ninety percent of the track sets intersected at least one deer track of similar age.* Single coyotes crossed the most deer tracks (44) but rarely pursued deer and made no kills. Paired coyotes crossed slightly fewer tracks (36) but pursued deer more often and were successful (11 kills) in 79% of the pursuits. The frequency of multiple coyotes crossing deer tracks was the lowest (18), but they pursued relatively often, and successfully killed 4 deer. Overall, for the 4-month-period coyotes followed 32% of the deer tracks crossed, and deer were found killed in 15% of the intersections; a success rate of 15 to 48% which is based on the number of kills/intersection (minimum) and number of kills/pursuit (maximum). Absolute predation efficiency (see Mech, 1970) could not be determined, because these were not known coyotes being monitored continuously. A total of 17 dead deer was examined in the study area during the study, only two of which apparently were not killed by coyotes. This suggests that direct predation by coyotes traveling in pairs or groups of 3–4 was responsible for much of the deer remains (over 60% frequency) found in coyote scats in that area during the same period.

Nonpredatory winter loss of deer was minimal during the study period because of mild winter conditions (unpublished dead-deer survey records and other winter-severity indices, Maine Dept. Fish. and Wildlife). Thus, a preference for fresh-killed deer or carrion could not be established. It would seem that Chambers' *et al.* (1974) contention that coyotes thrived on winter-killed deer in the Adirondacks is a fair evaluation. However, the question of whether or not eastern coyotes can accent a deer decline caused by severe

* See Hilton (1976) and Hilton and Richens (1975) for experimental design.

winters, successional changes in vegetation, etc., and can become a proximate factor in the absolute loss of deer remains unanswered.

2. Prey Selection and Hunting Effort

Of 38 whitetailed deer killed by coyotes during 1974–1976 in Maine and examined by myself and W. Noble, Maine Dept. Fish. and Wildlife. Biologist, 2 occurred in December, 5 in January, 10 in February, 21 in March and April. Of the 17 deer killed in December through February, 13 were fawns, while only 6 out of the 21 killed in March and April were fawns. The mean age of males killed was 5.0 years and of females, 7.5 years. Some of the adults killed exhibited abnormalities such as poor teeth, a badly healed broken leg and low marrow fat content. The evidence that predation increased as the winter progressed may be attributed to increased vulnerability of wintering deer, their concentrated numbers and weakened condition, and also to increased nutritional requirements of pregnant coyotes (see Gier, 1975). Interestingly, it was during the late-winter period that groups of 3–4 coyotes were recorded most frequently during the tracking study. Whether these groups represented temporary social groups, organized to increase the efficiency of hunting large prey, is a question that should be considered in the future.

3. Predation on Moose and Beaver

There is no evidence that moose (*Alces alces*) are exploited by coyotes in Maine. The only occurrences of moose in scats were directly attributed to roadkills and other nonpredatory sources. In view of the absence of moose in the diet of Algonquin wolves in Ontario (Kolenosky and Standfield, 1975), it is highly unlikely that this largest North American ungulate would be utilized by eastern coyotes.

It has been suggested that predation on beaver may represent a distinct difference between coyotes and wolves in feeding behavior (R. Chambers, personal communication). Observations have been made in Maine of coyote-killed beaver, and the occurrence of beaver in scats is not uncommon. Two wardens for the Maine Department of Inland Fisheries and Wildlife, flying over the St. John River in early spring, located a freshly killed adult beaver on the ice. There was a blood trail from a hole where the beaver was attacked, and evidence of considerable struggling at the scene of the kill. Several trappers in western Maine have reported similar incidents, but to my knowledge no one has actually observed such an attack.

Beaver remains occurred in coyote scats in New York (Hamilton, 1974) in trace amounts in summer and fall. In Maine (Hilton, 1976) beaver appeared in coyote scats in all seasons but occurred most frequently in spring (18%) and fall (8%). The occurrence of beaver remains in winter coyote scats likely resulted from eating beaver carcasses discarded by trappers. However, that source would not be available at other times of the year. Interestingly, several beavers killed by ice floes in the spring on the St. John River were approached by coyotes, and played with, but not consumed. I recorded several instances of coyotes bedding down within view of beaver "holes" in the spring ice, and of active beaver trails accompanied by signs of coyote investigation. If coyotes in Maine have developed the searching image for beaver, it may reflect a behavioral trait of wolves that has been achieved by the eastern coyote through either a learned or genetically assimilated disposition to develop the skill to successfully capture and kill a prey normally left alone.

4. Food Consumption

Studies of food consumption by eastern coyotes are just beginning. Among these, Litvaitis and Mautz of the University of New Hampshire are examining the use-efficiency of wild-food items by the Seven Islands Litter (as adults). Their preliminary data show that the digestible dry matter intake ranges from 13.93 to 19.04 gm/kg body weight/day of whitetailed deer, snowshoe hare, and laboratory mice (*Mus musculus*) (J. Litvaitis, personal communication). The same captive coyotes at 8 months old (Hilton, 1976) consumed three beaver carcasses with an edible weight of 21.6 kg in six days, a rate of 0.72 kg/coyote/day. A deer killed in northern Maine in March by 2 or 3 coyotes was consumed in three days at a rate of 3.7–5.6 kg of meat/day/coyote, a consumption expectedly higher than that for penned animals. Elapsed times between feedings elsewhere were not adequately determined, but the feeding rates of 0.11–0.16 kg of meat/day/kg of coyotes are comparable to Mech's (1970) estimate of 0.09–0.19 kg of food/day/kg of wolves. Conversion estimates of feeding rates of western coyotes (Gier, 1975) correspond to these wolves and coyotes. The cumulative data suggest that consumption of meat in the wild by eastern coyotes likely would not exceed 1 kg/day/coyote on a sustained basis.

VI. SUMMARY

A form of coyote, differing substantially from previously described coyote subspecies, now occupies or is pioneering the northeast United States and much of eastern Canada. This wild canid is referred to as the eastern coyote, *Canis latrans* var., and is a product of hybridization among wild *Canis* of coyote, wolf, and coyote–wolf types. Local populations of first-generation coyote–dog hybrids have occurred during pioneering stages of the expansion eastward, but currently do not appear to be common. Feral dog populations having coyote influence do not occur in sufficient numbers to be important. Where they may occur, such animals would resemble dogs in appearance and behavior and would not be considered a part of the coyote population.

The taxonomic status of the eastern coyote has been defined by linear discriminant function analyses. Morphological changes in populations over geographic areas or through time may be compared. Currently, the discriminant function values of coyotes from New Brunswick, to New York are similarly situated on coordinate axes, intermediate to coyotes and wolves. Coyotes from Quebec and Pennsylvania exhibit a closer affinity to western coyotes than do specimens from Maine and New Hampshire, indicating that the latter populations are influenced less directly by western coyotes, and have evolved through genetic swamping of wolf and coyote traits. This process may not be complete and will likely continue to evolve naturally in the absence of alien canid introductions.

In regions, or at times, when large prey are more or less exclusively available, direct predation on deer, and perhaps beaver, may become proportionately more frequent. Limited studies to date have not shown that predation by eastern coyotes is a limiting factor in whitetailed deer populations. Large increases in coyote numbers have occurred following severe deer mortality from winter conditions. The conditions under which coyotes might become a limiting factor in absolute deer numbers have not been determined, but would likely be associated with internal changes in the age structure of deer populations brought on by successional changes in vegetation, severe winter conditions, or other long-term influences.

ACKNOWLEDGMENTS

The author is indebted to T. A. May, M. W. Coulter, and H. T. Gier for reviewing the manuscript. Several authors whose published works are cited also provided helpful comments and suggestions; in addition much appreciation is extended to Ben Day, Jay Lorenz, Helen McGinnis, and Joe Wiley for much needed information. Rodney Sirois served invaluably as guide, tracker, trapper, and field advisor throughout my coyote study in northern Maine. Jean-Paul Blais provided the skull series from Quebec; and numerous Maine Warden Service personnel provided important material contained in this chapter. The Maine Cooperative Wildlife Research Unit and the Maine Department of Inland Fisheries and Wildlife supported in part my initial eastern coyote research.

REFERENCES

Aldous, C. M. (1939). *J. Mammal.* **20**(1), 104–106.
Bee, J. W., and Hall, E. R. (1951). *Trans. Kans. Acad. Sci.* **54,** 73–77.
Carson, G. S. (1962). *Maine Fish Game* **4,** 8–9.
Cartwright, D. J. (1975). *Can. Wildl. Admin.* (*N.B. Sect.*) **1**(1), 2 pp.

Chambers, R. E., Gaskin, P. N., Post, R. A., and Cameron, S. A. (1974). *(N.Y. State) Conservationist* Oct.–Nov., 29(2) pp. 5–7.

Cook, R. (1952). *J. Hered.* **43,** 71–73.

Georges, S. (1976). *Can. Field Nat.* **90**(1), 78–79.

Gier, H. T. (1968). *Kans. Agric. Exp. Stn. Bull.* No. 393, 118 pp.

Gier, H. T. (1975). *In* "The Wild Canids: Their Systematics, Behavioral Ecology and Evolution" (M. W. Fox, ed.), pp. 247–262. Van Nostrand-Reinhold, New York.

Glatz, R. G. (1976). The Coyotes of Connecticut. M.S. Thesis, 51 pp. Univ. of Connecticut, Storrs.

Hamilton, W. J., Jr. (1974). *N.Y. Fish Game J.* **21**(2), 169–181.

Hilton, H. (1976). The Physical Characteristics, Taxonomic Status and Food Habits of the Eastern Coyote in Maine. M.S. Thesis, 67 pp. Univ. of Maine, Orono.

Hilton, H. (1977). *Maine Fish Wildl.* **19**(1), 2–4.

Hilton, H., and Kutscha, N. P. (1978). *Amer. Mid. Nat.* (in press).

Hilton, H., and Richens, V. B. (1975). *Trans. N.E. Fish Wildl. Conf., 32nd, N.E. Sec. Wildl. Soc., New Haven, Conn.*

Howard, W. E. (1949). *J. Mammal.* **30**(2), 169–171.

Ilgin, N. A. (1941). *J. Genet.* **42,** 359–414.

Kennelly, J. J., and Roberts, J. D. (1969). *J. Mammal.* **50,** 830–831.

Kolenosky, G. B. (1971). *J. Mammal.* **52**(2), 446–449.

Kolenosky, G. B., and Standfield, R. O. (1975). *In* "The Wild Canids: Their Systematics, Behavioral Ecology and Evolution" (M. W. Fox, ed.), pp. 62–72. Van Nostrand-Reinhold, New York.

Lawrence, B., and Bossert, W. H. (1967). *Amer. Zool.* **7,** 223–232.

Lawrence, B., and Bossert, W. H. (1969). *Breviora* **330,** 1–13.

Lawrence, B., and Bossert, W. H. (1975). *In* "The Wild Canids: Their Systematics, Behavioral Ecology and Evolution" (M. W. Fox, ed.), pp. 73–86. Van Nostrand-Reinhold, New York.

McCarley, H. (1962). *Southwest. Nat.* **7,** 227–235.

Mech, L. D. 1970. "The Wolf: The Ecology and Behavior of an Endangered Species," 384 pp. Nat. Hist. Press, Garden City, New York.

Mengel, R. M. (1971). *J. Mammal.* **52**(2), 316–336.

Murie, A. (1939). "Ecology of Coyotes in the Yellowstone," Fauna Ser. No. 4, 206 pp. U.S. Dep. Agric., Washington, DC.

Ontario Department of Lands and Forests (1974). "Wolves and Coyotes in Ontario," 14 pp. Ontario Dep. Lands For., Toronto.

Pimlott, D. H. (1975). *In* "The Wild Canids: Their Systematics, Behavioral Ecology and Evolution" (M. W. Fox, ed.), pp. 280–285. Von Nostrand-Reinhold, New York.

Pringle, L. P. (1960). *J. Mammal.* **41**(2), 278.

Richens, V. B., and Hugie, R. D. (1974). *J. Wildl. Manage.* **38**(3), 447–454.

Seton, E. T. (1929). "Lives of Game Animals," Vol. 2. Doubleday, Doran, Garden City, New York.

Severinghaus, C. W. (1974). *N.Y. Fish Game J.* **21**(2), 117–125.

Silver, H., and Silver, W. T. (1969). *Wildl. Monogr.* **17,** 41 pp.

Sperry, C. C. (1941). *U.S. Fish Wildl. Serv., Wildl. Res. Bull.* **4,** 70 pp.

Standfield, R. O. (1970). *Proc. Symp. Wolf Manage. Selected Areas North Amer.*
U.S. Fish Wild. Serv., Twin Cities, Minn. pp. 32–38. (Mimeo.)

Young, S. P., and Jackson, H. H. T. (1951). "The Clever Coyote," 411 pp. Stackpole, Harrisburg, Pennsylvania.

10

Ecology of Coyotes in Northern Minnesota

William E. Berg and Robert A. Chesness

I. INTRODUCTION

The coyote (*Canis Latrans*) is the most abundant large predator in Minnesota. Historical records indicate that coyotes were common prior to the early 1900's in the southern and southwestern Minnesota prairies, but rare throughout the northern forests (Surber, 1932). During the homestead era a combination of logging, fire, and land clearing created suitable coyote habitat in northern Minnesota. As a result, the northern two-thirds of the state presently comprises our main coyote range, with densities approximating one coyote per 1.6 km^2 (1 mi^2), while the coyote has been largely extirpated from its former southern range due to intensive agricultural practices.

Until this study began in 1968, no research had been conducted on coyotes in Minnesota. Our coyote studies are of a continuing nature, with most phases continuing through at least 1977. Therefore, information contained herein will be updated pending completion of the study.

The principal objectives of this study are to determine: (1) the seasonal food habits of coyotes in northern Minnesota, (2) the coyote population dynamics from age, sex, and productivity data, and (3) the home range, movements, and social behavior of coyotes. This paper summarizes the results to date of all phases of the study.

II. STUDY AREA

The principal study area for the telemetry portion of this study was a 4-township (3750 km^2) area in northwestern Aitkin County, and a 2-township (1870 km^2) area in southern Itasca County in northcentral Minnesota (Fig. 1). Predominant vegetation types consist of aspen (*Populus tremuloides*), balsam fir (*Abies balsamea*), marsh, black spruce (*Picea mariana*), and tamarack (*Larix laricina*), all interspersed with small farms involved mainly in cattle and sheep raising. Seventy percent of the land is owned by the state and county. Topography is flat to gently rolling, with annual precipitation averaging 66 cm (26 in.), and a snowfall averaging 127 cm (50 in.).

III. METHODS

A. Food Habits

Coyote carcasses were obtained from December through March from trappers and fur buyers throughout northern Minnesota. Stomachs were removed and frozen prior to food-habits analyses according to methods outlined by Korschgen (1969).

Scats were collected on designated routes and winter trails, dried, and autoclaved prior to examination. A hair collection consisting of 33 mammalian species was obtained to facilitate identification of hairs found in the stomachs and scats.

Coyote winter hunting and feeding behavior was determined by tracking coyotes in snow, and observing radiomarked coyotes from aircraft.

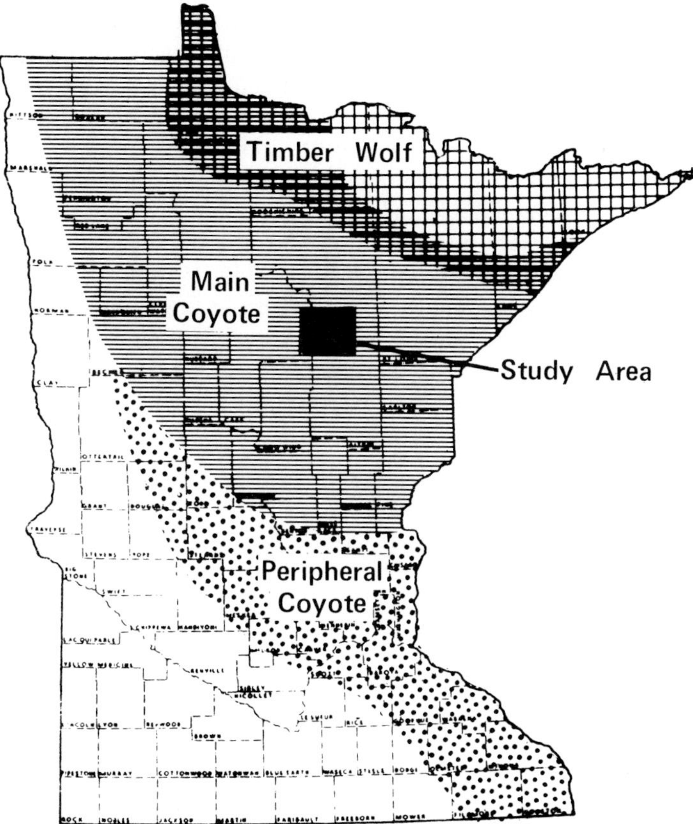

Fig. 1. Coyote study area in north-central Minnesota, with primary and peripheral coyote and timber wolf ranges.

B. Population Dynamics and Physical Parameters

Incisors were removed from lower jaws obtained from carcasses, and sectioned into 16 μm longitudinal sections using freeze-microtome. Ages were determined by microscopic examination of cementum layers as described by Linhart and Knowlton (1967). Other information obtained from carcass collections consisted of sex, weight of pelted and unpelted carcasses, and reproductive status.

C. Home Range, Movements, and Social Behavior

Coyotes were live-trapped in autumn using No. 3 and 4 steel leg hold traps. Padded jaws were tried but abandoned when injuries from unpadded traps were found to be minor. Animals were tranquilized with intramuscular injections of 10 mg/4.5 kg of live weight of phencyclidine hydrochloride (Sernalyn, Bioceutics, St. Louis, Missouri), and 20 mg/4.5 kg live weight of promazine hyrdochloride (Sparine, Wyeth Laboratories, Philadelphia, Pennsylvania).

Coyotes were weighed, measured, and eartagged with numbered monel metal tags (National Band and Tag Company, Newport, Kentucky). Transmitter collars were built by the Cedar Creek Bioelectronics Laboratory, University of Minnesota, and weighed 250–350 gm (9–13 oz). Aerial and ground telemetry techniques were used to locate coyotes on at least a weekly, and often more frequent, basis. Movement and home-range data were analyzed on the Wang 2200 Computer System, using the minimum area technique of home-range area determination (Dalke and Sime, 1938).

IV. RESULTS

A. Food Habits

A total of 1558 coyote stomachs were examined during the 8-year period 1968–69 to 1975–76. Remains of identifiable food items were found in 1204 (77.3%) of the stomachs.

Whitetailed deer was the predominant food item, occurring in 48.6% of the total stomachs (Table I) and comprising 41.8% of the total weight of all identifiable food items (Table II). Livestock, consumed by coyotes mainly as carrion, occurred in 18.9% of the stomachs and accounted for 23.3% of the total weight. Mice, while found in 23.1% of the stomachs, comprised only 4% of the total weight. Porcupine and snowshoe hare were found in 20.1 and 18.4%, respectively, of the stomachs, and comprised 4.0 and 12.8% of the total weight. Together, the five major food items comprised 85.5% of the total stomach content weight.

A total of 670 coyote scats were analyzed from 1970 through 1975 (Tables III and IV). Identifiable remains of deer were found in 40.9% of the scats, with the lowest frequency occurring in August and October. Deer remains were found in 54.8% of scats collected during the winter months (November–March), and 27.1% during the snow-free months. Adult and fawn deer hair was distinguished in the analysis of 541 scats collected from January–July, 1973–75, with adults and fawns found in 23.5 and 21.1%, respectively, of these scats. Fawn remains were most frequent in June and July scats (Fig. 2). Of those scats containing deer remains, fawns comprised the largest proportion (66.9%) of April–July scats (Fig. 2). Fawn hair found in April scats was likely prenatal.

TABLE I

Occurrence of Food Items in Coyote Stomachs from Northern Minnesota, 1968–1976

Winter:	1968–1969	1969–1970	1970–1971	1971–1972	1972–1973	1973–1074	1974–1975	1975–1976	Total
Total samples with food:	95	110	126	287	93	214	99	180	1204
Food items	Percent of occurrence								
Deer	54.7	46.3	43.6	44.9	49.5	49.1	50.5	50.6	48.6
Odocoileus virginianus)	2.1	26.3	23.8	26.8	28.0	14.6	13.1	16.2	18.9
Livestock									
Cattle (*Bos taurus*)	2.1	16.3	19.8	18.8	24.7	9.0	9.1	13.9	14.2
Hog (*Sus scrofa*)	0.0	8.1	8.7	12.2	4.3	4.2	0.1	1.7	4.9
Sheep (*Ovis aries*)	0.0	5.4	3.1	1.4	2.1	1.4	1.1	0.6	2.2
Mice (mainly *Microtus pennsylvanicus*)	14.7	27.2	20.6	25.7	14.0	45.4	34.3	28.3	26.3
Porcupine (*Erethizoadorsatum*)	25.2	22.7	23.8	34.8	22.6	12.1	12.1	7.8	20.1
Snowshoe hare (*Lepus americanus*)	21.0	6.3	16.7	16.7	28.0	31.8	9.1	17.2	18.4
Striped skunk (*Mephitis mephitis*)	3.1	0.9	3.9	8.3	3.2	1.4	7.1	3.9	4.0
Red squirrel	0.0	4.5	3.1	1.7	2.2	3.3	2.0	0.0	2.1
(*Tamiasciurus hudsonicus*)	1.0	0.9	0.0	1.0	1.0	1.9	4.0	3.3	1.6
Muskrat (*Ondatra zibethica*)	0.0	0.0	0.0	0.0	1.0	0.0	1.1	2.2	0.5
Beaver (*Castor canadensis*)	0.0	0.0	0.0	0.0	1.0	0.0	0.0	2.2	0.4
Raccoon (*Procyon lotor*)	3.1	12.7	10.3	10.4	12.9	9.8	0.0	1.1	7.5
Ruffed grouse (*Bonasa umbellus*)	7.3	15.3	10.2	11.9	9.7	8.9	3.1	7.2	9.2
Bird (passerine and unknown)	0.0	4.5	7.1	3.4	0.0	2.3	3.1	0.0	2.6
Poultry (mainly *Gallus domesticus*)	7.3	8.1	4.7	10.8	7.6	6.5	5.1	10.0	7.5
Unknown									

TABLE II

Weight of Food Items in Coyote Stomachs in Northern Minnesota, 1968–76

Winter:	1968–69	1969–70	1970–71	1971–72	1972–73	1973–74	1974–75	1975–76	Total
Total samples with food:	95	110	126	287	93	214	99	180	1204
Food items	Percent of total weight								
Deer	60.9	41.0	33.3	37.8	32.8	46.0	47.8	34.9	41.8
Livestock	3.0	24.0	37.6	28.8	33.7	11.8	20.5	27.2	23.3
Cattle	3.0	13.8	32.4	23.2	30.3	7.9	17.0	23.3	18.9
Hog	0.0	4.5	4.0	4.8	2.4	2.7	3.3	3.5	3.2
Sheep	0.0	5.7	1.2	0.8	1.0	1.2	0.2	0.4	1.3
Mice	1.7	1.2	1.3	4.4	1.3	10.0	6.3	2.4	3.6
Porcupine	5.7	4.6	4.9	5.2	3.2	0.4	5.7	2.6	4.0
Snowshoe hare	16.2	0.9	8.1	13.3	22.8	27.9	4.4	8.4	12.8
Striped skunk	3.1	T	5.0	2.3	0.3	0.1	2.1	3.2	2.0
Red squirrel	0.0	3.1	0.8	0.3	0.3	0.9	T	0.0	0.7
Muskrat	1.4	0.7	0.0	0.1	1.1	1.3	6.5	3.4	1.8
Beaver	0.0	0.0	0.0	0.0	T	0.0	0.6	4.7	0.6
Raccoon	0.0	0.0	0.0	0.0	0.5	0.0	0.0	1.2	0.2
Ruffed grouse	0.1	3.4	1.6	1.3	1.0	0.3	0.0	0.3	1.0
Bird (passerine and unknown)	*T*	0.1	0.1	0.1	0.1	0.1	0.2	0.2	0.1
Poultry	0.0	7.7	1.9	0.4	0.0	0.2	1.3	0.0	1.4
Unknown	5.9	3.1	3.0	0.3	0.4	0.3	0.5	3.5	2.0

TABLE III

Frequency of Occurrence of Major Food Items Found in 541 Coyote Scats in Northern Minnesota, January–July, 1973–1975[a]

Food item	Jan(44) %	Feb(80) %	Mar(19) %	Apr(36) %	May(95) %	June(177) %	July(90) %	Total(541) %
Deer								
Adult	54.6	50.0	47.4	16.7	13.7	15.2	8.9	23.5
Fawn	6.8	2.5	0.0	19.4	18.9	36.7	21.1	21.1
Total	61.4	52.5	47.4	36.1	32.6	52.0	30.0	44.5
Livestock	11.4	6.2	5.3	0.0	1.0	2.2	3.3	3.7
Mice	2.3	11.6	4.2	11.1	40.0	29.9	2.0	24.6
Porcupine	22.7	21.2	5.3	8.3	5.3	1.7	1.1	7.8
Snowshore hare	20.4	32.5	26.3	41.7	21.0	16.4	23.3	23.3
Striped skunk	0.0	0.0	5.3	2.8	0.0	1.1	0.0	0.7
Red squirrel	2.3	3.8	0.0	8.3	8.4	5.1	6.7	5.5
Muskrat	0.0	0.0	5.3	8.3	5.3	1.7	5.6	3.1
Beaver	0.0	0.0	0.0	0.0	3.2	2.2	1.0	1.5
Raccoon	0.0	0.0	0.0	0.0	1.0	0.6	2.2	0.7
Bird (all species)	6.8	7.5	5.3	2.8	3.2	1.7	6.7	4.2
Unknown	4.5	11.2	5.3	11.1	4.2	2.8	2.2	5.0
Plant (all items)	31.8	17.5	36.8	22.2	22.1	36.2	44.4	31.0

[a] Sample size in parentheses after month.

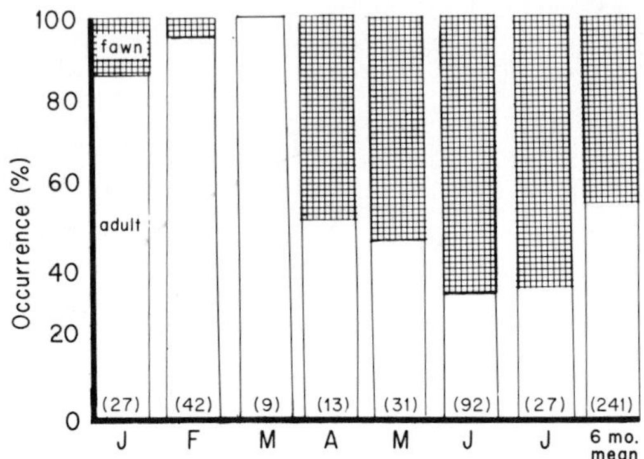

Fig. 2. Occurrence of adult and fawn whitetailed deer hair in 241 coyote scats containing deer remains, January–July, 1973–1975, in northern Minnesota.

Other remains most often found in scats were mice (which were less frequent in winter scats), snowshoe hare, bird (more frequent in winter scats), and porcupine (more frequent in winter scats) and plant material (Table III and IV). Plant items in the form of grass and seeds was found in approximately one-third of the scats each month.

Coyote trails in snow were followed for 509 km (318 miles) from 1968 to 1974. Deer, primarily in the form of carrion, was a major food source (Table V) and coyotes usually returned to the same carcass until it was almost consumed. Although the 509 km of coyote trails crossed deer tracks in 1656 instances, in only six of these did coyotes actually pursue the deer. A total of 17 definite and probable coyote deer kills were investigated during the study period, and of these, 11 (65%) were fawns. Snow tracking probably underestimated the consumption rate of small mammals due to their size. Coyote trails crossed snowshoe hare tracks 7508 times and of 54 actual chases, only three were successful (Table V).

B. Population Dynamics

During the period 1968–74, 960 coyotes were aged using the dental annuli technique (Table VI). Juveniles comprised 47.2% of the total sample, and varied annually from 40.1 to 53.0%. Yearlings comprised only 4.0 and 5.6%, respectively, of the 1972–73 and 1973–74 samples, as compared to a range of 16.2 to 32.3% during the 1968–69 to 1971–72 period. Coyotes between 2 and 3 years old accounted for 14.7% of the total, and varied annually from 4.0 to 32.3%. Seventy-four percent of the coyotes aged during the study were less than 3 years old. Six coyotes between 9 and 12 years old accounted for less than 1% of the total sample.

TABLE IV

Frequency of Occurrence (%) of Major Food Items Found in 129 Coyote Scats in Northern Minnesota, August–December, 1970–1973[a]

Food item	Aug(28)	Sept(54)	Oct(24)	Nov(3)	Dec(20)	Total(129)
Deer[b]	7.1	24.1	8.3	66.7	55.0	25.6
Livestock	0.0	5.6	12.5	0.0	5.0	7.0
Mice	21.4	29.6	50.0	0.0	10.0	31.0
Porcupine	17.9	18.5	25.0	0.0	0.0	20.9
Snowshoe hare	46.4	33.3	37.5	100.0	20.0	41.9
Striped skunk	7.1	5.6	8.3	0.0	0.0	5.4
Red squirrel	3.6	5.6	4.2	0.0	0.0	3.9
Muskrat	7.1	5.6	4.2	0.0	0.0	4.6
Beaver	0.0	1.9	0.0	0.0	0.0	0.8
Raccoon	0.0	1.9	4.2	33.3	0.0	2.3
Bird (All species)	28.6	29.7	20.8	0.0	5.0	27.1
Grass	35.7	35.2	50.0	66.7	10.0	40.3
Seeds	28.6	33.3	16.7	0.0	0.0	24.8

[a] During this period, fawns were not distinguished from adults.

TABLE V

Food Items Eaten by Coyotes in Northern Minnesota as Noted on 509 km (318 mi.) of Winter Coyote Trails, 1968–1974

Food item	Fresh kill	Probably killed by coyote	Carrion visit	Total
Deer	1[a]	1[a]	39	41
Deer (hunter gut pile)			6	6
Porcupine	1	2	12	15
Mice	30	274[b]		304
Shrew (*Soricidae*)	15[c]			15
Mole (*Condylura cristata*)	2[c]			2
Snowshoe hare	3	1	6	10
Red squirrel	4	1	4	9
Muskrat	1			1
Cattle			15	15
Sheep			1	1
Hog			3	3
Ruffed grouse	8	2	15	25
Passerine bird	5		3	8
House cat (*Felis catus*)			1	1
Dog (*Canis familiaris*)			1	1
Horse manure			4	4
Garbage dump			4	4

[a] Fawn.
[b] Many may be unsuccessful captures, some may be shrews.
[c] Not eaten.

The average sex ratio for 1558 coyotes collected from 1968–1976 was 109 males to 100 females (Table VII). Differences between years were not significant ($\chi^2_{(7\ \mathrm{d.f.})} = 12.900$, $p \geq 0.05$).

One-hundred four female reproductive tracts were examined. Placental scars were very evident in histological examination of coyotes more than 1 year old, but corpora lutea could only be positively identified in eight animals, all over 2 years old. Eighty percent of all reproductive tracts examined were from coyotes trapped between December and March, and all ovary pairs were between the small and medium stages of development during this period. For any given month, ovaries from adults were more developed than those from juveniles, and were characterized by crowded and numerous scars.

Weights of ovary pairs were not correlated to carcass weights ($r = 0.218$, $p \geq 0.05$). From December through March mean weights of ovary pairs from juveniles showed no change, but inadequate sample sizes prevented

TABLE VI

Age Structure of 960 Northern Minnesota Coyotes, 1968–69 to 1973–74[a]

Age class	Year						
	1968–69 (n = 68)	1969–70 (n = 136)	1970–71 (n = 127)	1971–72 (n = 279)	1972–73 (n = 101)	1973–74 (n = 249)	Total (n = 960)
$\frac{1}{2}$	45.5	50.7	48.8	40.1	46.5	53.0	47.2
$1\frac{1}{2}$	32.3	16.2	17.3	20.4	4.0	5.6	14.7
$2\frac{1}{2}$	10.3	11.0	11.0	17.6	6.9	9.6	12.1
$3\frac{1}{2}$	2.9	8.8	8.7	7.9	8.9	10.8	8.6
$4\frac{1}{2}$	5.9	5.9	7.9	7.5	11.9	9.6	8.2
$5\frac{1}{2}$	2.9	2.2	3.1	4.7	5.9	5.2	4.3
$6\frac{1}{2}$	0.0	3.7	0.8	0.7	6.9	3.2	2.4
$7\frac{1}{2}$	0.0	0.0	1.6	1.1	3.0	2.0	1.3
$8\frac{1}{2}$	0.0	0.0	0.8	0.0	3.0	0.0	0.4
$9\frac{1}{2}$	0.0	0.7	0.0	0.0	2.0	0.4	0.4
$10\frac{1}{2}$	0.0	0.7	0.0	0.0	0.0	0.0	0.1
$11\frac{1}{2}$	0.0	0.0	0.0	0.0	1.0	0.0	0.1
$12\frac{1}{2}$	0.0	0.0	0.0	0.0	0.0	0.4	0.1

[a] Expressed as the percent of each age class.

TABLE VII
Sex Ratios of Coyotes in Northern Minnesota, 1968–69 to 1975–76

Year	Males	Females	Males per 100 females
1968–69	32	55	58
1969–70	105	98	107
1970–71	86	92	93
1971–72	200	178	112
1972–73	62	58	107
1973–74	44	41	107
1974–75	88	80	110
1975–76	194	145	134
	811	747	108

analysis of ovaries from females more than 1 year old. Ovary weights were highly correlated ($r = 0.775, p \leq 0.05$) with animal age.

C. Physical Parameters

Whole weights as determined from pelted weights from the regression equation $N_y = 1.86 + 1.12x$ (Fig. 3) differed insignificantly with age (juvenile or adult) and sex ($\chi^2_{1\ \mathrm{d.f.}} = 0.337$, $p \geq 0.05$) as did differences between years ($\chi^2_{3\ \mathrm{d.f.}} = 0.089$, $p \geq 0.05$). Average weights for 204 coyotes were 12–13 kg (28–30 lb) for adult males, 11–12 kg (26–27 lb) for adult females, 10–11 kg (24–25 lb) for juvenile males, and 10 kg (23 lb) for juvenile females.

D. Home Range, Movements, and Social Behavior

A total of 100 coyotes fitted with radio transmitters between 1970 and 1975 provided sufficient data for analysis (Table VIII). Through 1975, 2434 relocations were obtained for 25 adult males, 25 adult females, 20 juvenile males, and 30 juvenile females. Twenty-one percent of the relocations during the autumn, winter and early spring were visually verified from aircraft.

Home-range sizes varied by age and sex (Table VIII). Home-range sizes averaged 68 km^2 (26.3 mi^2) and 16 km^2 (6.3 mi^2) for adult males and females, respectively. Whereas males occupied no exclusive territory and neighboring home ranges exhibited considerable overlap, females were essentially territorial and excluded other females, but not males, from their home range. Adult females occupied 54, 22, and 61% of their total home

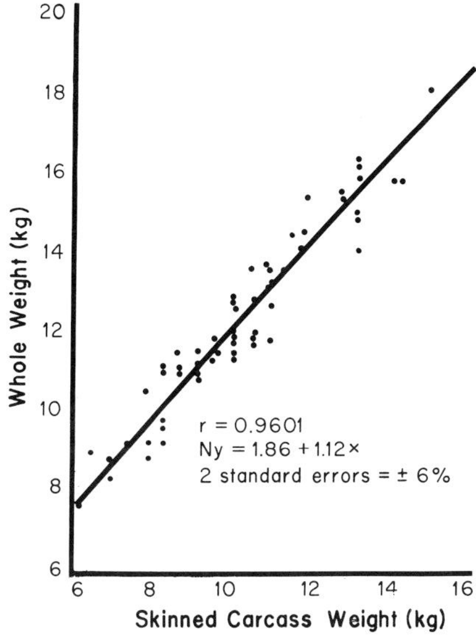

Fig. 3. Estimation of whole coyote weights from skinned carcass weights.

ranges, respectively, during the predenning (Jan. 15–Mar. 30), denning (Apr. 1–Jun. 10), and postdenning (Jun. 11–Aug. 15) periods.

Due to dispersal by more than 70% of the juvenile male and female coyotes from their parental home range, juvenile home-range sizes were more difficult to delineate. Prior to dispersal, juveniles averaged 5–8 km^2 (2–3 mi^2). Juveniles dispersed during October and November for distances of 16–68 km (10–55 mi), with an average of 48 km (30 mi). Dispersal was generally in a southeast to southwest direction, with the exception of two juveniles which dispersed 80 km (50 mi) east, apparently along a newly cleared powerline right-of-way.

TABLE VIII

Coyote Tagging and Relocation Data, 1970–1975, in Northern Minnesota

	Number radioed	Number relocations	Mean home range size	
			km^2	mi^2
Adult males	25	566	68	26.3
Adult females	25	784	16	6.3
Juvenile males	20	308	5–8	2–3
Juvenile females	30	776	5–8	2–3
	100	2434		

TABLE IX
Coyote Sociability during Winter, 1970–75, in Northern Minnesota

	Foot tracking		Aerial sightings	
Group size	Number of observations	Percent	Number of observations	Percent
1	108	60	254	62
2	61	34	123	30
3	8	4	25	6
4	3	2	4	1
5	0	0	2	1
	180	100	408	100

During the late autumn, winter, and early spring periods, coyotes were usually solitary (Table IX). Ground-tracking data indicated that 60% of the total 180 observations consisted of lone coyotes, whereas two coyotes together comprised 34% of the observations. Similarly, aerial observations of one and two coyotes, respectively, comprised 62 and 30% of the total. On two occasions five coyotes were seen together, and four groups of four coyotes each were recorded. Groups of coyotes in late autumn usually consisted of littermates, whereas male–female pairs accounted for most observations of two coyotes together during mid to late winter.

Nineteen timber wolves were trapped in a 281 km^2 (110 mi^2) area in and adjacent to the southeastern portion of our study area since 1970. Wolf numbers have varied from two to eight each year. Only six coyotes have been trapped during the study period in the area identified as being occupied by wolves, and radioed coyotes inhabiting the adjacent areas generally avoided the wolf-occupied range. Evidence of wolves chasing coyotes has been found, one fight between a wolf and a coyote has been seen from an aircraft, and two coyotes, one radioed, have been killed by wolves during the study period. Timber wolf densities averaging one per 27 km^2 (10 mi^2) in northeastern Minnesota likely prevent colonization by coyotes in that area (Fig. 1).

V. DISCUSSION

A. Food Habits

Whitetailed deer was found in nearly one-half of all coyote stomachs collected during the winter months, with livestock and snowshoe hare occurring in 18.9 and 18.4% of the stomachs, respectively. These items comprised 41.8, 23.3, and 12.8%, respectively, of the stomach contents by weight. Other studies have indicated higher use of livestock and rabbits (*Sylvilagus* and *Lepus*) (Sperry, 1941; Young and Jackson, 1951; Ferrel *et al.*, 1953; Fichter *et al.*, 1955; Korschgen, 1957; Hawthorne, 1972), while Nellis and Keith (1976) reported considerably lower use of snowshoe hare. A high winter use of deer similar to our study was also reported in Michigan (Ozoga and Harger, 1966) and Washington (Ogle, 1971). Poultry (mainly *Gallus domesticus*) was found in only 1.4% of Minnesote coyote stomachs during winter, as compared to 34% of stomachs during the winter in Arkansas (Gipson, 1974). Mice were important in our and other studies, but were noticeably low in Arkansas (Gipson, 1974).

Analysis of foodstuffs by frequency of occurrence and weight (Tables I and II) in Minnesota coyote stomachs showed obvious discrepancies. For example, 23.1% of the 1204 stomachs containing food items had mice in them, whereas mice only accounted for 3.6% of the total weight. Similarly, porcupine represented 4.0% of the total weight, but was found in 20.1% of all stomachs.

The biases and advantages of using identifiable remains in scats for food-habits studies were summarized by Brunner *et al.* (1976), and occurrence of food items in scats and stomachs was compared by Fichter *et al.* (1955) in California and Korschgen (1957) in Missouri. In Minnesota, whitetailed remains were found in 44.5% of the January–July scats examined, with fawns more frequent than adults in May, June, and July. A high incidence of fawn remains in early summer scats was also reported in California (Salwasser, 1974) and Washington (Ogle, 1971), with small mammals comprising the bulk of identifiable remains in central Manitoba (D. Pastuck and D. Glays, Manitoba Dept. Mines, Resources, and Environmental Management, personal communication) where during this period, low deer densities occur. Knowlton (1964) concluded that coyotes in Texas were involved in 75–80% of the total fawn mortality. Another Texas study (Cook et al., 1971), using telemetry, attributed coyote predation to 60–90% of all fawn losses due to predation, with the remainder attributed to bobcats (*Lynx rufus*).

It is important to note that in Minnesota, most deer eaten by coyotes in winter were consumed as carrion, with 47% of the carrion consisting of fawn remains. Of 17 definite and possible coyote-killed deer in our study, two (65%) were fawns.

B. Population Dynamics and Physical Parameters

Northern Minnesota coyote age ratios were similar to those reported in Kansas (Gier, 1968). Knowlton (1972) reported that 40% of Texas coyotes were young of the year, with 70–80% of the population less than 3 years old. Juvenile coyotes in New Mexico comprised 53% of the autumn population (Rogers, 1965). The oldest coyote aged in our study was an 11-year-old female, compared to a 13.5-year-old male in Alberta (Nellis and Keith, 1976) and a 14.5-year-old female in Texas (Knowlton, 1972).

Whereas some population studies indicate a 1 : 1 sex ratio (Knowlton, 1972; Nellis and Keith, 1976), two studies of heavily exploited populations documented sex ratios having a preponderance of females (Wetmore *et al.*, 1970; Knowlton, 1972). Most studies where human influence was not judged to be the controlling factor had sex ratios slightly favoring males (Young and Jackson, 1951; Gier, 1968; Wetmore *et al.*, 1970; Knowlton, 1972; Nellis and Keith, 1976; see also this study).

Weights of northern Minnesota coyotes were similar to those reported in Kansas by Gier (1968). However, weights in California of 10.9 kg (24 lb) and 9.5 (21 lb), respectively, for males and females (Hawthorne, 1971) and New Mexico of 10.9 and 10.0 kg (22 lb) (Van Wormer, 1964) were considerably lighter.

C. Home Range, Movements, and Social Behavior

Home ranges for adult coyotes in northern Minnesota were estimated at 68 and 16 km^2 for adult males and females, respectively, using radio telemetry. They were smaller than the 51–128 km^2 (20–50 mi^2) winter ranges estimated by snow tracking in Michigan (Ozoga and Harger, 1966). Ear-tagging studies in New Mexico and Wyoming indicated recovery distances of 35–45 km (20–28 mi) (Young and Jackson, 1951), and in Wyoming 11 km (7 mi) for adults, and 16 km (10 mi) for juveniles (Robinson and Cummings, 1951). The average recovery distance of 6 km (4 mi) in California (Hawthorne, 1971) is most comparable to Minnesota data. Longer distance recoveries based on tag-recovery data may be due to juvenile dispersal.

Dispersal of juvenile coyotes from parental home ranges played an unknown role in regulating population densities in our study area. Nearly all juvenile coyotes dispersed south; however, it is not known whether other coyotes to the north of our area also dispersed south to fill voids created by radioed juveniles. No other study noted a single direction dispersal pattern, and in fact Knowlton (1972) documented dispersal with no mention of ages from all directions into an area of intensive predator control.

Most dispersal in north-central Minnesota began in late October or November, with some taking place as late as January. The rate of movement averaged 11 km (7 mi) per week. Our dispersal dates were similar to those reported from Texas (Knowlton, 1972) and Iowa (Bogess, 1974), but later than the early October dispersal in Yellowstone Park (Robinson and Cummings, 1951) and Alberta (Nellis and Keith, 1976).

In our study, male coyotes occupied larger home ranges than did females, and juvenile males dispersed farther than juvenile females. This is in marked contrast to other studies in which females dispersed greater distances (Robinson and Grand, 1958; Knowlton, 1972; Nellis and Keith, 1976) or equal distances (Hawthorne, 1971) as compared to males. Two studies of fox dispersal in Iowa, however, documented far greater dispersal distances for juvenile males than juvenile females (Phillips *et al.*, 1972; Storm *et al.*, 1976).

VI. SUMMARY

From 1968 to 1976 (continuing) coyote (*Canis latrans*) food habits, population dynamics, and movements were studied in the forests of north-central Minnesota. Seasonal food-habits data obtained from 1558 stomachs, 670 scats, and 509 km (318 mi) of coyote trails indicated that whitetailed deer (*Odocoileus virginianus*) was the major food item, occurring in 48.6% of the total stomachs, and 40.9% of the scats. Adult deer was consumed mostly as carrion. Fawn hair was found in 66.9% of the April–July scats. Other major food items consisted of domestic sheep and cattle, snowshoe hare (*Lepus americanus*), mice (mostly *Microtus pennsylvanicus*), and porcupine (*Erethizon dorsatum*). Plant and fruit material was common in scats, but not stomachs, throughout the year. Ages of 960 coyotes indicated that 47.2% of the coyotes over a 6-year period were less than 1 year old, with 74% of the total sample being less than 3 years old. The sex ratio for the 1558 trapped coyotes was 109 males to 100 females. Weights of 104 ovary pairs were not correlated ($r = 0.218$, $p \geq 0.05$) with carcass weight, but were correlated ($r = 0.775$, $p \leq 0.05$) with age. Adult male coyotes averaged 12–13 kg (28–30 lb) in weight, compared to 11–12 kg (26–27 lb) for adult females, with juveniles weighing 10–11 kg (24–25 lb) and 10 kg (23 lb), respectively, for males and females. A total of 2434 relocations obtained from 100 radiotagged coyotes indicated home ranges averaging 60 km^2 (26.3 mi^2) for adult males, and 16 km^2 (6.3 mi^2) for adult females. Adult females were highly territorial, whereas adult male home ranges overlapped considerably. Juvenile males and females both occupied comparatively small home ranges of 5–8 km^2 (2–3 mi^2). Approximately two-thirds of the juveniles dispersed in late autumn, usually in a southerly direction, over distances averaging 48 km (30 miles). Sixty percent of 408 observations of coyotes from aircraft were of single individuals. Trapping and telemetry data indicated that coyotes generally avoided or were excluded from an adjacent area containing a pack of timber wolves (*Canis lupus*), and two coyotes, one radioed, were killed by wolves during the study period.

ACKNOWLEDGMENTS

We wish to acknowledge the skilled assistance of the three biological technicians on this study, Dennis Strom, Timothy Bremicker, and David Kuehn; trapper Leo Jewett; and the assistance of student interns Kenneth Patzoldt, Charles Cooper, Carol Engel, Debbera Ferretti on the scat analysis, Nancy Radio on ovary sectioning, and Kathleen Preece on the den work. Patrick Karns critically reviewed the manuscript.

REFERENCES

Bogess, E. K. (1974). *Coyote Res. Workshop, U.S. Fish Wildl. Serv., Denver, Colo.*

Brunner, H., Amor, R. L., and Stevens, P. L. (1976). *Aust. Wildl. Res.* **3,** 85–90.

Cook, R. S., White, M., Trainer, D. O., and Glazener, W. C. (1971). *J. Wildl. Manage.* **35**(1), 47–56.

Dalke, P. D., and Sime, P. R. (1938). *Trans. North Amer. Wildl. Conf.* **3,** 659–669.

Ferrel, C. M., Leach, H. R., and Tillotson, D. (1953). *Calif. Fish Game* **39**(3), 301–341.

Fichter, E., Schildman, G., and Sather, J. H. (1955). *Ecol. Monogr.* **25**(1), 1–37.

Gier, H. T. (1968). "Coyotes in Kansas." *Kans. Agric. Exp. Stn. Bull.* No. 393.

Gipson, P. S. (1974). *J. Wildl. Manage.* **38**(4), 848–853.

Hawthorne, V. M. (1971). *Calif. Fish Game* **57**(3), 154–161.

Hawthorne, V. M. (1972). *Calif. Fish Game* **58**(1), 4–12.

Knowlton, F. F. (1964). Aspects of Coyote Predation in South Texas with Special Reference to White-Tailed Deer. Ph.D. Thesis, Purdue Univ., Lafayette, Indiana.

Knowlton, F. F. (1972). *J. Wildl. Manage.* **36**(2), 369–382.

Korschgen, L. J. (1957). *J. Wildl. Manage.* **21**(4), 424–435.

Korschgen, L. J. (1969). *In* "Wildlife Management Techniques" (R. H. Giles, Jr., ed.), pp. 233–250. Wildl. Soc., Washington, D.C.

Linhart, S. B., and Knowlton, F. F. (1967). *J. Wildl. Manage.* **31**(2), 362–365.

Nellis, C. H., and Keith, L. B. (1976). *J. Wildl. Manage.* **40**(3), 389–399.

Ogle, T. F. (1971). *Northwest Sci.* **45**(4), 213–218.

Ozoga, J. J., and Harger, E. M. (1966). *J. Wildl. Manage.* **30**(4), 809–818.

Phillips, R. L., Andrews, R. D., Storm, G. L., and Bishop, R. A. (1972). *J. Wildl. Manage.* **36**(2), 237–248.

Robinson, W. B., and Cummings, M. W. (1951). *US. Fish Wildl. Serv., Spec. Sci. Rep. Wildl.* No. 11.

Robinson, W. B., and Grand, E. F. (1958). Comparative movements of coyotes as disclosed by tagging. *J. Wildl. Manage.* **22**(2), 117–122.

Rogers, J. G. (1965). Analysis of the Coyote Population of Dona Ana County, New Mexico. MS. Thesis, New Mexico State Univ., Las Cruces.

Salwasser, H. (1974). *Calif. Fish Game* **60**(2), 84–87.

Sperry, C. C. (1941). *U.S. Dept. Interior Wildl. Res. Bull. 4.*

Storm, G. L., Andrews, R. D., Phillips, R. L., Bishop, R. A., Siniff, D. B., and Tester, J. R. (1976). *Wildl. Monogr.* No. 49.

Surber, T. (1932). "The Mammals of Minnesota" Minn. Game Fish Dept. St. Paul.

Van Wormer, J. (1964). "The World of the Coyote." Lippincott, Philadelphia, Pennsylvania.

Wetmore, S. P., Nellis, C. H., and Keith, L. B. (1970). *Alberta Dep. Lands For. Wildl. Tech. Bull.* No. 2.

Young, S. D., and Jackson, H. H. T. (1951). "The Clever Coyote." Stackpole, Harrisburg, Pennsylvania.

11

Ecology of Coyotes in Iowa*

Ronald D. Andrews and Edward K. Boggess

I. HISTORY OF THE IOWA COYOTE

The prairie wolf or coyote *canis latrans* has been present in Iowa since the first settlers reached our present day boundaries. The timber wolf *canis lupus* probably outnumbered the coyote in the territory now considered Iowa, but their numbers were also comparatively small. The first bounty law in this territory was adopted in 1795 (Waller and Errington, 1961). This law imposed a 2 dollar reward for adult wolves, including the prairie wolf or coyote. Payment was made when the head was presented to the local justice

* These investigations were supported by funds from the Iowa Conservation Commission.

of the peace. Although the bounty law was mandatory throughout the territory, some counties could not stand the financial burden and in 1845, the legislature allowed optional bounty payments.

In 1858 the legislature, due to pressure from the state wool-growers association, enacted a new bounty law requiring all counties to pay $1.50 for coyotes of any age. Again, increased expense strained county budgets and the 1860 legislature reduced the bounty to 1 dollar and coyotes and timber wolves were lumped under one term, the "wolf." From that time until now, the two species have not been distinguished from one another despite the fact that the last authenticated timber wolf was killed in Iowa in 1925.

Bounties are still paid on coyotes on an optional county-by-county basis. Most of these are limited to counties in the coyote range of southern Iowa. In 1976, a few coyote range counties are discontinuing the optionally offered bounty payments. Fraudulent claims and tight county budgets may cause the bounty payments to become nonexistent despite the fact the bounty law may still be in the Code of Iowa.

II. RANGE AND HABITAT

During the course of a year a few coyotes can be found in all counties of the state; however, the highest populations are located in southern and western Iowa (Fig. 1). During the late 1950's coyotes began to increase significantly in Iowa. The increase coincided with changing farm practices which opened up small fields by clearing portions of timber away. About the same time a drastic decline in red fox (*Vulpes vulpes*) numbers occurred because of mange. Apparently, as the red fox population declined, the coyote population began to increase and fill the void left by the fox. Continued timber removal and piling brush in ditches and elsewhere, has apparently aided the coyote in establishing a strong foothold in southern and western Iowa.

Southern and western Iowa is characterized by gently rolling to hilly topography and represents remnants of an undulating to level plain which was modified by erosional processes following the retreat of the Kansas glaciers (Oschwald *et al.*, 1965). Vegetative cover estimates, based on information compiled from the Iowa Assessors Annual Farm Census (for 1973), indicate 50% of the area is in crop production including corn (*Zea mays*), soybeans (*Glycine max*), oats (*Avena sativa*), alfalfa (*Medicago sativa*), and red clover (*Trifolium pratense*). Approximately 35% of the area is permanent pasture with the major grasses being bluegrass (*Poa pratensis*) and smooth brome (*Bromus inermis*).

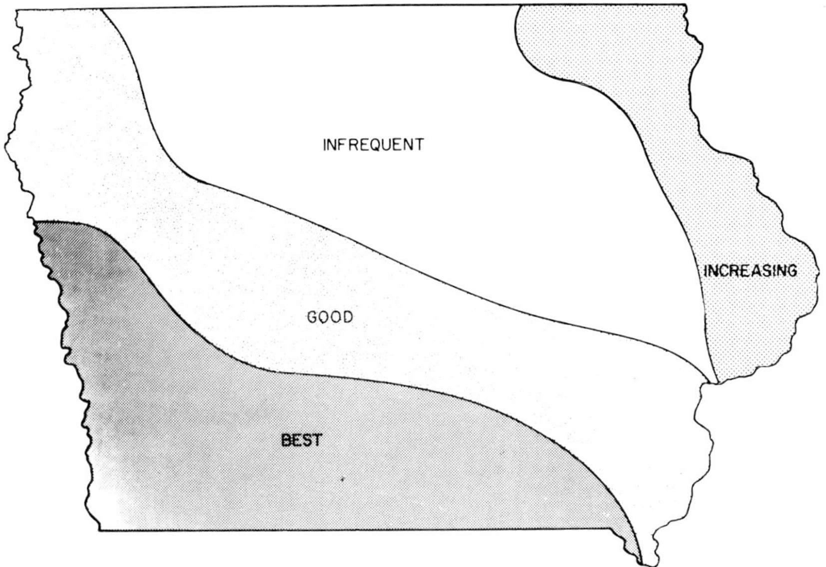

Fig. 1. Coyote population range and density.

Timbered draws and uplands make up approximately 15% of the area. The dominant canopy species in the upland areas are oak (*Quercus* sp.), and shagbark hickory (*Carya ovata*). The major components of the understory are ironwood (*Ostrya virginiana*), buckbrush (*Symphoricarpos orbiculatus*), hazelnut (*Corylus americana*), and gooseberry (*Ribes* sp.). Timbered draws are dominated by boxelder (*Acer negundo*), cottonwood (*Populus deltoides*), and dead American elm (*Ulmus americana*). Bottom land areas are composed primarily of silver maple (*Acer saccharinum*), American basswood (*Tilia americana*), and willow (*Salix* sp.).

The rural human population, although considerably higher than much of the North American coyote range, has decreased approximately 35% since 1960 (Iowa Assessors Annual Farm Census for 1960–1973).

III. IOWA COYOTE CHARACTERISTICS

Physical characteristics of the Iowa coyote are similar to coyotes in other states. The coyote is a rather shaggy, doglike animal with erect pointed ears and a bushy, bottle-shaped, drooping tail. The Iowa coyote is the characteristic gray color with yellowish tint and scattered black patches throughout the pelage.

Boggess (1975) found mean weights of 28.6 and 25.1 lb (13.4 and 11.4 kg) for adult male and female Iowa coyotes, respectively. These are comparable with values of 30 and 24 lb (13.6 and 11.3 kg) for male and female coyotes in Minnesota (Chesness, 1973) and with 31 and 26 lb (14.1 and 11.8 kg) averages for Kansas coyotes (Gier, 1968). Weights of Iowa coyotes were greater than the 24 and 21 lb (10.9 and 9.5 kg) for coyotes in California (Hawthorne, 1971) but less than the 34.8 and 30.2 lb (15.8 and 13.7 kg) values of coyotelike canids in Maine (Richens and Hugie, 1974). Iowa coyote weights in winter range from 21.0 (9.5 kg) to 38.4 lb (17.4 kg).

The incidence of coy–dogs (coyote–dog crosses), although quite small, appears to be increasing in Iowa. Each winter fur buyers, hunters, and trappers report handling a few of these animals. Interestingly enough, while actual data are not available, most reports of coy–dogs are received from the "fringe" area of the Iowa coyote range. This may reflect the fact that as coyotes expand into the "fringe" area and do not come in contact with a suitable mate, they will mate with roaming dogs. Coy–dogs generally are larger than the true coyote and most times they exhibit characters of both dogs and coyotes (Gipson *et al.*, 1974).

IV. DEN SITES

Iowa coyotes chose a variety of den sites. The more typical dens are short self-dug holes along a timbered creek bank. Other den sites include brush piles, tree roots, hollowed tree trunks, abandoned badger diggings, old farm buildings, and cupped-out pockets under the stems of gooseberry or other shrubs. Den sites are generally within or very near considerable amounts of timber and brush cover and for the most part, are fairly inconspicuous to man. Pasture renovation, where land is being cleared of timber and dozed into piles, has added greatly to the security of den sites. These brush piles are also havens for cottontail rabbits (*Sylvilagus floridanus*), voles (*Microtus* sp.), deer mice (*Peromyscus* sp.), and other wildlife considered important food sources for the coyote.

By the time the coyotes are 3–4 weeks old they become very mobile and many temporary dens are used. This mobility apparently adds to their security in that they do not remain at any one den long enough to become conspicuous to man. By 6 weeks of age the pups often do not den, but rather remain above ground except in periods of inclement weather.

V. REPRODUCTIVE STATUS

Reproductive data of the Iowa coyote has not been fully analyzed. It appears that the peak of the breeding season occurs in February; however, litters born as early as April 1 and as late as June 1 indicate that breeding spans the time from late January thru early April. According to Jackson (1976), at least 40 to 50% of yearling Iowa coyote females produce young the first year. This was based on microscopic examination of the ovaries of 75 coyotes. Jackson's data also indicated that average litter size was 5.6 pups. Data obtained at den sites provides inconclusive information on litter size. Average litter sizes for 1972, 1973, 1974, 1975, and 1976, based on the number of pups captured at den sites, were 5.25, 5.75, 6.90, 5.43, and 5.12 pups per litter. Sample sizes each year were small. In one instance we captured 12 pups all believed to be from the same litter. Generally there was only one family of coyotes per den; however, of the 35 dens where pups were captured, three had double litters or two females present. These were easily distinguishable by the size differences of the pups.

VI. POPULATION STRUCTURE

Ages from 389 coyotes, collected at fur buyer houses during January and February, were determined by the tooth sectioning technique described by Linhart and Knowlton (1967). Sex ratio information was obtained from 805 coyote carcasses checked at fur buyer houses during the winter. Over a 3-year period (1973–1975), 53.2% of the coyotes collected were males which was significantly different from an equal sex ratio ($p < 0.05$). From 191 coyote pups tagged at den sites during the spring, 97 were males and 94 were females.

Figure 2 shows the composite age–sex frequency distribution for all coyotes aged. A general preponderance of males is noted, particularly in the youngest and older age classes. This is in general agreement with findings of several other studies (Robinson and Cummings, 1951; Young and Jackson, 1951; Gier, 1968; Hawthorne, 1971; Mathwig, 1973; Nellis and Keith, 1976). Wetmore *et al.* (1970) and Knowlton (1972) found a greater proportion of females in areas of less intense harvest. This predominance of males may result from a greater vulnerability of male coyotes to some forms of human-caused mortality. All data were obtained from a sample of coyotes killed by hunters and trappers and may not be representative of the composition of the actual population. Behavioral or other differences between male and female coyotes and their responses to hunting and trapping could

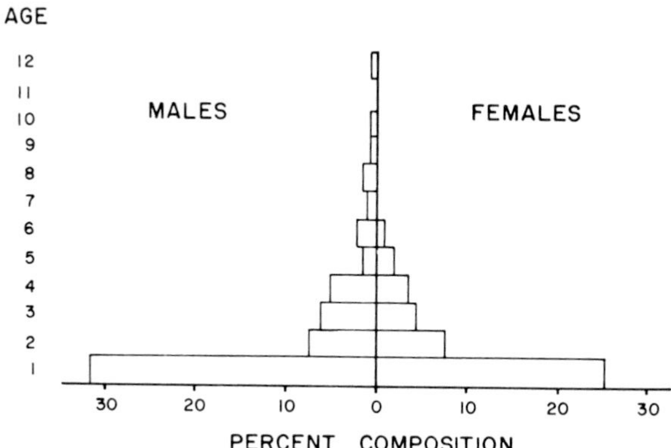

Fig. 2. Composite age–sex frequency distribution for all coyotes aged.

lead to an unrepresentative sample. An uneven sex ratio at birth or some type of sex-specific mortality of juvenile females could also explain the disparate sex ratio. Competition of female pups with larger and presumably more aggressive male littermates, could be a contributing factor to an uneven sex ratio.

From population age structure data from 1973 to 1975, we found a mean survival rate of 60.9%, calculated by the Chapman–Robson equation (Chapman and Robson, 1960), excluding the first age class which was inconsistent with the required assumption of a constant survival rate. This compares favorably with survival values calculated from data presented by Knowlton (1972) of 59.3, 71.9, and 69.9% for Texas, New Mexico, and Arizona, respectively. Mathwig's data (1973) gave a value of 40.5% survival when calculated by the Chapman–Robson method, but it was not consistent with the assumption of constant survivorship between age classes. The life table data from that study suggested that 2-year-old animals had higher survival than other age classes. Nellis and Keith (1976) estimated mortality from recoveries of marked animals at 36 to 42% (58 to 64% survival) near Rochester in central Alberta.

Iowa coyote populations appear to be fairly typical of exploited populations, with a survivorship between the extremes reported in other studies. The reason that observed survival in this study was higher than that found by Mathwig (1973) is not clear. It is interesting to note that in Knowlton's (1972) New Mexico and Arizona data, which had the highest survival rates and presumably the lowest exploitation, the number of juvenile animals was consistent with the assumption of a constant survival rate. This adds further support to the hypothesis that juvenile coyotes may be more susceptible to some forms of human-caused mortality than are older animals, as has been reported in Alberta (Wetmore *et al.*, 1970).

The differential survival between males and females noted in Iowa has not been reported previously. The major difference between the age structures of the two sexes was the absence of females in the upper age classes. The reason for shorter longevity in females is not clear, but may be related to greater reproductive stress in this sex throughout its lifetime.

VII. POPULATION DENSITY

A. Siren Surveys

Population densities for Iowa coyotes are difficult to determine because adequate techniques have not been developed or are at least in the early stages of experimentation. Siren surveys were conducted during 1973 and 1974 to determine if this was a practical technique to measure coyote population trends. Standardized routes were established similar to that suggested by Alcorn (1971). Such variables as weather, an individual's hearing sensitivity, surrounding noise, variability of coyote response, and human disturbances caused us to discontinue the Iowa siren survey. The main advantage of this technique is the probable reduction in observer bias because coyote and dog vocalizations are relatively easy to recognize, whereas with the scent-post track survey, many dog and coyote tracks are not readily distinguishable.

B. Scent-Post Survey

In 1972 the Division of Wildlife Services of the Fish and Wildlife Service implemented a 5-year study to determine coyote population trends based on what they call a scent-post survey. This involved placing a scent capsule in the center of a 3-foot-diameter circle of sifted dirt at 50 stops along a 15-mile standardized route. The tracks present were identified on the next 3 to 5 mornings and an index based on number of visits per route was calculated. It is hoped that increases or decreases in the number of visits per route from year to year will give an index to coyote populations. Iowa did not initiate the scent-post survey until 1974 and then only on a limited basis.

In 1975 and 1976, the scent-post survey was expanded in Iowa to evaluate it as a technique to monitor the coyote population. Analysis is incomplete but it appears that variables associated with the survey also create considerable question as to its value unless the technique is modified. The

Iowa scent-post survey is being conducted on rural county roads where human disturbances occur much more readily than on the ranch trails of the western states. This alone likely alters the coyote behavior in Iowa to the point that they do not travel along the rural roads like they do the ranch trails of western states. Also, free-roaming dog populations in Iowa make the survey more subjective. Personnel inexperienced in track identification may make the validity of the data questionable. Modification of the scent-post survey needs to be evaluated in Iowa to determine if this technique can reliably be used to monitor coyote population trends in midwest farm states.

VIII. COYOTE FOOD HABITS

Winter food habits were investigated by following procedures described by Korschgen (1971). Food items were identified to species when possible with the aid of a reference hair collection and hair keys by Stains (1958) and by Adorgan and Kolenosky (1969). A summary of food items is shown in Table I. Stomach contents of 291 coyotes were analyzed of which 69 (23.7%) were empty. It was usually difficult, if not impossible, to identify a food item as carrion. Livestock carrion was readily available to coyotes so it was assumed that a considerable portion of the livestock found in the analysis was carrion. By volume, rabbits accounted for 51.0% of the contents in the coyote stomachs, livestock 25.5%, mice 12.3%, other mammals 8.0%, birds 2.7%, and miscellaneous 0.5%.

The amount of livestock found in the diet of coyotes in the present study was higher than in several other studies in the midwest. This is probably accountable to the fact that in other midwestern food-habit studies, much of the livestock found was placed under the category of carrion. The 25.5% (by volume) figure for livestock in this study compares with 10.9% livestock and 12.8% carrion (mainly cattle and pig) in north-central Missouri (Korschgen, 1973), 25.4% carrion (including livestock) in Kansas (Tiemeier, 1955), 14.0% livestock in Iowa in 1971–1972 (Mathwig, 1973), and 12.5% livestock in Nebraska (Fichter *et al.*, 1955). Gipson (1974) found a low incidence of cattle and hogs but a high incidence of poultry in coyotes in Arkansas.

The proportion of livestock and carrion found in Missouri coyotes increased between the collections of 1957 and 1973 (Korschgen, 1957, 1973). A similar trend may also partially explain the greater amount of livestock in this study in comparison to that found by Mathwig (1973) and could be due to increased availability of cattle carcasses with increased cattle production and higher rendering costs.

The most important foods of coyotes in summer as determined from scats were rabbits and plant material followed by mice, livestock, and birds

TABLE I
Summary of the Contents of 222 Coyote Stomachs Collected Winter 1972–1973

Food items	Percentage[a]	
	Occurrence	Volume
Rabbits	(56.8)	(51.0)
Cottontail (*Sylvilagus floridanus*)	56.8	51.0
Livestock	(39.7)	(25.5)
Cattle	23.9	10.2
Pig	17.1	8.1
Sheep	4.5	7.3
Mice	(54.9)	(12.3)
Vole (*Microtus* sp.)	29.3	10.2
Deer mouse (*Peromyscus* sp.)	1.8	0.3
Harvest mouse (*Reithrodontomys megalotis*)	0.9	0.2
House mouse (*Mus musculus*)	0.5	tr[b]
Mouse, undetermined	24.3	1.7
Other mammals	(12.2)	(8.0)
Fox squirrel (*Sciurus niger*)	2.3	2.7
Whitetailed deer (*Odocoileus virginianus*)	3.6	2.6
Raccoon (*Procyon lotor*)	0.9	2.6
Muskrat (*Ondatra zibethicus*)	1.4	0.1
Coyote (*Canis latrans*)	1.8	tr
Shrew (*Blarina brevicauda*)	0.5	tr
Mink or weasel (*Mustela* sp.)	0.5	tr
Mammal, undetermined	2.3	0.1
Birds	(19.8)	(2.7)
Chicken (*Gallus gallus*)	8.6	1.9
Pheasant (*Phasianus colchicus*)	2.7	0.3
Bobwhite (*Colinus virginianus*)	0.9	0.2
Bird, undetermined	7.2	0.4
Plants	(35.1)	(0.3)
Grass	32.0	0.1
Corn (*Zea mays*)	3.2	tr
Oats (*Avena sativa*)	0.9	tr
Bark, leaves, twigs	2.7	0.2
Straw	0.9	tr
Carrot (garbage)	0.5	tr
Miscellaneous	(3.6)	(0.2)
Paper	1.4	0.2
Gravel	0.9	tr
Cloth	0.5	tr
Tape	0.5	tr
Fence barb	0.5	tr
Lead shot	0.9	tr

[a] Parentheses indicates totals for each major category.
[b] tr: Trace.

TABLE II

Summary of the Contents of 246 Scats Collected 1971–1974

Food Item	Percentage[a]	
	Occurrence	Volume
Plants	(80.8)	(25.2)
Mulberry (*Morus* sp.)	27.2	15.3
Wild Plum (*Prunus americana*)	8.5	5.3
Chokecherry (*Prunus virginiana*)	3.3	0.8
Corn (*Zea mays*)	2.8	1.4
Grass	59.3	2.0
Gooseberry (*Ribes* sp.)	0.4	0.1
Oats (*Avena sativa*)	1.2	0.1
Sticktight	0.4	tr[b]
Hazelnut (*Corylus americana*)	0.4	tr
Bark and twigs	1.2	0.1
Juniper (*Juniperus virginiana*)	1.2	tr
Alfalfa (*Medicago sativa*)	0.4	tr
Wild grape (*Vitis riparia*)	0.4	tr
Leaves, undetermined	1.6	tr
Seeds, undetermined	2.8	tr
Plant material, undetermined	0.8	tr
Rabbits	(42.3)	(33.0)
E. cottontail (*Sylvilagus floridanus*)	42.3	33.0
Mice	(35.0)	(19.5)
Vole (*Microtus* sp.)	23.6	17.3
Deer mouse (*Peromyscus* sp.)	2.8	0.6
Harvest mouse (*Reithrodontomys megalotis*)	0.9	0.1
Mouse, undetermined	9.3	0.7
Livestock	(33.7)	(12.4)
Cattle	24.4	9.5
Pigs	9.3	2.7
Sheep	1.6	tr
Livestock, undetermined	0.8	0.1
Other mammals	(20.3)	(3.2)
Raccoon (*Procyon lotor*)	2.8	1.6
Fox squirrel (*Sciurus niger*)	2.0	0.7
Muskrat (*Ondatra zibethicus*)	0.8	0.5
Coyote (*Canis latrans*)	2.4	tr
Shrew (*Blarina* and *Sorex*)	0.8	0.1
Woodchuck (*Marmota monax*)	0.4	0.1
Pocket gopher (*Geomys bursarius*)	0.4	0.1
Opossum (*Didelphis marsupialis*)	0.4	tr
Striped skunk (*Mephitus mephitus*)	0.4	tr
House cat (*Felis domesticus*)	0.4	tr
Mammal, undetermined	10.2	0.1
Birds	(32.5)	(4.4)
Chicken (*Gallus gallus*)	3.3	1.5

TABLE II ***(Continued)***

Food Item	Percentage[a]	
	Occurrence	Volume
Bobwhite (*Colinus virginianus*)	1.2	0.9
Meadowlark (*Sturnella magna*)	2.0	0.2
Eggshell, undetermined	5.3	0.3
Bird, undetermined	21.5	1.4
Invertebrates	(37.4)	(1.4)
Grasshoppers	15.0	1.1
June beetles	1.2	tr
Other beetles	7.7	tr
Insect, undetermined	11.0	0.2
Maggots	1.2	tr
Ticks	2.0	tr
Crayfish	0.8	tr
Snails	1.2	tr
Crickets	0.4	tr
Reptiles	(1.2)	(tr)
Lizards (six-lined racerunner)	0.4	tr
Snakes, undetermined	0.8	tr
Miscellaneous	(8.1)	(0.8)
Sand, gravel	5.7	0.2
Manure	0.4	0.2
Tinfoil	0.4	tr
Plastic	0.4	tr
Pan cover	0.4	0.1
Eebris, undetermined	0.8	0.4

[a] ( ) Indicates totals for each major category.
[b] tr: Trace.

(Table II). In general, rabbits and livestock were less important in the summer diet than in winter. Plants, mice, birds, and invertebrates were all important in the summer diet. Plants, primarily the fruit, became more important in August when they comprised nearly half the total food volume (Boggess, 1975). Grasshoppers were also present in greater frequency and volume in late summer.

IX. LIVESTOCK LOSSES

The Iowa coyote studies, like many others, have evolved primarily because of the controversy between coyotes and the livestock industry, particularly the sheep industry. Iowa is unique from most other states in that farmers incurring losses of livestock to either dogs or coyotes, can file domestic animal loss claims at the county courthouse and receive partial indemnification for those losses.

A producer is required to file the normal claim within 10 days of the loss. The claim must be signed by one or two unrelated witnesses verifying that the loss actually occurred and that they believed it was attributable to dogs or coyotes. In most instances it was the livestock producer and his witnesses who judged whether it was a coyote or dog kill. From field observations by the authors, it appears that the loss assessments by these producers were incorrect only 10% of the time. The general honesty of reporting on the part of the livestock producer has also been noted in other loss studies (Balser, 1974).

Denny (1974) reported at least 18 other states provide for indemnification to stockmen for damage done by dogs. He does not mention, however, whether any other state provides for compensation to producers for damage caused by "wolves" (coyotes). All of these states, except Texas and Washington, were eastern states.

A total of 5800 individual domestic animal loss claims were examined, representing data from 130 separate 1-year periods (some from as early as 1958). The claims were for a total of 18,309 sheep and lambs, 826 cattle, 2257 swine and 6839 chickens, turkeys, geese, and ducks. Of the 18,309 sheep claimed, 49.5% was attributable to dogs, 35.8% to coyotes, and the remainder was undetermined predator losses (Boggess *et al.* submitted for publication). Between 1960–1974, the proportion of sheep losses to coyotes increased while the proportion attributed to dogs decreased.

Schaefer (personal communication) indicated that of 141 sheep carcasses examined in 1976 in south-central Iowa, 56% were considered killed by dogs and 44% by coyotes. Twenty-four sheep producers experienced losses attributed to coyotes while 12 experienced losses attributed to dogs. Further information will be collected to provide insight into the losses of sheep, as well as other livestock, to dogs and coyotes. In addition, information on the husbandry practices associated with these losses is being evaluated.

X. IOWA COYOTE DISEASES

Diseases in Iowa coyotes have not been studied to any great extent. From field reports and observations, we know that coyotes do occasionally become infested with mange. A sarcoptic mite causes the mangey condition. Unlike the red fox, however, most coyotes appear to be able to survive mange infestations.

Franson *et al.* (1976) found 3.6% of 220 coyotes collected at fur buyers had heartworms (*Dirofilaria immitis*). Stomach worms (*Physaloptera* sp.), tapeworms (*Taenia* sp.), large roundworms (*Toxascaris leoma*), hookworms (*Ancylostoma canium*), and whipworm (*Trichuris vulpis*), were counted in 144 gastrointestinal tracts of Iowa coyotes (Franson *et al.*, 1977). Jorgenson *et al.* (1977) detected rabies antigen in 2 of 192 coyotes collected from fur buyers in southwestern Iowa. He found 5 of 14 sera samples collected from central Iowa coyotes to be positive for rabies antibodies. However, diagnostic reports from rabies laboratories in Iowa indicate very few coyotes are tested for rabies.

The liver, kidney, and brain from six coyotes were collected and analyzed for organochlorine insecticides. Low levels of dieldrin were found in the liver (34 to 223 ppm) and kidney (0 to 57 ppm). No dieldrin was present in the brains and no other insecticides were detected in any of the tissues collected.

XI. COYOTE MOVEMENTS AND MORTALITY

With the aid of local hunters who were adept at locating coyote dens, 191 coyote pups and 2 adult females were captured from 1972 through 1976. These animals were ear-tagged and released at the den sites. To increase the sample of tagged animals an additional 51 pups and 6 adults were captured with traps, ear-tagged and released. Sex was determined for all pups and they were tagged with small monel metal tags (National Band and Tag Co., Newport, Kentucky), button-type aluminum tags, or self-punching plastic rototags (Nasco, Inc., Ft. Atkinson, Wisconsin).

To date, 63 of 250 tagged coyotes have been recovered. Of the 250 animals, 57 tagged in 1976 have not yet lived through one fall–winter harvest period. The 63 recoveries from 193 animals tagged represents a known recovery rate of 35.8%. In addition, at least 2 tagged pups were known to have been killed at dens by farmers but were not reported and 5 other coyotes were reported to have lost both ear tags.

The overall mean recovery straight-line distance for the 63 recovered animals was 22.2 miles. A mean distance of 18.9 miles (30.2 km) was recorded for males and 19.5 miles (31.2 km) for females, excluding an exceptionally long 202-mile movement by one female. Male coyote movements ranged from 0 to 110 miles (0 to 176.0 km) and females ranged from 0 to 202 miles (0 to 323.2 km). The 202 mile (323.2 km) movement of an Iowa female coyote is the longest documented movement recorded in the literature. This animal was tagged as a pup in May of 1974 near Mt. Ayr, Iowa. It was shot in August of 1975 about 10 miles southeast of the Lake of the Ozarks in Missouri. Previously recorded long-distance movements were 100 miles

(160.9 km) in Wyoming (Garlough, 1940), 115 miles (185 km) in Montana (Robinson and Cummings, 1951), 87 miles (140 km) in California (Hawthorne, 1971), and 96 miles (154.5 km) in Alberta (Nellis and Keith, 1976). Young and Jackson (1951) had some undocumented evidence of a longer movement.

Of 26 coyotes recovered more than 10 miles (16.1 km) from initial tagging site, 14 males were recovered at a mean distance of 38.5 miles (61.6 km) and 12 females averaged 42.9 miles (68.6 km). Again, this average does not include the 202 mile (323.2 km) movement of one female coyote. The apparent onset of dispersal in November in Iowa is similar to findings in Minnesota (Chesness and Bremicker, 1974) and in Texas (Knowlton, 1972) but it was slightly later than reported dates for coyotes in Yellowstone Park (Robinson and Cummings, 1951) and Alberta (Nellis and Keith, 1976).

Preliminary recoveries indicate an apparent westward directional tendency. This directional movement tendency is similar to that reported in Minnesota (Chesness and Bremicker, 1974) and in Alberta (Nellis and Keith, 1976). The most plausible explanation for the apparent westward tendency in Iowa would seem to be differential hunting pressure (Boggess, 1975). Coyotes generally decrease in abundance from west to east across the southern part of the state and the hunting pressure seems to decline accordingly in the easterly direction. Habitat in the western part of Iowa has more open space interspersed with woodlands thus making the coyote more vulnerable to hunting. A tagged coyote dispersing west would probably encounter greater hunting pressure and be more vulnerable, increasing the chances of recovery.

Also, it is interesting to note that despite the recoveries being skewed in the westward direction, the coyotes are expanding and increasing their numbers north and eastward within the state (Fig. 1).

XII. MORTALITY

Mortality causes for all recovered coyotes included: shot, 53.3%; trapped, 30.4%; roadkilled, 8.4%; killed by dogs, 6.7%; and snared, 1.2%. Many of the animals that were shot were taken with the aid of dogs.

XIII. COYOTE HARVEST

Table III shows the coyote harvest figures based solely on fur buyer reports. These reports are believed to provide harvest trend information but they are not reflective of actual harvest due to conservative fur buyer

TABLE III
Coyote Harvest Data, 1960–61 through 1975–76

Season	No. of Animals purchased by fur buyers	Average price/ pelt ($)	Total value ($)
1960–61	97	1.09	105.73
1961–62	113	.98	110.74
1962–63	92	1.43	131.50
1963–64	61	1.67	101.87
1964–65	340	1.81	137.56
1965–66	732	4.22	3,089.40
1966–67	864	1.50	1,296.00
1967–68	512	1.95	998.40
1968–69	4,922	5.94	29,236.68
1969–70	3,678	5.17	19,014.26
1970–71	4,430	4.65	20,599.50
1971–72	5,240	5.58	28,715.20
1972–73	5,616	11.64	65,370.24
1973–74	8,713	13.60	118,496.80
1974–75	12,020	9.48	113,949.60
1975–76	9,444	15.73	148,554.12

reports. Prior to 1968, coyotes were of little fur value and hunters and trappers seldom sold the coyote pelt. As fur value increased, more and more animals were sold and during the last few years, nearly all coyotes taken were sold to fur buyers. The increasing number of coyotes, higher pelt prices, and the greater interest in coyote hunting explain the rising harvest figures. The reduced 1975–1976 harvest can be partially explained by very poor hunting conditions and perhaps a surpressed coyote population because of the excellent late season hunting conditions and thus high coyote kill of the previous season.

XIV. PERSPECTIVE

A year-round continuous open season has always existed for the Iowa coyote. It has not affected the population and presently, the coyote is increasing its numbers and expanding its range.

Increased alledged livestock losses from coyotes, particularly sheep, make it necessary for the Conservation Commission to closely monitor and collect factual data to place the coyote in proper perspective. It has been said that the coyote provides more hours of recreation to the southern Iowa sportsmen than any other game animal in the state.

Current information indicates that it would be economically infeasible and biologically unsound to attempt to reduce coyote damage to livestock by general population reduction. There does not appear to be sufficient justification to warrant a restricted season on Iowa coyotes at this time. The present continuous open season has not resulted in any apparent reduction in the coyote population, yet it allows the elimination of problem coyotes at any time and serves to reduce public concern about rising coyote populations.

Coyote damage to sheep can be controlled or reduced most effectively by practicing good animal husbandry and by selectively controlling problem coyotes when necessary. Livestock growers should be encouraged to properly dispose of dead livestock. This will aid in removing a major source of food for coyotes and thereby reduce the possibility of these predators becoming habituated to feeding on livestock. The important thing that we all must realize, whether we be sheep producer, hunter, trapper, wildlife biologist, or other outdoor enthusiast, is that the coyote does have an important role to play in the wildlife community as a predator, a game animal, and a fur resource. Documented facts and not hearsay, will lead to a better understanding of this wily animal.

REFERENCES

Adorgan, A. S., and Kolenosky, G. B. (1969). *Ont. Dep. Lands For. Res. Rep. Wildl.* No. 90, 64 pp.

Alcorn, J. R. (1971). "Directions for Censusing Problem Animal Populations," 6 pp. Rep. Div. Wildl. Serv., U.S. Fish Wildl. Serv., Fallon, Nevade. (Mimeo.)

Balser, D. S. (1974). *Trans. North Amer. Wildl. Nat. Resour. Conf.* **39,** 292–300.

Boggess, E. K. (1975). Some Population Parameters of Iowa Coyotes and an Analysis of Reported Livestock Losses. M.S. Thesis, 94 pp. Iowa State Univ. Ames.

Boggess, E. K., Andrews, R. D., and Bishop, R. A. "Domestic Animal Losses to Coyotes and Dogs in Iowa." (submitted for publication).

Chapman, D. G., and Robson, D. S. (1960). *Biometrics* **16**(3), 354–368.

Chesness, R. A. (1973). *Minn. Dep. Nat. Resour., Game Res. Q. Prog. Rep.* **33**(3), 151–177.

Chesness, R. A., and Bremicker, T. P. (1974). *Coyote Res. Workshop, Denver, Colo.* 17 pp. (Mimeo.)

Denny, R. N. (1974). *Trans. North Amer. Wildl. Nat. Resour. Conf.* **39,** 257–291.

Fichter, E., Schildman, G., and Sather, J. H. (1955). *Ecol. Monogr.* **25**(1), 1–37.

Franson, J. C., Jorgenson, R. D., and Boggess, E. K. (1976). *J. Wildl. Dis.* **12,** 165–166.

Franson, J. C., Jorgenson, R. D., Boggess, E. K., and Greve, J. H. (1977). *J. Parasitol.* (in press).

Garlough, F. E. (1940). "Study of the Migratory Habits of Coyotes," 5 pp. Denver Wildl. Res. Lab., US. Fish Wildl. Serv., Denver, Colorado. (Mimeo.)

Gier, H. T. (1968). *Kans. Agric. Exp. Stn. Bull.* No. 393, 118 pp.

Gipson, R. S. (1974). *J. Wildl. Manage.* **38**(4), 848–853.

Gipson, R. S., Sealander, J. A., and Dunn, J. E. (1974). *Syst. Zool.* **23**(1), 1–11.

Hawthorne, V. M. (1971). *Calif. Fish Game* **57**(3), 154–161.

Jackson, D. H. (1976). "The Use of Ovary Dissections to Examine the Reproductive Capacity of Iowa Coyotes," Honor Project Rep., 33 pp. Iowa State Univ., Ames.

Jorgenson, R. D., Boggess, E. K., Franson, J. C., and Gough, P. M. (1977). *Iowa State J. Res.* **52**(1), 1–3.

Knowlton, F. F. (1972). *J. Wildl. Manage.* **36**(2), 369–382.

Korschgen, L. J. (1971). analysis. Pages 233–250 *In* "Wildlife Management Techniques" (R. H. Giles, Jr., ed.), 3rd ed., 623 pp. Wildl. Soc., Washington, D.C.

Korschgen, L. J. (1973). "Food Habits of Coyotes in North-Central Missouri," Federal Aid Prog. No. W-13-R-27, 8 pp. Mo. Dep. Conserv., Columbia, Missouri.

Linhart, S. B., and Knowlton, F. F. (1967). *J. Wildl. Manage.* **31**(2), 362–365.

Mathwig, H. J. (1973). *Iowa State J. Res.* **47**(3), 167–189.

Nellis, C. H., and Keith, L. B. (1976). *J. Wildl. Manage.* **40**(3), 389–399.

Oschwald, W. R., Reicken, F. F., Dideriksen, R. I., Scholtes, W. F., and Schaller, F. W. (1965). *Iowa State Univ. Coop. Ext. Serv., Spec. Rep.* No. 42, 76 pp.

Richens, V. B., and Hugie, R. D. (1974). *J. Wildl. Manage.* **28**(3), 447–465.

Robinson, W. B., and Cummings, M. W. (1951). *U.S. Fish Wildl. Serv., Spec. Sci. Rep.: Wildl.* No. 11, 17 pp.

Stains, H. J. (1958). *J. Wildl. Manage.* **22**(1), 95–97.

Tiemeier, O. W. (1955). *Trans. Kans. Acad. Sci.* **58**(2), 196–207.

Waller, D. W., and Errington, P. L. (1961). *Proc. Iowa Acad. Sci.* **68,** 301–313.

Wetmore, S. P., Nellis, C. H., and Keith, L. B. (1970). *Alberta Dep. Lands For. Fish Wildl. Div. Wildl. Tech. Bull.* No. 2, 22 pp.

Young, S. P., and Jackson, H. H. T. (1951). "The Clever Coyote," 411 pp. Stackpole, Harrisburg, Pennsylvania and Wildl. Manage. Inst., Washington, D.C.

12

Behavioral Ecology of Coyotes on the National Elk Refuge, Jackson, Wyoming

Franz J. Camenzind

I. INTRODUCTION

The coyote (*Canis latrans*) is a conspicuous faunal resident of Central and North America. The earliest written reports of the coyote in Western North America are found in the Journals of the Lewis and Clark expedition (Thwaites, 1904–1905) and in the accounts of Long's expedition to the Rocky Mountains (Say, 1832). Both state that the coyote, or prairie wolf as it was often referred to, was abundant on the plains and frequently occurred in packs.

Few of the early fur trappers and explorers that passed through the Jackson Hole region in Northwestern Wyoming maintained journals and fewer make any mention of coyotes. One of the first biologists in the region, Preble (1911), while discussing the potential "enemies" of the Jackson Hole elk (*Cervus canadensis*) stated that "The coyote, unlike the wolf, is almost certainly native to the region, but has increased greatly with settlement." Murie (1940) presents a review of the coyote control practices conducted in Yellowstone National Park (80 km north of the study area) and hints that early coyote control was initiated ". . . because coyotes were numerous, not because they were injurious." From these and other accounts, it appears that the coyote is a bona fide member of the Jackson Hole environment and not a recent immigrant.

II. DESCRIPTION OF STUDY AREA

The National Elk Refuge is located in the east-central portion of Jackson Hole, a high mountain valley with an average altitude of 1980 m. The Refuge encompasses an area of 9656 hectares of which the northern one-half is dissected by steep rolling hills. The southern one-half consists primarily of glacial outwash material with one resistant formation (Miller Butte) rising approximately 150 m above the valley floor.

There are two major streams flowing through the study area. The Gros Ventre River forms much of the northern boundary of the Refuge, and Flat Creek, flowing from east to west, nearly bisects the study area. As Flat Creek approaches the western boundary of the Refuge, it turns and continues southward and eventually leaves the Refuge at its extreme southwestern corner. Numerous springs emerge from the northern edge of Miller Butte and form Nowlin Creek which flows to the northwest until it joins Flat Creek (Fig. 1).

The Refuge is bounded on the north by Grand Teton National Park, on the east by the Teton National Forest and on the south and east by the town of Jackson and mixed private and Bureau of Land Management lands, respectively. The boundaries between the Refuge and private lands are maintained by 2-m-high elk-proof woven wire fences.

The Refuge is the natural wintering ground for the Jackson Hole elk herd (Murie, 1951) and during the study period an average of 7600 elk spent the winter months (November to March) on the area. Of these, approximately 1% died of natural causes and provided a major part of the coyote's winter diet. Except for the annual fall elk hunt on the northern portion of the study area, the Refuge management plan grants full protection to the native flora and fauna and limits public access to the major roadways.

1. Vegetation

The vegetation occurring on the glacial outwash material consists predominately of an association of big sagebrush (*Artemisia tridentata*)–june-

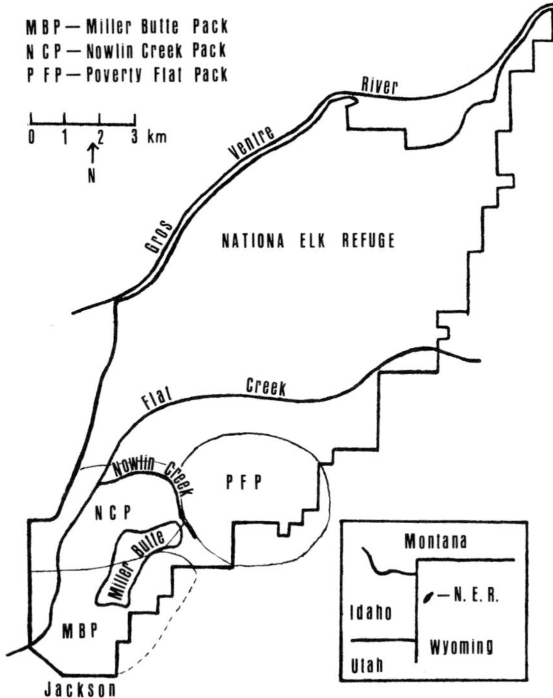

Fig. 1. National Elk Refuge, Jackson Hole Wyoming (96 km^2) including the approximate territorial boundaries for the Miller Butte, Nowlin Creek, and Poverty Flat coyote packs, 1970–1975.

grass (*Koeleria crisata*), and big sagebrush–bitterbrush (*Purshia tridentata*). A bunchgrass—shrub association occurs on the south, east and west facing slopes of foothills and buttes. Its major plant components are bluebunch wheatgrass (*Agropyron spicatum*) and douglass rabbitbrush (*Chrysothamnus viscidiflorus*). Approximately 10% of the Refuge is under irrigation and supports a mixed agriculture type of bromegrass (*Bromus* spp.), clover (*Trifolium* spp.), and alfalfa (*Medicago* spp.). Much of the southwestern portion of the Refuge is influenced by Flat Creek and supports a mixed sedge (*Carex* sp.) – rush (*Juncus* sp.) – cattail (*Typha* sp.) community (Houston, 1968; Dimmick, 1968).

2. Climate

The climate of the area is indicative of its geographic location. The summers are short and cool and the winters are long and cold with abundant snowfall. United States Department of Commerce Weather Bureau records for the period 1950 to 1972 report mean January and July temperatures of

-10° and 15°C, respectively. Snow depth often exceeds 1.5 m on the northern and western portion of the valley floor while on the Refuge snow seldom accumulates in excess of 0.5 m.

3. Objectives

My objective was to investigate pack, territorial, denning, and family group behavior. Population densities, flucutations, and reproductive parameters were also investigated coincidentally with the behavioral observations.

4. Methods

A limited trapping-and-marking program was carried out during the first years of the study on the elk Refuge. Twenty-six coyotes were captured using live traps and No. 4 coil spring traps with padded jaws. Traps were checked daily (often twice) to minimize disturbance and injury to the trapped coyotes. Also, six pups were captured and marked at den sites in Grand Teton National Park and the Teton National Forest. All captured coyotes were restrained by hand and were sexed, aged, and had standard measurements recorded. In 1969, 1970, and 1971 hair samples were cut from the midline of the back between the shoulders. These were analyzed for trace element content and the results were reported by Huckabee *et al.* (1973). Both plastic colored and aluminum ear tags were used to individually mark the coyotes. The metal tags were of the button type, approximately 2.2 mm in diameter, and stamped with a number and return address. The colored plastic tags, 4.5 mm by 1.8 mm, were white, red, yellow and green.

Observations were made with 7 × 26 binoculars and a 15–60 power spotting scope from a variety of locations. Under optimum viewing conditions, tagged coyotes were identified at distances up to 1.5 km. Some coyotes were identified by unusual color patterns or other physical features such as missing or damaged appendages.

Intensive observations were conducted on the Refuge from November 1970 until the summer of 1974. From September 1974 until the spring of 1976, only the southern two-fifths (37 km^2) of the Refuge were under observation and then only on a part-time basis.

III. POPULATION PARAMETERS

A. Spring Densities

Spring density estimates were determined from actual counts of coyotes present in the respective areas during the April to July denning season.

Whenever possible, dens were located and kept under observation until the number of resident adults and pups were determined. In several cases, 3 or 4 adults maintained joint occupancy of a den and shared the responsibilities of caring for the pups. These groups are referred to as packs (Section III,A). In several cases dens could not be located, although adults were consistantly seen in the areas. These are referred to as denning areas and are incorporated into the density estimates as representing only 2 adults and the otherwise determined number of pups per den. Consequently, all density estimates represent minimum values since not all coyotes may have been located.

Coyote densities are summarized in Table I. Spring densities for all of the National Elk Refuge for 1971, 1972, and 1973 were estimated to be 0.51 (N = 49), 0.58 (N = 56), and 0.46 (N = 44) coyotes/km^2, respectively. For both 1974 and 1975 the spring densities were estimated to be 0.54 (N = 20) coyotes/km^2 for the southern two-fifths of the Refuge. Similiar spring densities have been noted by many investigators. Knowlton (1972) reported that an area in Texas supported an average of 0.31 coyotes/km^2 and Gier (1968) reported an average of 0.58 coyotes/km^2 in an area of Kansas.

TABLE I
Coyote Population Parameters for the National Elk Refuge (96 km^2) from 1971 to 1976.[a]

Parameters	1971	1972	1973	1974[b]	1975[b]	1976[b]	Mean (standard deviation)
Peak coyote concentrations (February–March)	95	65	65	55	—	—	70 (17)
Spring coyote population	49	56	44	20	20	—	38 (17)
Spring coyote density	0.51	0.58	0.46	0.54	0.54	—	0.53 (0.04)
Total litters produced	21	25	19	5	4	4	13 (10)
Litter density	0.22	0.26	0.20	0.14	0.11	0.11	0.17 (0.06)
Average litter size	4.9	4.8	4.1	4.4	4.2	4.3	4.45 (0.33)
Pup density	1.07	1.24	0.81	0.59	0.46	0.46	0.77 (0.33)
Postwhelping population	152	176	122	44	37	—	106 (63)
Postwhelping density	1.57	1.82	1.26	1.19	1.0	—	1.37 (0.33)

[a] All density estimates are expressed as coyotes/km^2.
[b] From 1974 to 1976 only the southern two-fifths (37 km^2) of the Refuge was under observation.

B. Winter Concentrations

Winter concentrations of coyotes on the Refuge varied. It was estimated that peak concentrations were 95 (0.98/km^2), 65 (0.67/km^2), 65 and 55 (0.57/km^2) for the winters of 1970–71 through 1973–74, respectively. These concentrations occurred in January and February with the initial increase noted in early December.

Craighead (1951) reported the occurrence of similiar seasonal population fluctuations on the Refuge for the winter of 1949–50. The Quarterly Narrative Reports of the National Elk Refuge state that the estimated maximum coyote population for the years 1943 to 1973 fluctuated between 10 and 150. My work agrees with Craighead's (1951), who concluded that there was no correlation between coyote numbers and winter elk losses. Craighead believed that field mouse (*Microtus* spp.) availability may have played an important role in maintaining coyote populations.

C. Reproductive Parameters

Reproductive data from the Refuge are summarized in Table I. A total of 21 (0.22 litters/km^2), 25 (0.26 litters/km^2), and 19 (0.20 litters/km^2) litters were produced on the Refuge for the years 1971, 1972, and 1973, respectively. For 1974, 1975, and 1976 a total of 5 (0.14 litters/km^2), 4 (0.11 litters/km^2), and 4 litters were produced on the southern two-fifths of the Refuge. Knowlton (1972) is one of the few investigators to discuss coyote reproduction on a per unit area basis. He reported that 6 litters were produced within a 78 km^2 area of South Texas for an average of 0.08 litters/km^2. At Jackson, the total number of pups could not be counted for every litter. However, for each year from 1971 through 1976 the average litter size was determined to be 4.9 (7, 21), 4.8 (11, 25), 4.1 (7, 19), 4.4 (5, 5), 4.2 (3, 4), and 4.3 (4, 4), respectively. (The actual number of litters from which counts were made is represented by the first number in the parenthesis and the total number of litters known to be present is represented by the second number.)

An average of 1.07, 1.24, 0.81, 0.59, 0.46, and 0.46 pups were produced per square kilometer for the same period. The estimated pup production plus the adult population resulted in postwhelping densities of 1.57, 1.82, 1.26, 1.19, and 1.0 coyotes per square kilometer for the same 5 years. It should be noted how the last two sets of population estimates were derived. The total pup population figures were arrived at by multiplying the average litter size by the number of known litters. This figure was then added to the known adult coyote population and from these data the postwhelping densities were derived. Similiar results were reported by Knowlton (1972) from his study area in Texas. He estimated that 0.57 pups were produced per square kilometer and that the average litter size was 7.4 ($N = 6$).

The apparent decline in all population parameters measured during the 5-year study period cannot be satisfactorily accounted for. Only 11 dead coyotes were located on the Refuge during the study and 8 of these were found in January and February of 1973. Seven of these were partially eaten and/or carried away by scavengers before they could be examined. The eighth carcass was sent to the Utah State University Veterinary Laboratory. The cause of death was determined to be canine hepatitis. The age of 5 of these carcasses was determined to be less than 1 year and two were between 1 and 2 years. One coyote, whose skull could not be located, was estimated to be less than 1 year of age based on body size. During this same period many coyotes appeared to be in poor health; some were lethargic and easily approached while others had lost the hair from all but the tips of their tails.

The apparent high incidence of mortality during the winter of 1972–73 undoubtedly affected the decline in the various population parameters. However, if an inverse relationship exists between population density and litter size (Knowlton, 1972; Christian, 1959; Errington, 1946) one could have reasonably expected an increase in litter size following the mortality of 1972–1973. This did not occur. Undoubtedly many other factors were still influencing reproduction and survival.

IV. BEHAVIOR

A. Population Organization

The population of coyotes on the National Elk Refuge was divided into 4 major organizational types: nomads, aggregations, resident pairs, and resident packs.

1. Nomads

Nomadic coyotes were defined as those that were consistantly observed alone and did not defend a specific geographical area. Based on repeated observations of individual coyotes, it was determined that approximately 15% of the Refuge coyote population was nomadic. Of these, approximately one-half were judged to be less than 1 year of age. Many of the other animals were disabled (crippled or missing feet), while only a few appeared to be physically healthy adults. On only 1 occasion were disabled coyotes seen to be members of a pack, however, they occasionally appeared as members of aggregations (see below).

The home ranges of the nomadic coyotes were superimposed upon the territories of the resident coyotes. The intruders were consistantly driven from the occupied territories when they came into contact with territorial coyotes. Nomadic coyotes also were driven away from the elk carcasses by the residents in whose territory the carrion was located. Only after the carcass had been abandoned by the residents were the nomadic animals free to feed.

2. Aggregations

The second segment of the Refuge coyote population consisted of aggregations, large transient groups (from 7 to 22) that displayed no social organization beyond brief dominant–subordinate encounters. Aggregations were composed of winter migrants and nomadic coyotes interacting with the resident pairs and packs resulting in large numbers of coyotes occupying a small area for a short period of time. The movements of aggregations were at times influenced by leaders although leadership was not based on dominance. Most of the activity of the aggregations appeared to be a result of one coyote reacting to the behavior of the coyote next to it.

Aggregations were observed only from November to early April and only near carrion. The largest single aggregate was recorded on February 24, 1970 for 19 minutes when 22 coyotes were observed on the south edge of Miller Butte where 3 elk carcasses were located. Forty minutes later, on the north edge of Miller Butte, 17 additional coyotes were observed near another elk carcass. This second sighting was 2.5 km from the first aggregation and since none of the original group were seen moving north, it is unlikely that these 2 groups contained any of the same individuals.

As with the nomadic coyotes, aggregations moved over existing territorial boundaries. Resident coyotes, both pairs and packs, appeared unable to defend effectively their boundaries or carrion food sources from these large numbers of coyotes. No aggregation was seen to remain intact for more than 1 hour and 56 minutes (14 coyotes) with the average duration being 38 minutes for 9 observations.

3. Resident Pairs

The third group, resident pairs, comprised approximately 24% of the resident coyote population. Resident pairs were defined as those coyotes observed denning and spending the entire year together, in the absence of other adults.

All of the resident pairs of coyotes that were observed extensively occupied the northern one-half of the Refuge. This is an area of steep rolling hills and sage-covered valleys in which prolonged observations were difficult. However, sufficient observations were made of boundary markings, boundary disputes, and territorial vocalizations, to enable me to conclude that pairs occupied and defended distinct territories in the same fashion as did the packs. Four pairs of coyotes were known to remain intact for at least 2 denning seasons and one pair for 3 denning seasons. A total of 7 pairs were known to have included at least one new member sometime during the study. Of these, 4 included new males and 3 involved new females. In no case was I able to determine the origin of the new members or the fate of the departed individuals.

Dominance hierarchies were not always detectable within pairs of coyotes and the expression of such relationships was usually limited to greeting ceremonies. Of the 13 observations of greeting ceremonies involving known pairs, 9 clearly demonstrated male dominance, one female dominance, and in 3 situations, dominance could not be recognized. All of these observations were made at active dens between April 20 and July 9.

Leadership, or the initiation of different activities, was not synonymous with dominance. Many activities including territory and den defense were nearly as often initiated by females as by males (4 female, 5 male).

4. Packs

The last organizational group observed was the pack. On the Refuge, approximately 61% of the resident coyotes belonged to packs. A pack was defined as a group of coyotes (3–7) that occupied and defended the same territory, maintained social hierarchies, and often fed and denned together. They did not however always travel together. The data in this discussion of pack behavior originated primarily from 3 packs of coyotes observed intensively from the spring of 1971 to the spring of 1974 on the southern two-fifths of the Refuge. Additional observations were made during the denning seasons of 1975 and 1976. These 3 packs were the *Miller Butte Pack* (MBP), the *Nowlin Creek Pack* (NCP), and the *Poverty Flat Pack* (PFP).

a. The Miller Butte Pack (MBP). In 1971 and 1972 the MBP consisted of 4 and 5 adults, respectively, but I was unable to determine pack organization. In 1973 the MBP consisted of 4 adults, 2 males and 2 females. In March 1973, the first information on the pack hierarchy was obtained. Based on the postures and behavior evident during greeting ceremonies (Lehner, Chapter 6, Section III,C), it was determined that the adult male and the nursing female held the first and second highest ranks, respectively. The relationship of the other 2 adults was not determined. In 1974 this pack consisted of 5 adults, 2 males, 2 females, and one adult of unknown sex. The highest rank within this pack was maintained by the same male from the spring of 1973 until the fall of 1975 when the last observations were made. The nursing female was dominant over the other female but the position the second male and unknown adult held in relation to the 2 females could not be determined.

In December 1973, the above mentioned dominant male was captured and fitted with a radio collar as part of a coyote mortality study (under the direction of W. Tzilkowski). For the next 8 days this coyote was not seen with his pack but did remain in the territory. On the tenth day after being collared, he was again observed with his pack and in the position of dominance that he held at least until November of 1975. This male retained his position of dominance for a minimum of 23 months. He was shot by a hunter approximately 6 km south of his territory in November of 1976, still wearing his collar.

The amount of time that the pack members spent together varied seasonally and was expressed as pack cohesiveness. The variation in pack cohesiveness appeared to be related to changing feeding patterns. During the winter months when elk carcasses provided the major food source, the entire pack often fed and defended the carcass from intruders. During the remainder of the year, rodents were the major food source and were captured and consumed independently. Sightings were recorded whenever positive identification could be made. If, for example, six coyotes of a pack were observed in close proximity then the pack size, or measure of cohesiveness was recorded as 6. If however, the pack was divided into 3 groups of 1, 2, and 3 coyotes each, then pack sizes of 1, 2, and 3 were each recorded once. The pack size figures were totaled for each month and divided by the total number of sightings made for the same month. The result was a monthly average pack size figure which represented a measure of pack cohesiveness.

A total of 76 sightings were made of the MBP from November to May 1972 and 1973 (Table II). Pack cohesiveness was at its greatest during the winter when average pack sizes of 3.5 and 3.6 were recorded for January and February, respectively. Results from the remainder of the months for

TABLE II

Average Monthly Pack Size (Pack Cohesiveness) for the Miller Butte Pack (MBP) Based on 76 Sightings from November to May of 1972 and 1973.

	Nov.	Dec.	Jan.	Feb.	Mar.	Apr.	May
Average	2.1	2.7	3.5	3.6	2.4	2.3	1.6
Range	1–3	1–5	2–5	2–5	1–5	1–4	1–3
Mode	2	2	3	3 and 4	2	3	1
Sightings	8	9	11	13	15	11	9/76

which there are data available indicates that pack cohesiveness was at its lowest level in May when the average pack size was 1.6.

b. The Nowlin Creek Pack (NCP). The first extensive observations of this pack were made in the spring of 1971. At this time, 3 adults, 2 females and 1 male were recognized, however, no observations were made concerning pack hierarchy. In 1972 the NCP consisted of 2 pairs of coyotes. The dominant coyote was an adult male, and his mate, a nursing female, was dominant over the other younger female and other male. The relationship of this second male to the second female was not determined (Ryden, 1974, 1975). In both 1971 and 1972, only one litter was produced although 2 females were present. In 1973 the same male and female retained their pack dominance and again produced the only litter. However, in 1973 there was a total of 6 adults in this pack, the original dominant pair, an additional adult male, 1 yearling female, and 3 yearling males (Ryden, 1974, 1975). The dominance relationships of these additional 4 coyotes was not clear.

In 1974 the same male held the position of dominance but I could not determine if he retained his mate of the previous year, although she was clearly dominant over the second female. Both of these females nursed the 9 pups. A second adult male appeared to be the same individual as the additional male in 1973. Two other unknown adults were seen with this pack, but their sex and hierarchial relationships were not determined.

Pack cohesiveness was determined from a total of 87 sightings collected from December 1970 to November 1973 (Table III). The results were similiar to those observed with the MBP; the greatest degree of pack cohesiveness occurred during the winter and the lowest occurred during the summer.

c. The Poverty Flat Pack (PFP). The Poverty Flat Pack (PFP), was observed intensively from December 1970 to June 1974. In the spring of 1971 when the first determination of pack hierarchy was made, the pack was made up of 2 pairs of coyotes: 1 pair of adults and another pair consisting of a 2-year-old male and a 1-year-old female. The 1-year-old female was trapped and eartagged as a juvenile in this same territory in September of 1970 and may have been born into the pack in April of 1970. The adult male was clearly the dominant male while the adult female was dominant to both the younger male and young female. The young male dominated his mate. In May of 1971, these 4 coyotes denned together and produced a total of 9 pups which were nursed by both females and fed solid foods by both males with no apparent segregation of the pups into individual litters. By the denning season of 1972, an additional pair of coyotes were seen with the

TABLE III

Average Monthly Pack Size (Pack Cohesiveness) for the Nowlin Creek Pack (NCP) Based on 87 Sightings from December 1970 to November 1973.

	Jan.	Feb.	Mar.	Apr.	May	Jun.	Jly.	Aug.	Spt.	Oct.	Nov.	Dec.
Average	3.1	3.9	3.0	2.7	2.0	1.7	1.5	1.6	1.2	1.7	3.7	3.4
Range	1–5	1–6	1–5	1–5	1–4	1–2	1–2	1–3	1–2	1–3	2–5	1–5
Mode	2 and 5	4	2 and 4	1	1	1	1 and 2	1	1	1	4	4
Sightings	12	13	7	6	9	6	4	5	4	6	6	9/87

original 2 pairs. In May of the same year these 6 coyotes produced a total of 16 pups in 2 seperate dens. The same dominant pair denned in the same den used in 1971 but shared it with the new pair. This den contained 10 pups who were cared for in the same fashion as in 1971. The other pair denned in an area less than ½ km northwest of the main den and produced 6 pups. By late June, all 16 pups and 6 adults were together constituting the largest number of coyotes in 1 pack, including offspring, observed during the study. The hierarchial relationship of the 2 dominant coyotes remained unchanged as did the relationship of the original subordinate pair. The relationship of the new pair to the lower ranking male was unknown but they were clearly dominant to the original low-ranking female.

In October 1972 an additional male was trapped and ear-tagged in this territory and was frequently seen in the company of this pack bringing the total number of adults in the PFP to 7. During the winter of 1972–1973 major changes took place in the composition of this pack. The dominant female and the subordinate male that had been with the pack for 2 years, and the new unmarked male of 1972, were not seen again. This was the same winter that many coyotes were found dead due to canine hepatitis.

At the onset of the 1973 denning season the PFP consisted of the original dominant male, the new female of 1972, the female born in 1970, the ear-tagged male of 1972, and an additional male of unknown origin, as well as a new female estimated to be 1 year old. The order in which the individuals are listed represents their hierarchial relationship. In 1973 this pack denned at the site used the previous year but on May 2, it is believed that the pups were destroyed by three members of the pack immediately to the north (Section III,C). For the remainder of the year, the PFP was not seen engaged in any denning activities.

In 1974 the PFP consisted of six individuals with the ear-tagged female of 1970 being the dominant member of the pack. The pair of new coyotes from 1973 were the only other members recognized from previous observations, and the fate of the other three coyotes is unknown. The three new coyotes were of unknown origin and rank. In this pack then, the female born in 1970, the lowest ranking coyote in the pack in 1971, became the dominant coyote in the PFP in 1974. This female was still the dominant animal of the PFP when last seen in March of 1977.

Pack cohesiveness was determined from 380 sightings from December 1970 to November 1973 (Table IV). As with the previous two packs, the PFP displayed seasonal variations in Pack cohesiveness with the greatest pack sizes occurring from November to March (2.3 to 3.7). The smallest pack, occurred in June, July, and August with averages of 1.3, 1.7, and 1.3, respectively.

TABLE IV

Average Monthly Pack Size (Pack Cohesiveness) for the Poverty Flat Pack (PFP) Based on 380 Sightings from December 1970 to November 1973

	Jan.	Feb.	Mar.	Apr.	May	Jun.	Jly.	Aug.	Spt.	Oct.	Nov.	Dec.
Average	3.4	3.7	2.2	2.6	1.6	1.3	1.7	1.3	1.9	1.8	2.3	3.3
Range	1–7	1–6	1–5	1–5	1–3	1–3	1–3	1–2	1–4	1–4	1–4	1–6
Mode	5	2 and 4	1	1	1	1	1	1	1	1	2	4
Sightings	36	38	60	22	42	35	20	19	17	27	18	46/380

5. Discussion: Population Organization

The Refuge coyote population was divided into four categories based on the degree of social organization. The individuals in the population that displayed the least amount of social organization were referred to as nomads. These were coyotes of all age classes, including disabled individuals. They ranged over large geographical areas but maintained rather stable home ranges. The occurrence of young and disabled individuals in this portion of the population is probably a result of their inability to compete successfully in the dynamic hierarchial structure of the resident pairs and packs. That some apparently healthy adults appear in this segment of the population probably represents nothing more than the variation in the "personalities" of the individual coyotes. Similiar factors appear to play a significant role in determining which wolves exist as loners and which maintain a position within the socially organized packs (Zimen, 1975; Mech, 1970). Although probably not in themselves a part of the reproducing population, nomadic coyotes undoubtedly serve as pools from which individuals are recruited into the resident and reproductively active segments of the population.

The second category of coyotes was referred to as aggregations. Scott (1972) described aggregations of animals as having no social organization but behaving as a result of one member reacting to the activities of the one next to it. This results in group coordination but with no differentation of individual social position. Coyotes belonging to aggregations seem to have at least one advantage over nomadic individuals, namely, their numbers frequently make it possible for them to feed on carrion that the nomadic coyotes can not approach due to defensive behavior of resident coyotes.

Packs, the third category, represented the largest number of coyotes that existed intact throughout the year. They had well-defined hierarchies, shared the duties of maintaining their common territories, reared their offspring together, and fed as a group whenever large carrion food sources were available. Based on the interactions visable during greeting ceremonies, it was clear that coyote packs maintained dominance hierarchies similiar to those described for the wolf (Zimen, 1975; Mech, 1966; Jordan *et al.*, 1967; Pimlott *et al.*, 1969; Rabb *et al.*, 1967; Scott, 1967). These and other authors indicated that perhaps the major selective advantage of the pack is its ability to capture and kill large ungulate prey species. On the Refuge, the apparent major advantage of the coyote pack lies in its ability to maintain ownership of the carrion food source and not in actual depredation of that animal. Thus, with both species, it appears that a major evolutionary advantage of the pack lies in its ability to ensure the successful acquisition and maintenance of an adequate food source.

The cohesiveness of coyote packs fluctuated seasonally in the same manner as did wolf packs in northern Minnesota (Stenlund, 1955). The decline in pack cohesiveness occurred simultaneously with the changing feeding patterns of the coyotes. In winter, carrion provided the major source of food and pack size was largest while in the summer, when only small prey items were available, coyotes were more often observed alone or in pairs. Both Stenlund (1955) and Murie (1944) state that wolves were most often observed as singles or pairs during the summer probably as a result of their feeding on small prey items.

The common occurrence of more than one pair from one pack denning together is similiar to that described for wolves by Mech (1966) and others, and undoubtedly could account for many of the large litters reported by Young and Jackson (1951) and other investigators. These authors often reported large litters as double litters, resulting from the mating of 1 male to 2 females (possibly a mother and her daughter). They never suggested that his might have represented the offspring of 2 pairs or a pack of coyotes.

Resident pairs formed the nucleus of the breeding population on the Refuge. They appeared as parts of packs and as individual pairs maintaining exclusive territories identical to the large packs. Pair bonds often lasted several years but the mechanism by which they were formed, maintained, or broken, remains unknown.

B. Coyote Territories

Information on territories was collected from the above mentioned three packs. The Miller Butte Pack occupied the southern portion of the Refuge (Fig. 1) and had their eastern territorial boundary on the Teton National Forest. This area rises abruptly from the Refuge and is dissected by several steep, forested canyons, which made prolonged observations difficult. As such, the eastern boundary was never determined nor was the exact territory size known. The southern and western boundary of the MBP was constant throughout the study period coinciding with the town of Jackson on the south and the western Refuge boundary and north–south valley highway on the west. The northern boundary remained constant from the winter of 1970–1971 through the early winter of 1972–1973. This line coincided with the southern and eastern divide on Miller Butte, and formed a common boundary with the NCP. Here, the crest of the butte formed a distinct geographic divide upon which the coyotes established a narrow line of overlapping activity, in some cases as little as 100 m.

During the late winter of 1972–1973 the northern MBP boundary shifted north to the north end of Miller Butte, and disputes with the NCP continued until the following winter (1973–1974) when this shift was solidified and maintained through the spring of 1975. The shift coincided with the outbreak of canine hepatitis and the subsequent death of many coyotes. The western portion of the boundary dividing the MBP and the NCP crossed a low wetlands area through which Flat Creek flowed. In this area the boundary was not distinct and activities of the two packs overlapped by as much as 0.75 km.

In 1971 and 1972 the activity of the MBP suggested that the den was on the rough southeastern portion of their territory, but I was unable to locate the den or determine its reproductive success. In 1973 the den was located on the boundary between the forest and Refuge and extremely close (300 m) to the northeastern boundary. Simultaneous with the northward shift of the boundary in the winter of 1972–1973, much of the activity of the MBP also shifted northward. The 1973 den was situated further north than the presumed dens of the previous 2 years. The first den of 1974 was located on the south facing slope of Miller Butte, midway between the east and west pack boundaries. However, early in July, the litter of 4 pups was moved approximately 1 km to the northeast, placing it in the disputed zone between this and the NCP.

In 1975 the den was located atop the north end of Miller Butte within 400 m of their northern boundary. During the winter of 1975–1976 the northern boundary shifted southward coinciding with the same boundary used from 1971 to 1973. The 1976 MBP litter was located in the same den that was used in 1974. In July the pups were moved atop the south end of the butte where they remained through the summer.

The Nowlin Creek Pack (NCP) was the only pack investigated that maintained a territory exclusively on the Refuge. The location of their southern boundary has already been described in conjunction with the MBP. Their western boundary coincided with the western Refuge boundary which paralleled the north–south valley highway. In 1971 and 1972 the western portion of their northern boundary coincided with the channel of Flat Creek. The northern portion of their territory occupied an area of wetlands between Nowlin Creek and the northeastern base of Miller Butte.

In the winter of 1972–1973, as the southern boundary moved northward, the NCP also shifted much of their activities to the north across Flat Creek. Exactly what shifts were made by the pack occupying the territory north of Flat Creek are unknown, but the abandonment of their southern boundary was witnessed. In 1971 and 1972, the NCP dens were located on the north end of Miller Butte less than 600 m north of their southern boundary. In 1973, their first den was located on a slight rise along Flat Creek. This den was relocated back to Miller Butte at the time observations were begun by Ryden (1974, 1975). By the end of June, less than 2 weeks after the constant surveilence by Ryden was halted, the NCP again moved their pups to the northern portion of their territory. In 1974 and 1975 the NCP again moved their pups to the northern portion of their territory. In 1974 and 1975 the NCP denned and reared their pups on this same northern area of their territory. Thus, by the spring of 1974, the shift northward was completed and maintained until the winter of 1975–1976. With the southward shift of the common boundary between the MBP and NCP in the winter of 1975–1976, the 1976 den was located on the north face of Miller Butte, where it was in 1971, 1972, and a portion of 1973. Throughout the study period the NCP territory was estimated to be approximately 5 km^2 in size. Even with the boundary shifts, there was no significant change in the size of the territory.

The other pack observed was the Poverty Flat Pack (PFP). This pack occupied the territory east of the NCP (Fig. 1) and shared the common boundary along Nowlin Creek from its origin at the base of Miller Butte northward across a wet sedge meadow. From these wetlands the boundary turned to the northeast and east across the featureless, dry glacial deposits constituting Poverty Flats. This area of the territory was contested by both the PFP and by the Flat Creek pack (FCP) immediately to the north. The area of overlap varied in width from ½ to ¾ km. The eastern portion of the PFP boundary continued along the open hillsides stradling the eastern Refuge boundary. The southeastern boundary line crossed the private property of the Twin Creek Ranch and included a large (0.9 km^2) irrigated hay meadow. The southern boundary of the PFP territory coincided with the east–west portion of the main graveled Refuge road. To the south of this and extending to the east of the MBP territory resided the Twin Creek pack (TCP). The activities of this pack were only observed as they occurred on the open area of the Refuge. The portions of the boundary which followed Nowlin Creek and the Refuge road appeared to be well defined. The overlap of activities between the respective packs in these locales was restricted to an area of less than 200 m.

From 1971 to 1975 the PFP den was on the extreme northeastern portion of their territory. The only boundary changes observed during the study occurred along this same eastern boundary. During the winter of 1972–1973 there was an eastward movement of about 0.6 km which was maintained to the end of the observation period in the winter of 1975–1976. This extension coincided with the heavy coyote mortality previously reported. The winter of 1972–1973 was also the first winter that I became aware of coyote trapping activities on the Teton National Forest immediately adjacent to the PFP boundary. The exact number of coyotes harvested is not known. In 1971 and 1972 the PFP territory was approximately 6 km^2 in size. With the extension of the eastern boundary, the territory increased to 7.2 km^2.

C. Territorial Behavior

Territorial behavior was divided into 2 types. Type I involved actual physical contact between members of different territories (fighting and chasing), while type 2 included activities such as scent-marking and vocal behavior and involved no actual physical contact between members of different territories.

1. Direct Territorial Behavior: Fighting and Chasing

Thirteen cases of direct territorial defense were observed during the entire study period, eight from December to April and five near active dens from May to July. No direct encounters were witnessed from late July to early December.

A direct territorial encounter, typical of the rest, occurred during the breeding season (February) of 1971. Five members of the PFP were resting together approximately one km southeast of their northwest boundary when 3 members of the Fish Hatchery Pack (FHP) entered the PFP territory from the northwest. After the FHP had crossed the disputed area, they began a short group howling session (Section III,C,2,b) which lasted less than 1 minute. The PFP immediately rose from their beds and replied with their own group howl which lasted about 70 seconds. As soon as the vocalizations ended, four of the PFP coyotes began running toward the intruders who then ran south, deeper into the PFP territory. When less than 200 m separated the combatants, the FHP coyotes individually turned westward toward the PFP–NCP boundary. As each individual turned, one PFP coyote also turned and continued the chase. The fourth PFP coyote stopped and returned to the one pack member that did not enter the chase (an estrous female). As each pair of combatants approached the territorial boundary, all chasing ceased, the intruders slowed to a walk and began moving north toward their own territory. The defenders scent-marked (Section III,C,2,a) in the boundary area and then returned to the original resting area. When all had reunited, the PFP coyotes initiated a group yip-howl session (Section III,C,2,b). All encounters ended at the respective territorial boundaries and in no case did I ever witness an encounter that proceeded across a boundary.

Eight of the 13 encounters witnessed began with vocalizations. An incident that occurred on March 24, 1974 is typical of the encounters that started without vocalizations. At 10:45 A.M. 3 members of the PFP were moving slowly southwestward from their northern boundary. At the same time a lone unknown coyote was moving from west to east midway through the PFP territory. When the PFP coyotes first became aware of the lone coyote, 2 of the 3 began chasing the intruder to the east along a Refuge road. After they had traveled slightly over 1.28 km, they reached the boundary area. Here, as always, all chasing ceased and both defenders scent-marked the area. At no time did any of the coyotes actually come in contact with one another, but they dramatically portrayed their respective roles. The defenders ran with their tails held out horizontally and occasionally slightly higher. As the pace slowed and the combatants approached one another the backs of the defenders were arched slightly and the legs were outstretched giving the appearance of a slightly larger than normal coyote. When these body postures predominated, their tails were held slightly above the horizontal and wagged stiffly back and forth with high amplitude. Some piloerection was observed along the dorsal-median line from the base of the skull to the base of the tail. The facial expressions became intense as the combatants neared; canine teeth were exposed by means of a vertical retraction of the lips (see Lehner, Chapter 6, Fig. 4c).

The intruder assumed a submissive posture that became more exaggerated as the defender neared. Initially the tail was held below the horizontal. The head of the fleeing coyote was held lower than that of the defenders. The ears were held tightly back against the head with the opening oriented downward and slightly covered by the top or median edge of the ear. As the combatants neared one another, the tail of the intruder was held against the back of the hind legs and partially tucked between the legs. In this situation the back of the intruder was arched and piloerection was evident. Facial expressions included "submissive grins" (see Bekoff, Chapter 5, Fig. 2i) which involved retraction of the corners of the mouth and a slight lifting of the lips which partially bared the canines. The posture of the intruder contained both submissive (tucked tail, submissive grin and, flattened ears) and aggressive features (arched back and piloerection) (Lehner, Chapter 6, Fig. 4). As in the previously described encounters, no actual body contact was made with the intruder and when the marking sequences were completed, the defenders returned to their original course of travel and the intruder continued away from the area of the encounter.

Five successful defensive encounters occurred near active dens from May 6 to July 17. For example, on May 28, 1971, the dominant male and the lowest ranking female (yearling with pups) were the only adults at a den containing 9 pups when a single yearling of unknown sex was observed just inside the PFP territory and 350 m northwest of the den site. The yearling female was the first to respond to the presence of the intruder. She assumed an alert posture and slowly approached the intruder to within 75 m. At this distance the female began running toward the intruder who responded by retreating. When the female came to within 45 m of the intruder, the latter individual assumed a submissive posture (tail tucked, back arched, and neck and head lowered; Lehner, Chapter 6, Fig. 4a). The chase continued for another 50 m at which time the intruder jumped into a narrow irrigation ditch which contained approximately 0.25 m of water. At this time, the dominant male arrived and both defenders attacked with swift bites and lunges. They never maintained any extended body contact with the intruder who remained in the ditch and on his back and sides snapping at the defenders. After 2 minutes and 50 seconds, the defenders moved several meters away from the intruder and scent-marked the area. When they had moved about 60 m the intruder emerged from the ditch and walked north into the FCP territory.

Two similiar incidents were observed in both 1973 and 1974. In each case a female at the den led the defense. Twice, males joined the females, once, a male remained behind, and once no male was present. I could not identify the intruders in any of the situations although 3 of the 5 appeared to be yearling coyotes.

Ryden (1975) describes an incident in 1973 at the NCP den where a yearling female made repeated appearances at the den only to be driven away by the dominant female. However by late June she was accepted into the area and allowed to bring food to the pups. Ryden (1975) concluded that this represented the recruitment of this yearling into the pack. No similiar incident was observed by me during the study.

There were 2 additional instances of coyotes entering adjacent territories, both resulting in the destruction of the resident pups by the invading pack. In 1973 the PFP whelped their pups in a den approximately 350 m south of the northern boundary that separated their territory from that of the FCP. The FCP had their den approximately one km north of the PFP den. On May 11, 3 members of the FCP were seen at the PFP den. They immediately retreated to their own territory when I approached the denning area. Since I witnessed only the retreat, I have no record of what transpired prior to my arrival. At the same time the PFP was along the southern boundary of its territory feeding on a deer carcass that had been entrapped in a woven wire fence. This was one of the few times that I was aware of a den being completely unattended by the adults. When the PFP coyotes returned to their den their behavior became cautious and deliberate; their bodies were stiff and they moved slowly with their tails elevated to slightly below horizontal. Then, for the first and only time throughout the study, I witnessed the adults scent-mark their den. For the remainder of the year, the PFP was not seen engaged in any denning activities.

In May of the following year the dominant male and female and the second ranking male of the PFP were seen at the den of the Twin Creek Pack (TCP) (200 m south of the TCP–PFP boundary) which contained 4 pups. The dominant female of the PFP walked about 300 m back into her territory carrying a dead pup in her mouth. She then disappeared from view for 7.5 minutes after which she reappeared and returned to the TCP den without the pup. The 3 PFP coyotes spent an additional 26 minutes investigating and scent-marking the surrounding area. They returned to their denning area by following their boundary and scent-marking. Thirty-five minutes later, one pup emerged from the den and produced a howl similiar to that of an adult lone howl (see Lehner, Chapter 6, Section IV,C,1). The following day, the female of the TCP was at this den nursing the one remaining pup. By the next day, May 16, the pup had been moved 500 m south to a new den.

I searched the area where the PFP female disappeared with the one dead pup but found no evidence of its remains and concluded that she ate it. The other 2 pups were similiarly unaccounted for and may have disappeared in the same manner. That one pup survived may be due in part to the construction of the den. A den that I examined in 1969 consisted of a single tunnel that spiraled downward 1 m ending in a narrow pointed tunnel not large enough to accomodate an adult coyote. If this den was of similiar construction, it is possible that the pup could have remained in the narrow portion of the den and inaccessible to the raiding adults. These were the only 2 cases of possible cannibalism observed during the study period.

Both of the destroyed litters were located in dens in close proximity to the territorial boundaries as were nearly all of the dens observed throughout the study. Whether the placement of dens near boundaries indicated a preference on the part of the coyotes or was strictly a function of the available denning habitat remains unknown. Other than the cases where territory boundaries shifted, all denning areas, and in some cases the same dens, were used throughout the years of this study.

2. Indirect Territorial Behavior

Scent-marking and vocalizations constituted the only indirect territorial activities witnessed during this study.

a. Scent-Marking. Kleiman (1966, p. 167) defined scent-marking as ". . . urination, defecation, or rubbing of certain areas of the body which is (1) oriented to specific novel objects, (2) elicited by familiar conspicuous landmarks and novel objects or odours, and (3) repeated frequently on the same object." With coyotes, both urination and defecation fit this definition.

Because of the great distance at which most observations were made, it was often impossible to determine if any or all of the 3 criteria were met. Therefore, for the sake of separating basic eliminative behavior from scent-marking, I have incorporated a fourth criteria to the above definition, that of scratching at the ground with the feet after elimination. The "scratching" sequence provided a visible feature which I believe to be unique to the scent-marking regime. That is not to say that scent-marking does not occur without "scratching," but rather that scratching provides a positive indication, one that is clearly visible over a long distance. (Editors note: By defining scent-marking in this way, Camenzind's data almost definitely are an underestimate. I have observed numerous instances of scent-marking by free-ranging coyotes at the Rocky Mountain National Park, Estes Park, Colorado, that are consistant with Kleiman's criteria.)

Coyote scent-marking by urination was performed differently by the sexes and involved one of two postures. Males lifted one hind leg laterally, keeping it stretched slightly forward while urinating on either the ground or a vertical surface. While doing this, the other hind leg was often placed slightly behind the perpendicular.

In the second method of scent-marking employed by males, all four feet were kept on the ground but slightly separated laterally as well as from front to back. In this posture the urine was always sprayed on to the ground.

Females always used a leg lift while scent-marking (as defined above). But instead of lifting the leg laterally, they lifted a hind leg straight up under the body and sometimes crouched with the other hind leg. Females also crouched while urinating but bent both hind legs and placed the genitals nearly on the ground.

Fifty-seven cases of scent-marking by urination were observed. Of these, 39 (68%) were located on boundary areas (within the overlap areas) while the remainder were inside the territories. Of the 57 observations, 23 (40%) involved females, 27 (47%) involved males, and 7 (13%) involved animals of unknown sex. Of the 27 cases of male scent-marking, 20 (75%) were performed with the hind leg lifted and the remainder from a crouched position. The lowest incidence of urine scent-marking occurred in the fall months of September and October when only 4 markings were observed; 9 were sighted in May and June and 11 in each of the other 2 month periods.

Both sexes employed the same posture when scent-marking with feces. The hind legs were moved forward under the abdomen and crouched to nearly a sitting position while the forelegs remained upright causing the back to bend sharply downward toward the base of the tail. The tail was held horizontally from the base with the tip of the tail dropping. This was no different from the elimination defecation posture that was not followed by ground scratching.

Defecation scent-marking was less frequently observed than marking by urination. Only three observations were made of the actual process and in only one case was the sex of the coyote determined (male). Three times during the summer months I found two separate coyote scats of different age on or very near dried domestic cow feces. Sixteen other locations were found where 2–5 coyote scats of different ages were all within an area of less than 4 m^2.

In the winter of 1972–1973 a coyote "latrine" was located in a partially empty Refuge hay shed. It was estimated that in excess of 500 separate coyote scats were located in an area of less than 500 m^2. The exact number of scats could not be determined because of the broken condition of most and the mixing of these fragments which occurred as a result of the heavy coyote traffic. K. Levitt (personal communication) reported to me that in the mid-1960's another "latrine" was found on the refuge under a dilapidated wooden bridge crossing a dry creek channel. Several hundred coyote scats were in the ditch within an area of only 30 m^2. Ozoga and Harger (1966) reported finding 13 separate coyote scats on a small knoll while following coyote tracks in the winter. They did not mention whether this might have represented a scent station or if it was on a boundary area. Kruuk (1972) described the "latrines" formed by spotted hyenas (*Crocuta crocuta*) as always being on or very near territorial boundaries and playing a significant role in maintaining these boundaries. The one coyote "latrine" found in the hay shed was not near a boundary and both were in inconspicuous and sheltered areas. I do not think that these coyote "latrines" served territorial functions.

b. Vocal Behavior. Two vocalizations, the group howl and group yip-howl, appear to play significant roles in maintaining coyote territories. They are performed by two or more members of the packs, are often given in apparent response to similiar vocalizations of adjacent packs and frequently preceed and/or follow direct territorial defense activities (discussed previously). Lehner (Chapter 6, Sections IV,C and D), Camenzind (1974, 1976), and Camenzind and Lehner (1975) describe these and other vocalizations in detail. During both types of vocalizations, the subordinate individuals frequently oriented themselves around the dominant individual. The group howl was usually given from a standing position although there were several instances in which coyotes remained lying or rose only to a sitting position. The group yip-howl was always performed from a standing position and as the intensity of the call increased, the tails were elevated to the horizontal position and wagged rapidly back-and-forth. Pups as young as 5 weeks of age joined the adults in group yip-howling with high pitched yips. Both vocalizations were most often heard from November to April and again in June and July.

D. Territorial Behavior: Discussion

The coyote population on the National Elk Refuge demonstrates both home range and territorial systems of land tenure. The nomadic segment of the population appeared to occupy true home ranges. They regularly traveled over large geographic areas and defended only a limited "individual distance" (Klopfer, 1973, p. 59).

Pairs and packs of coyotes were strictly territorial in their activities on the Refuge. Recently, telemetry studies (Chesness, 1972; Gipson and Sealander, 1972) have revealed the presence of minimal or nonoverlapping areas of activity in other coyote populations. Unfortunately none of these studies included behavioral observations and as such no conclusions can be made as to whether the geographic areas represented home ranges or true territories. I suspect that when behavioral observations can be made in other areas, they will demonstrate the presence of territories.

Considering the infrequency with which boundary crossings were observed, it appears that the coyotes recognized and respected the various signals used to deliniate territories. Fighting and chasing provided a direct, short-lived, and local means of driving intruders from occupied territories. Vocalizations were immediate and short-lived but covered a large geographic area while scent-marking produced a local but long-lasting signal of territorial occupancy. Very few boundary crossings were witnessed and I do not think that these activities invalidate the conclusion that the Refuge coyotes occupied virtually exclusive nonoverlapping territories.

In addition to the observations made on the Refuge, research was conducted in Grand Teton National Park. The results from the Park agree with those from the Refuge. Packs were frequently observed engaged in territorial activities in areas which remained essentially unchanged for 5 years. Territories were known to emcompass denning areas which were reused annually, as on the Refuge.

In areas where prey items were less abundant, such as the extensive glacial outwash region of the west-central portion of the Park (Weaver, 1977), the territories were larger then on the Refuge, and it appeared that home ranges might extend beyond the territories. The exact sizes of these home ranges was not determined but adult spring densities were estimated to vary from 0.23 to 0.32 coyotes/km^2 or approximately one-half of that on the Refuge. In other portions of the Park where the habitat more closely resembled that of the southern portion of the Refuge, spring densities were within the range expressed for the Refuge.

In conclusion it appears that a portion of the resident Jackson Hole coyote population maintains exclusive, high density territories. Where (and when) food resources are less abundant, the territories are larger and home ranges may extend beyond the actual territories. Superimposed on this land use scheme are the nomadic individuals that travel over even larger areas in a pattern indicative of a home range.

V. CONCLUSIONS

The Jackson Hole coyotes are highly organized and utilize an elaborate land tenure system to achieve their ecological requirements. They occupy clearly defined territories which are maintained through a combination of direct (fighting and chasing) and indirect (scent-marking and vocalizations) behavioral activities. On the National Elk Refuge, where an abundant food supply exists, these territories are compact and apparently satisfy virtually all of the resident coyote's needs. In other areas of the valley where food resources are less abundant, the coyotes have responded by occupying larger territories possibly with home ranges extending beyond the defended boundaries.

Superimposed upon the range of the territorial coyotes are a group of nomadic individuals that travel within extensive home ranges and do not defend territorial boundaries. They probably serve as a reservoir from which new members are recruited into resident pairs and packs.

Territoriality varies seasonally. All territorial activities reach their high point during the winter; scent-marking occurs most frequently, territorial vocalizations are heard most often, actual boundary conflicts are apparent, and pack cohesiveness is at its highest level. Breeding activities also reach their peak in February and March (personal observations). This coincides with the time of the harshest weather conditions and can only add to the intensity with which resident coyotes can be expected to defend their territories, including their food sources and their mates. During the spring and summer denning season, territorial activity lessens in boundary areas but remains at a moderately high level near the active dens.

With the abundant rodent population, food during the denning season did not appear to be a limiting factor. In fact, boundary crossings by territorial coyotes during the denning season did not involve the acquisition of food as they did in winter months. Instead, litters in adjacent territories were destroyed. These results do not prove that territories in themselves regulate population size, but in conjunction with the behavioral activities observed, the net result is a population spacing regime that inevitiably must affect population levels. The coyote population appears to have partitioned the resources through a strict land tenure system.

Over much of the present range of the coyote, man is attempting to control coyote numbers. This undoubtedly keeps the population in "social flux," and any social organization may be unnatural and/or difficult to detect due to the wariness of the individual animals. The flux in pack composition and territorial boundaries that occurred during the winter of 1972–1973 when canine hepatitis was prevalent is indicative of the effect such disturbances may have on population and social stability. The results of this study suggest that there can be some plasticity in the social organization of free-ranging coyotes in relatively unexploited populations.

ACKNOWLEDGMENTS

This work was supported in part by grants from the Welder Wildlife Foundation, the New York Zoological Society, the American Museum of Natural History, and the University of Wyoming. Grateful cooperation was received from the biologists and administrators of the National Elk Refuge and Grand Teton National Park, and from the faculty at the University of Wyoming. To all these organizations and individuals I extend a sincere thank you.

Special thanks must be given to Philip N. Lehner and the Department of Zoology and Entomology, Colorado State University, who supported me through the final portions of this work.

REFERENCES

Camenzind, F. J. (1974). *Teton Mag.* **7,** 10–13, 40–42.

Camenzind, F. J. (1976). *Persimmon Hill* **6,** 12–17.

Camenzind, F. J., and Lehner, P. N. (1975). *Coyote Res. Newsl.* **3,** 14–15.

Chesness, R. A. (1972). *Midwest Fish Wildl. Conf., 34th* 20 p.

Christian, J. J. (1959). *In* "Comparative Endocrinology" (A. Gorbman, ed.), pp. 71–97. Wiley, New York.

Craighead, F. C. (1951). "A Biological and Economic Evaluation of Coyote Predation," pp. 1–23. N.Y. Zool. Soc. and Conserv. Found., New York.

Dimmick, R. W. (1968). "Canada Geese of Jackson Hole." Wyo. Game Fish Comm., Cheyenne, Wyoming.

Errington, P. L. (1946). *Q. Rev. Biol.* **21,** 144–177, 221–245.

Gier, H. T. (1968). "Coyotes in Kansas." Agric. Exp. Stn., Kans. State Coll., Manhattan, Kansas.

Gipson, P. S., and Sealander, J. A. (1972). *Proc. Southeast Assoc. Game Fish Comm.* **26,** 82–94.

Houston, D. B. (1968). "The Shiras Moose in Jackson Hole." Grand Teton Nat. Hist. Assoc., Moose, Wyoming.

Huckabee, J. W., Cartan, F. O., Kennington, G. S., and Camenzind, F. J. (1973). *Bull. Environ. Contam. Toxicol.* **9,** 37–43.

Jordan, P. A., Shelton, P. C., and Allen, D. L. (1967). *Am. Zool.* **7,** 233–252.

Kleiman, D. (1966). *Symp. Zool. Soc. London* **18,** 167–177.

Klopfer, P. H. (1973). "Behavioral Aspects of Ecology," 2nd Ed. Prentice-Hall, Englewoods Cliffs, New Jersey.

Knowlton, F. F. (1972). *J. Wildl. Manage.* **36**, 369–382.

Kruuk, H. (1972). "The Spotted Hyena." Univ. of Chicago Press, Chicago, Illinois.

Mech, L. D. (1966). "The Wolves of Isle Royal." U.S. Dept. of Interior Fauna Series 7, Washington, D.C.

Mech, L. D. (1970). "The Wolf." Nat. Hist. Press, Garden City, New York.

Murie, A. (1940). "Ecology of the Coyote in the Yellowstone." U.S. Gov. Printing Office, Washington, D.C.

Murie, O. (1944). "The Wolves of Mt. McKinley." U.S. Dept. of Interior Fauna Series 4, Washington, D.C.

Murie, A. (1951). "Coyote Food Habits on a Southwestern Cattle Range." *J. Mamm.* **32**, 291–295.

Ozoga, J. J., and Harger, E. M. (1966). *J. Wildl. Manage.* **30**, 809–818.

Pimlott, D. H., Shannon, J. A., and Kolenosky, G. B. (1969). "The Ecology of the Timber Wolf in Algonquin Provincial Park." Ont. Dep. Lands For., Toronto.

Preble, E. A. (1911). "Report on the Condition of Elk in Jackson Hole, Wyoming in 1911. U.S. Gov. Printing Office, Washington, D.C.

Rabb, G. B., Woolpy, J. H., and Ginsburg, B. E. (1967). *Am. Zool.* **7**, 305–311.

Ryden, H. (1974). *Nat. Geogr.* **146**, 278–294.

Ryden, H. (1975). "God's Dog." Coward, McCann, Geoghegan, New York.

Say, T. (1832). "Early Western Travels: S. H. Long's Expedition," (R. G. Thwaites, ed.), Vol. 14. A. H. Clark, Cleveland, Ohio.

Scott, J. P. (1967). *Amer. Zool.* **7**, 373–381.

Scott, J. P. (1972). "Animal Behavior." Univ. of Chicago Press, Chicago, Illinois.

Stenlund, M. H. (1955). "A Field Study of the Timber Wolf (*Canis lupus*) on the Superior National Forest, Minnesota," Minn. Dep. Conserv., Minneapolis, Minnesota.

Thwaites, G. G., ed. (1904–1905). "Original Journals of the Lewis and Clark Expedition," Vol. 1. Antiquarian Press, New York.

Weaver, J. L. (1977). Coyote-Food Base Relationships in Jackson Hole, Wyoming. M.S. Thesis (unpublished), 88 pp. Utah State Univ., Logan, Utah.

Young, S. P., and Jackson, H. H. T. (1951). "The Clever Coyote." Stackpole, Harrisburg, Pennsylvania and The Wildlife Management Institute, Washington, D.C.

Zimen, E. (1975). *In* "The Wild Canids" (M. W. Fox, ed.), pp. 336–362. Van Nostrand-Reinhold, New York.

Section IV

MANAGEMENT

13

Coyote Damage-Control Research: A Review and Analysis

Ray T. Sterner and Stephen A. Shumake

I. INTRODUCTION

For over a century, the coyote of North America (*Canis latrans*) has been extensively controlled (see Young and Goldman, 1944; Young, 1946; Young and Jackson, 1951; McNulty, 1971; Olsen, 1971). Since the 1960's, however, public attitudes and values regarding environmental resources—particularly wildlife resources—have changed. An increased awareness of environmental factors and renewed concern for the maintenance of all species had led to numerous inquiries of relevant governmental policies. Noteworthy are certain events related to predator and rodent control activities.

In 1963, Secretary of Interior, Stuart Udall, directed the Advisory Board on Wildlife Management to consider the extent of predator and rodent control in the United States. This led to publication of the first of several reports evaluating the activities of the Fish and Wildlife Service in predator management—the "Leopold Report" (Leopold *et al.*, 1964). Briefly, these authors stated that:

> All native animals are resources of inherent interest and value to the people of the United States. Basic governmental policy therefore should be one of husbandry of all forms of wildlife. At the same time, local population control is an essential part of a management policy, where a species is causing significant damage to other resources or crops, or where it endangers human health or safety. Control should be limited strictly to the troublesome species, preferably to the troublesome individuals, and in any event to the localities where substantial damage or danger exists.

Leopold *et al.* (1964) concluded their report with six recommendations for improving predator and rodent control, one of which was increased research and development of damage-control methods.

Subsequently, two important federal legislative actions were signed into law: the 1969 Environmental Policy Act and the 1969 Endangered Species Act. These established guidelines for the protection of certain species judged to be threatened or in danger of extinction. Indirectly, these acts affected predator control, because of their implied restrictions on the widespread use of chemical toxicants and on the use of damage-control activities which might have adverse effects on endangered species.

In 1971, following two additional hearings on predator control activities (the 1966 Congressional Hearings on Predatory Mammals and the 1970 National Academy of Sciences report on animal damage), the Advisory Board on Wildlife Management—the "Cain Report" (Cain *et al.*, 1972)—reemphasized and extended the recommendations of Leopold *et al.* (1964). Cain *et al.* (1972) cited 15 points intended to further improve the environmental safeguards associated with predator management.* Like Leopold *et al.* (1964), these authors also concluded that research and development of selective, intensive control devices and techniques should receive funding priority. On February 8, 1972, within 1 month after publication of the Cain Committee's report, an Executive Order (11643) restricting the use of toxicants on Federal lands and in Federal programs of mammal- or bird-damage control was signed into effect. This resulted in a reemphasis on alternative methods of coyote management (e.g., trapping, denning, and hunting), and further stimulated research to develop safer, more selective, lethal or nonlethal techniques (Wagner, 1975).

The current chapter reviews research and technological developments in coyote-damage control since the 1960's. In organizing the available

* Wagner (1975) discussed organizational and procedural events surrounding establishment of the Cain Committee (Cain *et al.*, 1972), noting that the absence of representatives from the livestock industries has been a major criticism of this report.

materials, we found that the recent scientific literature has dealt largely with attempts to (a) quantify the magnitude of coyote–sheep predation and (b) develop and evaluate potential nonlethal or selective lethal methods of coyote damage control. Essentially, we have limited our review to studies directly involving these two topics; studies involving behavioral, biological, and ecological variables—data of obvious importance to the eventual development of new techniques (see Knowlton, 1972)—were omitted so as to keep our treatise of chapter length. Furthermore, although numerous studies relevant to coyote damage control are now in progress (Balser, 1974b; see Section III), many remain unpublished. Because methodological considerations are essential to research evaluations in any field, we have mainly limited our review to formal published reports which include details of experimental procedures. Where possible, however, we have tried to footnote major unpublished research so as to help the interested reader locate these sources in the future.

II. COYOTE-DEPREDATIONS SURVEYS

The recommendations of both Leopold *et al.* (1964) and Cain *et al.* (1972) acknowledged the need for localized damage control in situations where coyotes cause significant destruction of other resources. Although the occurrence of coyote predation on various wildlife and livestock species is documented,* current damage-control research stems mainly from the coyote–sheep problem. In addition, much of the controversy over coyote damage-control activities reflects the lack of scientific data available on the frequency and nature of coyote depredations (Balser, 1974a). In this section, we review accounts of recent trends in the United States sheep industry, as well as recent surveys which have attempted to quantify the extent of coyote–sheep predation.

A. Sheep-Industry Trends

Pearson (1975) reviewed the status of the sheep industry, concluding that the stock sheep population in the United States has undergone drastic decline since 1947. The states west of the Mississippi still stock 80% of the

* A number of articles describing the occurrence and/or extent of coyote predation on various game and livestock species have been published; the following represent only a partial list for the interested reader: antelope (Knowlton, 1968); deer (Cook *et al.*, 1971; Jackson *et al.*, 1972; White *et al.*, 1972; Beasom, 1974); elk (Craighead, 1951); cattle (Anonymous, 1972); chickens (Anonymous, 1972); goats (Shelton, 1972); sheep (see text; Section II). Additional references on coyote-caused damage to various agricultural crops are cited by Wade in Chapter 15.

nation's sheep, but the 17 western and 31 eastern states currently maintain only 58.5 and 44.2%, respectively, of their 1960 totals. Development of synthetic fibers (Spurlock *et al.*, 1972; Early *et al.*, 1974a), increased production and labor costs (Goodsell, 1971), and predation losses (Baker, 1971; Goodsell, 1971) are some of the factors various researchers have cited as influencing this decline. More recently, however, coyote–sheep predation has become the primary cause expressed by stockmen. According to Nesse *et al.* (1976), for example, the majority of California sheepmen contend that coyote predation is the main problem facing their industry. Such arguments have led to recent attempts to estimate the extent of coyote–sheep predation.

B. Estimates of Coyote–Sheep Predation

Table I lists estimates of sheep loss due to coyotes and other predators obtained in major questionnaire, interview, and biological surveys since 1970. These include two questionnaire surveys (Reynolds and Gustad, 1971; Early *et al.*, 1974a,b), three interview surveys (Nielson and Curle, 1970; Dorrance and Roy, 1976; Nesse *et al.*, 1976) and eight biological surveys (Davenport *et al.*, 1973; Henne, 1975; Nesse, 1975; DeLorenzo and Howard, 1976; Klebenow and McAdoo, 1976; Munoz, 1976; Nass, 1977; Tigner and Larson, 1977). In general, questionnaire surveys are based on stockmen's written responses to a set of questions regarding production practices, marketing matters, predator problems, and predator controls. Interview surveys typically cover the same information, but are collected in personal question–answer sessions between the researchers and ranchers. Finally, biological surveys are based on daily field searches for dead sheep and necropsies of these carcasses by the researchers in order to determine cause of death. Whereas questionnaire and interview procedures are subject to different forms of sampling and response biases, biological surveys frequently yield data for only a portion of missing sheep (see Davenport *et al.*, 1973; Tigner and Larson, 1977).

1. Questionnaire Surveys

Reynolds and Gustad (1971) compiled U.S. Department of Agriculture (USDA) production records (questionnaire reports) for select years from Colorado, Montana, Texas, and Wyoming in order to derive statewide economic information on losses caused by predators. Early *et al.* (1974a,b) mailed two questionnaires to 150 Idaho ranchers (44% response) to estimate statewide economic losses caused by predators. As shown in Table I, the resulting estimates were somewhat variable. Estimates of sheep losses to all

TABLE I

Select Sheep-Loss Estimates Obtained in Major Questionnaire, Interview, and Biological Surveys Since 1970[a]

Survey	Location	Period(s)	Total sheep	Sheep-loss data			
				Percent lost to all causes (estimated loss)	Percent lost to predators (estimated loss)	Percent lost to coyotes (estimated loss)	Percent of predator-caused loss due to coyotes
Questionnaire							
Reynolds and Gustad (1971)	Colorado	1966	1,560,000	17.3 (270,000)	6.7 (104,300)	5.0 (77,500)	74.3
	Montana	1967	1,351,000	31.3 (423,000)	4.5 (61,400)		
		1968	1,275,000	23.8 (303,000)	6.7 (85,000)		
		1969	1,225,000	36.2 (444,000)	5.6 (68,000)		
	Texas	1967	4,802,000	14.6 (700,000)	3.6 (172,500)		
	Wyoming	1966	2,029,000	19.8 (401,000)	5.8 (118,400)		
		1968	1,847,000	20.4 (377,000)	4.6 (85,200)	3.0 (56,300)	66.1
		1969	1,782,000	26.4 (470,000)	7.9 (140,100)	5.3 (94,900)	67.7
Early *et al.* (1974a,b)[b]	Idaho	1970–1971	914,280	14.8 (135,556)	3.4 (30,641)	2.5 (22,661)	74.0
		1972–1973	1,004,607	12.5 (125,870)	3.4 (34,230)	2.8 (28,354)	82.8
Interview							
Nielson and Curle (1970)	Utah	1969	157,491		6.1 (9,607)	4.8 (7,507)	78.0
Dorrance and Roy (1976)[c]	Alberta, Canada	1974	25,494	11.3 (2,885)	2.2 (571)	2.0 (508)	88.0
Nesse *et al.* (1976)[d]	California	1973–1974	980,000	4.1 (40,358)	1.1 (11,175)	0.9 (10,175)	82.1

TABLE I (Continued)

Select Sheep-Loss Estimates Obtained in Major Questionnaire, Interview, and Biological Surveys Since 1970[a]

Survey	Location	Period(s)	Total sheep	Sheep-loss data: Percent lost to all causes (estimated loss)	Percent lost to predators (estimated loss)	Percent lost to coyotes (estimated loss)	Percent of predator-caused loss due to coyotes
Biological							
Davenport *et al.* (1973)	Southwest Utah	1972	17,308	9.5 (1,649)	1.5 (269)		
Henne (1975)[e] (limited predator control)	Southwest Montana	1974–1975	2,041	31.6 (644)	21.5 (449)	21.3 (436)	97.1
Nesse (1975)	Northcentral California	1972	30,510		1.2 (359)		
		1973	31,886	7.1 (2,273)	0.5 (160)		
DeLorenzo and Howard (1976)[f] (limited predator control)	Southeastern New Mexico	1974	994	14.5 (144)	5.3 (53)	4.1 (41)	77.4
		1975	977	11.7 (114)	5.3 (52)	5.3 (52)	100.0
Klebenow and McAdoo (1976)[g]	Northern Nevada	1973–1974	2,466	8.5 (210)	4.9 (121)	3.8 (96)	45.7
Munoz (1976)[h]	Southwest Montana	1975–1976	3,712	21.7 (807)	16.3 (606)	16.2 (602)	99.3
Nass (1977)	Southern Idaho	1973	21,586	9.5 (2,050)	1.3 (282)		93.0 (1973–1975, bracketed)
		1974	22,881	11.5 (2,632)	1.2 (272)		
		1975	5,630	11.1 (624)	1.0 (54)		

Tigner and Larson (1977)[i]	Southern Wyoming	1973	36,438	3.2 (1,152)	0.6 (213)
		1974	33,284	4.8 (1,609)	1.2 (412)
		1975	24,331	6.9 (1,679)	1.7 (405)

[a] Numbers cited refer to combined lamb and ewe losses. More lambs than adults were lost to predators in every study; for example, Henne (1975) reported losses of 349 lambs vs 76 ewes; DeLorenzo and Howard (1976) reported losses of 53 and 52 lambs vs 0 ewes or rams in 1974 and 1975, respectively; and, Nass (1977) reported losses of 1455, 2104, and 399 lambs vs 595, 528, and 225 ewes in 1973, 1974, 1975, respectively. Some of the cited estimates may differ slightly from reported statistics due to the use of actual percentages—not average percentages. In addition, certain estimates were difficult to reconstruct because insufficient detail was provided in the publications; these situations are footnoted. Omitted entries indicate that data were not reported or not presented in a way which would allow reconstruction. We regret any errors in tabled values, however, estimates should be accurate to ±10 sheep. Two additional sources of damage assessment data not included in this table are reports by Stevens and Hartley (1976) and Gee and Magleby (1977).

[b] Data represent estimated values as prepared by Early *et al.* (1974[a,b]) from a subsample of questionnaire responses.

[c] Dorrance and Roy (1976) do not present actual sheep loss counts; rather, data are cited in percentages of ewe and lamb losses for several selected factors: ecosystem (i.e., mixed forest, northern parkland, foothills, prairie, and southern parkland) and flock management (i.e., confined, semiconfined, and range). The cited estimates were computed by us from percentage estimates and total sheep reported in Table 2 of Dorrance and Roy (1976).

[d] Data represent the combined results of questionnaire responses for six regions of California and are based only on 1974 results of Nesse *et al.* (1976); results of a preliminary series of subexperiments are omitted.

[e] Henne (1975) conducted damage assessment for 12 months on the approximately 6000-acre Eight Mile Ranch (Cook) near Florence, Montana. During the first 7 months, predator control was restricted on the ranch and for several miles around; the rancher was compensated for predator kills. Compensation became so expensive, however, that nine coyotes were removed during the final 5 months. The cited loss estimates are those reported in Table II of Henne (1975).

[f] DeLorenzo and Howard (1976) conducted a 2-year biological survey in which the rancher was compensated for predator kills and predator control was not in effect on the actual test area (a 3840-acre ranch); however, predator control activities were practiced on adjacent ranches.

[g] Klebenow and McAdoo (1976) present a variety of statistics based on specific combinations of select data; the cited estimates are those from Table III of their report.

[h] Munoz (1976) reported a second year of measurements on the same ranch covered by Henne (1975). However, predator control was used during this survey. Slight numerical discrepancies occur between Henne's and Munoz's reports for the first year's data.

[i] Tigner and Larson (1977) surveyed range-lambing operations on several ranches. Over 3 years, a total of 4440 losses were examined, of which predators killed 1030 (23%); however, missing sheep (numbers not recovered from docking—tail cutting and counting—until end of the production cycle or grazing periods) comprised a sizable portion of the original herds, and were impossible to estimate in this range survey.

causes (disease, predator, lambing, injury, etc.) for the two surveys ranged from 12.5 to 36.2% of total sheep, whereas estimates of losses due to all predators ranged from 3.4 to 7.9% of total sheep (i.e., approximately one-fourth of all losses). Coyotes were estimated to cause between 2.5 and 5.3% of all losses (i.e., approximately two-thirds to four-fifths of all losses to predators).

2. Interview Surveys

Nielson and Curle (1970) interviewed approximately 20% of Utah's range sheep operators; Dorrance and Roy (1976) interviewed 89 members (5%) of the Alberta Provincial Sheep Breeders Association; and Nesse *et al.* (1976) interviewed 140 California sheep ranchers. As shown in Table I, the resulting estimates of sheep losses to all causes ranged between 4.1 and 11.3% of total sheep; and losses attributed to predators ranged between 1.1 and 6.1% of total sheep (again, about one-fourth of all losses). Noteworthy are the estimates that coyote-caused losses accounted for 4.8% (Nielson and Curle, 1970), 2.0% (Dorrance and Roy, 1976), and 0.9% (Nesse *et al.*, 1976) of total sheep (i.e., three-fourths to four-fifths of all predator kills).

3. Biological Surveys

The eight biological surveys involved daily searches for dead sheep and necropsies of sheep carcasses. In such studies, identification of the predator that attacked and killed the sheep is based on wound and consumption patterns, as well as predator signs evident at the kill site (see Davenport *et al.*, 1973). As one would expect, performing necropsies before decomposition is advanced greatly enhances the validity of such data. If it can be assumed that discovered losses are a representative sampling of all losses, biological survey data can be viewed as the least biased of the available survey methods.

Inspection of Table I shows that magnitudes of losses were highly specific to given surveys, and often fluctuated within the same survey from year to year. Total losses from all causes ranged from 3.2 to 31.6% (Tigner and Larson, 1977; Henne, 1975). Sheep losses to predators ranged from 0.5 4.9% in surveys with predator control in effect (Nesse, 1975; Klebenow and McAdoo, 1976), but from 5.3 to 21.5% with limited control (DeLorenzo and Howard, 1976; Henne, 1975). Losses due solely to coyotes varied from 3.8% with control (Klebenow and McAdoo, 1976) to 21.3% with control activities restricted (Henne, 1975). In four out of six cases, coyote kills accounted for over 90% of all predator-caused losses (see Henne, 1975; DeLorenzo and Howard, 1976; Munoz, 1976; Nass, 1977).

C. Discussion

Despite the noted and expected variability of certain sheep loss estimates listed in Table I, several general patterns in these data merit note. First, questionnaire-based percentage estimates of total sheep losses were greater than either interview or biological survey estimates (except for Henne, 1975; DeLorenzo and Howard, 1976; Munoz, 1976). Second, with the same three exceptions (i.e., Henne, 1975; DeLorenzo and Howard, 1976; Munoz, 1976), predators accounted for less than one-fourth of total losses. However, whereas losses to predators were rather uniform for questionnaire surveys (i.e., between about 4 and 6%), variation was greater for interview data (i.e., between about 1 and 6%), and sizable for biological data (i.e., between 0.5 and 21.5%). Third, where estimates of coyote-caused losses could be computed, all three survey procedures yielded highly variable estimates between 0.9 (Nesse *et al.*, 1976) and 21.3% (Henne, 1975) of all losses. Finally, where computed, coyote-caused losses relative to predator-caused losses were extremely high across all surveys, ranging from 45.7 (Klebenow and McAdoo, 1976) to 100% (DeLorenzo and Howard, 1976). Thus, at the very least, available estimates confirm that: (a) the coyote is the main predator of domestic sheep in North America, and (b) in specific situations, coyote predation can result in sizable sheep production losses.

Of course, as Balser (1974a) pointed out, the manner in which data are collected, summarized, and presented greatly influences the perceived magnitude of predation effects. In particular, percentage estimates of loss can be misleading. Percentages of predator-caused losses based on total losses are much greater than estimates based on total sheep, and total flock sizes obviously determine percent loss magnitudes. Either type of estimate also conveys little, if any, information as to how economically significant the reported losses are to given producers (i.e., a 1% loss can be more or less significant depending on the operation's profit margin and the amount of money already invested in the livestock at the time they are killed). Additionally, although questionnaire, interview, and biological surveys provide useful information regarding the overall impact of predation, comparisons among means and variances of loss estimates are not possible because either these data are unavailable or coyote depredations are unlikely to be normally distributed. While the systematic collection of balanced data from a variety of livestock situations would facilitate comparisons among surveys, this is both impractical and unlikely. In fact, the high cost of recent surveys, particularly biolgical surveys, places additional collection of such data in doubt. Thus, the problem for researchers may become one of attempting to characterize livestock predation from the results already available.

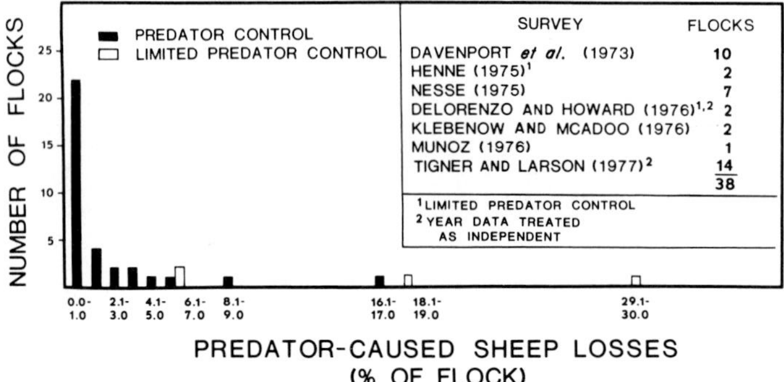

Fig. 1. Distribution of verified, predator-caused sheep losses (expressed as percent of total sheep in each flock) for 38 separate flocks as reported in seven recent biological surveys. Estimates for two flocks reported by Henne (1975) and two by DeLorenzo and Howard (1976), surveys in which predator control was limited, are shown with open bar lines.

Wagner (1975) has suggested that the pattern of predation probably reflects a Poisson distribution, with most ranchers experiencing a few losses and a small number receiving varying degrees of intense damage. Recently, Dorrance and Roy (1976) have partially confirmed this hypothesis from the results of their interview survey. In order to further examine Wagner's concept, we have plotted the percent loss to predators based on total sheep for each of 38 flocks cited in seven of the biological surveys (Fig. 1).* As can be seen, this histogram is positively skewed. Modal losses (i.e., 22 flocks) ranged between 0.0 to 1.0% of total sheep for the compared flocks. Thirty flocks received between 0.0 and 4.0% losses, five flocks received between 4.1 and 9.0% losses, and three flocks showed very high loss estimates (greater than 16%); these latter three estimates were obtained for flocks surveyed on a single ranch—formerly the Eight Mile Ranch (Cook Ranch), Florence, Montana (Henne, 1975; Munoz, 1976). In addition, of the four flocks with limited predator control, two had 5.3 and 5.8% losses (DeLorenzo and Howard, 1976) and two had 17.7 and 29.3% losses (Henne, 1975). Thus, although we have not statistically described the cited distribution, current results appear to support Wagner (1975) and Dorrance and Roy (1976). That is, sizable losses of sheep to coyote predation are likely for a few flocks, with most experiencing far less severe losses.

Some of the biological surveys provide additional predator-loss informa-

* Although Fig. 1 is a plot of predator-caused losses, inspection of Table I statistics reveal the majority of predator-caused losses to be attributable to coyotes. Hence, in order to graph actual flock estimates as most frequently reported in the cited surveys, we elected to plot percent of predator-caused losses, rather than percent of coyote-caused losses (i.e., both graphs are essentially the same).

tion related to: (a) yearly variation, (b) lamb–ewe loss ratio, and (c) predator control. Nesse (1975), Nass (1977), and Tigner and Larson (1977) analyzed year-to-year variation. Depending on the study areas and different investigators, predator losses were found to vary as much as 50 to 200% from the previous year(s). The most consistent finding in all surveys was that far more lambs than ewes were killed by predators. For example, Henne (1975) reported 349 lamb kills versus 87 ewe kills, and Nass (1977) reported 3958 lamb kills versus 1351 ewe kills over 3 years. These disproportionate ratios occurred despite approximately equal numbers of lambs and ewes on the range. Except for the reports of Henne (1975) and DeLorenzo and Howard (1976), predator control was in effect during all surveys. However, whereas Henne's (1975) survey involved restriction on control activities over an extensive area, DeLorenzo and Howard's (1976) involved limited control on a 3840-acre ranch with control measures in effect on surrounding areas. Henne (1975) conducted a 1-year damage assessment study in which predator control was absent for the first 7-month period. The predator loss figure (21.5%) was the highest estimate reported for this type of survey. However, removal of nine coyotes from the area over the next 5-month period produced no change in the predator-loss level, a result somewhat confirmed by Munoz (1976) who reported a 16.3% predator loss estimate for the succeeding 12-month period with control. Of course, whether this coyote-damage situation was anomalous or typical is unknown.

In conclusion, although these 13 surveys of predation losses permit certain interpretations, a number of questions remain. Rarely are reliability or validity coefficients reported for questionnaire and interview responses, and randomness of questionnaire and interview respondents, or of biological survey locations, is unlikely. Questionnaire and interview techniques are subject to numerous sampling and response biases; but, biological surveys involve varying numbers of undetermined losses, degrees of predator control, and potential effects of field disturbance. In all surveys, statistical considerations related to how data are collected and presented greatly influence the perceived magnitude of predation effects (see Balser, 1974a). However, even if these inherent difficulties were resolved, the central problem would remain: justification of coyote control rests on evidence that coyotes cause a *significant* portion of livestock losses. Specification of what are *significant levels of damage* rests on the cost return ratio of control efforts and sheep losses. Although several surveys have dealt with economic effects of predation (i.e., Early *et al.*, 1974a,b; Nesse *et al.*, 1976), these reports omit or make numerous assumptions regarding control costs and the savings to be gained by such activities. Objective estimates of either costs or savings are lacking. Until these data are available the economic benefits accrued from damage-control activities simply cannot be evaluated.

III. COYOTE DAMAGE-CONTROL RESEARCH

With the increased coyote research since the 1960's, there has been a proliferation of terms used to describe damage-control research. Although these have been intended to clarify the functions and rationale underlying development of new methods, many have led to confusion. Thus, before reviewing the recent research literature on nonlethal and lethal methods of coyote damage control, we believe that some clarification of terms and damage-control concepts would be helpful.

A. Terms and Concepts in Damage-Control Research

From a research standpoint, we find it useful to view the development of new damage-control methods as involving a hierarchy of approaches, strategies, substrategies, and methods. Basically, two approaches are thought to guide research: *preventive* (application of methods beforehand to alleviate expected damage) and *corrective* (application of methods after damage starts, to reduce it). (Cain *et al.*, 1972, refer to these as prophylactic and troubleshooting, respectively.) Either of these approaches can be pursued using a lethal or nonlethal strategy. With a *lethal strategy,* methods such as traps, guns, or toxicants are used to alleviate damage by reducing a population or destroying one or more "problem coyotes" (see Gier, 1968; Henderson, 1972). With a *nonlethal strategy,* methods such as exclusion fences, aversive agents, and chemosterilants would be used to reduce damage without the elimination of coyotes.

Either strategy is viewed to reduce damage by reducing the overall coyote population density, by reducing the number of coyotes in localized areas, or by affecting individual coyotes. With nonlethal strategies, these ways of reducing damage correspond to three substrategies: (a) reproductive inhibition, reducing population density by interfering with the coyote's breeding biology or behavior; (b) area avoidance, reducing coyote numbers in a local area by the use of repellents, barriers, herders, or guard dogs; and (c) prey avoidance, affecting individual coyotes by pairing a noxious or repellent stimulus with the prey. Lethal strategies have three analogous substrategies: (a) population reduction, the continual, wide-scale use of lethal methods such as bounty programs in order to reduce population density; (b) intensive reduction, the intensive use of lethal methods for a limited period and/or over a limited area (see Cain *et al.*, 1972; Knowlton, 1972; Hornocker, 1972); and (c) specific reduction, the application of a lethal method in such a way that only coyotes responsible for depredations are eliminated (see Gier, 1968; Henderson, 1972; Wagner, 1972). Although some researchers consider attempts to develop this third substrategy premature, we believe it has become a goal of many damage-control research programs.

Finally, each substrategy can be pursued by either *chemical methods* (the use of toxicants, chemosterilants, emetics, repellents, tranquilizers, etc., to either eliminate coyotes, or alter their activities) or *nonchemical methods* (the use of mechanical, manual, electrical, or other nonchemical devices to achieve the same ends).* In practice, a few methods combine chemicals with nonchemical devices, but most can still be classified (e.g., a steel trap with tranquilizer tabs attached for purposes of humaneness is still mainly mechanical).

Finally, in addition to these classifications, control methods can be characterized as *selective* (affecting mainly coyotes) or *nonselective* (affecting both coyotes and nontarget species), as well as *specific* (affecting an individual coyote that causes damage) or *nonspecific* (affecting any coyote in the population). Although these terms have come into general use (Cain *et al.*, 1972), they imply dichotomies that rarely exist. Selectivity and specificity represent continua, and each control method has greater or lesser degrees of selectivity and specificity depending on how, when, and where it is applied. We will discuss these and other problems of interpretation after summarizing recent damage-control research.

B. Research on Nonlethal Methods

Recently, nonlethal methods have received major emphasis in coyote damage-control research (Balser, 1974b). Considerable work is currently in progress†,‡ and numerous studies aimed at evaluating various aspects of

* Some researchers may recognize a third category of damage-control methods labeled *Biological.* These would refer to methods which utilize natural behavioral or biological functions of coyotes in order to reduce damage (e.g., coyote diseases, primer pheromones, etc.). To date, however, very little research has been conducted towards the development of such biological methods.

† Several general sources of informally published research dealing with coyote damage-control are: (a) abstracts of 1974, 1975, and 1976 annual meetings of the USDA Technical Committee of the Western Regional Research Project W-123; (b) Coyote Research Newsletter, particularly abstracts of the 1974 Coyote Research Workshop (Nov. 14–17, 1974, Denver, Colorado) in Vol. **2**(1), circulated by the U.S. Fish and Wildlife Service (FWS); (c) select copies of the Monthly Narrative of the Denver Wildlife Research Center (DWRC), FWS, Denver, Colorado. A general source of published research citations is Predator Data Base (a computerized reference file), assembled and updated under the direction of S. Linhart, DWRC, FWS; currently, this file is accessible for a nominal fee through the Conservation Library, Denver Public Library, 1357 Broadway, Denver, CO 80203.

‡ Considerable research that is either directly or indirectly related to development of nonlethal and lethal methods is currently in progress or has recently been completed. Projects of FWS (Section of Predator Damage, DWRC, Denver, Colorado) include contractual or in-house work to assess: (a) field evaluation of the toxic sheep collar and improved chemicals for use in the collar; (b) relative importance of coyote sensory stimuli in eliciting and inhibiting predatory behavior; (c) effectiveness of physiological aversive agents in reducing predation; (d)

(*Continued*)

nonlethal techniques, both chemical and nonchemical, have been published. Chemical research has dealt with: (a) drug-induced aversions, (b) repellents, and (c) chemosterilants; whereas, nonchemical research has centered on: (a) sheep-confinement procedures, (b) herding practices, (c) guard-dog effects, and (d) exclusion fences. At present, with the possible exceptions of sheep-confinement procedures, herding practices, and exclusion fences, these methods remain experimental—none are field operational.

1. Chemical

a. Drug-Induced Aversions. Research aimed at development of aversive conditioning techniques for nonlethal control of sheep-attacking coyotes can be traced to Gustavson and his co-workers (Gustavson *et al.*, 1974, 1975, 1976). These authors have hypothesized that: If coyotes eat *baits* treated with an emesis-inducing drug (lithium chloride), they will associate the taste of this meat (as well as secondary cues to odor, sight, and texture) with the subsequent gastrointestinal disorders and will generalize (transfer) this association to live sheep and therefore suppress predatory attacks.

Briefly, Gustavson *et al.* (1974) fed rabbit- or lamb-bait packets containing lithium chloride to six pen-reared coyotes before pairing them with the corresponding live prey. Four coyotes attacked the prey after one baiting (two for rabbits and two for lambs). These four were than presented with a second lithium bait and also injected with the agent. Results showed that the coyotes suppressed prey attacks for several 15-minute periods following this *bait plus injection* trial. Gustavson *et al.* (1974) concluded that one or two trials with a given meat and lithium chloride specifically suppressed coyote attacks on the corresponding prey. Bekoff (1975), however, correctly criticized this interpretation, pointing out that use of an injection procedure was not a test of the baiting approach.

Gustavson *et al.* (1975, 1976) later presented additional data on the use of lithium chloride baits. In one experiment, five of six coyotes eventually avoided killing rabbits following two lithium chloride baitings (i.e., mainly

---

effectiveness of electric fencing in reducing predation; (e) potential of sheep-carried agents to induce anaphylactic shock in coyotes; (f) relative effectiveness of select control tools on coyote–sheep depredations; (g) evaluation and development of coyote attractants; (h) factors influencing efficacy and selectivity of lethal, placed baits (S. Linhart, 1977, personal communication). Projects of the Agricultural Research Service (U.S. Sheep Experiment Station, Dubois, Idaho) include work to assess the potential effectiveness of: (a) chemosterilants; (b) chemical repellents; (c) electrical fences (N. Gates, 1977, personal communication). A limited sampling of other research includes assessments of (a) sound repellents (A. Dracy, 1977, personal communication); (b) chemical repellents (R. Teranishi, 1977, personal communication, R. McColloch, 1977, personal communication; M. Botkin, 1977, personal communication); (c) guard dogs (D. Humphrey, 1977, personal communication).

chickens were killed and eaten following emesis from two different rabbit baits). Gustavson *et al.* (1975, 1976) interpreted these data as supportive of bait-induced prey aversion; however, the fact that two successive baitings and the simultaneous presence of an alternative prey were used are important qualifications to these data. In later parts of their reports, they also cited results of a limited field test of the lithium chloride bait procedure. Fleece-covered lithium baits and lamb carcasses were distributed over a 3000-acre sheep ranch. By comparing the number of lambs and ewes lost after baiting with rancher estimates of earlier losses, Gustavson *et al.* (1975, 1976) concluded that losses had been reduced by 49 to 62%. Unfortunately, during the test (see Gustavson *et al.*, 1975), a variety of lethal control methods were also used, and the extent of yearly fluctuations in coyote-caused losses was not reported.

Despite the reported effectiveness of this method, data either confirming or rejecting the potential usefulness of lithium chloride baiting for producing livestock aversion have yet to be published. Work aimed at development of aversive conditioning remains a major area of nonlethal research. Furthermore, baiting represents only one mode for delivering aversive agents to coyotes. Use of longer lasting, more intense drugs, as well as delivery during actual sheep attacks could enhance these aversion effects.

b. Repellents. Published studies of repellents have dealt almost exclusively with chemical irritants and olfactory agents (Swanson and Scott, 1973; Jankovsky *et al.*, 1974; Lehner *et al.*, 1976). As used in the present context, repellency refers to direct effects of noxious stimuli that produce *unlearned avoidance reactions* upon initial exposure. Although the need to investigate sound, light, and mechanical repellents has been noted (Sander and Dracy, 1972), we were unable to locate any formal publications of such work.

The Gerhardi Livestock Protector is the only commercially available coyote-repellent device for use with livestock. This device is a cup-shaped ear tag which contains mercaptan in a napthalene carrier. The mercaptan is formulated as a slow-release agent and intended to repel neck-attacking coyotes. To date, however, results of field trials with the device have been equivocal (Swanson and Scott, 1973); only minor nonsignificant reductions in coyote-caused losses of mercaptan-tagged lambs were noted during a 60-day test.

More recently, Jankovsky *et al.* (1974) conducted a field study to reevaluate the repellent properties of three chemical mixtures using collar configurations instead of ear tags. Napthalene, napthalene plus cyclohexyl mercaptan, and *trans*-cinnamaldehyde plus motor oil were compared either simultaneously or successively on flocks of sheep expected to experience coyote predation. Control flocks without collars and with water-filled collars were also included. Results were again equivocal: coyote-caused sheep losses were not reduced in two of the three test flocks (as compared to uncollared controls) but were significantly reduced in the third flock. The authors inferred that differences in predation may have influenced the effectiveness of these repellents, i.e., that the repellent effect occurred for the flock having the fewest total losses.

Lehner *et al.* (1976) conducted a pen-test evaluation in which five coyotes were trained to traverse an enclosed area for food rewards. A total of 45 olfactory repellents were then presented adjacent to the food compartment in order to assess the delay in coyote food-getting responses produced by these agents. Chloroacetyl chloride showed the most consistent repellency; however, Lehner *et al.* (1976) stated that the irritant properties of this agent make it impractical for use with livestock. *Trans*-cinnamaldehyde and a commercial animal repellent (Off Limits) also delayed the coyotes from obtaining food, but these effects were somewhat inconsistent and of brief duration. Lehner *et al.* (1976) postulated that neophobia (the avoidance of novel stimuli) could have accounted for certain of the observed effects.

Behaviorally, effects of repellents are prone to habituation. Thus, although a number of repellents can be identified that produce short-term avoidance, few, if any, have been found which will produce continued avoidance for long periods. Researchers must be careful to delineate the potential novelty effects (neophobic reactions) from actual repellency (see Lehner *et al.*, 1976).

c. Chemosterilants. Work to develop an effective technique for inhibiting reproduction in coyotes was a major research activity of the 1960's (e.g., Balser, 1964; Linhart *et al.*, 1968). However, this work was later abandoned because of the short duration of reproductive inhibition often associated with early chemosterilants and the difficulty of delivering an agent to a sufficient segment of the coyote population. Linhart *et al.* (1968), for example, reported a maximum bait pickup of only 36% based on capture estimates of marked coyotes, a result believed insufficient to provide for long-range reduction of the population. A further difficulty was the complexity of supporting Environmental Protection Ageny (EPA) requirements for registration of chemosterilants, such as diethylstilbestrol (Linhart, 1977, personal communication).

Recently, Gates *et al.* (1976) have reported results of a laboratory study of cadmium chloride as a reproductive inhibitor. They administered different oral dosages to two groups of coyotes (an untreated control group was also used). Histological inspections of tissue removed from the testes of these animals yielded essentially negative results; no histopathological changes were found at 60, 120, or 240 days posttreatment for any group. Thus, despite this renewed interest in chemosterilant methods (preferably one that is coyote-selective, effective in a single dose, and capable of preventing reproduction for one or more years), discovering an acceptable agent and delivering such an agent to large numbers of coyotes still plague this strategy. Connolly and Longhurst (1976) implied that at least 70 to 95% of the coyote population would have to be treated in order to significantly reduce natality.

2. Nonchemical

a. Sheep-confinement procedures. In their recent interview survey (see Section II), Dorrance and Roy (1976) compared reports of predation losses for Alberta sheep ranchers using confined, semiconfined, and range (unconfined) management practices. Results indicated that predation losses for ewes and lambs, respectively, were 4,3 [sic 4.3%] and 4.4% for confined flocks, 2.1 and 4.3% for semiconfined flocks, and 1.4 and 1.5% for range flocks. Thus, predation was greatest under confinement and least on the range. Dorrance and Roy (1976) explained this apparent paradox by postulating that confinement leads to killing of greater numbers of sheep once coyotes breach the confinement barriers, whereas range management tends to be practiced in areas where predation is thought to be less severe. It should be recognized that the use of interview data, coupled with a high percentage of unexplained missing sheep under range conditions (see Tigner and Larson, 1977), could influence such results.

b. Herding Practices. Davenport *et al.* (1973), in a biological survey of coyote–sheep depredations (see Section II), attempted to assess the effects of sheep-herding practices on predation. Briefly, these authors compared coyote–sheep depredations during the spring and summer of 1972 for 10 independent flocks of sheep, five unherded and five tended by full-time herders. The two sets of flocks were roughly equated for numbers of sheep. Predator losses of total sheep averaged 2.2% for the unattended flocks as compared to 0.9% for the tended flocks. While herder costs are often cited as prohibitive by many operators, these data demonstrate the potential for sheep-management procedures to alter predation.

c. Guard-dog effects. Although numerous articles have mentioned the potential application of guard dogs to protect sheep (Gerber, 1974; Newbold, 1974), objective evidence of guard-dog effectiveness is limited to a single study (Linhart *et al.*,1977). Briefly, Linhart *et al.* (1977) trained two pairs of Komondor dogs to attack coyotes (see Fig. 3) and remain inside fenced pastures with sheep for extended periods. Tests were conducted on

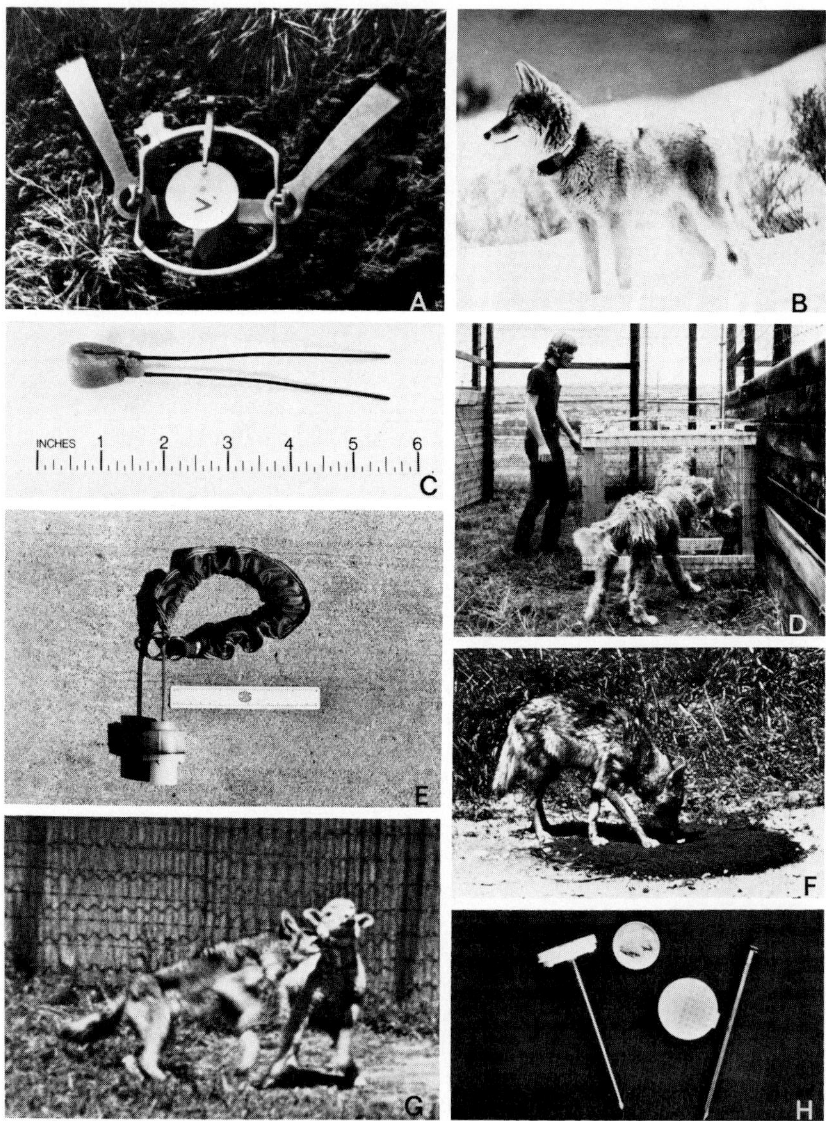

Fig. 2. A montage showing several recent coyote damage-control and ecological research innovations. A and C: A tranquilizer tab attached to a leg-hold trap; a high percentage of captured coyotes ingest the tab, apparently lessening the incidence of leg damage (humaneness). B: A locator transmitter for studying movements and home-range patterns of coyotes. D: Komondor guard dogs being trained to act aggressively towards coyotes; since these dogs are probably too slow to catch coyotes in field situations, the

three ranches utilizing fenced pastures of less than 1 mi^2 in area; one pair of dogs was used on two ranches and the second pair on one ranch. Biological surveys of coyote-caused sheep losses were conducted for the 20 days preceding and during the continuous, 24-hour introduction of the Komondors. The ranchers were compensated for coyote-caused losses, and coyote-control activities were discontinued in the vicinity of each ranch throughout the study. Results for the three ranches indicated that sheep losses to coyotes decreased 70, 35, and 35%, respectively, after the dogs were introduced. Despite these reductions, however, several problems were reported (e.g., one dog attacked sheep and strayed from test pastures). Although improved breeding, rearing, and training practices could alleviate these problems, the utility of this approach remains questionable, particularly its applicability to unconfined flocks ranging over extensive areas. To date, the protective action of Komondors reported by Linhart *et al.* (1977) remains unspecified; pheromones, barking, and actual coyote–dog encounters are only three possible ways that the dogs could serve to reduce losses. Further studies seem warranted.

d. Exclusion fences. Despite recent emphasis upon development of exclusion fences to prevent coyote–sheep contact (Shelton, 1972, 1973), published studies regarding this topic are limited. In one of the few studies reported, B. C. Thompson (1976) conducted a laboratory test in which trained coyotes ran a standard pathway with different fence configurations blocking return to their home cages. In other tests, an attempt was made to exclude coyotes from rabbits within a fenced enclosure. When allowed overnight for several days, coyotes managed to cross practically all of the 34 fence configurations tested. B. C. Thompson (1976) concluded that an effective fence for deterring coyotes should be at least 66 inches high, be made of woven mesh (less than 6 × 4 inch weave), have a 38-inch perpendicular overhang, and include a 12-inch woven wire apron beneath the

---

mode by which their presence deters coyote–sheep predation (if any) is unknown. E: A sheep-mortality transmitter used in biological surveys of coyote-sheep depredations; following some preset delay period of sheet inactivity, the device starts transmitting a signal, permitting early discovery and necropsy of dead sheep (see Kolz *et al.*, 1973). F and H: A scent station used to index local coyote populations by counts of coyote visits; the plastic capsule containing an attractant is placed in the center of a cleared circle, and a series of such stations are then checked daily for signs of coyote visitation (see Linhart and Knowlton, 1975). G: Coyote attack and puncture of an experimental toxic-collar device which is fitted about the neck of a lamb; this lethal chemical method could afford a highly selective, specific technique for eliminating sheep-attacking coyotes. (Photos by: R. Belton, G. Dasch, R. Henderson, F. Knowlton, L. Kolz, and R. Sterner; montage prepared by L. Ropes; we thank *The Wildlife Society Bulletin* for permission to print Photo F.)

ground. Although extrapolation of these data to field situations is difficult, such an "ideal" fence would be impractical and the cost prohibitive. Simple, inexpensive designs are needed if exclusion fences are to receive general application. Currently, research to develop and assess both electric and wire fence designs as coyote-excluding barriers is increasing (Linhart, 1977, personal communication; Humphrey, 1977, personal communication).

C. Research on Lethal Methods

It is difficult to delineate the extent of research activities on lethal damage-control methods. Attempts to improve effectiveness can range from minor modifications in an existing lure, device, or formulation to development of a major new technique or device. Since 1970, only limited data concerning this class of methods have been published. Largely, work on lethal chemical methods has involved: (a) studies to collect improved efficacy, safety, and selectivity data for registration of the sodium cyanide spring loaded ejector mechanisms, or M-44 (Matheny, 1976), and (b) studies to evaluate a toxicant-filled sheep collar as a selective, specific technique for the removal of sheep-attacking coyotes (Connolly, 1976; Savarie and Sterner, 1976, 1977). Reports and work concerning lethal-nonchemical methods have been limited to short-term assessments of the effectiveness of aerial and ground shooting, and selectivity, and effectiveness of traps and snares (Beasom, 1974; Matheny, 1976).

1. Chemical

a. M-44 Registration. Matheny (1976) summarized an extensive survey designed to assess the efficacy, safety, and selectivity of the M-44, a tube containing a sodium cyanide capsule, and used to orally dose coyotes that investigate and pull the exposed end of the buried device (Poteet, 1967). Most of the survey was carried out by various state departments of agriculture, universities, and the U.S. Fish and Wildlife Service (FWS) in order to obtain registration data for the M-44.

During the survey, over 315,000 M-44's were placed in selected regions of the western U.S. Matheny (1976) reported the following breakdown of recovered animals from these M-44 sites: 4970 (73.4%) coyotes, 925 (13.6%) foxes, 91 (1.3%) feral dogs, and 794 (11.7%) various noncanid species. Among the noncanid species, FWS data revealed that raccoons (1.7%), skunks (4.5%), and opossums (4.5%) were the most vulnerable. California Department of Food and Agriculture data showed that M-44 placements at old sheep-kill sites, along coyote-traveled trails, and old carcass dumps (bone piles) afforded the greatest numbers of coyote kills. Montana Department of Agriculture data on effectiveness and cost efficiency indicated that it required an average of 409.3 average-use days and cost an average of $19.32 for each M-44 elimination of a coyote, fox, or feral dog.

This study serves as an example of the extensive effort required to collect *adequate* data for evaluating effectiveness, safety, selectivity, and cost of a damage-control method. At face value, results tend to verify that the M-44 can be used in a generally safe and selective manner for eliminating wild canids (i.e., 5986 or 88.3% of all animals were canids) from designated areas. Nevertheless, the enormity of the problem addressed by Matheny is apparent; guidelines for acceptable safety, selectivity, and effectiveness of control methods remain largely unspecified. Funding and manpower limitations may ultimately determine the extent to which these factors are studied.

b. Toxic sheep collar. Although several patents for livestock protective collars had been issued since 1920 (Duncombe, 1920; McBride, 1974), data regarding the effectiveness of this technique were lacking. Renewed interest in such a method was stimulated by biological survey data indicating that between 72 to 96% of coyote-caused sheep losses involved head and neck wounds (e.g., Henne, 1975; Nesse, 1975). Savarie and Sterner (1976, 1977) reported on a series of pen trials designed to evaluate the potential for orally dosing sheep-attacking coyotes by polyethylene or polyvinylchloride sheep collars filled with sodium cyanide.

Briefly, Savarie and Sterner (1976, 1977) separately paired four sheep-attacking coyotes with individual collared sheep in a fenced enclosure (see Fig. 2). Three different collar designs were evaluated with four coyotes each. Altogether, 9 out of 12 test coyotes received lethal doses of cyanide during attacks of collared sheep. Times to death for these coyotes ranged from 2 to 25 minutes, but immobility always occurred within 3 minutes. From these findings, the authors concluded that the toxic collar offered potential as a selective, specific technique for the control of sheep-attacking coyotes.

Since collection of these data, however, preliminary field trials involving sodium cyanide collars have failed to confirm the field applicability of the technique (Connolly *et al.*, 1976). In 12 attacks upon tethered sheep wearing sodium cyanide collars, 11 of 12 collars were punctured, but no coyote carcasses recovered. The rapid toxic action of cyanide (1 to 3 minutes) indicated that lethally dosed animals should have been recovered in the vicinity of such attacks. Currently, these data are best explained by the repellent properties of sodium cyanide; it has a caustic pH of +11, and was observed to repel sublethally dosed coyotes in the aforementioned tests.

More recently, Connolly (1976) reported on a series of additional field trials involving diphenadione, a less repellent but relatively slow-acting toxicant. Although the use of this anticoagulant produced no repellency, the 8- to 16-day lethal action implied that dosed coyotes could continue to attack and kill sheep for several days or weeks. This delayed action may have obscured the collar's effectiveness in reducing predation. The presence of several sheep killers, the immigration of new killers, and the sublethal dosing of coyotes are only a few of the factors that can prevent unequivocal assessments when slow-acting toxicants are employed.

Thus, despite such advantages as the specific dosing of only those coyotes that prey on sheep, limited environmental contamination and secondary hazards, and the potential of recovering lethally dosed sheep killers for biological study, the toxic collar is not a panacea. Its future seems to hinge on elimination of the repellent properties of sodium cyanide or the discovery of an alternate nonrepellent, fast-acting toxicant.

2. Nonchemical

Only scattered reports and very limited studies have been published concerning data on lethal nonchemical methods. Sampson and Brohn (1955) found an 81% reduction in sheep losses to coyotes during a 6-year trapping program in Missouri; rancher-interview data were used to measure the losses. R. A. Thompson (1976) roughly estimated a cost-benefit ratio of 1:3.9 for a California predator program that used trapping as a primary control method. However, damage reduction was not measured but extrapolated from depredation data collected in other states. In computing this ratio, Thompson assumed sheep losses to coyotes would double in the absence of the program.

As part of the Matheny (1976) M-44 survey, the California Department of Food and Agriculture reported that steel traps were quite unselective in comparison to the M-44. Still, over 60% of the trapped nontarget species were released unharmed. Again, these selectivity data for trapping are extremely limited, and as Beasom (1974) pointed out, selectivity of traps depends on many variables, such as bait material, scent material, trap placement, season, weather, food supplies, as well as the relative abundance of both target and nontarget species. Additionally, trapping skill is important; selectivity of trapping can be increased through knowledge of coyote behavior and the habits of nontarget species (Linhart, 1977, personal communication). Like traps, snares may be quite a bit less selective than the M-44. Matheny (1976) reported limited data from Texas showing that of 103 animals caught with snares, 19 were coyotes; these results, however, were probably influenced by a high abundance of rodents and rabbits in the study area.

Most reports dealing with aerial shooting of coyotes have indicated that this method can be used to quickly correct local coyote–sheep depredations; for example, in southwest Texas, 21 coyotes were taken within 12 hours by aerial shooting from a helicopter (Matheny, 1976). Montana Department of Livestock data have shown helicopter shooting to cost around $45 per coyote and fixed-wing aircraft shooting around $25 per coyote. Again, because of the limited sample sizes in these estimates, most of the published data regarding efficacy, selectivity, and cost-efficiency of damage-control methods remain tentative.

D. Discussion

This sampling of current coyote damage-control studies suggests a trend toward development of nonlethal methods (e.g., Gustavson *et al.*, 1974, 1975, 1976; Swanson and Scott, 1973; Jankovsky *et al.*, 1974; Lehner *et al.*, 1976; Linhart *et al.*, 1977) and highly selective lethal methods (e.g., Connolly, 1976; Savarie and Sterner, 1976, 1977). As with any research, adequacy of experimental designs, sample sizes, measurement reliability, etc., greatly affect the confidence and generality of given results. Where possible in the preceding review, we have attempted to point out methodological considerations which ultimately must be weighed in evaluating the validity of cited data. However, we have not discussed the criteria necessary to compare different damage-control methods. The following discussion outlines some of the kinds of information needed before a new method can be adequately evaluated and registered with EPA for use by individuals or wildlife-damage-control agencies.

Cain *et al.* (1972) proposed that several factors be used in evaluating coyote-damage-control methods, among which were effectiveness, safety and selectivity, and cost-efficiency. *Effectiveness* would be evaluated by quantifying or estimating the extent of damage reduction associated with a new method. *Safety and selectivity* refers to an evaluation of potential dangers to man, nontarget wildlife, domestic animals, and environmental quality. *Cost-efficiency* involves measurement of the cost of control per unit reduction in damage. While the need to assess certain aspects of these and other factors is generally recognized, several methodological considerations warrant note.

Typically, the effectiveness of damage-control methods has been measured by the number of coyotes taken (e.g., Robinson, 1948; Beasom, 1974), or by reductions in sheep losses, either from rancher and herder reports (e.g., Sampson and Brohn, 1955) or use of biological survey procedures (e.g., Linhart *et al.*, 1977). All three measures have their drawbacks. For example, measures based on number of coyotes taken assume that depredations are positively correlated with coyote densities—

this has not been thoroughly tested. Sheep rancher and herder reports are subject to bias and often lack quantitative precision. Biological survey measures of damage are presumably the least biased, but they are very costly and often report recovery and examination of only one-fourth to one-half of all missing sheep (Balser, 1974a). Thus, among the unrecovered sheep, the proportion lost to coyotes versus other causes remains unknown.

In addition to problems with measurement techniques, other variables can confound the assessment of a damage-control method: (a) coyote movements into and from the treated or untreated test areas, (b) nonrecovery of coyotes affected by a given method, and (c) inherent variability in measures used to assess the effects produced by a new method (e.g., sheep loss, coyote-density reduction). New coyotes are known to migrate into low-coyote-density areas during certain seasons (Knowlton, 1972). With lethal control methods, reductions in depredations can sometimes only be expected for short periods. Conversely, with a new nonlethal control method that caused area avoidance or reduced availability of livestock prey, emigration from the treated area might be expected; thus, sheep losses might be reduced in the localized treated areas, but actually increase in surrounding areas. Finally, reliable estimates of a control method's effectiveness are frequently difficult to obtain because of extreme variability in local coyote populations or sheep depredation levels; in other words, the effects of introducing the method may be partially or totally obscured by normal fluctuations in sheep losses (see Table I) or coyote recoveries.

Mechanical devices used in coyote-damage control are generally covered by safety standards not unique to control applications (e.g., safety guidelines for firearms, aircraft, electric-fence chargers). However, safety aspects of toxicants and other chemicals (e.g., tranquilizers, chemosterilants) used in predator control are of greater concern (Cain *et al.*, 1972). Typically, chemical properties such as solubility, stability, biodegradability, and availability of antidotes are used to estimate safety. Chemical residues in the affected animals and the resulting secondary hazards to nontarget species are also important considerations. Secondary hazards are influenced by the speed with which a chemical acts, the speed with which it is absorbed and metabolized, the biological activity of its metabolites, and the availability of affected animals to nontarget predators and scavengers. Relatively fast-acting toxicants permit recovery of affected animals [although, as Robinson (1948) has pointed out, seldom, if ever, are all target and nontarget animals recovered]. In general, toxicants like sodium cyanide that are fast-acting and are also quickly metabolized and degraded are less likely to cause secondary hazards than slower-acting, less degradable compounds such as 1080 (sodium monofluoroacetate) and thallium. Although the effects are difficult to measure, the way a chemical is applied also influences its safety. As a hypothetical example, using 10 gm of strychnine in a bait might present more of a safety hazard than using the same quantity in an M-44 device. Research and development of new control chemicals is often guided by existing data related to potential carcinogenic, teratogenic, and mutagenic effects. Where specified, EPA, Food and Drug Administration (FDA), and USDA requirements dictate that these effects also be within acceptable safety limits.

The selectivity of a control method is also affected by many variables such as the time, place, rate, and method of application and species composition of the treated area. For example, Beasom (1974) found that meat-baited traps could pose a potential danger to raptors in Texas, that traps scented with coyote urine were somewhat more selective, and that blind-set traps were the most selective for coyotes. However, coyote takes were also very low with this latter technique. Currently, the term selectivity is ill-defined and difficult to measure. As Beasom (1974) noted, nontarget species in one area may be target species in another area. Cain *et al.* (1972) suggested that the public regards rodents as having less value than songbirds, and raptors as more important than magpies. No quantitative values or relative weights have been assigned to the vast majority of potentially affected nontarget species. A selectivity measure derived by simply forming a ratio between the number of target and nontarget animals affected by a given control method (total percent selectivity, Matheny, 1976) equates the value of all nontarget species recovered and is therefore inadequate. Furthermore, the numbers of individuals of a species (or the number of nontarget species for that matter) affected by a given damage control method means little without an understanding of that species' population dynamics and ecology. Population trends of nontarget species affected should therefore be studied in order to give a clearer indication of selectivity. Unless criteria for evaluating these effects in specific nontarget species are established, selectivity measures will continue to have limited meaning.

The costs associated with a damage-control method, up until recently (e.g., Clark, 1976; R. A. Thompson, 1976; Matheny, 1976), have been rather infrequently reported. Although these data can usually be objectively measured, problems arise when new control methods, not fully perfected, are assessed economically. Large-scale production and manufacturing processes will almost invariably lower the cost of well-established techniques. In certain studies (e.g., Robinson, 1948; Sampson and Brohn, 1955), direct physical costs have been measured (e.g., cost of the toxicant, M-44 devices, helicopter and pilot). However, comprehensive totals covering time and cost estimates for personnel (including salaries, benefits, and training), transportation, equipment, and miscellaneous materials and supplies are difficult to obtain. As mentioned, measuring the effectiveness of a control method, and therefore the savings gained by its use, is even more difficult. Nevertheless, the cost : benefit ratios associated with a given method must be recognized as an important justification for continued development and/ or registration work.

IV. CONCLUDING REMARKS

In conclusion, we have tried to review the published literature concerning sheep-depredations and damage-control research. Where possible, we have also attempted to outline some of the problems involved in collecting such data, as well as in developing coyote damage-control methods. Although far from conclusive, we believe that quantification of the nature and extent of coyote-caused sheep losses has been greatly enhanced by recent depredations surveys. Furthermore, our review indicates that several new nonlethal and lethal methods have been tested under laboratory and limited field conditions. Contrary to popular belief, however, development of animal damage-control methods rarely involves an unheralded breakthrough. Numerous details concerning species biology, behavior, ecology, and method application must be considered in the development of a new method. In addition, standards of nontarget safety and environmental quality imposed by EPA, particularly with regard to the registration of chemicals, have greatly increased the research effort needed to evaluate new methods. *Although there is an urgent need for the development of an effective, safe, selective, cost-efficient, socially-acceptable, and easily-used technique, our review indicates that no quick solution to the coyote damage-control problem is imminent.* Traditional methods such as trapping, denning, and hunting will probably continue to characterize damage-control efforts for a number of years. The most encouraging points are the diversity of current research and the collection of objective data.

ACKNOWLEDGMENTS

We sincerely thank Sam Linhart and Erwin Pearson for their invaluable help with literature search and retrieval activities, as well as critical readings of the manuscript. Thanks are also extended to Ann Bean for her helpful editorial comments, and Florence Powe for her painstaking typing of the manuscript. Finally, we acknowledge the contributions of the numerous researchers whose publications have provided the basic information for this review.

REFERENCES

Anonymous. (1972). "Nebraska Livestock and Chicken Losses: October 1, 1970–September 30, 1971," 41 pp. Nebr. Dep. Agric. Rep., Lincoln.

Baker, N. F. (1971). "Rep. West Assoc. Agric. Exp. Stn. Dir.," 26 pp. *U.S. Dep. Agric. Rep.*, Washington, D.C.

Balser, D. S. (1964). *J. Wildl. Manage.* **28,** 352–358.

Balser, D. S. (1974a). *North Am. Wildl. Natur. Resour. Conf.* **39,** 292–300.

Balser, D. S. (1974b). *Proc. Vertebr. Pest Conf.* **6,** 171–177.

Beasom, S. L. (1974). *J. Wildl. Manage.* **38,** 837–844.

Bekoff, M. (1975). *Science* **187,** 1096.

Cain, S. A., Kadlec, J. A., Allen, D. L., Cooley, R. A., Hornocker, M. G., Leopold, A. S., and Wagner, F. H. (1972). "Predator Control—1971," Rep. to Counc. Environ. Qual. Dep. Inter. by Advis. Comm. Predator Control, 207 pp. Univ. of Michigan Press, Ann Arbor.

Clark, J. P. (1976). *Proc. Vertebr. Pest Conf.* **7,** 139–145.

Connolly, G. C. (1976). *In* "The Toxic Collar for Selective Control of Sheep-Killing Coyotes," 131 pp. Final Rep. to Environ. Prot. Agency, Washington, D.C.

Connolly, G. C., and Longhurst, W. M. (1975). 37 pp. *Div. Agric. Soc., Bull.* No. 1872, *Univ. Calif., Davis.*

Connolly, G. C., Savarie, P. J., Sterner, R. T., Griffith, R., Eliss, D., Garrison, M., Johns, B. and Okuno, I. (1976). *In* "The Toxic Collar for Selective Control of Sheep-Killing Coyotes," 131 pp. U.S. Fish Wild. Serv. Final Rep. to Environ. Prot. Agency, Washington, D.C.

Cook. R. S., White, M., Trainer, D. O., and Glazener, W. C. (1971). *J. Wildl. Manage.* **35,** 47–56.

Craighead, F. C. (1951). "A Biological and Economic Evaluation of Coyote Predation," 23 pp. N.Y. Zool. Soc. and Conserv. Found., New York.

Davenport, J. W., Bowns, J. E., Workman, J. P., and Nielsen, D. B. (1973). *In* "Final Report to Four Corners Regional Commission Predator Control Study," 47 pp.

DeLorenzo, D. G., and Howard, V. W., Jr. (1976). "Evaluation of Sheep Losses on a Range Lambing Operation without Predator Control in Southeastern New Mexico," 34 pp. Final Rep. to U.S. Fish Wildl. Serv., Washington, D.C.

Dorrance, M. J., and Roy, L. D. (1976). *J. Range Manage.* **29,** 457–460.

Duncombe, J. (1920). U.S. Patent No. 1,349,665.

Early, J. O., Roethli, J. C., and Brewer, G. R. (1974a). *Idaho Agric. Res. Prog. Rep.* No. 182, 49 pp.

Early, J. O., Roethli, J. C., and Brewer, G. R. (1974b). *Idaho Agric. Res. Prog. Rep.* No. 186, 46 pp.

Gates, N. L., Card, C. S., Eroschenko, V., and Hulet, C. V. (1976). *Theriogenelogy* **5,** 281–288.

Gee, C. K., and Magleby, R. S. (1977). *U.S. Dep. Agric. Econ. Res. Serv., Agric. Econ. Rep.* No. 345, Washington, D.C.

Gerber, P. (1974). *Natl. Wool Grower* **64,** 22.

Gier, H. T. (1968). *Kans. State Univ. Agric. Exp. Stn. Bull.* No. 393, Lawrence.

Goodsell, W. D. (1971). *U.S. Dep. Agric. Econ. Res. Serv.*, 28 pp. *Agric. Econ. Rep.* No. 195, Washington, D.C.

Gustavson, C. R., Garcia, J., Hankins, W. G., and Rusiniak, K. W. (1974). *Science* **184,** 581–583.

Gustavson, C. R., Kelly, D. J., Sweeney, M., and Garcia, J. (1975). "An Evaluation of Taste Aversion Coyote Control," 36 pp. Final Rep. to Wash. State Dep. Agric., Pullman.

Gustavson, C. R., Kelly, D. J., Sweeney, M., and Garcia, J. (1976). *Behav. Biol.* **17,** 61–72.
Henderson, F. R. (1972). *Kans. State Univ., Coop. Ext. Serv. Bull.* No. C-397.
Henne, D. R. (1975). Domestic Sheep Mortality on a Western Montana Ranch. M.S. Thesis, 53 pp. Univ. of Montana, Missoula.
Hornocker, M. G. (1972). *J. Wildl. Manage.* **35,** 401–404.
Jackson, R. M., White, M., and Knowlton, F. F. (1972). *Ecology* **53,** 262–270.
Jankovsky, M. J., Swanson, V. B., and Cramer, D. A. (1974). *Proc. West. Sect. Am. Soc. Anim. Sci.* **25,** 74–76.
Klebenow, D. A., and McAdoo, K. (1976). *J. Range Manage.* **29,** 96–100.
Knowlton, F. F. (1968). *Proc. Antelope States Workshop* **3,** 65–74.
Knowlton, F. F. (1972). *J. Wildl. Manage.* **36,** 369–382.
Kolz, A. L., Corner, G. W., and Johnson, R. E. (1973). *U.S. Bur. Sport Fish. Wildl., Spec. Sci. Rep. Wildl.* No. 163, 11 pp.
Lehner, P. N., Krumm, R., and Cringan, A. T. (1976). *J. Wildl. Manage.* **40,** 145–150.
Leopold, A. S., Cain, S. A., Cottam, C. M., Gabrielson, I. M., and Kimball, T. L. (1964). *Trans. North Am. Wildl. Nat. Resour. Conf.* **29,** 27–49.
Linhart, S. B., and Knowlton, F. F. (1975). *Wildl. Soc. Bull.* **3,** 119–124.
Linhart, S. B., Brusman, H. H., and Balser, D. S. (1968). *Trans. North Am. Wildl. Nat. Resour. Conf.* **33,** 316–327.
Linhart, S. B., Sterner, R. T., Carrigan, T. C., and Henne, D. R. (1977). "Komondor Guard Dogs Reduce Sheep Losses to Coyotes: A Preliminary Evaluation." In preparation.
McBride, R. (1974). U.S. Patent No. 3,842,806.
McNulty, F. (1971). "Must They Die?" Doubleday, New York.
Matheny, R. W. (1976). *Proc. Vertebr. Pest Conf.* **7,** 161–177.
Munoz, J. R. (1976). "Causes of Sheep Mortality at the Cook Ranch, Florence, Montana, 1975–1976," 44 pp. Final Rep. to U.S. Fish Wildl. Serv., Washington, D.C.
Nass, R. D. (1977). *J. Range Manage* (in press).
Nesse, G. E. (1975). Predation and the Sheep Industry in Glenn County, California. M.S. Thesis, 127 pp. Univ. of California, Davis.
Nesse, G E., Longhurst, W. M., and Howard, W. E. (1976). 63 pp. *Div. Agric. Sci., Bull.* No. 1878, Univ. Calif. Davis.
Newbold, V. F. (1974). *Natl. Wool Grower* **64,** 8.
Nielson [sic, Nielsen], D., and Curle, D. (1970). *Natl. Wool Grower* **60,** 14–22.
Olsen, J. (1971). "Slaughter the Animals, Poison the Earth." Simon & Schuster, New York.
Pearson, E. W. (1975). *J. Range Manage.* **28,** 27–31.
Poteet, J. L. (1967). U.S. Patent No. 3,340,645.
Reynolds, R. N., and Gustad, O. D. (1971). *U.S. Bur. Sport Fish. Wildl.,* 22 pp. *Div. Wildl. Serv. Rep.,* Washington, D.C.
Robinson, W. B. (1948). *J. Wildl. Manage.* **12,** 279–295.
Sampson, F. W., and Brohn, A. (1955). *J. Wildl. Manage.* **19,** 272–280.
Sander, E., and Dracy, A. E. (1972). *Natl. Wool Grower* **62,** 15.
Savarie, P. J., and Sterner, R. T. (1976). *In* "The Toxic Collar for Selective Control of Sheep-Killing Coyotes," 131 pp. Final Rep. to Environ. Prot. Agency, Washington, D.C.
Savarie, P. J., and Sterner, R. T. (1977). *Science* (submitted).
Shelton, M. (1972). *Natl. Wool Grower* **62,** 20–22.
Shelton, M. (1973). *Proc. Manage. Pract. Evade Predatory Losses, Tex. A & M Univ. Agric. Res. Ext. Cent., San Angelo,* 31–38.
Spurlock, G. M., Ellis, K., and Bell, M. (1972). *Calif. Livestock Symp.* 19 pp.
Stevens, D. W., and Hartley, D. R. (1976). *Wyo. Agric. Exp. Stn. Res. J.* No. 104, 41 pp.
Swanson, V. B., and Scott, G. E. (1973). *Proc. West. Sect. Am. Soc. Anim. Sci.* **24,** 34.

Thompson, B. C. (1976). Evaluation of Wire Fences for Control of Coyote Depredations. M.S. Thesis, 59 pp. Oregon State Univ., Corvallis.

Thompson, R. A. (1976). *Proc. Vertebr. Pest Conf.* **7**, 146–153.

Tigner, J. R., and Larson, G. E. (1977). *J. Range Manage.* (in press).

Wagner, F. H. (1972). "Coyotes and Sheep," 44th Fac. Assoc. Honor Lect., 59 pp. Utah State Univ., Logan.

Wagner, F. H. (1975). *J. Range Manage.* **28**, 4–10.

White, M., Knowlton, F. F., and Glazener, W. C. (1972). *J. Wildl. Manage.* **35**, 897–905.

Young, S. O. (1946). "The Wolf in North American History." Capton Printers, Caldwell, Idaho.

Young, S. P., and Goldman, E. A. (1944). "The Wolves of North America." Am. Wildl. Inst., Washington, D.C.

Young, S. P., and Jackson, H. H. T. (1951). "The Clever Coyote." Stackpole, Harrisburg, Pennsylvania.

14

Predator Control and Coyote Populations: A Review of Simulation Models

Guy E. Connolly

I. INTRODUCTION

Since pioneer days coyotes (*Canis latrans*) have been killed regularly throughout the western United States because of their depredations on domestic animals. Yet, after decades of destruction by a wide variety of schemes and devices, the coyote remains abundant today. Late in the nineteenth century the efforts of ranchmen to destroy the coyote were supplemented by bounties paid from public funds (Young and Jackson, 1951).

But Lantz (1905, p. 8–9) pointed out that:

> Some of these [bounty] laws have been in operation for a score of years or even more and, except locally, no diminution in the general numbers of the animals has resulted . . . in most sections of its range [the coyote] is either increasing or no substantial decrease has been observed . . . it has thrived upon civilization and is practically as numerous as it was before settlements began. Indeed, in many parts of the West coyotes are said to be increasing in spite of a constant warfare against them.

Lantz's observations set the stage for what was to follow. The coyote survived and even thrived locally in spite of all efforts to exterminate it. In 1915 the Federal government appropriated $125,000 for the destruction of wolves, prairie dogs, and other animals injurious to agriculture and animal husbandry (Young, 1944). This was the origin of the present Federal–Cooperative Animal Damage Control Program administered by the U. S. Fish and Wildlife Service. The coyote is one of the main species taken.

The known number of coyotes removed by the Federal–Cooperative Animal Damage Control Program from 1916 through 1975 was 3,973,558 (compiled from Presnall, 1948; Cain *et al.*, 1972; Johnson, 1976 personal communication from ADC Program Manager). This is a minimum estimate because many of those destroyed by toxicants were probably not found. Even greater numbers may have been taken by ranchers, sport hunters, and fur trappers. In addition, many State and local governmental agencies conducted predator control work outside the auspices of the Federally supervised program. In 1974 at least 295,000 coyotes were killed in the 17 western states (Pearson, 1976). Some 71,000 of these were taken by the Federal Animal Damage Control Program and the remainder by sport hunters, fur trappers, and local control or bounty programs. Pearson's (1976) survey indicated that for each coyote taken by Federal agents at least three more were killed by others.

During this century millions of coyotes have been destroyed in the western United States, yet a large and healthy coyote population remains (Balser, 1974). Cain *et al.* (1972) suggested that control measures other than toxicants were of limited effectiveness in reducing coyote populations. The most effective toxicant, compound 1080 (sodium monofluoroacetate), apparently reduced coyote numbers in proportion to the amount used and may have been more effective in northwestern than in southwestern states (Wagner, 1972). With the 1972 Presidential ban (Executive Order No. 11643) against the use of all poisons for predator control on public lands, Gier (1975) forecast that coyote populations throughout the Rocky Mountain states would reach a higher level than had been maintained for the previous half century. In spite of claims that the lack of effective coyote control since the ban has caused economic crises in some sheep producing areas of the West (Johnson and Gartner, 1975), no drastic, general increase in coyote numbers has been documented (Roughton, 1975). This may be partly due to a substantial increase in control by aerial means since 1972 (Wade, 1976).

It is clear that coyotes can survive intensive efforts to eradicate them, but the biological mechanisms which permit such resilience have received surprisingly little study considering the magnitude of the control effort. This chapter seeks to summarize existing knowledge of the factors which regulate coyote numbers both with and without control. Recent simulation modeling efforts to elucidate the responses of coyote populations to predator control are also reviewed.

II. NATURAL LIMITATIONS ON COYOTE POPULATIONS

Nearly all animal populations fluctuate irregularly within limits that are extremely restricted compared with what is theoretically possible. It follows that natural populations are in some way regulated, and that the controlling factors act more severely when numbers are high than when they are low. Population levels of several species of carnivores have been shown to fluctuate in response to variations in the abundance of their principal prey (Lack, 1954; Keith, 1974). Therefore, it is not surprising that most studies of the factors limiting coyote populations have identified food as the predominant constraint (McLean, 1934; Murie, 1940; Robinson, 1956; Gier, 1968; Clark, 1972; Wagner, 1972; Nellis and Keith, 1976). Cain *et al.* (1972) and Gier (1975) suggested that predator numbers are commonly limited by available food within levels of social tolerance, while other authors implicated disease as well as food limitations (Murie, 1940; Nellis and Keith, 1976).

One of the more illuminating studies on this point is that of Clark (1972), whose coyote population declined from its highest index value in 1963 to one-seventh of that value in 1968 and then increased substantially to 1970. These changes appeared to have been correlated with the density of black-tailed jack rabbits (*Lepus californicus*) in the previous year. Jack rabbits made up three-fourths or more of the coyote diet during the period of study.

The mechanisms by which food supplies might limit coyote numbers have been considered by several workers. Gier (1975) suggested that if food is inadequate, as is true following rabbit–rodent crashes, multiple occupation of the same hunting areas results in many conflicts between hungry coyotes. If such food shortages and intraspecific strife do not result in death, they may be debilitating enough to severely reduce reproduction the next year. Murie (1940) believed food scarcity to operate in two ways to control coyotes: through death of individuals, and through reduced reproduction (fewer and smaller litters). Conversely, when rodents are abundant, food is plentiful for predators, and they respond by raising more young until the carrying capacity of their habitat is reached (Robinson, 1956).

The carrying capacity of coyote habitat, in terms of available prey, is extremely variable, both seasonally and geographically. As envisioned in Kansas by Gier (1968, p. 83)

> Proper food during the winter results in large litters from a high proportion of the coyotes and, if the food supply holds out, a high survival of pups is probable. As long as climatic conditions and the food supply permit, both the reproductive rate and survival are high and the population continues to increase year after year. However, neither rabbits nor rodents maintain high populations for more than 3 consecutive years. If both rodents and rabbits hit the 'low' in their cycles at the same time, a high population of coyotes will be left without adequate food supply and they are thrown again onto carrion and domestic animals for sustenance. This condition results in increased hunting pressure, and, within the year, in a reduced birth rate and greater mortality among the young, again bringing the coyote population in line with the available food supply after several months lag.

A similar analysis was given for coyote population changes in the Curlew Valley, Utah, where the fluctuations were attributed in part to the effect of jack rabbit density on the coyote reproductive rate. The annual percentage changes in coyote population indices, the mean number of unborn fetuses per female coyote, and the percentage of females breeding all seemed to be positively correlated with the density of jack rabbits, which were the predominant coyote food in this area (Clark, 1972). In south Texas, with a relative abundance and diversity of coyote food items, Knowlton (1972) likewise noted that the conditions which favor a high percentage of females breeding also lead to larger litters.

It is noteworthy that the major studies documenting a relationship between food supplies and coyote reproductive success are from populations subject to intensive control. In both Curlew Valley, Utah (Clark, 1972), and Kansas (Gier, 1968), coyotes were subjected to heavy, man-caused mortality but were not regulated by such mortality. The inference is that, even under intensive control, food supplies are an important if not the decisive factor limiting coyote numbers. In Kansas, where the annual take was at least 40% and possibly 50% of the maximum population, Gier (1968, p. 85) stated:

> The real limiting factors in coyote populations . . . are (1) food supply determines litter size and the proportion of females that will breed; (2) parasites, disease, and internal strife remove a certain amount of excess population, and (3) man removes coyotes selectively or *en masse* to make the final determination of how many coyotes are left at breeding time.

The relationship between food supplies and birth rates in coyote populations presumably is nutritional. Death rates probably are similarly related to food supplies, but relatively little information is available on this point. The lack of such data may result from the difficulty of securing it. Reproductive data may be collected by examining coyotes killed by control workers, but it is nearly impossible to find coyotes that have died of natural causes in the field. Even if dead coyotes are found the true cause of death may be hard to discover. Lack (1954) generalized that the main density-dependent control of numbers probably comes through variations in the death rate, even though density-dependent mortality has rarely been measured in the field. Despite the lack of such measurements, variations in food supplies are considered to have a major impact on natural mortality rates in coyote populations.

The concept emerging from this analysis is that, in addition to the normal, annual cycle of numbers, coyote populations fluctuate in response to environmental conditions, of which food supplies seem to be most important. The population fluctuations probably result from variations in both natality and mortality rates. Intensive control may hold coyote numbers below the carrying capacity of the land (Knowlton, 1972), but even then the populations continue to fluctuate in response to environmental constraints.

III. HOW COYOTE POPULATIONS COMPENSATE FOR CONTROL LOSSES

Irrespective of whether coyote populations are harvested by man, they appear to have high annual mortality rates (Rogers, 1965; Clark, 1972; Knowlton, 1972). It follows that the killing of some coyotes does not necessarily reduce their population density, at least not permanently. The deaths so induced might simply replace mortality that otherwise would have resulted from other causes. This notion of compensatory mortality originated with Errington (1967, p. 229), who wrote:

> Intercompensatory trends in rates of population gains and losses go a long way toward conferring a singular degree of biological safety upon species that are subject to vicissitudes. In a resilient population, severe loss rates may in effect substitute for each other without mounting up excessively high in total. Extraordinary losses through one agency may automatically protect from losses through other agencies. The death of one individual may mean little more than improving the chances for living of another one. Furthermore, in some species, extraordinary losses may be compensated by accelerated reproduction, more young being produced in consequence of more being destroyed.

This principle seems to apply to many animal species. Thus, Keith (1974) noted that the striking features of wolf (*Canis lupus*) population dynamics are the immediacy and magnitude of compensatory changes in reproduction and survival in response to human exploitation and to changes in their own population density. Wolves, like coyotes, seem able to withstand high rates of killing by humans (Mech, 1970).

It is one thing to theorize on the resilience of coyote populations to control, and quite another to produce documentation of the population mechanisms causing such resilience. An outstanding work on this subject is that of Knowlton (1972) who showed that the average litter size among coyotes in Texas varies with the intensity of control. He found 2.8–4.2 uterine swellings per female under light control and 6.2–8.9 where control was intensive. In South Texas, where coyotes are extremely abundant, reported litter sizes averaged 4.3. Near Uvalde, where coyote numbers are drastically reduced by control, the average litter size was 6.9. In addition, the greatest adjustments in productivity of local populations were believed to result from significant changes in the percentage of females bearing young, with the percentage of juveniles that become sexually mature in their first year of life being particularly important. Robinson (1956) also showed that average litter size may vary with the intensity of control, from about 4 in Yellowstone Park where coyotes apparently have reached the carrying capacity of their habitat to 9 in a controlled population in the state of Washington.

The concept of compensatory mortality implies that mortality as well as natality rates could be influenced by predator control. "The deaths so induced might simply replace mortality that would have occurred by other means" (Wagner, 1975, p. 7). "Reducing the numbers of predators makes it easier for the remaining predators to survive the winter and come through in better shape" (Henderson, 1972, p. 7). This principle has been documented for a number of animal species although not, to my knowledge, for the coyote. As a general rule, however, it seems applicable to coyote populations.

At the present state of knowledge, the responses of coyotes which survive control seem basically similar to the responses attributed to abundant food. Increases in prey populations augment the food supply available to coyotes, while predator control reduces the number of coyotes which compete for limited food supplies. Regardless of whether food supplies increase or coyote numbers decrease the net effect is the same: more food available to each coyote. Neither food supplies nor coyote numbers are static in natural ecosystems, and the birth and death rates observed at any given time undoubtedly reflect the composite effects of both influences. Therefore in any given situation it is difficult to determine whether food variations or changes in coyote density is the primary cause of subsequent fluctuations in birth or death rates. Definitive research on this subject is stymied by the impossibility of controlling food supplies or hunting pressure under field conditions. The picture may be further complicated by other factors such as parasites and diseases, competition for space, or behavioral constraints such as social intolerance. Given the difficulties of elucidating such relationships under field conditions (Lack, 1954), it is not surprising that practically no data exist on their regulating effects.

IV. SIMULATION MODELS OF COYOTE POPULATIONS

One of the major unanswered research questions is what level of control mortality is needed to reduce coyote densities (Wagner, 1975). A direct approach to this question would require the application of control at varying intensities to previously uncontrolled populations while the resulting changes in density, immigration, emigration, natality, and mortality are monitored. Such a study would be all but impossible on any sizable area. However, several workers have approached this issue through the use of simulation models; these models are reviewed here.

A simulation model of an animal population mimics or reproduces the numerical behavior of that population over time. Simulation is a systematic way to integrate sets of data on biological processes, such as natality and mortality, which otherwise are available only in fragments. The practical result of such integration is that when one aspect of the biosystem is changed (in the model), the effects of this change on other aspects can be estimated. Simulation models of coyote populations permit estimation of the changes in numbers, pregnancy rates, litter sizes, and other parameters which might result from changes in the intensity of control. Such information is not presently available from field studies.

A number of simulation models have been constructed to explore the relationships between "predator control" (killing coyotes) and coyote population dynamics (Pyle, 1972; Connolly and Longhurst, 1975; Gum, 1975; Sheriff *et al.*, 1976). To the best of my knowledge this list includes all such models developed to date.

A. Structure and Assumptions

Each of the four models begins with an arbitrarily specified number of coyotes. This number changes through time due to births and deaths. Deaths result either from control (killing by man) or natural causes. In each model the population is stable in the absence of control, although Sheriff *et al.* (1976) included a stochastic element to simulate normal variations about a mean population level. Figure 1 shows the logic and sequence of events of

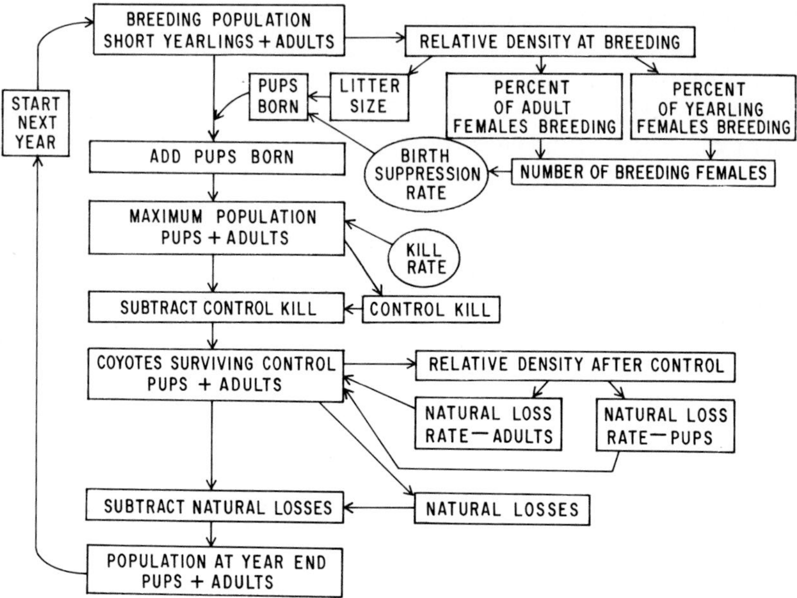

Fig. 1. Sequence of events in the coyote population simulation model of Connolly and Longhurst (1975). (Reproduced by permission of the University of California, Division of Agricultural Sciences.)

Connolly and Longhurst (1975); the other models are somewhat similar. In three of the models births and deaths are computed once each year, with the surviving coyotes at year end constituting the breeding population for the next year. Gum (1975) calculated births yearly and deaths quarterly.

In each of these models the coyote population is at maximum density, or at the limits of habitat carrying capacity, in the absence of control. If sufficient numbers of coyotes are killed the populations decline. Since birth and natural death rates are density dependent, the reduction of coyote numbers by control causes birth rates to increase while natural death rates decrease. If the control kill rate is held constant over a period of years the population stabilizes, usually at a lower density than when no control is practiced, and the number of coyotes in the population at stability is inversely related to the annual kill rate. At the highest rates of control, coyote numbers do not stabilize until they decline to zero. This result indicates that the population was exterminated by the simulated level of control.

In each model the response of the population to control is governed by functions which relate birth and natural death rates to coyote numbers or coyote density. The simulation of density-dependent birth and natural death rates relies heavily on the documented relationships of food supplies (Gier,

1968; Clark, 1972) and intensity of control (Knowlton, 1972) to reproduction, as discussed earlier. The models equate reduced densities (from control) with good reproductive conditions and low natural mortality since intraspecific competition for food is low and food-resource availability high. Conversely, high densities (when control is light) can be equated with poor reproductive conditions (Pyle, 1972) and high juvenile mortality.

To use density-dependent birth and death rate functions in a simulation model an expression of relative coyote density is needed. Each model approaches this problem differently although the end results are similar. Pyle (1972) proposed densities ranging from 4.5 coyotes/mi^2 (with no control) to 0.5 coyotes/mi^2 (at maximum control), with intermediate densities at intermediate levels of control. Connolly and Longhurst (1975) used a "relative density" concept, relative density at any time being the number of coyotes present divided by the number which would have been present in the absence of control. Gum (1975) considered his uncontrolled population of 1000 coyotes to utilize 100% of the habitat carrying capacity, and calculated the percentage use of carrying capacity at lower population levels as the total number of surviving coyotes divided by 1000 (the maximum population). This approach is virtually identical with that of Connolly and Longhurst (1975). The most straightforward procedure was that of Sheriff *et al.* (1976) whose model was structured around an initial population of 1000 coyotes with all functions related directly to population size.

Regardless of whether the measure is called "density," "percentage use of carrying capacity," "relative density," or "population size," it is used in each model as a proxy variable encompassing food supplies and any other density-dependent factors that may affect birth and death rates in wild coyote populations. Without such an abstraction separate functions would be needed for each variable believed to influence coyote density.

In each of the coyote simulation models, the birth and natural death rate functions are based largely on the data of Gier (1968) and Knowlton (1972). Consequently, it is not surprising that the models treat these subjects, especially births, quite similarly. The Pyle, Gum, and Connolly–Longhurst models all estimate the numbers of pups born from the percentage of yearling females with litters, percentage of older females with litters, and the average litter size. Each of these three measures is functionally related to some measure of density, as discussed previously. Sheriff *et al.* (1976) also relate natality to density, but express natality directly in terms of pups per adult or yearling female without estimating litter size or percentages of females bearing young.

The functions relating these natality parameters to density differ among workers, as might be expected given their speculative nature. Connolly and Longhurst (1975) specified that the average litter size could reach 9.0

whereas the limit in other models is 7.0. The Connolly–Longhurst model also employs thresholds to imply that maximum pregnancy rates and litter size are reached when coyote density is reduced to half (0.5) the precontrol level. Gum (1975) sets similar thresholds at the 0.1 density level, whereas Pyle (1972) varies these parameters through the entire range of possible densities. The functions in all these models are linear, but Sheriff *et al.* (1976) used curvilinear functions. Each model assumes a 50:50 sex ratio, consistent with the data of Knowlton (1972) and Nellis and Keith (1976).

As a starting point for natural mortality functions, each of the 4 models utilized Knowlton's (1972) estimated 40% adult mortality rate in an uncontrolled population. Gum (1975) adjusted this rate against his birth functions to achieve population stability in the absence of control. The resulting natural death rate was kept constant in early runs of the model, but was later replaced by a function relating natural mortality to percentage use of carrying capacity. This is similar to the functions of Connolly and Longhurst (1975) which showed 40 and 61% natural mortality rates for adults and pups, respectively, in the uncontrolled population. Both functions declined linearly to 10% as relative density approached zero. Sheriff *et al.* (1976) used curvilinear functions to relate mortality directly to population size. The most complicated mortality functions were devised by Pyle (1972), with separate curves for adults in age classes 1, 2, 3, and 4–11 years, and additional, corresponding functions for pups produced by female coyotes within each of these age classes. Whether such elaborations offer any advantage over the simpler procedures of other workers is not clear.

B. Simulation of Control

Three of the models reviewed here permit control (killing) of coyotes at varying levels of intensity. Both Connolly and Longhurst (1975) and Gum (1975) specified "control" rates as fractions of each age class to be killed. These models permit an infinite combination of kill rates on the various sex and age classes, but in practice a single rate applied to all classes seemed adequate. Through the relationships expressed in the density-dependent birth and natural death functions, each level of control alters coyote numbers, birth rates, natural death rates, and all related features of the simulated populations. By comparison with values generated in the absence of control, these alterations are interpreted as effects of the particular control strategy under consideration.

In contrast to the specification of a single "control" kill rate applied to the entire population, as described above, Pyle (1972) used eight hunting rate functions to vary the percentages of animals killed from each of five age classes according to coyote density. At any given density these functions specified different control rates for each age class. The control rate could be changed as an experimental variable, although not as readily as in the Connolly–Longhurst and Gum models.

Sheriff *et al.* (1976) did not specify control kill rates separately from natural death rates. Instead they empirically varied the general mortality rates for pups and adults and monitored the resulting changes in coyote numbers.

C. Simulation of Birth Suppression

The traditional approach to predator control has been to kill predators in the problem areas. General suppression of coyote populations, where desired, was attempted by killing as many coyotes as possible. But birth prevention may be an attractive alternative to the killing of animals, at least in theory (Balser, 1964).

Each of the models reviewed here except that of Gum (1975) considered the effects of birth suppression, both alone and in combination with killing coyotes. Birth suppression was entered in the calculations as a percentage decrease in net productivity (Pyle, 1972) or as a percentage of normally breeding females prevented from having litters (Connolly and Longhurst, 1975; Sheriff *et al.*, 1976). Either approach yields similar results.

D. Findings from Simulation Models

1. Effectiveness of Killing in Reducing Coyote Numbers

The simulation models reviewed here differ in format and output, but they all indicate that coyote populations can withstand high levels of control. Pyle (1972) showed that annual kill rates of approximately 40% of the pups, 45% of the yearlings, 36% of the 2 year olds, 26% of the 3 year olds, and 20% of the 4 to 11 year old coyotes would hold the population density at 0.5 coyotes/mi^2. (In the absence of control the density would be 4.5 coyotes/mi^2.) Heavier control rates were not attempted. These results are hard to interpret because the model allows only the above combination of kill rates at the density of 0.5 coyotes/mi^2.

Controlled mortality experiments by Sheriff *et al.* (1976) were accomplished by varying the mortality rates for pups and adults. Set mortality rates of 78% for pups and 50% for adults reduced the population by half over a 25 year period. The population increased slightly with mortality rates set at 80% for pups and 40% for adults, but declined 74% in 25 years under pup and adult annual mortality rates of 85 and 40%, respectively. These results cannot readily be related to the effects of killing more or fewer coyotes, because this model does not estimate the control kill separately from natural losses.

Gum (1975) found that his simulated coyote population declined steadily as the annual control kill rate increased from 0 to 30%. At higher levels of control the rate of decline increased. The Connolly–Longhurst model behaved similarly. The highest control rate Gum tested was 40%. At this level, 62% of the equilibrium population consisted of yearlings. The comparable value of Connolly and Longhurst (1975) was 58%.

Connolly and Longhurst (1975) found that their coyote population could withstand an annual control kill of 70% but not 75% of the maximum (postwhelping) population. But even at the 75% level of control the population persisted for more than 50 years. This model also showed that to maintain the breeding population below half of the precontrol level would require a control kill of three coyotes for every animal in the breeding population. In this model the changes in reproductive parameters with increasing control substantiated Knowlton's (1972) suggestion that the greatest potential for increased reproduction lies with the yearling age class. Yearling females produced 9% of the pups in the uncontrolled population, compared with 71% of the pups at the 70% annual control rate.

Although their model did not consider the efficiency relationships of various control methods, Connolly and Longhurst (1975) pointed out that control efforts aimed at the breeding population would probably decline in effectiveness as the intensity of control increases, due to a reduced catch per unit effort as coyote numbers decrease. But the estimated number of females with litters, and presumably the number of dens, declined only slightly with increasing control. Therefore, it seemed that den hunting, where feasible, should remain quite effective even at high rates of control.

All of the coyote modeling work to date indicated that intensive and persistent control is needed to reduce coyote numbers significantly. Thus the models verify the opinion of the Arizona rancher who told Young and Jackson (1951, p. 156), ". . . I poisoned and trapped the coyotes all out but it was like trying to dig a hole in the sea; they came right back again."

2. Effectiveness of Birth Suppression in Reducing Coyote Numbers

Limiting coyote numbers by inhibiting reproduction with chemosterilants might be preferable to direct killing under some circumstances. Livestock losses to coyotes are particularly serious during spring and summer because of the food requirements of the pups (Wade, 1973), and a reduction in the number of pups born would presumably reduce the depredations associated with the feeding of pups.

The effects of birth suppression (without other control) upon coyote numbers have been simulated in 3 models. Pyle (1972) tested decreases of 30, 50, and 70% in net productivity. Sheriff *et al.* (1976) simulated applications of chemosterilants to reduce breeding by 30 to 70% of the females, in increments of 10%. Connolly and Longhurst (1975) prevented from 0 to 95% of the normally breeding females from having litters. These tactics reduced coyote numbers in all 3 models, but stable populations remained even at the highest rates of reproductive inhibition. Birth suppression reduced the numbers of pups born but had little effect on the size of the breeding populations except at the highest levels of suppression. Therefore, chemosterilants alone might be relatively effective in reducing coyote predation associated with the feeding of pups during spring and summer, but ineffective against predation losses in late winter.

Birth suppression combined with conventional control was tested by Pyle (1972) and Connolly and Longhurst (1975). These experiments showed that to simultaneously minimize both the breeding population and the number of births is especially difficult. The breeding population was reduced by a heavy control kill, but at the cost of increased reproduction among the survivors. Conversely, the number of births was minimized by birth control in a breeding population at or near the carrying capacity of the habitat. Thus, the goals of minimizing births and minimizing the breeding population are somewhat mutually exclusive.

The relative merits of birth suppression and lethal control methods are only theoretical at present because effective chemosterilant techniques for field use do not exist. Initial trials were promising (Balser, 1964) but later tests were less successful. The proportions of females prevented from breeding were low, possibly because many baits were apparently consumed by nontarget animals (Linhart *et al.*, 1968). Also the drug used, diethylstilbestrol, is effective only if ingested during a limited period within the reproductive cycle. Improved baiting procedures and drugs which sterilize both males and females might improve the efficacy of this technique, but at present birth control is not a viable alternative to existing lethal methods. If an effective chemosterilant scheme is ever developed, it will have to be registered with appropriate governmental agencies before operational use.

3. Recovery of Coyote Populations from Control

The ability of coyotes to recover from reductions by intensive control was tested in two models (Pyle, 1972; Connolly and Longhurst, 1975). Both models showed coyotes to increase rapidly from low densities when control was stopped. Connolly and Longhurst (1975) found that a reduced, stabilized population with a 50% annual control kill recovered to its precontrol level in 3 years after control was stopped. Even when the breeding population was reduced to 9% of its precontrol density it recovered fully in 5 years without control. Coyote populations reduced by chemosterilants also may recover rapidly if the birth control program is stopped (Sheriff *et al.*, 1976).

The above estimates are based only on reproduction and survival within the controlled population. In nature the immigration of surplus animals from surrounding areas might permit faster rates of recovery. On the other hand, as coyotes are reduced, their ecological role may be assumed, in part, by increasing populations of other carnivores (Robinson, 1956). High populations of other species utilizing the prey formerly used by coyotes might retard the recovery of coyote populations from control.

Following the Presidential ban in 1972 on the use of toxicants for predator control, many observers forecast an increase in coyote numbers. This concern is based on the supposition that toxicants have been the most effective means of generalized coyote population control (Cain *et al.*, 1972; Wagner, 1972). The only comprehensive estimates of relative coyote densities are the scent station surveys conducted annually since 1972 by the U.S. Fish and Wildlife Service and cooperators. The overall coyote visitation index for the Western United States increased 10% between 1972 and 1973. An additional 10% increase occurred between 1973 and 1974, with a 5% decrease from 1974 to 1975 (Roughton, 1975). Unfortunately these surveys do not permit correlation of population trends with the intensity or type of predator control.

E. Critique of Simulation Models

Every simulation model is an abstraction of the real world. The degree of abstraction is a value judgement made by the investigator who must strike a balance between reality and available data. The main avenue of simplification is the use of assumptions. In simulations of coyote population dynamics these assumptions are particularly important because the models exceed the bounds of available data.

The lack of data becomes particularly apparent when the investigators construct functions relating births and natural losses to coyote density. For example, each model incorporates the notion that the average litter size in coyotes increases as coyote density is reduced by control. This idea seems generally correct (Knowlton, 1972), but it can be incorporated into a model only by means of a function specifying average litter sizes at all possible coyote densities. The details of such a function are well beyond present knowledge and, in fact, the relationship may be so variable from place to place that a representative function is impossible. Nevertheless, in each of the models reviewed here the missing information has been fabricated through the use of simplified assumptions which may be only generally correct. Thus, the models express the general relationship in numbers which cannot be taken literally. The resulting output will appear in specific terms, but can be interpreted only generally. The reports describing these models usually include caveats to this effect:

> The paucity of data for coyotes . . . made it necessary to speculate in developing this model. For this reason, caution is urged in using the results. The general relationships expressed . . . are believed to be reasonable. However the actual values need verification from additional studies (Pyle, 1972, p. 43).

In addition to the problem of general principles stated in unduly specific form, the use of assumptions introduces an element of circular logic to the model: the assumptions may be retrieved as conclusions. Therefore, a careful comparison of assumptions with conclusions is in order.

Yet another problem with simulation models arises from misplaced confidence in the computer. It is a curious phenomenon that computer-generated numbers enjoy higher credibility than hand-written ones. Laymen confronted with simulation models will do well to keep in mind that the computer performs only the accounting chores, and the investigator alone is responsible for the logic and validity of the model.

One omission of the coyote modeling work to date is the lack of study of the relative effectiveness of control at different seasons of the year. The literature contains differences of opinion on this point. Gier (1968) stated that den hunting has proved to be the most effective way to reduce coyote numbers, while Knowlton (1972) suggested that removal of coyotes just prior to whelping is more effective than at any other time because part of the annual production is removed simultaneously. This question is well within the capabilities of existing models. It seems probable that, in terms of achieving maximum control for the number of coyotes taken, Knowlton's contention is correct. But in comparison with den hunting, the removal of animals just before whelping would require greater effort per animal taken. The relative cost effectiveness of these approaches undoubtedly would vary locally, as den hunting is more feasible in some areas than others. The removal of adult coyotes in late winter, especially by aerial methods, is also possible only in certain areas.

An outstanding discrepancy of existing simulation models, in my judgement, is that they fail to consider dispersal. While dispersal provides the mainspring for restocking heavily hunted areas (Knowlton, 1972), existing models treat the simulated populations as isolated units with no immigration or emigration. In practice, predator control agencies concentrate their limited resources in areas where depredations are most severe. As a result only 10 to 25% of the land area in the West is subject to the governmental control program (Balser, 1974). Coyotes in the surrounding areas receive lighter hunting pressure, so that surplus animals are always available to repopulate the areas where control is intensive. Reproductive success, and hence population density, in surrounding areas may be an important factor in determining infiltration rates (Knowlton, 1972).

F. The Value of Simulation Models in Coyote Management

While the models reviewed here are oversimplified and speculative, they provide a reasonable synthesis of some of the mechanisms permitting coyote populations to withstand heavy hunting pressure. The models also offer credible, though unvalidated, numerical estimates of population responses to control at various levels. The importance of habitat carrying capacity in determining coyote numbers is emphasized, although variations in habitat carrying capacity are ignored in most models. Rather than yielding new insights for predator management, the models tend to reinforce the outstanding field studies by Gier (1968), Clark (1972), Knowlton (1972), Nellis and Keith (1976), and others. The models also pinpoint deficiencies in existing field data.

Given the correlation between environmental conditions and reproductive success in coyote populations, Connolly and Longhurst (1975) suggested that reproductive rates could be routinely monitored in coyote populations to determine population status relative to habitat carrying capacity. However, Sheriff, Cringan, and Dyer (personal communication) have identified some practical limitations to this concept. The carrying capacity of the coyote habitat would have to be quantified as well and monitored along with the coyote population. Failing this, one would be uncertain whether observed changes in the population resulted from changes in the intensity of control or from normal environmental fluctuations. Also it seems likely that intensively controlled populations would be held to low levels, where changes in reproductive rates would be minimal unless coyote numbers changed drastically. Nevertheless, the prospect of assessing control intensity through examination of population statistics collected from the animals killed would seem to merit further study.

Although the models reviewed here differ in many details, all show that coyote populations can withstand high mortality rates. Such results lead to the conclusion that predator control as presently practiced is not effectively limiting coyote numbers in the West. However, the goal of the present Federal–Cooperative Animal Damage Control Program is not to limit coyote numbers but rather to control depredations as selectively as possible, and to direct control at the depredating individual or local depredating population (Cain *et al.*, 1972, p. 121). Existing simulation models do not consider selective, localized control nor do they evaluate the impact of control on livestock losses due to coyote depredations. Therefore, the models are of limited value in assessing the effectiveness of current control programs.

V. POPULATION SUPPRESSION VS SELECTIVE REMOVAL OF PROBLEM ANIMALS

There are two general approaches to predator control: (1) overall reduction of coyote numbers on the assumption that depredation losses correlate directly with coyote abundance, and (2) selective control of the depredating individual or local depredating population. As noted above, the current Federal control program espouses the latter approach, in keeping with its goal of limiting control to areas where the social and economic benefits are judged to offset the cost of the control work and the loss of the controlled species. It is worth noting that, aside from policy considerations, the current governmental program probably lacks the resources to reduce coyote numbers generally throughout the West, given the current restrictions on methods.

This is not to imply that control of coyote populations is impossible. Some regions, such as the Edwards Plateau in Texas (Shelton and Klindt, 1974), were kept free of coyotes for many years by intensive control, and this was accomplished before the advent of such effective tools as 1080, the M-44, and aerial hunting.

Although the Federal control program is committed to selective control of problem animals or local populations, there is some question whether livestock depredations in all areas can be effectively controlled with this approach:

> . . . there are animals which can be considered offending individuals, . . . Yet the correlation between coyote densities and level of sheep losses . . . suggest that such offending animals may be some relatively constant fraction of the population. If so, generalized population control ("prophylactic" control) may be a valid means for reducing sheep loss. And if our surmise is correct that pre-1080 control had limited effectiveness, "prophylactic" control may be the most effective approach" (Cain *et al.*, 1972, p. 55).

One question influencing the relative merits of selective control vs population reduction is the proportion of coyotes which actually kill sheep. Gier (1968, p. 108) proposed that "A few coyotes become habitual predators on domestic stock just as a few men become thieves." The current government policy of selective control is consistent with the "killer" coyote concept; i.e., that most depredations are committed by a relatively few individuals. This notion is challenged by sheepmen and many animal damage control workers, and even Gier (1968) acknowledged that no "killer" control system has been successful in any state without some numerical control. Field data to support or refute the "killer" coyote concept are nonexistent, but Connolly *et al.* (1976) tested 11 naive, penreared coyotes and found 8 of them willing and able to kill sheep. Despite the small sample size it is reasonable to suppose that most wild adult coyotes can kill sheep. What proportion of the coyotes actually does so under field conditions is unknown, and this proportion may well vary seasonally, annually, or geographically. Clarification of this subject seems essential to the development of a realistic predator management policy.

VI. CONCLUSION

Most animal species possess some population resilience by virtue of density-dependent responses in their reproductive and mortality patterns. The history of predator control in the western United States shows the coyote to be a prime example of this general rule. Field studies find coyote populations to be regulated primarily by environmental conditions, especially food supplies, even when 40 to 50% of the coyotes are killed annually. Simulation experiments verify that coyote populations can endure much higher annual kill rates than are likely to be obtained over broad geographical areas with the funds, manpower, and methods currently available.

It is abundantly clear that indiscriminant killing of coyotes, with the techniques presently available, is not a very feasible means of reducing populations over large areas. This is not to imply that predator control as currently practiced is ineffective in reducing livestock losses due to predators. In my opinion, the present governmental program is reducing livestock depredations significantly even though it does not materially affect coyote numbers in most areas of the West. To the degree that this is true, the program may be considered to serve the interests of both ranchers and preservationists.

ACKNOWLEDGMENTS

I thank the University of California, Division of Agricultural Sciences, for permission to reproduce Fig. 1 from Connolly and Longhurst (1975). A. T. Cringan, W. R. Dryer, M. I. Dyer, S. B. Linhart, W. M. Longhurst, E. W. Pearson, W. L. Pyle, S. L. Sheriff, R. N. Smith, and D. A. Wade offered helpful comments on early drafts of the manuscript.

REFERENCES

Balser, D. S. (1964). *J. Wildl. Manage.* **28**, 352–358.

Balser, D. S. (1974). *Trans. North Am. Wildl. Nat. Resour. Conf.* **39**, 292–300.

Cain, S. A., Kadlec, J. A., Allen, D. L., Cooley, R. A., Hornocker, M. G., Leopold, A. S., and Wagner, F. H. (1972). "Predator Control—1971," Rep. to Council Environ. Qual. Dep. Inter., by Advis. Comm. Predator Control. Univ. of Michigan Press, Ann Arbor.

Clark, F. W. (1972). *J. Wildl. Manage.* **36**, 343–356.

Connolly, G. E., and Longhurst, W. M. (1975). *Univ. Calif., Davis, Div. Agric. Sci., Bull.* No. 1872.

Connolly, G. E., Timm, R. M., Howard, W. E., and Longhurst, W. M. (1976). *J. Wildl. Manage.* **40**, 400–407.

Errington, P. L. (1967). "Of Predation and Life." Iowa State Univ. Press, Ames.

Gier, H. T. (1968). *Kans. Agric. Exp. Stn. Bull.* No 393. (Rev.)

Gier, H. T. (1975). *In* "The Wild Canids" (M. W. Fox, ed.), pp. 247–262. Van Nostrand-Reinhold, New York.

Gum, R. (1975). "Coyote Population Sub-Model," Prog. Rep., U.S. Dep. Agric., Econ. Res. Serv., Tucson, Arizona.

Henderson, F. R. (1972). *Kans. State Univ., Coop. Ext. Serv. Bull.* C-397.

Johnson, J., and Gartner, F. R. (1975). *J. Range Manage.* **28**, 18–21.

Keith, L. B. (1974). *Proc. Int. Congr. Game Biol., 11th, Stockholm, 1973* pp. 17–58.

Knowlton, F. F. (1972). *J. Wildl. Manage.* **36**, 369–382.

Lack, D. (1954). "The Natural Regulation of Animal Numbers." Oxford Univ. Press, London.

Lantz, D. E. (1905). *U.S. Dep. Agric. Biol. Surv., Bull.* No. 20.

Linhart, S. B., Brusman, H. H., and Balser, D. S. (1968). *Trans. North Am. Wildl. Nat. Resour. Conf.* **33**, 316–326.

McLean, D. D. (1934). *Calif. Fish Game* **20**, 30–36.

Mech, L. D. (1970). "The Wolf." Nat. Hist. Press, Garden City, New York.

Murie, A. (1940). *U.S. Natl. Park Serv. Fauna Natl. Parks U.S. Fauna Ser.* Bull. No. 4.

Nellis, C. H., and Keith, L. B. (1976). *J. Wildl. Manage.* **40**, 389–399.

Pearson, E. W. (1976). "A 1974 Coyote Harvest Estimate for 17 Western States." U.S. Fish Wildl. Serv., Denver Wildl. Res. Cent., Denver, Colorado.

Presnall, C. C. (1948). *J. Mammal.* **29**, 155–161.

Pyle, W. M. (1972). A Coyote Population Dynamics Model. M.S. Thesis, Univ. of Washington, Seattle.

Robinson, W. B. (1956). *Am. Cattle Producer* **38**(4), 8–12.

Rogers, J. G. (1965). Analysis of the Coyote Population of Dona Ana County, New Mexico. M.S. Thesis, New Mexico State Univ., Las Cruces.

Roughton, R. D. (1975). "Indices of Predator Abundance in the Western United States." U.S. Fish Wildl. Serv., Denver Wildl. Res. Cent., Denver, Colorado.

Shelton, M., and Klindt, J. (1974). *Tex. Agric. Expt. Stn., Misc. Publ.* MP-1148.

Sheriff, S. L., Cringan, A. T., and Dyer, M. I. (1976). "A Coyote Population Model for Testing Management Strategies." Colorado State Univ., Fort Collins.

Wade, D. A. (1973). *Colo. State Univ., Coop. Ext. Serv., Bull.* No. 482a.

Wade, D. A. (1976). *Proc. Vertebr. Pest. Conf.* **7**, 154–160.

Wagner, F. H. (1972). "Coyotes and Sheep," 44th Fac. Honor Lect. Utah State Univ., Logan.

Wagner, F. H. (1975). *J. Range Manage.* **28**, 4–10.

Young, S. P. (1944). "The Wolves of North America," Part I. Am. Wildl. Inst., Washington, D.C.

Young, S. P., and Jackson, H. H. T. (1951). "The Clever Coyote." Stackpole, Harrisburg, Pennsylvania.

15

Coyote Damage: A Survey of its Nature and Scope, Control Measures and their Application

Dale A. Wade

I. INTRODUCTION

Major objectives of animal damage control programs are protection of agriculture and other natural resources, urban and industrial facilities, and human health and safety. Economic, social, and aesthetic concerns are the primary reasons for such programs, each having varying degrees of importance from different points of view. Widely varying opinions are held regarding the desirability of these programs and the methods which should be employed in damage control. The result over the past decade has been greater emphasis on removal of only specific offending animals, particularly in rural areas and where carnivores are involved. This approach is far more difficult in problems caused by wild and commensal rodents where populations are large and may be vectors of disease as well as the cause of economic damage. The relatively rapid changes of the past decade in laws, regulations, and policies related to damage control and the methods employed are likely to continue. There has been extensive dissent from environmental groups regarding the need for control of damage for economic reasons and this too will continue. Typically, hazards to humans generate greater concern and support for control; zoonoses such as plague and rabies are examples of these.

Rabies is endemic to many areas of the United States and periodically erupts in populations of bats (*Myotis* spp., etc.), skunks (*Spilogale putorius, Mephitis spp*), raccoons (*Procyon lotor*), foxes (*Urocyon cinereoargenteus, Vulpes* spp), and other species, including coyotes (*Canis latrans*). Birds, rodents, and carnivores are also vectors of other diseases which may be transmitted to man and domestic animals (Young and Jackson, 1951; Herrick, 1963; Johnson, 1964; California State Department of Public Health, 1971). Occasionally, the large carnivores are a direct hazard to human life. Attacks on camping and hiking parties by bears are perhaps the most common and dramatic example (Herrero, 1970).

In some instances, other wild species may require protection from depredation. The whooping crane (*Grus americana*), Hawaiian goose (*Branta sandvicensis*), and Attwater's greater prairie chicken (*Tympanuchus cupido attwateri*) are examples of threatened species for which protection has required control of resident carnivores to encourage increased populations (U.S. Department of the Interior, 1973).

II. TYPES OF DAMAGE

Protection of livestock, poultry, and crops from carnivores is one of the major components of damage control programs, since depredation by various species occurs throughout the United States during all seasons of the year (Berryman, 1973). Coyote depredation on sheep has received the greatest attention by the news media but cattle, goat, hog, and poultry producers are also affected (Gier, 1968; Shelton, 1973; Thompson, 1976) by coyotes and other carnivores. Less common but still of concern to individual producers is coyote damage to melon and fruit crops (Sperry, 1941; Young and Jackson, 1951). In some areas, coyotes and other species disrupt irrigation by chewing holes in plastic pipe. Avocado producers who rely on drip irrigation systems indicate that this is a substantial problem for which no satisfactory solutions are now evident (Cummings, 1973).

The extent and severity of coyote damage has been argued at length but only recently has research begun to assemble this information (Balser,

1974a). Historically, coyote depredation has been considered a problem of the western states but reports of damage in the eastern United States are becoming more frequent (Ross, 1975). Complaints of pets being killed by carnivores, particularly by coyotes, have also increased with urbanization (Swick, 1974).

Most available data on coyote depredation are related to the sheep industry. The Statistical Reporting Service, United States Department of Agriculture, summarized loss data reported in fifteen western states for 1974 (California Crop and Livestock Report, 1975). Average reported losses were 2.5% of total stock sheep and 8.1% of docked lambs. Nesse *et al.* (1976) reported average statewide losses in California of 1.9%. Klebenow and McAdoo (1976) recorded a confirmed loss of 4% to predators from a band of range sheep in Nevada. Nielson and Curle (1970) reported average losses to predators of 6.1% in Utah. Reynold's and Gustad's (1971) data from four states (Montana, Wyoming, Colorado and Texas) indicated average losses due to predation of 5.3%, with a range of 3.6% in Texas to 7.9% in Wyoming. Early *et al.* (1974) estimated 3.4% as the average loss to predators in Idaho.

Averages give little indication of the severity of individual losses which range from none to extremely high levels (Balser, 1974b). In addition, most data are gathered from operations in areas where predator control is conducted. Some indication of potential losses with limited control is provided by Henne (1975), who recorded the causes of all sheep mortality on a Montana ranch from March 1974 to March 1975 based on necropsy of the carcasses. He reported that predators killed 20.8% of the original herd and 29.3% of the 1974 lamb crop exposed. Coyotes caused 97.1% of these deaths. Munoz (1976) repeated this study from 1975 to 1976. He recorded depredation losses of 19.9% of the original herd and 24.4% of the 1975 lamb crop exposed. Coyotes were responsible for 99.3% of predator kills. During these 2 years the ranch operator lost a total of 1027 animals to predators, primarily to coyotes, compared to 279 lost to all other causes of field mortality, including 43 to undetermined causes. No predilection of coyotes for sick or disabled sheep was found. DeLorenzo and Howard (1976) from a similar study in New Mexico recorded lamb mortality on pasture of which 46% was caused by predators in 1974 and 67% in 1975, primarily by coyotes.

Predators also cause significant loss to other classes of livestock and poultry (Young and Jackson, 1951; Gier, 1968, Free, 1973; Stanfeld, 1973; Shelton and Klindt, 1974). Producers surveyed by mail in Lassen County, California reported calf losses to predators which were equivalent to 8.7% of the calves marketed from Lassen County in 1974. Response rate to the survey was 28.7% and coyotes were considered responsible for 96.7% of these losses

(Rimbey and Wade, 1975). Since many producers did not respond, total losses in the county were not established. Extensive testimony has been provided in numerous congressional hearings that segments of agriculture other than the sheep industry are affected by such depredation (U.S. Congress, 1973a,b,c), and the predator of major concern is the coyote.

III. FACTORS AFFECTING DAMAGE

Climate, season, and weather are factors which affect depredation by altering energy requirements for carnivores and their young. Coyotes, for example, tend to kill more domestic animals while raising litters during spring and summer months than they do at other seasons (Berryman, 1973; Lemm, 1973). Terrain and vegetation types also affect depredation by imposing limits on the number and species of predators and prey which can successfully compete for survival. Both natural and domestic components are influenced by all of these factors and thus affect the carnivore food base and diet. Competition among individuals and with other species provides additional pressure to restrict populations. Perhaps the most significant of all elements, however, is habitat change since this commonly affects all species in the system (Howard, 1974a).

Land development progressively limits populations and species as natural areas are altered by agricultural practices and more severely by urbanization. However, various rodents and birds benefit from agricultural development and some carnivores also may increase in numbers. Carnivores which readily adapt to urban areas include raccoons, skunks, foxes, and coyotes. Urbanization is much less favorable for most other species except for commensal rodents, pigeons (*Columba livia*), starlings (*Sturnis vulgaris*), and other pest birds.

Economic considerations are obviously of major importance to prevention or reduction of damage and the methods employed should provide benefits at least equal to the costs of application. Mechanical exclusion, for example, is possible for protection from most species but may be prohibitively expensive, particularly for large land areas (Nesse *et al.*, 1976). Rough topography, climatic conditions, and other physical factors can increase costs far beyond economic margins. Such factors also increase the costs of applying other control methods (Berryman, 1973; Nesse *et al.*, 1976; Wade, 1976).

In addition, social and political factors must be considered in planning and application of control (Howard, 1974b; Swanson, 1976). It is not likely that any aspect of wildlife management elicits greater interest and opposition than damage control programs. The carnivores are species of concern to many interest groups. Some who represent themselves as environmentalists urge total protection of carnivores while agricultural and other interest groups demand their control. In general, opponents of control cite the aesthetic and ecological benefits of these species while proponents point to economic losses and increased carnivore populations, (U.S. Congress, 1973a,b,c). Objections to lethal control methods are common, and other social interests may receive higher priority even for the application of exclusion techniques if they are believed to interfere with public enjoyment and use of the environment (Scheffer, 1976).

All of these factors, physical, biological, social, and political, have contributed to immense change in the United States in the past three centuries and have had substantial impact on wildlife populations. Many species have decreased and some have become extinct while other more versatile species have bettered their position. Among these, few have demonstrated greater ability to compete than the coyote. A high degree of intelligence, excellent sensory capabilities, and ability to adapt to change are characteristics of the species. These qualities coupled with ready acceptance of a wide variety of foods have ensured its survival and have permitted the coyote to greatly expand its range in North America. Originally, it was primarily a plains and desert species, but now is found in all of the continental states of the United States, much of Canada, and south to Central America (Young, 1951; Howard, 1974a). No current control method or program seems likely to affect its survival (Young and Jackson, 1951; Berryman, 1973; Howard, 1974b; Connolly and Longhurst, 1975).

IV. DAMAGE-CONTROL PROGRAMS

Current control operations include a wide range of effort and funding levels. Individual producers may do their own control or form associations for this purpose. Private control agents are sometimes hired by producers on these associations. In most western states, producers and livestock associations cooperate with government agencies in providing assistance and financial support to organized professional programs. The U.S. Fish and Wildlife Service (FWS), Department of Interior (USDI), is the responsible federal agency and has direct operational programs in most of the western states. The FWS operates primarily to extend information and advice in states east of the Mississippi river and in western states in which it does not carry out direct control (Berryman, 1973). Some states confine their efforts largely to Cooperative Extension Service programs which inform producers of available control methods and demonstrate their use. Iowa, Kansas, and Missouri are examples (Smith, 1973; Henderson, 1973; Dickneite, 1973). South Dakota combines these systems with a state-operated program west of the Missouri River and an Extension program east of the River (Van Ballenberghe, 1973). Washington and Colorado have statewide operational programs conducted by state agencies.

Historically, bounties on wildlife species have been a popular approach to damage control but with rare exceptions have consistently failed to achieve their goal (Young and Jackson, 1951). Those who hunt or trap because of bounties are interested in economic benefits. In general, these benefits are greatest when and where animal populations are high and often do not coincide with periods and areas where damage control is needed. Where coyotes cause damage adults are typically the major cause and are much more difficult to capture than young of the year. Those that survive their first year of life become progressively more wary and may not offer sufficient economic returns to attract the bounty hunter. In addition, transportation of animals to other localities and states with higher bounties has been a perennial problem (Young and Jackson, 1951).

Sport hunting and trapping of coyotes is done for a variety of reasons, among them being interest in the outdoors, the challenge of hunting an extremely wary species, improving relations with landowners, and other interests. Fur values and bounties are often an added incentive (Young, 1951), but furs are suitable for harvest for only a short period during winter months, typically from November through January, and provide no incentive during other seasons. In hot southern areas, coyote pelts may have little market value. In addition, fur values are subject to fashion demands and often find an unstable market (United Fur Brokers, 1975). Also, the sport hunter or trapper normally has another means of support and is often not available nor sufficiently skilled to remove individual depredating coyotes. Coyotes exposed to control methods applied with inadequate skill rapidly learn to avoid traps and other devices. Therefore, there is often a residue of coyotes which are difficult to control when they cause depredation. Where coyote numbers are low, and consist primarily of cautious and wary adults, there is little economic incentive for hunting or trapping except to the producer suffering loss.

Varying levels of control are carried out by producers themselves. Some may offer bounties, others may hunt or trap for the challenge, sport, or economic reasons, and some hire hunter-trappers. Some producers are highly competent and fully capable of controlling depredation but many have limited experience in this activity. Historically, many producers used toxic chemicals but increased opposition to and regulation of these practices have greatly restricted their use (U.S. Congress, 1973a,b,c). As a result, private control efforts are limited primarily to mechanical methods except in states which have intrastate registration for such chemicals. This is permitted for some chemicals until federal regulations are fully implemented, as currently scheduled, in 1977.

The Cooperative Extension Service of the land grant universities has been heavily involved in vertebrate animal damage control in some states. Typically, this includes cooperative efforts by federal, state, and county Extension personnel with other agencies at these same levels to provide informational programs and workshops on specific problems and problem-solving methods (Howard, 1976). A few states have Extension specialists in this field to provide information and to demonstrate damage control methods and techniques (Berryman, 1972). The emphasis is on technical assistance and advice to urban residents, industry, producers, and landowners for solving their problems. Thus, although such efforts are frequently referred to as "Extension animal damage control," it should be recognized that they are primarily educational in nature and are not control or management methods (Berryman, 1972), or direct operational programs.

Organized professional damage control programs now in existence have developed in response to requests from individuals, organizations, and agencies for assistance in damage reduction. Cooperative agreements, funding and effort at county, state, and federal levels are commonly involved (Berryman, 1973). Federal involvement began with damage surveys and became operational in 1915 under the Bureau of Biological Survey, U.S. Department of Agriculture. Prior to 1915, this was entirely a local and state responsibility. The federal program was transferred in 1939 to the U.S. Fish and Wildlife Service (FWS), Department of Interior (USDI), where it has remained (Wade, 1975). Both extension education and direct operational control are utilized in the FWS cooperative program. Extension and technical assistance are the primary methods used in the eastern states, but are also an integral part of western state programs.

It is common that total efforts in damage control include various combinations of private producer, sport hunting, Extension and organized professional programs. Bounties paid by private organizations, counties, or states are sometimes included. Thus, it is difficult in most areas, often impossible, to assess the total effort and cost. Effort from the private sector varies with economic interest. Professional effort is typically more uniform in specific areas but does fluctuate with funding and is subject to extensive social and political pressures (U.S. Congress, 1973a,b,c). This is evident in the numerous bills that have been introduced annually in state and federal legislatures to limit control and to prohibit control methods. Agricultural interests apply their influence to retain control programs while preservationist groups demand less control and the use of "humane nonlethal methods" (U.S. Congress, 1973a,b,c, 1975).

V. NONLETHAL DAMAGE-CONTROL METHODS

The only nonlethal control method which is consistently effective is total exclusion of predators. Production of poultry and hogs in total confinement are examples (Henderson, 1973). This can be done on a limited basis in some areas with other classes of livestock where forage production and land values provide a sufficient economic margin. However, fencing is impractical for large land areas and for the arid ranges of the western states due to costs of construction and maintenance (Nesse *et al.*, 1976). In addition, effective exclusion implies and requires removal of predators from within the confines of such fences. Physical, legal, social, and political factors prohibit this approach for much of the United States. Opposition to fencing which could affect migration of antelope, deer, and elk herds is one example of social and political pressures (Outdoor News Bulletin, 1975).

Various sonic devices have been developed in the hope that they would be useful since many species are repelled by new and strange sounds. Propane exploders, sirens, and recorded distress calls are examples. These have been partially effective in repelling pest birds and game animals but show only limited short-term effects on rodents and carnivores. There is little doubt that the presence of humans and strange sounds tends to repel coyotes but they rapidly adapt. The need for a continued variety of sound and 24-hour coverage over vast land areas would present a monumental problem in application and energy requirements. The nature of many agricultural operations prohibits these methods. Moreover, even if this were theoretically possible, the noise would likely be opposed for social and environmental reasons.

Historically, guard dogs were used to protect humans, domestic animals, and other property, and their current use by the military services, law enforcement, and in guarding households is well established. However, most historical accounts of the Komondor, Great Pyrenees, and other breeds as livestock protectors deal with their use in Europe and Asia under conditions much different from those that exist in the United States. It is quite likely that individual dogs with such aptitude and ability can be found. It is also likely that conditions under which they are effective occur on smaller farms with close human attention, but it is evident that many thousands of dogs would be needed for protection of range livestock in the United States and close personal attention on a 24-hour basis would be impossible. Suggestions to release them on the range with livestock they are to guard could lead to problems greater than those that now exist. Dogs at large are a common cause of damage to wild and domestic animals and frequently a threat to human life (Denney, 1974). The use of metal collars for protection on guard dogs and on other domestic animals to repel carnivores has been known for centuries. However, predators readily adapt to killing by other means than attacking the throat, and there is little evidence now available to suggest that such an approach would be effective or practical.

Chemical methods of repelling carnivores seem to be slightly more useful. These have included body sprays, collars containing odorous chemicals, and surrounding certain areas with odor stations. The Gherhardi device, a small plastic capsule containing chemicals for attachment to the ear or a collar on domestic animals has been tested extensively but has failed to demonstrate consistent effects with the chemicals used (Swanson and Scott, 1973). Other tests of the chemical-collar method have shown similar inconclusive results (Jankovsky *et al.*, 1974). Perhaps more effective chemicals will be discovered but none appear imminent. Proof of efficacy is required for registration by the Environmental Protection Agency (1975) (EPA) of such methods and none tested to date show sufficient promise to encourage the extensive testing required to provide these data.

Attempts have also been made to avert predators from live domestic animals by treating meat and dead animals of the same species with chemicals that cause illness following ingestion (Gustavson *et al.*, 1974). This approach is based on the belief that the predator will associate the unpleasant effects of eating treated meat with the live prey and thus be prevented from killing. Although the concept is attractive, there are numerous problems to solve before these can become effective control methods (Bekoff, 1975; Conover *et al.*, 1976). Physical factors related to livestock management and application of this method, as well as the intelligence of the predator species, are not the least of these. Efficacy data required by the EPA also includes documentation of the effects on nontarget species and proof that the method is effective. At present, data available are insufficient to meet these criteria and no chemicals are registered by the EPA for this purpose (Matheny, 1976, personal communication).

Among the nonlethal coyote control methods which have been proposed are chemical inhibitors of reproduction. The potential for nonlethal control of populations to levels more compatible with a food base that excludes domestic animals is highly attractive (Connolly and Longhurst, 1975). Field tests of synthetic estrogens and delivery methods have shown some promise for regulating coyote and fox populations (Balser, 1964; Oleyar and McGinnes, 1974). Other trials (Linhart and Enders, 1964) demonstrated that the chemicals tested were only effective on females and that there is a critical period in the estrus cycle when they must be ingested. Delivery systems tested were found inadequate for various reasons (Linhart *et al.*, 1968). Much more research is needed to thoroughly evaluate this approach as a control method but it does present an interesting possibility as an acceptable nonlethal method to supplement other controls (Linhart *et al.*, 1968; Connolly and Longhurst, 1975).

VI. LETHAL DAMAGE-CONTROL METHODS

With the exception of aerial hunting, lethal coyote control methods have changed very little in the past century. Equipment has been improved somewhat but intimate knowledge of animal behavior, experience in the methods and techniques of control, and intelligent effort are still prerequisites to selective, efficient damage control (U.S. Department of the Interior, 1950; Berryman, 1973). Unfortunately, mechanization and the shift from a rural society to one that is primarily urban have removed much of the opportunity for gaining such knowledge and experience. Many urban and rural residents are unprepared or unable to cope with coyote depredation.

Hunting with firearms for problem animals typically involves careful searching for evidence of their activity and may require substantial effort to get within shooting range of the animals. A high-powered rifle with telescopic sights is the best choice for relatively open areas but a shotgun is often better in wooded or brushy area and is frequently used when calling predators under these conditions. Mouth-blown predator calls which simulate distress calls of prey animals are widely used in some areas. They can be very effective under some conditions but are often used to excess resulting in animals that are wise to this method. Two hunters working together are often more effective than one alone. This is particularly true when calling and hunting in brushy and wooded areas. Many predators circle the caller downwind before coming in to the call and escape unseen when they smell human odors. Two hunters can watch a wider area for approach of these animals.

Den hunting for adult coyotes and their young is often combined with still hunting and calling. Dependent on terrain, vegetation, weather, and other factors, this may be done by walking, from horseback, or with motor vehicles. Good binoculars are often essential for observation of denning areas and in following animals. Careful hunting and observation from vantage points in areas where coyotes are heard or have been seen in midday during the denning season will often reveal the den. Dogs are also used to find coyotes and dens by scent, and it is common for adult coyotes to follow and attack them in the denning area. Some dogs learn rapidly to lead coyotes back within shooting range and can provide a great deal of help to the hunter (U.S. Department of the Interior, 1950; Lemm, 1973).

Coursing with greyhounds and other breeds that hunt by sight is an ancient hunting method but is most suitable in open terrain. These dogs are released in sight of and as close as possible to coyotes to catch and kill them. Trail hounds that follow the predator's body scent are also used but normally are too slow to catch coyotes. Hunters using them normally take stands where the coyote is expected to travel when chased and are able to do effective shooting. This practice is little used in open range areas of the west but is much more useful in farmed and wooded areas. One negative aspect of hunting with hounds is that young and poorly trained dogs may trail and attack nontarget animals, both wild and domestic species.

All of these methods require the presence of humans, vehicles, and/or dogs for varied periods during application. Consequently, their presence frequently prohibits effective control by warning coyotes and permitting them to escape. Thus, there is a need for methods that operate in the absence of these disturbing influences. Pit traps and deadfalls to capture animals have been known and used for centuries (Bateman, 1973) but are rarely used for damage control in the United States. They have very limited application for this purpose, particularly for coyotes, and present substantial hazards if used incorrectly. Other traps are much more useful. Modern animal traps are variations of three basic types; cage traps and leghold traps that capture animals alive and body-gripping traps which kill the animals as they are captured. The common snap trap for mice and rats is one example of the latter. With rare exceptions, leghold traps are the only useful type in capturing coyotes. Cage and killer traps can be used with some success on young naive coyotes and those in urban areas that have become accustomed to man-made objects. With those exceptions, coyotes are far too wary to be enticed into cages and killer traps that cannot be concealed. Moreover, the large killer traps present a serious hazard to pets and humans (Berryman, 1973; Thompson, 1976) and are not designed for safe release of nontarget animals which may be caught.

The modern leghold trap was first made by Sewell Newhouse in New York State in 1820 (Bateman, 1973) and retains the same basic form today. Its effective use in coyote control requires knowledge of coyote habits and behavior, in addition to awareness of other species in the area and many other factors. Leghold traps carefully concealed under a thin layer of dirt or duff can be used to capture the most cautious of adult coyotes. They are much less useful and effective in rain, snow, and freezing weather but are probably the single most useful control method known under most conditions even though our methods may be more effective in some situations. It is essential that the trapper have some knowledge of scents attractive to coyotes and, occasionally, competence in preparing specific scents needed to attract some wary animals to trap sets (U.S. Department of the Interior,

1950). A significant advantage of the leghold trap is that it does permit safe release of nontarget animals which may be captured.

Snares made of flexible wire cable are occasionally used where coyotes crawl under or through fences to prey on domestic animals. They are most used and useful during wet weather and in winter when snow and ice interfere with effective trapping. A loop in the snare is placed to encircle the coyote neck as it passes through the fence and the snare is anchored to a solid object. A simple locking device holds the loop closed on the animals neck (Bateman, 1973; Wade, 1973).

The use of aircraft in coyote control is a comparatively recent development in mechanical methods (Young and Jackson, 1951), apparently first used in the plains states. Records indicate that aerial hunting began in North and South Dakota at least as early as 1923 (Wade, 1976). The first official use of aircraft in professional control programs appears to have been in 1942 by the FWS, also in North Dakota (Hamm, 1944). Aerial hunting is employed primarily as a supplemental method where coyote damage is severe and other methods require excessive time or costs for reduction of loss. The use of light fixed-wing aircraft and helicopters has increased in the past few years, partially due to restrictions placed on chemical control methods (Berryman, 1973; Wade, 1976). Good visibility is required for effective and safe aerial operations; therefore, relatively clear and stable weather conditions are necessary. Hot summer weather limits effective aerial hunting by reducing coyote activity and visibility from aircraft. High temperatures also reduce air density and the safety of low-level flight to further restrict aerial hunting.

Aircraft are used to intercept and shoot coyotes at locations where they kill and in searching for dens (U.S. Department of the Interior, 1950; Berryman, 1973; Lemm, 1973). They may also be used to reduce local coyote populations on lambing and calving areas with a history of coyote depredation (Berryman, 1973; Wade, 1976). Normally, a 12-guage shotgun is used to shoot the animal as the aircraft is brought within range. Some private pilots may do both the flying and shooting but this is not a safe practice. In most cases, the pilot has an assistant to do the shooting (U.S. Department of the Interior, 1950; Gottschalk, 1970a; Wade, 1976).

When it can be employed, aerial hunting is unsurpassed as an immediate and selective control method where livestock losses are severe. However, it is prohibited in many states and rigidly controlled in those areas where it is allowed. In addition, it is not effective during inclement weather, in dense vegetation, and in extremely rough terrain, therefore it is supplemental to other methods in professional damage control programs (Berryman, 1973; Wade, 1976).

The use of toxic chemicals for predator control in the U.S. began at least as early as 1847 when strychnine was introduced. Both the alkaloid and sulfate forms were used extensively in wolf and coyote control (Young and Jackson, 19751; Crabtree, 1962) until 1972 (Berryman, 1973). Thallium salts (commonly the sulfate) were first used experimentally for coyote control during field studies in 1937. These gradually expanded to limited operational use some ten years later, primarily by the FWS in the mountain states (Robinson, 1948). However, the discovery of sodium monofluoroacetate (Compound 1080) as an effective pesticide and the more hazardous aspects of thallium limited its use. As an operational method, thallium was officially cancelled by the FWS in 1967 although its use had been discontinued much earlier (Gottschalk, 1967; Berryman, 1973).

Compound 1080 was found to be as effective as thallium, more selective toward the canid species, and safer to handle and use. It was developed during World War II as a rodenticide to replace other compounds in short supply due to the war. Experimental use of 1080 for coyote control began in 1944 in Colorado. Successful field experiments led to its operational use in impregnated meat baits for coyote control from 1946 to 1972 (Robinson, 1948; U.S. Department of the Interior, 1950; Berryman, 1973).

Experimental use of sodium cyanide for coyote control began before 1940. Its use employed various experimental devices, settling finally on the Humane Coyote Getter*, a mechanical device partially buried in the ground which utilizes a .38 Special pistol cartridge case containing the cyanide compound. The cyanide is fired into the coyote's mouth when it lifts the top of the device with its teeth. This device came into operational use during World War II when its effectiveness became apparent. It was used extensively in both professional and private control programs until 1972. However, its potential hazards led to development of a completely mechanical device, called the M-44**, from which the cyanide is ejected by a spring-loaded plunger. The M-44 was officially adopted by the FWS as a replacement for the Humane Coyote Getter in 1970 (Gottschalk, 1970b).

During the past several decades, the use of these chemicals by the FWS was restricted primarily to western states and west of the one-hundredth meridian. The use of strychnine, Compound 1080, and sodium cyanide in programs conducted or supervised by federal employees and on all federal lands was prohibited except under specified emergency conditions, on February 8, 1972, by order of President Nixon (1972). The EPA issued orders cancelling registration and suspending interstate shipment of the chemicals on March 9, 1972 (Ruckelshaus, 1972). Immediately following these actions

* Humane Coyote Getter Inc., Pueblo, Colorado.

** M-44 Safety Predator Control Company, Midland, Texas.

the FWS issued policy statements to implement the orders and to remove all chemicals from federal field operations. These administrative actions were accompanied by statements that the chemicals created hazards in the environment and were neither necessary nor justified for damage control since effective mechanical alternatives existed (Reed, 1973a,b).

Somewhat later, following requests for emergency use of chemicals received from several western states by the President, the EPA, and the FWS, the administration discovered that mechanical methods alone were inadequate to solve many damage problems (Berryman, 1973). In 1974, the EPA granted several experimental use permits to assemble data related to the use of the M-44 sodium cyanide device and a permit for emergency use of the M-44 by the FWS. Data gathered under these permits led to two modifications of the Executive Order by President Ford (1975, 1976) and registration of sodium cyanide by the EPA in 1975 for operational use by the FWS and some state agencies. More restrictions are imposed under the current registration than were applied in the past. With the exception of the M-44 sodium cyanide capsules, no other chemicals are now registered by the EPA for control of predators (Matheny, 1976, personal communication) although there is limited use in some states under state registration. This, however, will become subject to EPA control when the Pesticide Act of 1972 is fully implemented.

Various other chemicals used to kill rodents in their burrows and to fumigate buildings have occasionally been used as fumigants in coyote dens but none are currently registered by the EPA for this purpose (Matheny, 1976, personal communication).

Among the many suggestions for more effective and selective methods to remove problem coyotes, exposure of sacrificial sheep wearing toxic collars around the neck (where coyotes normally attack their prey) is one proposal. The collars containing toxic chemicals would in theory remove the animals causing damage without harming others. The concept, although not new, has been proposed as a solution to coyote depredation (Peterson, 1975; Willson, 1975), but extensive field tests have revealed numerous difficulties in its application, partially due to lack of suitable registered chemicals which can be used (Connolly *et al.*, 1976). Some coyotes continue to kill but will not attack the collared sheep. These and other factors indicate that, at present, there are several limitations to effective use of the toxic collar.

Suggestions for biological control of coyotes causing damage frequently include proposals for habitat modification, introduction of larger carnivores to increase competition, a return to the "balance of nature," and other simplistic approaches. These fail to recognize the varied and complex nature of this issue from the lack of simple problems to which simple solutions apply.

VII. CONTROL APPLICATION

Knowlton (1972) has pointed to different circumstances in which coyote depredation occurs and control may be necessary, with the understanding that situations encountered are seldom so clear and distinct. These include:

1. An occasional need for general population suppression to avoid epizootics or harassment of livestock by large numbers of coyotes
2. Local problems of generally short duration such as depredation on calves or ripening watermelons
3. High risk areas such as lambing ranges and sheep pastures
4. A need to restrict coyote infiltration from adjacent areas

Understanding of how, when, where, and why various control methods and techniques might be applied in these differing situations requires consideration of coyote ecology and population dynamics. These concepts are reviewed at length by Connolly and Longhurst (1975) and by other authors in this text. This discussion will consider coyote control only as it relates to and is affected by other physical and biological factors.

Preventive control typically consists of local population reduction and may be applied for one or several of the reasons listed by Knowlton. The intent is to reduce populations to levels more compatible with wild prey and thus reduce loss of domestic products. Aerial hunting can accomplish desired control in areas where it is effective if weather and funds for operation are not limiting factors. Other mechanical methods typically require more time and effort to achieve a similar degree of control (Berryman, 1973). High fur prices contribute by encouraging private efforts which supplement control programs. This is limited primarily to fall hunting and fur seasons and may have little effect on the numbers of coyotes that raise young (Knowlton, 1972; Connolly and Longhurst, 1975) although it may cause added future difficulty in removal of individual animals. Moreover, fur prices fluctuate according to fashion demands and frequently are not sufficient to attract extensive private effort (Swick, 1974). Historically, coyote population reduction over substantial areas required intensive application of all available methods, including the use of toxic baits in open range areas (Robinson, 1948; Berryman, 1973). In general, only limited control of local coyote populations is possible with mechanical methods as they are currently used (Berryman, 1973; Connolly and Longhurst, 1975).

All methods are adversely affected by various physical factors, including climate, temperature, and terrain, and their application must be flexible for the most efficient use of equipment and personnel. Hunting with dogs, calling and shooting, and snares are used under such limited conditions in professional control that they are not considered significant to population control. Traps are the most useful single method available for depredation control (Thompson, 1976) but trapping requires massive effort to reduce populations. Aerial hunting requires clear stable weather, suitable terrain, and limited vegetative cover. It is most effective with snow or short green vegetation as a background and least useful during hot summer weather. Its use in summer months is primarily for locating dens and for hunting adult coyotes during early morning hours (Berryman, 1973; Lemm, 1973; Wade, 1976).

Chemical methods are also much less useful during summer months although they can be effective in some situations. They become more effective as weather cools in the fall, typically in September, and coyotes begin to disperse (Robinson, 1943, 1948; U.S. Department of the Interior, 1974). M-44 or Coyote Getter stations become more attractive to coyotes at this time and continue to be relatively effective until spring, occasionally into early May if temperatures remain cool. Meat baits containing toxic chemicals are most effective from November through March when food is less plentiful, weather is cold, and energy demands are greatest. Some variations occur, but, in general, these principles apply throughout much of the coyote's range. Currently, only the M-44 sodium cyanide capsules are registered for coyote control by the EPA and interstate shipment of nonregistered restricted-use chemicals for this purpose is prohibited by the Federal Environmental Pesticide Control Act of 1972 (Environmental Protection Agency, 1975).

Selective removal of animals causing damage has received greater emphasis in professional control programs in recent years. In most instances, mechanical methods are employed although the M-44 device can be effective and may be the most selective of all techniques under some conditions (Berryman, 1973; Beasom, 1974a; U.S. Department of the Interior, 1974).

Individual coyotes may have experience in avoiding traps or other control tools and most are wary of humans. Removal of problem animals may, therefore, require application of several methods and techniques. Traps are probably the most reliable and are the most commonly used method. In specific cases, calling and shooting, or the use of snares, can be highly successful. In some circumstances the M-44 is the best tool. Aerial hunting to intercept coyotes at or near sites where they kill can be highly selective and successful, particularly if trained dogs are used to trail and find individual killers (Berryman, 1973; Lemm, 1973). However, hot, dry weather limits effective aerial hunting to early morning hours and sharply reduces the amount of deposited body scent by which dogs follow the predator. Winds also decrease effectiveness of dogs by causing rapid dispersal and loss of scent trails.

In addition to physical factors, time and cost also affect the choice of control methods. Where conditions are suitable, two or more methods may be applied simultaneously to expedite removal of the target animal to hold depredation losses to a minimum. This frequently permits more efficient use of time and equipment by the control agent who may be involved in depredation control at numerous locations over large land areas (Berryman, 1973).

VIII. COYOTE BEHAVIOR

Coyote depredation on livestock and poultry varies by season and is typically more severe during spring and summer, from birth of the young until dispersal begins in the fall (Berryman, 1973). In many areas this coincides with birth of young domestic animals, some of which are more vulnerable to predators than are the adults. However, in areas where livestock reproduction occurs at other seasons, depredation may be more severe during fall and winter months (Nesse *et al.*, 1976). Coyote feeding on watermelon, canteloupe, and other fruits coincides with ripening of these crops.

Control of coyote damage requires understanding of basic coyote biology and behavior. During spring and summer months, lone animals and pairs without young are somewhat less likely to prey on domestic animals than pairs with young. Kills made by those without young may be fewer and more irregular since they require less food and are not compelled to return for daily feeding of young at a single location. Those raising litters are known to travel extensive distances to secure prey. Lemm (1976, personal communication) reported aerial observation of one pair of adults that travelled approximately 15 air miles (24 km) from kill sites to their den. He further reported that adults commonly travelled 5–10 miles (8–16 km) from den sites to their hunting areas as confirmed by aerial observation and tracking. However, with few exceptions adult pairs return and remain near their young from midmorning to evening, and the den is their center of activity. Therefore, finding the den confirms the daily location of adults and aids substantially in their removal by allowing more intensive effort in a limited area. As described by the USDI (1950), Lemm (1973), and Wade (1976) it is possible to follow adults to the den under some conditions. More commonly, however, finding dens requires intensive searches of probable travel routes, hunting areas and watering sites for animals, tracks, feeding sites, and other evidence of activity. Close to the den, travel routes become much more evident from continued daily use of the trails. Howling by coyotes in the same location on a daily basis during the denning season is also a strong indication that a den exists.

IX. DISCUSSION

Selective control is based on securing as much information as possible for each case of depredation and selecting the control tools which are most suitable for each set of conditions. Intimate knowledge of the terrain involved, coyote and livestock behavior, recent history of depredation in the area, and experience in applying this knowledge in choosing control methods are necessary for selective and efficient control. It is important to recognize that availability is the rule that governs the coyotes' diet as demonstrated by numerous food-habits studies (Sperry, 1941; Ferrel *et al.*, 1953; Gier, 1968). Moreover, the coyote is not confused by the need to define "natural" or "unnatural" prey, but is satisfied by any palatable food. Numerous domestic animals and crops fit the "suitable and available" category, not excluding dogs, cats, and garbage in urban areas.

A general increase in loss of domestic animals during the coyotes reproductive period is not surprising. The natural cycle dictates a greater chance of survivial for carnivore young if they are born when weather is least severe, food is most plentiful, and energy demands are least. This is common to most wild species. It seems logical to assume that this similarity to other species, for which environmental carrying capacities have been measured and are better known, extends to overpopulation as well. Knowlton (1972), Beason (1974b), and Howard (1974a) have indicated that coyote numbers likely are regulated primarily by their food base and density-dependent factors which may induce competition, intensify social stress, and thus affect reproduction and survival. A relationship of higher reproductive and survival rates to the food base is indicated by these and other reports (Connolly and Longhurst, 1975). If this relationship is real, artificial reduction and control of coyote numbers should lead to reduced levels of predation on prey species, including domestic animals within the system. Arguments for the concept that population reduction reduces depredation on domestic animals may, therefore, be valid. The limited research data available (Robinson, 1948; Shelton and Klindt, 1974; Henne, 1975; Klebenow and McAdoo, 1976; Nesse *et al.*, 1976; DeLorenzo and Howard, 1976; Munoz, 1976), suggest this possibility is real. Whether or not this is true, coyote depredations do occur and their importance varies with the personal interests of the individual. Individuals naturally exhibit greater concern for direct personal loss than for the losses of others.

Professional control receives greater emphasis when human health and safety are threatened, particularly in urban and recreational areas, and in circumstances where reduction of damage to acceptable levels is difficult. It should not be surprising that such emphasis occurs. Nor should it lead to wonder that damage control is typically more efficient, selective, and safe under all conditions when carried out by personnel trained in this field. Increased ability to develop and apply solutions is characteristic in any discipline when more intimate knowledge, extensive training, and greater experience are brought to bear in problem areas. It would be unfortunate, therefore, if cooperative professional programs were abandoned since the need for damage control will continue wherever humans exist. Despite disagreement on methods and their application, in many circumstances professional control is essential.

REFERENCES

Balser, D. S. (1964). *J. Wildl. Manage.* **28**(2), 352–358.

Balser, D. S. (1974a). *Proc. Sixth Vertebr. Pest Conf.,* Div. Agric. Sci., Univ. Calif., Davis, Calif., 171–177.

Balser, D. S. (1974b). *Trans. North Am. Wildl. Nat. Resour. Conf.* **39,** 292–300.

Bateman, J. A. (1973). "Animal Traps and Trapping." Stackpole, Harrisburg, Pennsylvania.

Beasom, S. L. (1974a). *J. Wildl. Manage.* **38**(4), 837–844.

Beasom, S. L. (1974b). *J. Wildl. Manage.* **38**(4), 854–859.

Bekoff, M. (1975). *Science* **187,** 1096.

Berryman, J. H. (1972). *Proc. Nat. Ext. Wildl. Workshop., Colorado State Univ., Fort Collins.* pp. 15–16.

Berryman, J. H. (1973). *In* "Hearings before the Committee on Agriculture," House of Representatives, Ninety-Third Congress, First Session. Serial No. 93-DD, pp. 204–317. Washington, D.C.

California Crop and Livestock Report (1975). "Sheep Losses due to Predators and Other Causes in the Western United States, 1974." Dep. Food Agric., Sacramento, California.

California State Department of Public Health (1971). "A Manual for the Control of Communicable Diseases in California." State Dep. Public Health, Berkeley, California.

Connolly, G. E., and Longhurst, W. M. (1975). *Univ. Calif., Davis, Div. Agric. Sci., Bull.* No. 1872.

Connolly, G., Sterner, R., Savarie, P., Griffith, R., Elias, D., Garrison, M., Johns, B., and Okuno, I. (1976). "The Toxic Collar for Selective Control of Sheep-killing Coyotes," 119 pp. Final Prog. Rep. to Environmenal Protection Agency, Agreement No. IAG-D6-0910. U.S. Fish Wildl. Serv., Denver Wildl. Res. Cent., Denver, Colorado.

Conover, M. R., Francik, J. G., and Miller, D. E. (1976). "Coyote Predation Control through Aversive Conditioning; an Experimental Evaluation of its Plausibility." Dep. Zool., Washington State Univ., Pullman.

Crabtree, D. G. (1962). *Proc. Vertebr. Pest Control Conf., Natl. Pest Control Assoc., Elizabeth, N.J.* pp. 327–361.

Cummings, M. W. (1973). *Proc. Fourth Drip Irrig. Semin., Fallbrook, Calif.; Univ. Calif., Agric. Ext. Serv., San Diego County* pp. 25–30.

DeLorenzo, D. G., and Howard, V. W., Jr. (1976). "Evaluation of Sheep Losses on a Range Lambing Operation Without Predator Control in Southeastern New Mexico," Final Rep. U.S. Fish Wildl. Serv., Denver, Wildl. Res. Center, Denver, Colorado.

Denney, R. N. (1974). *Trans. North Am. Wildl. Nat. Resour. Conf.* **39,** 257–289.

Dickneite, D. F. (1973). *Proc. Great Plains Wildl. Damage Control Workshop, Kans. State Univ., Manhattan* pp. 57–60.

Early, J. O., Roethali, J. C., and Brewer, G. R. (1974). *Idaho, Agric. Exp. Stn., Prog. Rep.* No. 186.

Environmental Protection Agency (1975). *Fed. Regist.* **40**(123), Part II, 26802–26928.

Ferrel, C. M., Leach, H. R., and Tillotson, D. F. (1953). *Calif. Fish Game* **39**(3), 301–341.

Ford, G. R. (1975). Executive Order 11870. *Fed. Reg. 40(141)*, 30611–30613.

Ford, G. R. (1976). Executive Order 11917. *Fed. Reg. 41(107)*, 22239.

Free, D. H. (1973). *In* "Hearings before the Committee on Agriculture," House of Representatives, Ninety-Third Congress, First Session. Serial No. 93-DD, pp. 88–104. Washington, D.C.

Gier, H. T. (1968). *Kans. Agric. Exp. Stn. Bull.* No. 393.

Gottschalk, J. S. (1967). "Thallium Sulfate-Discontinued Use by the Division of Wildlife Services," Memo. U.S. Bur. Sport Fish Wildl., U.S. Dep. Inter., Washington, D. C.

Gottschalk, J. S. (1970a). "Aerial Predator Hunting Policy," Memo. U.S. Bur. Sport Fish. Wildl., U.S. Dep. Inter., Washington, D.C.

Gottschalk, J. S. (1970b). "Use of the M-44 Predator Control Device," Memo. U.S. Bur. Sport Fish. Wildl., U.S. Dep. Inter., Washington, D.C.

Gustavson, C. R., Garcia, J., Hankins, W. G., and Rusiniak, K. W. (1974). *Science* **184,** 581–583.

Hamm, A. S. (1944). *In* "Biennial Report," July 1, 1942–June 30, 1944. U.S. Dep. Inter., Fish Wildl. Serv., State North Dakota.

Henderson, F. R. (1973). *Proc. Great Plains Wildl. Damage Control Workshop, Kans. State Univ., Manhattan* pp. 75–80.

Henne, D. R. (1975). Domestic Sheep Mortality on a Montana Ranch. M.S. Thesis, Univ. of Montana, Missoula.

Herrero, S. (1970). *Science* **170,** 593–598.

Herrick, J. B. (1963). *Iowa State Univ. Ames, Coop. Ext. Serv., Pamph.* No. 295.

Howard, W. E. (1974a). "The Biology of Predator Control." Cummings Publ., Menlo Park, California.

Howard, W. E. (1974b). *BioScience* **24**(6), 359–363.

Howard, W. E. (1976). *Proc. Seventh Vertebr. Pest Conf.*, Div. Agric. Sci., Univ. Calif., Davis, Calif., 116–120.

Jankovsky, M. J., Swanson, V. B., and Cramer, D. A. (1974). *Proc. West. Sect. Am. Soc. Anim. Sci.* **25,** pp. 34–37.

Johnson, H. N. (1964). *Proc. Second Vertebr. Pest Control Conf.*, Div. Agric. Sci., Univ. of Calif., Davis, Calif. 138–142.

Klebenow, D. A., and McAdoo, K. (1976). *J. Range Manage.* **29**(2), 96–100.

Knowlton, F. F. (1972). *J. Wildl. Manage.* **36**(2), 369–382.

Lemm, W. C. (1973). *Proc. Great Plains Wildl. Damage Control Workshop, Kans. State Univ., Manhattan* pp. 39–44.

Linhart, S. B., and Enders, R. K. (1964). *J. Wildl. Manage.* **28**(2), 358–363.

Linhart, S. B., Brusman, H. H., and Balser, D. S. (1968). *Trans. North Am. Wildl. Nat. Resour. Conf.* **33,** 316–326.

Munoz, J. R. (1976). "Causes of Sheep Mortality at the Cook Ranch, Florence, Montana, 1975–76," Ann. Rep. Mont. Coop. Wildl. Res. Unit, Univ. of Montana, Missoula.

Nesse, G. C., Longhurst, W. M., and Howard, W. E. (1976). *Univ. Calif., Davis, Div. Wildl. Fish. Biol., Bull.* No. 1878.

Nielson, D., and Curle, D. (1970). *Natl. Wool Grower.* **60**(12), 14–22.

Nixon, R. M. (1972). *Fed. Regist.* **37**(27), 2875–2876.

Oleyar, C. M., and McGinnes, B. S. (1974). *J. Wildl. Manage.* **38**(1), 101–106.

Outdoor News Bulletin (1975). (L. L. Williamson, ed.). Wildl. Manage. Inst., Washington, D.C. June 20.

Peterson, R. (1975). *Science* **189,** 361.

Reed, N. P. (1973a). *In* "Hearings before the Subcommittee on the Environment of the Committee on Commerce," U.S. Senate, Ninety-third Congress, First Session. Serial No. 93-28, pp. 32–55. Washington, D.C.

Reed, N. P. (1973b). *In* "Hearings before the Subcommittee on Fisheries and Wildlife Conservation and the Environment of the Committee on Merchant Marine and Fisheries," House of Representatives, Ninety-third Congress, First Session. Serial No. 93-2, pp. 44–88. Washington, D.C.

Reynolds, R. N., and Gustad, O. C. (1971). "Analysis of Statistical Data on Sheep Losses Caused by Predation in Four Western States during 1966–1969." U.S. Bur. Sport Fish. Wildl., U.S. Dep. Inter., Washington, D.C.

Rimbey, C. W., and Wade, D. A. (1975). "Predation on Domestic Animals and Wildlife, Lassen County, California, 1974." Coop. Ext. Serv., Univ. of Calif., Davis.

Robinson, W. B. (1943). *J. Wildl. Manage.* **7**(2), 179–189.

Robinson, W. B. (1948). *J. Wildl. Manage.* **12**(3), 279–295.

Ross, N. E. (1975). *Calif. Livestock News* Vol. 50 (2), 10–12.

Ruckelshaus, W. D. (1972). "PR Notice 72-2." Environ. Prot. Agency, Washington, D.C.

Scheffer, V. R. (1976). *Wildl. Soc. Bull.* **4**(2), 51–54.

Shelton, M. (1973). *BioScience* **23**(12), 719–720.

Shelton, M., and Klindt, J. (1974). *Tex., Agric. Exp. Stn., Bull.* MP-1148.

Smith, R. A. (1973). *Proc. Great Plains Wildl. Damage Control Workshop, Kans. State Univ., Manhattan* pp. 45–46.

Sperry, C. C. (1941). *U.S. Dep. Inter., Wildl. Res. Bull.* No. 4.

Stanfeld, E. (1973). *In* "Hearings before the Committee on Agriculture," House of Representatives, Ninety-third Congress, First Session. Serial No. 93-DD. pp. 104–106. Washington, D.C.

Swanson, G. A. (1976). *Proc. Seventh Vertebr. Pest Conf.,* Div. Agric. Sci., Univ. of Calif., Davis, Calif., 7–10.

Swanson, V. B., and Scott, G. E. (1973). *Proc. West. Sect. Am. Soc. Anim. Sci.* **24,** 34–36.

Swick, C. D. (1974). "Operational Management Plan for the Coyote." Calif. Dep. Fish Game, Sacramento, California.

Thompson, R. A. (1976). *Proc. Seventh Vertebr. Pest Conf.,* Div. Agric. Sci., Univ. of Calif., Davis, Calif., 146–153.

United Fur Brokers (1975). *Market Bull.* (*N.Y.*) December 17.

U.S. Congress (1973a). "Predator Control," Hearings before the Subcommittee on Fisheries and Wildlife Conservation and the Environment, Committee on Merchant Marine and Fisheries. House of Representatives, Ninety-third Congress, First Session. Serial No. 93-2. Washington, D.C.

U.S. Congress (1973b). "Predator Control," Hearings before the Subcommittee on the Environment, Committee on Commerce. U.S. Senate, Ninety-third Congress, First Session. Serial No. 93-28. Washington, D.C.

U.S. Congress (1973c). "Problems of Predator Control," Hearings before the Subcommittee on Public Lands, Committee on Interior and Insular Affairs. U.S. Senate, Ninety-Third Congress, First Session. Washington, D.C.

U.S. Congress (1975). "Painful Trapping Devices," Hearings before the Subcommittee on Fisheries and Wildlife Conservation and the Environment, Committee on Merchant Marine and Fisheries. House of Representatives, Ninety-Fourth Congress, First Session. Serial No. 94-18. Washington, D.C.

U.S. Department of the Interior (1950). "Handbook for Hunters of Predatory Animals" (C. C. Presnall, ed.). U.S. Bur. Sport Fish. Wildl., Washington, D.C.

U.S. Department of the Interior (1973). "Threatened Wildlife of the United States," Resour. Publ. No. 114. U.S. Bur. Sport Fish. Wildl., Washington, D.C.

U.S. Department of the Interior (1974). M-44 Efficacy Data. A report on emergency use of the M-44 Cyanide Ejector for canid damage control by the U.S. Department of Interior, June–October 31, 1974. U.S. Fish and Wildl. Ser., Wash., D.C.

Van Ballenberghe, V. (1973). *Proc. Great Plains Wildl. Damage Control Workshop, Kans. State Univ., Manhattan* pp. 61–63.

Wade, D. A. (1973). *Colo. State Univ., Coop. Ext. Serv., Bull.* WRP-11.

Wade, D. A. (1975). *Proc. Semin. Adv. Pestic., Mont. State Dep. Health Environ. Sci., Helena* pp. 100–119.

Wade, D. A. (1976). *Proc. Seventh Vertebr. Pest. Conf.*, Div. Agric. Sci., Univ. of Calif., Davis, Calif., 154–160.

Willson, P. D. (1975). *Conserv. News* **40**(16), 1–4.

Young, S. P. and H. H. T. Jackson. (1951). "The Clever Coyote." Wildl. Manage. Inst., Washington, D.C.

Index

Q

R

S

T

W

X

Y

Z

A 8
B 9
C 0
D 1
E 2
F 3
G 4
H 5
I 6
J 7